Here are your
2006 SCIENCE YEAR
Cross-Reference Tabs

For insertion in your WORLD BOOK

Each year, SCIENCE YEAR, THE WORLD BOOK ANNUAL SCIENCE SUPPLEMENT, adds a valuable dimension to your WORLD BOOK set. The Cross-Reference Tab System is designed especially to help you link SCIENCE YEAR's major articles to the related WORLD BOOK articles that they update.

How to use these Tabs:

First, remove this page from SCIENCE YEAR.

Begin with the first Tab, **Ape**. Take the A volume of your WORLD BOOK set and find the **Ape** article. Moisten the **Ape** Tab and affix it to that page.

Glue all the other Tabs to the corresponding WORLD BOOK articles.

2006 SCIENCE YEAR

The World Book Annual Science Supplement

A review of science
and technology
during the
2005 school year

World Book, Inc.

a Scott Fetzer company
Chicago

www.worldbook.com

World Book, Inc.
233 N. Michigan Ave.
Chicago, IL 60601

ISBN: 0-7166-0559-7
ISSN: 0080-7621
Library of Congress Control Number: 65-21776
Printed in the United States of America.

STAFF

▪ EDITORIAL

Editor in Chief
Paul A. Kobasa

Executive Editor
Sara Dreyfuss

Managing Editor
Maureen Mostyn Liebenson

Contributing Project Editor
Barbara A. Mayes

Senior Editors
Timothy D. Frystak
Kristina A. Vaicikonis

Staff Editors
Heather McShane
S. Thomas Richardson
Marty Zwikel

Contributing Editor
Alfred J. Smuskiewicz

Editorial Assistant
Ethel Matthews

Cartographic Services
H. George Stoll, Head
Wayne K. Pichler, Manager,
    Digital Cartography
John M. Rejba,
    Senior Cartographer

Indexing Services
David Pofelski, Head
Aamir Burki, Staff Indexer

Permissions Editor
Janet Peterson

▪ GRAPHIC DESIGN

Manager, Graphics and Design
Sandra M. Dyrlund

Project Design Coordinator
Brenda B. Tropinski

Senior Designers
Don Di Sante
Isaiah W. Sheppard, Jr.

Contributing Designers
Sandy Newell
Ann Tomasic

Photographs Editors
Tom Evans
Kathryn Creech

Contributing Photographs Editor
Carol Parden

Production and Administrative Support
John Whitney

▪ LIBRARY SERVICES

Library Services
Jon Fjortoft, Head

▪ PRODUCTION

Director, Manufacturing and Pre-Press
Carma Fazio

Manufacturing Manager
Barbara Podczerwinski

Senior Production Manager
Madelyn S. Underwood

Production Manager
Anne Fritzinger

Print Promotional Manager
Marco Morales

Proofreading
Anne Dillon

Text Processing
Curley Hunter
Gwendolyn Johnson

▪ MARKETING

Director, Direct Marketing
Mark R. Willy

Marketing Analyst
Zofia Kulik

CONTRIBUTORS

Baine, Celeste, B.S., M.Ed.
Director, Engineering Education
Service Center. [*Engineering*]

Blunk, Dan, B.A.
Free-Lance Writer. [**Consumer
Science,** *Brightening Your Smile*]

Bolen, Eric G., B.S., M.S., Ph.D.
Professor Emeritus, Department of
Biological Sciences, University of
North Carolina at Wilmington.
[*Conservation*]

Brett, Carlton E., M.S., Ph.D.
Professor, Department of Geology,
University of Cincinnati.
[*Fossil Studies*]

Burchett, Andrew, B.A.
Chemicals and Seeds Editor, *Farm
Journal Media*. [*Agriculture*]

Carpenter, Siri J., B.A., M.S., Ph.D.
Free-Lance Science Writer.
[**Special Report,** *Advances in
Understanding Asthma*]

Chiras, Daniel, B.A., Ph.D.
Visiting Professor, Colorado College.
[*Environmental Pollution*]

Cooper, Irene, B.J., M.L.S.
Children's Books Editor, *Booklist*.
[*Books About Science for Younger
Readers*]

Crist, Darlene Trew, B.A.
Science Writer, Office of Marine
Programs, School of Oceanography,
University of Rhode Island. [**Special
Report,** *Fishing Poll: The Census of
Marine Life*]

Despres, Renée, Ph.D. Free-Lance
Writer. [*Medical Research;* **Consumer
Science,** *The Power of Tea*]

Disterhoft, John F., Ph.D.
Professor of Physiology, Feinberg
School of Medicine, Northwestern
University. [**Science Studies,**
Remembering and Forgetting]

Ferrell, Keith, Free-Lance Writer.
[*Computers and Electronics*]

Gorman, Jessica, B.A.
Free-Lance Science Writer. [**Special
Report,** *Clearing the Way for a
Hydrogen Economy*]

Graff, Gordon, B.S., M.S., Ph.D.
Free-Lance Science Writer. [*Chemistry*]

Hay, William W., B.S., M.S., Ph.D.
Professor Emeritus, Geological
Sciences, University of Colorado at
Boulder. [*Geology*]

Haymer, David S., M.S., Ph.D.
Professor, Department of Cell and
Molecular Biology, John A. Burns
School of Medicine, University of
Hawaii at Manoa. [*Genetics*]

Hester, Thomas R., B.A., Ph.D.
Professor Emeritus of Anthropology,
University of Texas at Austin.
[*Archaeology*]

Hurley, Daniel J., B.S., M.D.
Director, Physical Medicine and
Rehabilitation, CINN Medical Group.
[**Special Report,** *Straight Talk About
Back Health*]

Johnson, Christina S., B.A., M.S.
Science Writer, California Sea
Grant College Program, Scripps
Institution of Oceanography.
[*Oceanography*]

Konrad, Rachel, B.A.
Silicon Valley Correspondent, The
Associated Press. [**Consumer Science,**
Byte Back: Protecting Your Computer]

Kowal, Deborah, M.A., P.A.
Adjunct Assistant Professor, Emory
University Rollins School of Public
Health. [*Public Health*]

Kramer, Thomas, A.M., M.D.
Associate Professor of Psychiatry;
Director, Student Counseling and
Resource Service, University of
Chicago. [**Science Studies,**
Remembering and Forgetting]

Lunine, Jonathan I., B.S., M.S., Ph.D.
Professor of Planetary Science and
Physics, University of Arizona Lunar
and Planetary Laboratory.
[*Astronomy*]

March, Robert H., A.B., M.S., Ph.D.
Professor Emeritus of Physics
and Liberal Studies, University of
Wisconsin at Madison. [*Physics*]

Marschall, Laurence A., B.S., Ph.D.
Professor of Physics, Gettysburg
College. [*Books About Science*]

Mateja, Jim, B.S.
Auto Columnist, *Chicago Tribune*.
[**Consumer Science,** *Shifting Gears to
Hybrid Cars*]

Milius, Susan, B.A.
Life Sciences Writer, *Science News*.
[*Biology*]

Milo, Richard G., B.A., M.A., Ph.D.
Associate Professor of Anthropology,
Chicago State University.
[*Anthropology*]

Morring, Frank, Jr., A.B.
Senior Space Technology Editor,
Aviation Week & Space Technology.
[*Space Technology*]

Moser-Veillon, Phylis B., B.S.,
M.S., Ph.D.
Professor Emerita, Department of
Nutrition and Food Science,
University of Maryland at College
Park. [*Nutrition*]

Murphy, Michael J., M.D., M.P.H.
Assistant Psychiatrist, McLean Hospital;
Instructor, Harvard Medical School.
[*Psychology*]

O'Dor, Ron, A.A., A.B., Ph.D.
Senior Scientist, Census of Marine Life,
Consortium for Oceanographic Research
and Education. [**Special Report,** *Fishing
Poll: The Census of Marine Life*]

Riley, Thomas N., B.S., Ph.D.
Professor of Medicinal Chemistry,
School of Pharmacy,
Auburn University. [*Drugs*]

Sforza, Pasquale M., B.Ae.E.,
M.S., Ph.D.
Professor of Mechanical and Aerospace
Engineering, University of Florida.
[*Energy*]

Smuskiewicz, Alfred J., B.S., M.S.
Free-Lance Writer. [*Anthropology*
(Close-Up), *Geology* (Close-Up),
Physics (Close-Up), *Public Health*
(Close-Up)]

Snow, John T., B.S.E.E., M.S.E.E., Ph.D.
Dean, College of Geosciences,
Professor of Meteorology, University of
Oklahoma. [*Atmospheric Science*]

Snow, Theodore P., B.A., M.S., Ph.D.
Professor of Astrophysics, University
of Colorado at Boulder. [*Astronomy*]

Spilker, Linda J., B.A., M.S., Ph.D.
Cassini Deputy Project Scientist/
Principal Scientist, Jet Propulsion
Laboratory. [**Special Report,** *Close
Encounters with Saturn*]

Stanford, Craig, B.A., Ph.D.
Professor of Anthropology and Biological
Sciences, University of Southern
California. [**Special Report,** *Great Apes:
Culture and Conservation*]

Tamarin, Robert H., B.S., Ph.D.
Dean of Sciences, University of
Massachusetts Lowell. [*Ecology*]

Teich, Albert H., B.S., Ph.D.
Director, Science and Policy
Programs, American Association
for the Advancement of Science.
[*Science and Society*]

Turner, Michael, B.S., M.S., Ph.D.
Rauner Distinguished Service Professor of
Astrophysics, University of Chicago.
[**Special Report,** *The Dark
Side of the Universe*]

Wergin, William P., B.S., Ph.D.
Research Cytologist, Agricultural
Research Service, U.S. Department of
Agriculture. [**Special Report,** *A Chance
(Discovery) of Snow*]

Winter, Alison, B.A., Ph.D.
Historian of Science, Department of
History, University of Chicago. [**Science
Studies,** *Remembering and Forgetting*]

EDITORIAL ADVISORY BOARD

Joshua Frieman is a theoretical astrophysicist at Fermi National Accelerator Laboratory near Batavia, Illinois, and a Professor of Astronomy and Astrophysics at the University of Chicago, where he is also a member of the Kavli Institute for Cosmological Physics. He earned the B.S. degree in physics from Stanford University and the Ph.D. degree from the University of Chicago. Specializing in cosmology, he has carried out theoretical and observational research on the early history of the universe; the large-scale structure of the universe; gravitational lensing; and the nature of dark energy, which is causing the expansion of the universe to speed up. His current research projects include work on the Sloan Digital Sky Survey, the most ambitious mapping of the universe yet undertaken.

Jinger G. Hoop is Senior Fellow at the MacLean Center for Clinical Ethics, and Psychiatric Genetics Fellow at the Department of Psychiatry, both at the University of Chicago. She received the B.A. degree in creative writing from California State University at Long Beach in 1981; the M.F.A. degree in creative writing from Wichita State University in 1985; and the M.D. degree from the University of Chicago Pritzker School of Medicine in 2000. She is a former managing editor of *Science Year*. Her major research interest is assessing and influencing the ethical behavior of psychiatrists, particularly in the area of genetic research and testing.

Kelly E. Mayo is Professor and William Deering Chair of Biochemistry, Molecular Biology and Cell Biology and Director of the Center for Reproductive Science, both at Northwestern University in Evanston, Illinois. He received the B.S. degree from the University of Wisconsin and the Ph.D. degree from the University of Washington, both degrees in biochemistry. He did postdoctoral training at the Salk Institute for Biological Studies. His current research focuses on gene regulation in the mammalian endocrine system and the synthesis and actions of hormones that control such physiological processes as growth and reproduction.

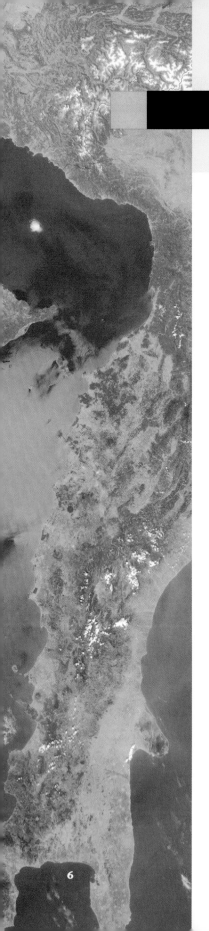

CONTENTS

■ **CROSS-REFERENCE TABS**

A tear-out page of Cross-Reference Tabs for insertion in *The World Book Encyclopedia* appears before page 1.

■ **SPECIAL REPORTS**   **10**

In-depth coverage of significant and timely topics in science and technology.

■ **SCIENCE STUDIES**   **128**

REMEMBERING AND FORGETTING:
THE SCIENCE OF HUMAN MEMORY

This special feature explores the latest research on the biochemical basis of memory as well as problems that can affect memory and ways to improve our ability to remember.

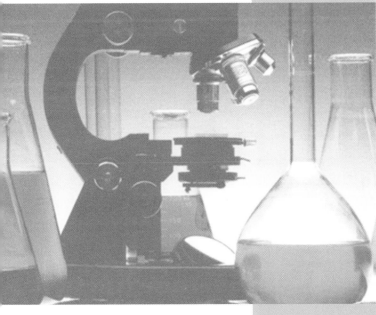

MAJOR SCIENCE STORIES

From new discoveries about Saturn and its rings and moons to scientific findings about the most devastating tsunami in history, a variety of topics made the year eventful in science and technology. These two pages present highlights of the stories chosen by the editors of *Science Year* as the most memorable or important of the year, along with information on where in the book to find details about them.

CASSINI–HUYGENS AT SATURN

The Cassini–Huygens spacecraft has provided scientists with the most spectacular images and most detailed information about Saturn ever recorded. The Huygens probe became the first human-made object to land on Titan, Saturn's largest moon. In the Special Reports section, see **CLOSE ENCOUNTERS WITH SATURN**, page 12.

DEADLY WAVES

An earthquake near the Asian island of Sumatra in December 2004 caused the most devastating tsunami in history, killing at least 175,000 people and leaving millions more injured and homeless. In the Science News Update section, see the Close-Up **TREMBLING EARTH AND TROUBLED WATERS**, page 240.

TINY PEOPLE MAY REPRESENT A NEW HUMAN SPECIES

Anthropologists were astounded in October 2004 by a report announcing the discovery in Indonesia of what may be a previously unknown species of human being. These people, who stood only about 1 meter (3.3 feet) tall, may have lived until about 18,000 years ago. The dwarf people were named *Homo floresiensis*—and nicknamed "Hobbits"—by the researchers who found them. In the Science News Update section, see **ANTHROPOLOGY**, page 177.

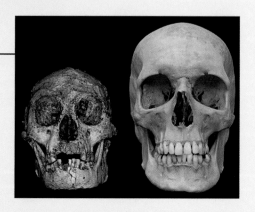

"EXTINCT" BIRD FOUND

Researchers discovered that the ivory-billed woodpecker, also known as the "Lord God bird," is not extinct as scientists had thought since 1944. Ornithologists reported in April 2005 that sightings of the bird had been confirmed in Arkansas. In the Science News Update section, see **CONSERVATION,** page 209.

"WORLD YEAR OF PHYSICS"

Celebrations in 2005 marked the 100th anniversary of Albert Einstein's "miracle year," in which he wrote five papers—including one proposing the special theory of relativity—that established the foundations of modern physics. In the Science News Update section, see **PHYSICS**, page 256.

NEW DIETARY AND EXERCISE GUIDELINES

The United States Departments of Health and Human Services and Agriculture announced a new set of dietary guidelines in January 2005 that, for the first time, stressed the importance of exercise as well as a balanced diet. In the Science News Update section, see **NUTRITION**, page 250.

FIRST PRIVATE CRAFT REACHES SPACE

SpaceShipOne in 2004 became the first privately owned rocket plane to fly in outer space. The craft won the $10-million Ansari X Prize for reaching outer space and returning to Earth safely twice within a two-week period. In the Science News Update section, see **SPACE TECHNOLOGY**, page 272.

DEATH OF FRANCIS CRICK

Francis Crick, the British Nobel Prize-winning biologist who, with James D. Watson, discovered the molecular structure of DNA, died on July 29, 2004. In the Science News Update section, see **DEATHS OF SCIENTISTS**, page 213.

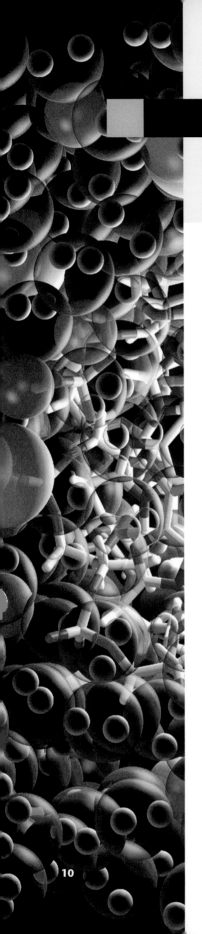

SPECIAL REPORTS

These feature articles take an in-depth look at significant and timely subjects in science and technology.

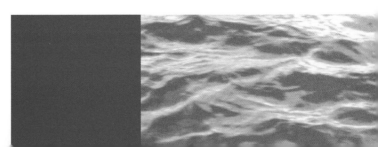

Close Encounters with
SATURN

Findings from the Cassini–Huygens mission are shedding light on the mysteries of Saturn, its dazzling rings, and its many moons.

By Linda J. Spilker

Descriptions of the international Cassini–Huygens mission to Saturn tend toward superlatives. The Cassini orbiter and the Huygens probe, which slid into orbit around this famously ringed planet in July 2004, represent the most ambitious effort in the history of interplanetary space exploration. Three probes launched by the United States National Aeronautics and Space Administration (NASA) had already flown by Saturn in the 1970's and 1980's. But the Cassini–Huygens spacecraft, the first to orbit Saturn, dwarfs all three in size and weight and in the complexity and power of its instruments. Scientists from NASA, the European Space Agency (ESA), and the Italian space agency, Agenzia Spaziale Italiana (ASI), spent more than 20 years and billions of dollars to complete the mammoth spacecraft, which stands 7 meters (22 feet) tall and weighs 5,700 kilograms (12,600 pounds). In fact, the spacecraft is so huge that it needed to swing by three planets—Earth, Venus, and Jupiter—to get the energy boost it needed for its seven-year journey to Saturn.

Instruments on the Cassini spacecraft have given us the most spectacular images as well as the most detailed information ever collected about Saturn. For example, Cassini's instruments recorded hurricane-like storms a million times stronger than those on Earth as well as the sudden appearance of a strange oxygen cloud that surrounded the planet. Cassini's cameras caught Saturn's moon Prometheus stealing particles from one of the planet's rings. A camera also spotted a

The author:
Linda Spilker is the Cassini deputy project scientist/principal scientist at the Jet Propulsion Laboratory in Pasadena, California.

previously unknown moon hidden within the rings. Cassini scientists were delighted to confirm that Titan, Saturn's planet-sized moon, has methane rain and an upper atmosphere with complex compounds similar to the chemical building blocks of life on Earth.

In January 2005, the ESA's Huygens probe—carried piggyback on Cassini during the journey from Earth—became the first human-made object to land on Titan. The probe, which collected and transmitted data for twice as long as anyone had expected, revealed its share of amazing discoveries, including detailed images of Titan's surface. As the probe floated through Titan's haze-choked atmosphere, its cameras revealed a hauntingly Earthlike landscape, complete with streamlike drainage channels, evidence of erosion, features that look like shorelines, and rocks (though the rocks are made of ice).

The Cassini mission is scheduled to last until at least 2008, by which time it will have orbited Saturn 76 times. The data the orbiter collects will keep scientists busy for years. Perhaps these data will answer some of the questions intriguing scientists. Where, for example, did the material in Saturn's rings originate? Why are the rings subtly colored? How many more moons does Saturn have? (By mid-2005, the count had reached 47.) How does the moon Enceladus produce particles for one of Saturn's rings? Why does the moon Iapetus have a huge mountain range around its equator? And where are the lakes and oceans of liquid methane and hydrocarbons that scientists expected to see on Titan?

A surprising turn

Saturn, which can be seen in the night sky with the unaided eye, was the farthest planet from Earth known to ancient astronomers. But studying this intriguing planet is not easy. When we look at Saturn through telescopes or even from spacecraft, we see only its dense cloud-covered atmosphere, partially obscured by a brightly lit high-altitude haze. The Italian astronomer and physicist Galileo (1564–1642) discovered Saturn's rings in the early 1600's. However, he thought he was seeing three satellites—and was annoyed to discover, when he looked at Saturn again a few months later, that two of the "satellites" had disappeared. (In fact, the angle of the rings relative to Earth had changed.) In the 1650's, Dutch astronomer Christiaan Huygens (1629–1695) discovered Titan and also concluded that what astronomers called "Saturn's arms" was actually a ring. Italian-born French astronomer Giovanni Domenico Cassini in 1675 discovered that Saturn had more than one ring.

Saturn is one of the oddest planets in the solar system. For example, although Saturn is the second largest planet (after Jupiter), it has the lowest *density* (amount of matter per unit volume) of all the planets. Saturn is the only planet that is, on average, less dense than water. In fact, if you could find a bathtub big enough to hold Saturn, the planet

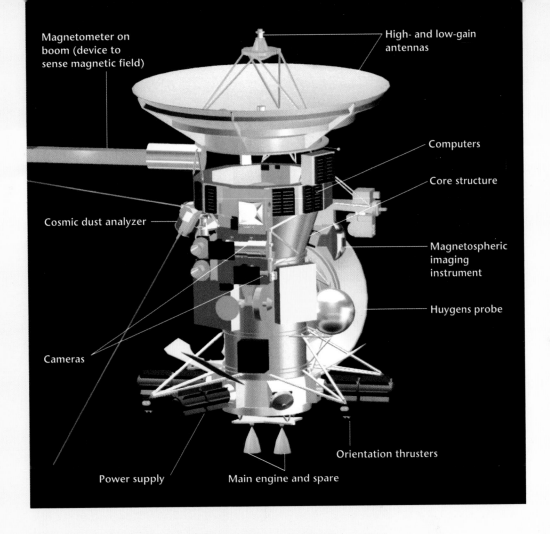

Magnetometer on boom (device to sense magnetic field)

High- and low-gain antennas

Computers

Core structure

Cosmic dust analyzer

Magnetospheric imaging instrument

Huygens probe

Cameras

Orientation thrusters

Power supply

Main engine and spare

would float. This low density results from Saturn's composition, which is mostly hydrogen and helium, the two lightest elements. The planet gets its white and golden hues from the small amounts of ammonia and other, less common chemicals in its atmosphere.

Some of Cassini's findings have strengthened Saturn's reputation for strangeness. For example, Saturn is the only planet whose exact rotation rate continues to be a mystery to scientists. As the two Voyager spacecraft flew by Saturn in 1980 and 1981, they measured intense radio waves coming from an area of the planet near the equator. Because the most energetic of these radio waves had *wavelengths* about 1 kilometer (0.6 mile) in length, they were called Saturn Kilometric Radiation (SKR). (Wavelengths measure the distance between one peak or crest of a wave and the next.) Scientists believe the SKR are caused by *ions* (electrically charged particles) interacting with a magnetic field that originates deep inside Saturn. In the 1980's, NASA scientists used the Voyager measurements of the SKR to calculate that Saturn took 10 hours 39 minutes and 24 seconds to spin on its axis (compared with 23 hours 56 minutes and 4 seconds for Earth).

The Cassini–Huygens spacecraft is about the size of a 30-passenger school bus. The 12 scientific instruments on the Cassini orbiter, some of which are shown above, and 6 on the Huygens lander were scheduled to carry out 27 scientific investigations.

Cassini's measurements of the planet's SKR, taken by the probe's Radio and Plasma Wave Science (RPWS) instrument, however, suggested the amazing possibility that Saturn was spinning more slowly than it had in the 1980's. According to Cassini's data, Saturn was spinning on its axis once every 10 hours 45 minutes 45 seconds, about six minutes slower than in 1981. Scientists were astounded. If all Saturn's rings and all its moons had crashed into the planet, the collisions would not have decreased Saturn's spin by that much. And at any rate, astronomers on Earth certainly would have noticed any event monumental enough to affect this huge planet to such an extent.

Rather than conclude that Saturn has slowed down, Cassini scientists settled on another possibility. They speculated that Saturn's magnetic field might not rotate at the same rate, the way all of Earth's or Jupiter's does. Instead, the field's—and, thus, the planet's—rotation rate might vary with latitude, like the sun's. That is, regions nearer the poles spin at a slower rate than regions nearer the equator. Support for that idea came from RPWS data indicating that the source area for the SKR had moved

The seven-year journey of the Cassini–Huygens spacecraft from Earth to Saturn totaled about 2 billion kilometers (3.2 billion miles), though Saturn is actually about one-half that distance from Earth. The spacecraft was so big and heavy that mission scientists plotted swingbys of three planets—Earth, Venus, and Jupiter. A swingby allows a spacecraft to take advantage of a planet's gravity to gain speed. The deep space maneuver slowed Cassini–Huygens so that it could go into orbit around Venus.

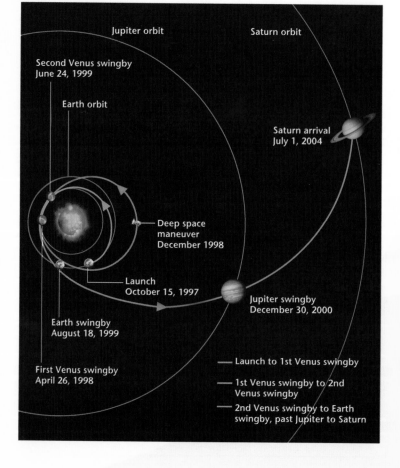

Jupiter orbit   Saturn orbit

Second Venus swingby
June 24, 1999

Earth orbit

Saturn arrival
July 1, 2004

Deep space
maneuver
December 1998

Launch
October 15, 1997

Jupiter swingby
December 30, 2000

Earth swingby
August 18, 1999

First Venus swingby
April 26, 1998

—— Launch to 1st Venus swingby

—— 1st Venus swingby to 2nd
Venus swingby

—— 2nd Venus swingby to Earth
swingby, past Jupiter to Saturn

to a region above Saturn's southern pole. As the mission progresses, scientists will examine additional data to try to solve Saturn's rotation-rate puzzle.

Cassini also found that Saturn's storms seem to have changed dramatically since the Voyager visits. Storms on Saturn develop along the edges of high-altitude bands of wind that encircle the planet at various latitudes. Some of these bands blow eastward; some blow in the opposite direction. The Voyager probes clocked the winds in the bands at about 1,600 kilometers (1,000 miles per hour), almost 10 times as fast as Earth's high-altitude winds. Along the boundaries between bands, the conflicting winds can churn into hurricanelike storms. The storms detected by the Voyager probes appeared almost exclusively near Saturn's equator and lasted for many months.

Cassini searched for storms using its RPWS instrument, which can detect a type of radio wave generated by lightning. On Earth, these radio waves cause the crackle and pop that you hear when listening to AM radio during a thunderstorm. The RPWS instrument found that the

Saturn appears in unprecedented detail (left, above) in a mosaic of 126 images taken by the Cassini spacecraft in 2004 at a distance of about 6.3 million kilometers (3.9 million miles). A less detailed image of Saturn taken by the Pioneer-Saturn spacecraft in 1979 (left) thrilled scientists by providing their first close-up look at the ringed planet. This image was taken at a distance of about 2.8 million kilometers (1.8 million miles).

A huge thunderstorm called the Dragon Storm (bright area in this false-color image) rages across the surface of Saturn in September 2004. Scientists discovered that lightning from the storm, which was 10,000 times as intense as lightning on Earth, was the source of the powerful bursts of radio waves (blue and yellow streaks in the artist's illustration, far right) detected by instruments on Cassini.

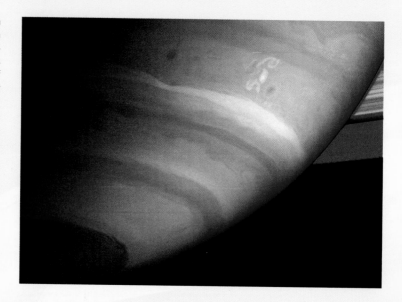

storms were widely distributed over mid- to high-latitude areas of Saturn's Southern Hemisphere.

Scientists think that the differences in storm patterns may be linked to the location of the shadow cast by Saturn's rings. As Saturn orbits the sun, the degree to which its axis tilts toward or away from the sun varies from 0 degrees to 26 degrees. The rings circle Saturn around its equator, and so they tilt with respect to the sun at the same angle as the planet.

In the 1980's, Saturn had almost no tilt with respect to the sun, and, thus, the rings cast a narrow, deep shadow near the equator. The result was turbulence between the cold, shadowed region near the equator and the warmer sunlit regions elsewhere. (In general, winds are fueled by differences in regional atmospheric temperatures based on the amount of energy received from the sun. The greater the temperature difference, the more violent the winds.) In 2004 and 2005, however, Saturn was tilting at its maximum angle with respect to the sun, and so the ring shadow covered most of its Northern Hemisphere. As a result, storms occurred over a broader region. In addition, because the temperature differences between regions were less, the storms lasted for shorter periods.

Storms on Saturn can blow for weeks, months, or even years. Storms on Earth rarely last more than one week, fading as they lose energy. On Saturn, storms tend to merge and continue their sweep across the planet. These combined storms also fade. But because Saturn does not have a solid surface to create friction, the storms fade more slowly than they do on Earth. On March 20, 2004, Cassini photographed the merger of two hurricanelike storms, each 370 kilometers (600 miles) in diameter. Both lasted for about a month before they approached each other, spun counterclockwise around each other, and then combined into an even larger storm.

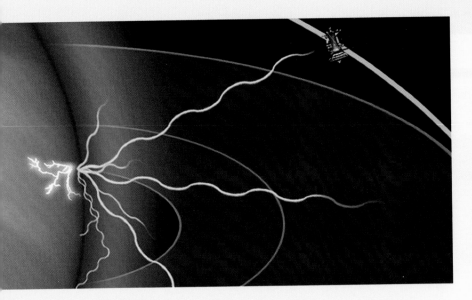

New belt

Another of Cassini's unexpected discoveries was a radiation belt existing much closer to the planet than scientists had thought possible. Saturn has one other radiation belt, outside the rings. Cassini's magnetospheric imaging instrument (MIMI) discovered the new belt encircling the planet between the cloud tops and the inner edge of the D ring, the innermost ring. Before the Cassini mission, scientists had thought that a radiation belt could not exist between the D ring and Saturn's atmosphere because Saturn's magnetic field would prevent the ions from entering the rings. Apparently, however, as particles trapped in the main radiation belt collide with Saturn's upper atmosphere, some of those particles "leak" into the region inside the innermost ring, creating a second radiation belt.

In early 2004, while Cassini was still en route to Saturn, the spacecraft's ultraviolet imaging spectrometer (UVIS) detected the sudden and surprising appearance of an immense cloud of oxygen surrounding Saturn. Scientists theorized that the oxygen atoms emerged from ice particles created as small moonlets in Saturn's E ring collided and broke apart. Radiation given off by Saturn freed the oxygen atoms from the ice particles. The oxygen cloud, equivalent to the total material in Saturn's E ring, dissipated within about two months. Cassini scientists will be watching to see if this startling process occurs again.

Remarkable rings

Saturn's magnificent rings are one of the greatest mysteries of the solar system. Other planets—Uranus, Neptune, and Jupiter—have rings. But none are as massive, complex, or diverse as Saturn's rings, which make them the solar system's best laboratory for studying planetary rings in

A stunning natural-color mosaic of six images taken by the Cassini spacecraft (top) shows three of Saturn's seven rings (inset) in exquisite, unprecedented detail—A, B, and C. The rings, which were named in the order of their discovery, extend about 137,000 kilometers (85,000 miles) from the planet's center. Cassini's narrow-angle camera created the images at a distance of about 1.8 million kilometers (1.1 million miles). The Cassini division is a large gap in the ring system discovered by astonomer Giovanni Domenico Cassini.

action. Cassini's mission includes orbits ideally suited to studying the rings, especially during the last year of its four-year tour. At that time, the spacecraft will orbit almost directly over Saturn's poles, providing scientists with excellent views of the rings.

Scientists using Earth-based telescopes discovered five of Saturn's seven rings, including the four main rings (A, B, C, and D), which extend from Saturn's upper atmosphere outward about 64,000 kilometers (40,000 miles). The fifth ring is the scattered E ring, which extends from just inside the orbit of Enceladus to as far away as Titan's orbit. NASA's Pioneer–Saturn spacecraft, which flew by Saturn in 1979, found the narrow F and G rings.

The Voyager probes discovered that the rings look like thousands of narrow ringlets. However, the main rings (except for a few gaps) are actually continuous rings that change in *optical depth* (the number of ring particles per unit area), giving the appearance of individual ringlets. In other words, the main rings' particles orbit closer together in some places and farther apart in other places, creating areas that look like alternating dense and less dense ringlets. The apparent ringlets range in size from about 2 to 100 kilometers (1 to 60 miles) in diameter. Cameras aboard the Voyager spacecraft also revealed that Saturn's rings consist of icy particles that may be as tiny as dust grains or as large as chunks the size of large houses or even mountains. The rings themselves, however, are paper-thin, no more than 90 meters (300 feet) thick in most places.

Cassini's cameras have photographed Saturn's rings in greater detail than ever seen before. At their best, the cameras can obtain a *resolution* of about 90 meters (300 feet), about the length of a football field. (Resolution is the ability of a lens to produce separate images of objects

A

Cassini division

that are close together.) The images have revealed, for example, the existence of seven new ringlets, five orbiting within gaps between main rings.

Cassini scientists have marveled at the images of such unexpected and intriguing ring features as straws and ropy areas. These structures appear to be long clumps of particles that, for some unknown reason, have become jammed together. The straws extend from 1 to 2 kilometers (0.62 to 1.2 miles) in length, while the ropy areas may be 9.6 to 19 kilometers (6 to 12 miles) long.

Cassini's cameras also revealed the "wake" created by the tiny moonlet Pan, Saturn's innermost moon, as it speeds like a motorboat in water through a passage in the A ring known as the Encke Gap. In the images, the wake appears as scalloping along the inner edge of the gap. Scientists believe that Pan maintains the Encke Gap by sweeping away any particles that fall into it. After Cassini entered Saturn's orbit, the cameras discovered three faint new ringlets in the Encke Gap. These ringlets suggest that Pan is not the only moonlet maintaining openings through the Encke Gap. Cassini's cameras also discovered a new moonlet in the Keeler Gap, a gap near the outer edge of the A ring.

Cassini has shed some light on the development of the rings. The rings may have formed from fragments of one of Saturn's moons after a collision with another moon or with a comet, meteor, or other object traveling through space. They also may be the remains of comets or meteors that ventured too close to Saturn and were captured and then torn apart by Saturn's gravity.

Before Cassini, scientists knew that the rings are only a few hundred million years

Waves created by the effects of gravity (below) resemble corrugated paper in a detail from an image of one of Saturn's rings. Bending waves (upper right in image) appear when the gravitational force of a moon orbiting within a ring lifts some of the particles from the plane in which the other particles orbit. Spiral density waves (lower left in image) appear when the gravitational force of a moon causes particles to collide.

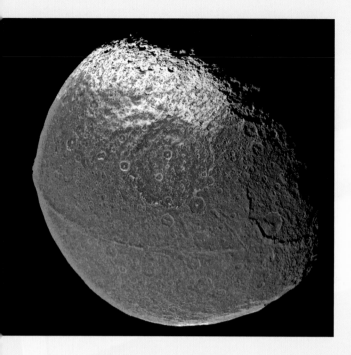

The bright and dark sides of Iapetus meet at a long, narrow ridge that lies almost exactly along the moon's equator, in a mosaic of four images. Cassini's cameras gave scientists their first look at the ridge, some of whose mountains soar 20 kilometers (12 miles) high, three times the height of Mount Everest on Earth.

old, much younger than Saturn and the rest of the solar system, which formed about 4.6 billion years ago. However, Cassini found that some regions of the rings contain fresh material that was released in the last 10 million to 100 million years. Where did these additions come from? The fresh material might have been created when a larger ring particle was broken apart, releasing cleaner, purer material.

Cassini also discovered that the rings might lose material to Saturn's moons. On Oct. 29, 2004, Cassini cameras caught the moon Prometheus stealing particles from the slender F ring. Prometheus—and its partner, Pandora—are among Saturn's *shepherd moons*, pairs of moons that orbit a short distance apart, keeping ring material confined between them. As Prometheus reached its closest approach to the F ring, a thin streamer of ring particles linked the two. These images showed, for the first time, the complex interaction between the shepherding moons and the F ring.

Saturn's icy satellites

Except for Titan, Saturn's moons are usually referred to as icy satellites because of their rock-hard surfaces consisting mainly of water ice. Scientists have long believed that the icy satellites were too small to have enough gravity to hold on to a substantial atmosphere. For many years, scientists also thought Saturn's icy satellites were geologically dead. They assumed that any internal source of heat the satellites might have was too limited to affect the surface in any way. (On Earth, radioactive decay in the core produces heat that fuels volcanic activity and powers the movement of the tectonic plates that make up Earth's outer surface.)

Images from the Voyager probes picked up clues that the moon Enceladus was ejecting material that became part of the scattered E ring, Saturn's outermost ring. In March 2005, Cassini discovered that Enceladus, which has a diameter of only about 500 kilometers (300 miles), actually has an atmosphere. The spacecraft's cosmic dust analyzer revealed that this atmosphere consists of tiny pieces of water ice only about 1 micron (0.0000394 inch) in diameter. Because of Enceladus's light gravitational force, however, these particles float away over time, becoming part of the E ring. Thus, scientists have speculated, Enceladus must have geysers or volcanoes or another means of replenishing its atmosphere.

Cassini also gave scientists their first close look at Phoebe, one of Saturn's darkest moons. Voyager 2 saw Phoebe in 1981 from a distance of 2.2 million kilometers (1.4 million miles). The Cassini spacecraft, however, flew within 2,060 kilometers (1,285 miles) of Phoebe on June 11, 2004. It was Cassini's only opportunity to fly that close to Phoebe. But that one flyby provided more information about Phoebe than scientists had learned since the moon's discovery in 1898.

Cassini's images of Phoebe revealed a battered world scarred with impact craters and littered with landslides and small boulders. In the bottom of some of the craters lay boulders hundreds of meters (thousands of feet) wide. Cassini's visual and infrared mapping *spectrometer* confirmed Earth-based conclusions that Phoebe's dark surface consists of water ice darkened by a covering of carbon compounds and other material. (A spectrometer is an instrument that spreads out light and other types of electromagnetic waves into a spectrum and displays it for study.)

Impact craters, landslides, and boulders mark the surface of Phoebe, one of the most primitive objects in the solar system. Phoebe is typical of the icy bodies that formed the building blocks of the outer planets billions of years ago.

Scientists were elated to see images showing bright streaks on the walls of Phoebe's largest craters and bright rays originating from its small craters. They believe these features were created as meteors or other objects broke through Phoebe's dark crust during bombardments, exposing the moon's deeper layers. Cassini's infrared and ultraviolet instruments also discovered that the bright streaks are water ice with some carbon dioxide ice.

We now know that Phoebe is a mixture of water ice, rock, carbon dioxide, and primitive *organic* (carbon-containing) compounds, much like Pluto and Neptune's moon Triton. Scientists believe that icy bodies like Phoebe were plentiful in the outer regions of the solar system about 4.6 billion years ago and were the building blocks of the outer planets—Jupiter, Saturn, Uranus, and Neptune. As these planets formed, gravitational forces ejected most of the leftover blocks to orbits outside the solar system. Phoebe became trapped in Saturn's orbit instead. As a result, we have the first detailed images of such a primitive object.

Saturn's oddest moon, Iapetus, also revealed some of its secrets to Cassini. One side of this moon is bright, while the other side is dark.

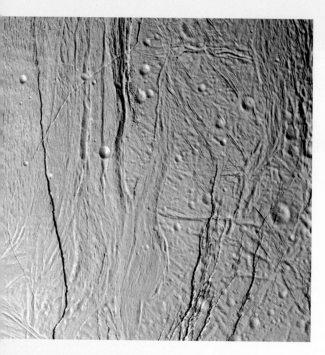

Rifts up to 3 kilometers (2 miles) wide and grooved terraces 20 kilometers (12 miles) wide separate remarkably different regions of Enceladus in a false-color mosaic image. The presence of a large number of impact craters suggests that the region on the right is geologically older than the region on the left. The younger region has apparently been smoothed by geologic processes that have left the other side unaffected.

Voyagers 1 and 2 flew by Iapetus, but the dark side appeared only as an inky blackness in the probes' cameras. Cassini's more sophisticated cameras returned images of both sides. The dark-side images showed startling surface features, including a long, narrow, soaring ridge that lies almost exactly on Iapetus's equator. The ridge is about 1,300 kilometers (800 miles) long, with some mountains at least 20 kilometers (12 miles) high, about three times higher than Earth's Mount Everest. The ridge narrows as it rises, from a base that is perhaps 20 kilometers (12 miles) wide to peaks only 2 kilometers (1.2 miles) across.

At the boundary between the bright and dark materials, the images show craters with bright walls on one side and dark walls on the other. The colors most likely relate to the material making up the moon. The dark material is probably organic compounds. The light-colored material is probably water ice and carbon dioxide ice, which are very bright.

Also at the boundary between the bright and dark material, the images show feathery-looking black streaks. Scientists disagree whether this dark material spews from the interior of Iapetus or rains down onto Iapetus from elsewhere, perhaps from nearby Phoebe. From looking at the meteorites that fall to Earth, we know that carbonaceous chondrites, the most primitive type of meteorite, are rich in dark materials like those from which the sun and planets formed. Perhaps at one time, Iapetus went through a cloud of this material. Scientists hope that Cassini's next flyby of Iapetus in 2007 will uncover more clues to this mystery.

Titan's pull

Titan, Saturn's largest moon, has exerted its own pull on Earth's scientists, independent of their fascination with its mother planet. Scientists and science-fiction writers alike have long speculated that Titan's methane-rich atmosphere might be similar to Earth's 4 billion years ago, before life appeared here.

One of the most exciting days of the Cassini-Huygens mission occurred on Jan. 14, 2005, when the Huygens probe became the first spacecraft to land on Titan. Mission scientists burst into cheers when the Green Bank radio telescope in West Virginia—1 of 17 radio telescopes around the world listening for signals from Huygens—picked up a faint but unmistakable crackling sound. The signal indicated that the probe had awakened from a 20-day "sleep" following its launch from Cassini and had come within about 1,300 kilometers (800 miles) of Titan's surface.

At that point, one exciting event happened after another. Within three minutes, Titan's dense atmosphere slowed the descending craft's speed from about 20,000 to 1,400 kilometers (12,300 to 900 miles) per hour. A small parachute deployed, further slowing the probe and pulling its main chute from its storage pack. At 120 kilometers (75 miles), another small parachute replaced the main chute for the final descent.

At an altitude of about 170 kilometers (100 miles), the probe's heat shield popped off, and its instruments began collecting and transmitting data. Then, as the probe descended for the next 2 hours and 30 minutes, Titan revealed some of its secrets.

During its descent, Huygens's instruments recorded sounds, measured wind speeds, and analyzed Titan's atmosphere. Observations by the Voyager spacecraft had revealed that nitrogen makes up most of Titan's atmosphere, as it does Earth's. In 1944, however, American astronomer Gerard Kuiper had discovered, using a spectrometer, that Titan had an atmosphere that included methane. Methane is a type of hydrocarbon, a compound of carbon and hydrogen. On Earth, hydrocarbons are found in large quantities in coal, natural gas, and petroleum. In the moon's upper atmosphere, ultraviolet sunlight breaks apart the methane molecules, the

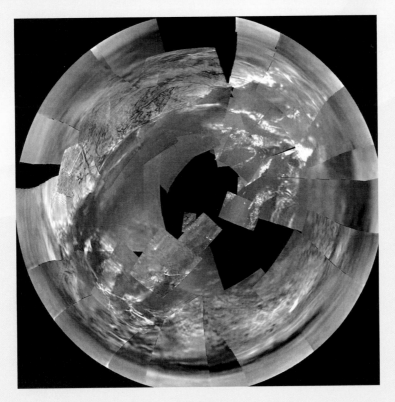

A mosaic of 60 images, taken by the Huygens probe as it descended through Titan's atmosphere, reveals the moon's surface in unprecedented detail. The bright areas at the top and left of the image are higher than other regions. The dark lines in these elevated regions may represent drainage channels created by the flow of liquid methane.

Objects the size of pebbles dot Titan's surface in an image taken during Huygens's descent. The color of the image closely resembles the actual color of the moon's surface.

way ultraviolet light destroys ozone molecules in Earth's upper atmosphere. The fragments of methane then recombine to form propane, acetylene, benzene, and the other molecules that make up Titan's smoggy atmosphere.

Methane gas in Titan's atmosphere provides the building blocks to produce complex organic molecules that might form life. However, because of the intense cold (-178 °C [290 °F]) at the surface, all water is frozen as hard as a rock and the chemical reactions that might have occurred on Earth and resulted in the development of life couldn't happen there.

The haziness of Titan's atmosphere surprised us. We had expected the probe to drop out of the haze when it reached an altitude of from 50 to 70 kilometers (30 to 45 miles). But the haze did not thin enough to give the probe's cameras a relatively clear view of the landscape until about 30 kilometers (20 miles) above the surface. At 20 kilometers (12 miles), Huygens found methane clouds. In fact, the Huygens probe discovered that the haze continues all the way to the surface.

As the probe descended, it took hundreds of pictures. Titan's surface, Huygens discovered, has intricate geologic features that scientists believe were shaped by physical processes similar to those that have shaped—and continue to shape—Earth. These include erosion caused by wind and, particularly, flowing liquids. On Titan, liquid methane plays the role that water does on Earth, scientists believe. The methane evaporates, condenses, forms clouds, and rains down, creating streams and rivers. The atmosphere, however, would run out of methane unless it was continually being replenished. These observations indicate that Titan's surface has been modified and changed over its history.

Finally, Huygens landed with what NASA called "a splat"—into Titanian mud. The first instrument to hit the surface was a long, sticklike device called a *penetrometer,* which was attached to the bottom of the probe. This device measured the force of the probe's impact and the properties of the material on the surface. Data from the penetrometer indicated something rigid—solid crust or a pebble—at the surface and clay or wet sand just below the surface.

Heat given off by Huygens warmed the landing surface, and the probe's spectrometer measured a sudden increase in methane gas boiling out of the surface. This event reinforced the idea that methane forms clouds and produces rain that erodes the surface. Much to scientists' surprise, Cassini's instruments have not detected any lakes or oceans of liquid

A river channel with many branches cuts through an area of high ridges in a mosaic created from three images taken by Huygens. The channel may have been created by liquid methane flowing over the moon's surface.

hydrocarbons. Before Cassini's arrival at Titan, models predicted that liquid methane and ethane should have been accumulating on Titan's surface for a long time, creating large oceans and lakes. Titan's rivers and lakes appeared dry at the Huygens landing site, but methane rain may have occurred not long before the landing.

Where did all of this liquid go? Did it even ever exist? What are the details about the unusual bright spot on Titan that scientists spotted in May 2005? These are some of the questions that scientists hope to answer after reviewing the Cassini–Huygens data. These unanswered questions provide even more reason to be intrigued with the mysteries that lie behind Saturn, its dazzling rings, and its numerous moons.

▓ FOR ADDITIONAL INFORMATION:

Periodicals

Battersby, Stephen. "The Petrolheads of Titan." *New Scientist,* October 23, 2004, pp. 43–46.

Dornheim, Michael A. "Capturing Saturn." *Aviation Week & Space Technology,* April 11, 2004, pp. 51–53.

Guterl, Fred. "Saturn Spectacular." *Discover,* August 2004, pp. 37–43.

Talcott, Richard. "Cassini Targets." *Astronomy,* February 2005, pp. 72–77.

Zarnecki, John C. "Destination: Titan." *Natural History,* December 2004/January 2005, pp. 26–32.

Web sites

European Space Agency—http://www.esa.int

Jet Propulsion Laboratory—http://saturn.jpl.nasa.gov

National Aeronautics and Space Adminstration—http://www.nasa.gov

On a winter morning, scientists testing a new microscope created the first three-dimensional images of freshly fallen snow crystals.

A Chance (Discovery) of Snow

By William P. Wergin

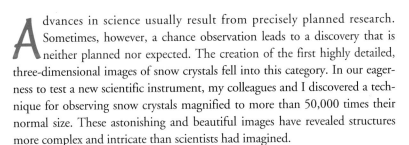

A dvances in science usually result from precisely planned research. Sometimes, however, a chance observation leads to a discovery that is neither planned nor expected. The creation of the first highly detailed, three-dimensional images of snow crystals fell into this category. In our eagerness to test a new scientific instrument, my colleagues and I discovered a technique for observing snow crystals magnified to more than 50,000 times their normal size. These astonishing and beautiful images have revealed structures more complex and intricate than scientists had imagined.

My research laboratory was in Beltsville, Maryland, at the Agricultural Research Service, an agency of the United States Department of Agriculture (USDA). I led a team of researchers working to develop and evaluate new imaging techniques using the scanning electron microscope (SEM). A SEM uses a beam of *electrons* (negatively charged subatomic particles) to illuminate and magnify objects tens of thousands of times. In my research, I used a SEM to study how the cells of plants grown for food and fiber react to such harmful organisms as viruses, fungi, and insects. I also explored the cells' reactions to pollution, drought, and other environmental conditions.

To see these cells under a SEM, however, we had to treat them with harsh chemicals and thoroughly dry them out. These chemical preparations shrank the cells and caused other changes in their shape. As a result, our *micrographs* (photographs taken with a SEM) frequently revealed distorted images.

To avoid this problem, my colleagues and I began working on the development of a *low-temperature stage* we could attach to a SEM. (A stage is a platform on which a sample is placed for observation. A low-temperature stage is a platform whose temperature can be lowered to that below room temperature.)

William Wergin (standing) and Eric Erbe, scientists at the U.S. Department of Agriculture's Agricultural Research Service, study images of snow crystals captured by a low-temperature scanning electron microscope.

We theorized that if we could simply freeze the cells by dipping them in liquid nitrogen and then keep them at a low temperature—about −196 °C (−320 °F)—while we were viewing them, the micrographs would appear more true to life.

The prototype of our cold stage arrived on a snowy morning in 1993. After my colleague, Eric Erbe, had installed the stage on our microscope, we realized that we had no cells to image. Perhaps a look outside might reveal a hardy plant or insect that had escaped the winter weather? In desperation, we opened the door and peered alongside the building. Nothing there—unless we wanted to image snow. Snow! Why not?

We grabbed a tray of collection plates—small pieces of copper about the size of a penny—and headed outside. Within a few minutes, gently falling snow had covered the plates. We plunged the plates into liquid nitrogen and eagerly returned to the laboratory.

The images we obtained using the low-temperature SEM astonished us. Six-armed "snowflakes," hexagonal plates, ornate columns, and long needles emerged in breathtaking detail never seen before.

Snow has long fascinated scientists. Robert Hooke, an English scientist, became the first to publish drawings of snow crystals. The drawings, which were based on observations using an optical microscope, appeared in Hooke's 1665 book *Micrographia.* (An optical microscope has one or more lenses that *refract* [bend] the light rays that shine through or are reflected by the object being observed.) From 1900 to 1930, Wilson Bentley, a dairy farmer and an amateur meteorologist, photographed more than 5,000 snow crystals using a camera attached to an optical microscope. These photos were published in his 1931 book *Snow Crystals.* During the 1900's, other scientists studied snowflakes using the optical microscope to determine how atmospheric conditions, particularly temperature and humidity, influenced the shape of the developing crystal.

As useful as the optical microscope was in such research, however, the instrument also presented some problems. For example, optical microscopes would typically magnify no more than 100 times their origi-

The author:
William P. Wergin is a biological science collaborator with the Agricultural Research Service, U.S. Department of Agriculture, in Beltsville, Maryland.

nal size. Furthermore, because microscopic stages were not temperature controlled, the snow crystals often melted, *sublimed* (evaporated), or *recrystallized* (developed new crystals atop existing crystals)—all of which changed the crystals' appearance. To prevent such changes, investigators were forced to work in frigid laboratories maintained at –30 to –45 °C (–22 to –49 °F). In addition, the snow crystals reflected and refracted the light used for illumination. As a result, the images showed both the outer surface and the inner features of crystals at the same time. Studying such an image would be like trying to examine the surface of your hand in an image that also revealed the bones, tendons, and nerves. Our observations of snow crystals with a cold stage SEM neatly overcame these problems.

At first, I worried that our fascination with snow crystals was too removed from our agriculture mission. One day, in a desperate effort to justify the study, I consulted *hydrologist* Albert Rango, also with the USDA. (A hydrologist studies the movement and distribution of Earth's waters.) I explained what we had been doing and asked whether our technique might be useful in his research. When he came to our laboratory to see the micrographs, he was dumfounded. These images had important uses for National Aeronautic and Space Administration (NASA) research, which assists scientists in climate studies and hydrology.

At that time, Rango and NASA scientists were using measurements of microwave radiation scattered by winter snowpacks and detected by Earth-orbiting satellites to estimate the amount of water the snowpacks contained. Melting snow contributes a large percent of the annual water supply in many parts of the world, including the western United States. Estimating how much water the melting snow will produce is important for calculating how much moisture will be available for the upcoming growing season, predicting floods, and managing water levels in dams. Rango soon discovered that being able to accurately determine the shape of crystals in the snowpack might greatly improve NASA's ability to predict the amount of meltwater.

Our research has proved helpful to colleagues in several other areas, including the study of avalanches worldwide and of seasonal polar icecaps on Mars. However, I never forgot that the mission of my laboratory was to develop new techniques for solving problems in agriculture. During the early phases of our study, we may have been somewhat distracted from this mission by the beauty and diversity of snow crystals. However, we have since used the low-temperature SEM to study numerous insects and other harmful organisms that affect crop production. No doubt many more uses of this technology will follow.

The complex surface features of a six-armed stellar dendrite—the most familiar type of snowflake—appear in unprecedented three-dimensional detail (above) in one of a series of revolutionary images of snow crystals made using a low-temperature scanning electron microscope (LT-SEM). The crystal is magnified to 40 times its normal size. An image of a stellar dendrite created using an optical microscope (above, left)—magnified 30 times—reveals the distortion and lack of detail that had limited scientists' study of snow crystals.

SNOW CRYSTALS

A snow crystal is a single crystal of ice that typically has six sides. A snowflake consists of up to 100 snow crystals clumped together. The main types of snow crystals include hexagonal plates, columns, stellar dendrites, and needles. Studies of snow crystals using a low-temperature scanning electron microscope (LT-SEM) have also revealed fascinating details about other types of frozen precipitation, including hail; ice pellets; and depth hoar, which are crystals associated with avalanches.

0.5 mm

HEXAGONAL PLATES

An image of a hexagonal plate made using the LT-SEM and magnified 60 times reveals the crystal's "arms," which consist of six smaller, identical plates. Hexagonal plates have either smooth or indented edges that descend in steps toward a common center. Temperature and humidity determine the shape of all snow crystals. Hexagonal plates are formed in two temperature ranges: -3 to 0 °C (27 to 32 ° F) and -15 °C (5 °F) or colder.

COLUMN

A column-shaped snow crystal, known as a *Tsuzumi* (right), magnified 80 times, tapers to a slender center. Tapered columns generally occur in sets of four and feature caps of hexagonal plates. Columns, which typically form at temperatures near -5 °C (23 °F) or below -25 °C (-13 °F), may have either solid or hollow cores, depending on atmospheric conditions. The sides of a column display layers that seem beautifully ornamental.

0.4 mm

0.1 mm

STELLAR DENDRITE

An extreme close-up of a stellar dendrite (left), magnified 200 times, reveals the amazing similarity of two of the crystal's arms. The six arms of a stellar dendrite are always nearly identical, probably because the atmospheric conditions immediately surrounding each tiny crystal affect all sides in the same way. Dendrites form at air temperature of about -15 °C (5 °F).

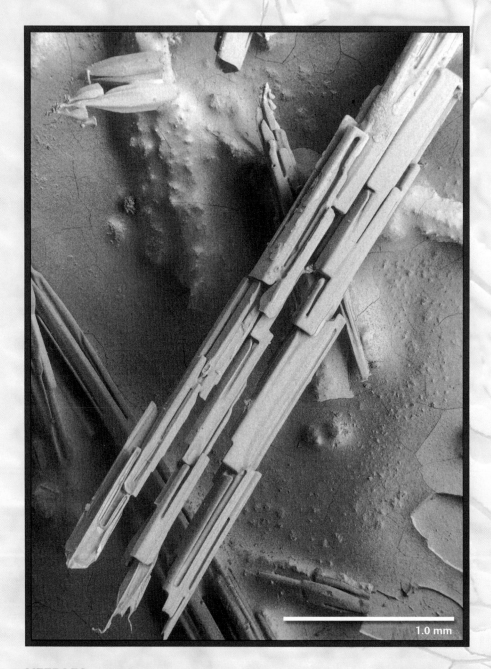

1.0 mm

NEEDLES

Needles, magnified 50 times, display the irregular lengths and carved features typical of this form of snow crystal. Needles do not always develop the sharp edges or smooth surfaces found on other types of snow crystals, probably because they form at temperatures near freezing—from -5 to -3 °C (23 to 27 °F). As they fall through the atmosphere, they probably thaw somewhat and then freeze again, a process that softens their edges and sculpts their surfaces.

IRREGULAR CRYSTALS

Hundreds of irregular snow crystals form an *aggregate* (mass) in an LT-SEM image magnified 50 times. LT-SEM technology has given scientists their first clear view of these snow crystals, which, they have discovered, are usually tiny hexagonal plates. These crystals were difficult to see under an optical microscope because they are so small, vary so greatly in their shape, and bend the light rays that shine on them. Single irregular crystals sometimes form on dendrites or plates. Aggregates, however, usually form only on needles, which suggests that the two shapes may form under similar atmospheric conditions.

1.0 mm

GRAUPEL

Graupel (right), magnified 30 times, consists of thousands of frozen cloud droplets mixed with air spaces. Graupel forms by *accretion*—that is, as droplets of *supercooled water* freeze to the surface of a snow crystal. (Supercooled droplets remain liquid at temperatures below freezing.) Eventually, the frozen droplets completely cover the crystal. LT-SEM images of graupel have provided the first sharp, three-dimensional views of these particles. The lenses of optical microscopes are not strong enough to reveal details on such a small scale. Graupel is soft and may disintegrate when it hits a hard surface.

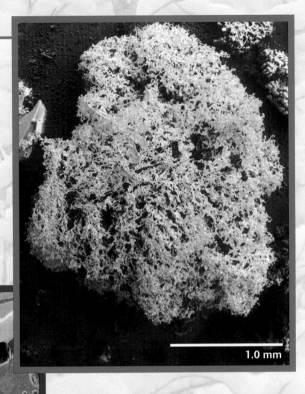

1.0 mm

HAIL

A section of a hail particle (left), magnified 130 times, reveals gas bubbles (rounded areas) that, scientists speculate, may give hail its characteristic milky appearance. Hail begins to form in thunderstorm clouds as frozen raindrops called *embryos*. As supercooled water droplets accrete to the embryos, the hailstones grow larger. Some may reach the size of golf balls or even baseballs.

0.3 mm

0.3 mm

ICE PELLET

Two cracked ice pellets, magnified 150 times, show no evidence of gas bubbles, the single characteristic that distinguishes pellets from hail. Usually associated with sleet, ice pellets are small, transparent *spheroids* (solid figures that resemble a sphere but are not perfectly round). Scientists have not determined if ice pellets are formed by frozen rain or by melting snow crystals re-forming into spheroids and then refreezing.

0.5 mm

DEPTH HOAR

An LT-SEM image, magnified 60 times, reveals the layering commonly found in a type of snow crystal known as depth hoar. These crystals form at the base of a *snowpack* (large accumulation of snow) as heat moving upward from the ground deposits water vapor on the lowest layers, causing these crystals to grow. Depth hoar crystals may be 10 times as large as the average snowflake. Depth hoar crystals are only weakly bound together and so are unstable. Eventually, the depth hoar may not be able to support the weight of the snowpack above, and a slight disturbance—such as a skier passing over—may cause a layer of the depth hoar crystals to give way. If the snowpack lies on a mountainside, the breakdown of depth hoar results in an avalanche.

MARTIAN SNOW

"Martian snow," created on Earth using the LT-SEM and magnified 2,500 times, consists of octagonal crystals of carbon dioxide (CO_2). To produce the crystals, CO_2 gas was subjected to the atmospheric pressures and temperatures found on Mars. NASA scientists used the crystals, believed to be similar to those in the icecaps that form during the Martian winter, to study that planet's atmosphere.

0.02 mm

Scientists are making fascinating discoveries about apes' intelligence and behavior. But scientists also warn that these amazing creatures may soon be lost to poaching and deforestation.

I am sitting on a grassy hillside, surrounded by 20 close relatives. No, it's not a family picnic. I'm in the East African nation of Tanzania, and I am watching an extended family of wild chimpanzees. As I sit quietly taking notes and shooting video, the chimpanzees go about their day. Three males sit side by side grooming one another, their long fingers combing through one another's black hair. A mother lies on her back, using her legs to dangle her infant above her. A few yards away, several females groom the *alpha* (top-ranking) male, whom researchers have named Frodo. Frodo has ruled this family group for three years. He has successfully fought off several challenges to his leadership, although some day another male chimpanzee will likely overthrow him.

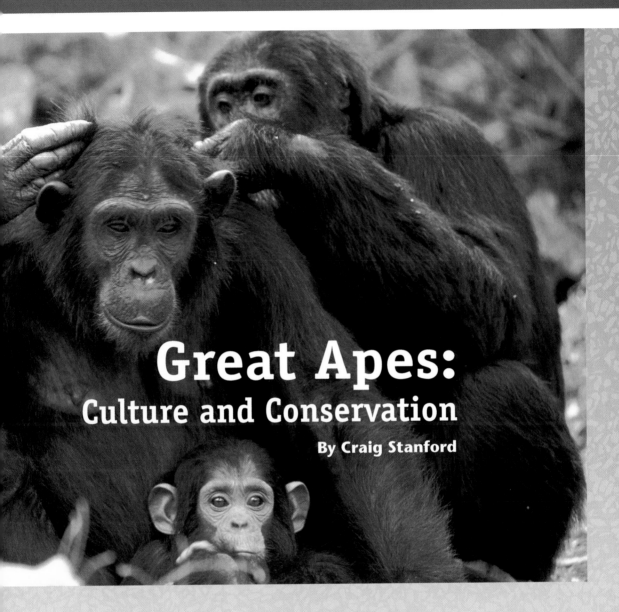

Great Apes:
Culture and Conservation
By Craig Stanford

Suddenly we hear a pant-hoot—a loud, wailing call—from the next valley. Everyone in the group leaps up and replies with the same call. Another group of chimpanzees is announcing its approach. When the newcomers arrive, they exchange excited greetings with members of the first group before settling down to more grooming.

Among the arrivals is Freud, Frodo's older brother, a lifelong ally and occasional rival. Freud is as different from Frodo as night is from day. Frodo is aggressive and macho. Freud is laid back, easygoing, and good-natured. I have nearly stepped on Freud a few times as I walked through thickets where he lay dozing in the shade. Getting that close to Frodo would be a mistake that he would punish with a hard slap on my leg.

Chimpanzees groom one another at the Jane Goodall Research Center in Gombe, Tanzania.

The author:
Craig Stanford (inset) is a Professor of Anthropology and Biology at the University of Southern California and co-director of the Jane Goodall Research Center.

MEET THE GREAT APES

Bonobos: The smallest of the great apes, bonobos live in a section of African rain forest in the Democratic Republic of the Congo. Adult bonobos weigh from 34 to 45 kilograms (75 to 100 pounds).

Chimpanzees: One of the best-known great apes, chimpanzees live in tropical Africa from Gambia in the west to Lake Victoria in the east. Adult chimpanzees are from 1 meter to 1.7 meters (3.25 to 5.5 feet) tall, and weigh from 40 to 50 kilograms (88 to 110 pounds).

Gorillas: The largest of the great apes are the gorillas. Mountain gorillas live in western and central Africa, mostly in lowland rain forests. The eastern gorilla lives at higher elevations. Gorillas can weigh up to 177 kilograms (390 pounds) and stand 1.8 meters (6 feet) tall.

Orangutans: The only Asian great apes, orangutans live on the Indonesian islands of Sumatra and Borneo. Adults weigh about 80 kilograms (180 pounds) and stand about 1.4 meters (4.5 feet) tall.

This difference in personalities is one reason chimpanzees are so fascinating to study. Their personalities influence the way they live their life, just as ours do.

I have spent about one-fourth of my adult life in remote forests of Africa and Asia studying *primates* (the group of mammals including apes, monkeys, and human beings). On my 35 research trips into the wild, I have usually focused on chimpanzees, which are, to me, the most fascinating of all the apes.

According to the theory of evolution, apes are our closest relatives in the animal kingdom. I think of them as my evolutionary cousins. Most scientists, including me, believe that human beings and apes developed from a common ancestor. We believe that if you went back in

time 7 million to 10 million years ago, you would find this so-called *missing link*. Studies beginning in the 1960's have found that human and chimpanzee DNA (*d*eoxyribo*n*ucleic *a*cid, the molecule that directs the development of all living things) is nearly identical.

This close genetic relationship alone makes apes intriguing to scientists. We have learned a great deal about our early apelike human ancestors from the many fossils we have found. For clues to how these early ancestors probably lived, however, we often study the behavior of modern apes. My own special area of research, for example, is the meat-eating habits of chimpanzees. This subject is of great interest to *primatologists* (scientists who study primates) because it helps us understand the origins of the modern human diet.

Another vitally important reason we study apes is their uncertain future. Without stepped-up local and international efforts to protect them, the apes will disappear from the wild within the next 50 years. Destruction of their forest habitat, *poaching* (illegal hunting), and disease are all taking a terrible toll on these creatures.

Three of the four kinds of great apes live in central Africa. These include gorillas (opposite page), chimpanzees (above, left), and bonobos (above). All these apes are highly social creatures.

Orangutans are the only Asian great ape. Unlike their African relatives, orangutans are highly solitary.

ASIA

Pacific Ocean

Borneo

Sumatra

Equator

Indian Ocean

Orangutans

AUSTRALIA

Which primates are known as the great apes?

About 250 species of primates live in the world today. However, there are only five main types of apes. Scientists divide these five into two categories, based chiefly on size. *Great apes* include gorillas, chimpanzees, bonobos, and orangutans. Three of the great apes—the bonobo, chimpanzee, and gorilla—live in the tropical equatorial forests of Africa, while the fourth—the orangutan—lives in Indonesia on the islands of Sumatra and Borneo. The gibbon, which lives in Southeast Asia, is the only *lesser ape.*

Although apes and monkeys appear similar, apes share certain characteristics that set them apart. Apes lack tails, which most monkeys possess. Apes have rotating shoulder joints that allow them to hang or swing by their arms. (You have the same kind of rotating shoulder, which allows you to throw a football or swing from a gymnastics high bar.) Apes also have a specialized way of walking, placing the weight of their forearms on their knuckles.

The most important trait shared by all great apes, however, is a large brain. Great apes top the list of brainy creatures, exceeded only by human beings. For this reason, ape intelligence has become an important focus for scientists seeking to understand the evolution of human intelligence. Some scientists study apes' intellectual abilities in laboratories, giving them tests similar to the intelligence tests given in school. My approach, however, is to try to understand ape intelligence in nature, by studying apes' strategies for using tools, finding mates, or hunting. Some primatologists also try to understand whether the emotions apes display—such as guilt, shame, fear, and anger—are the same as human emotions.

Among the great apes, the chimpanzee is probably the best known. An estimated 150,000 to 200,000 chimpanzees live in the wild—more than all the other great apes combined. Chimpanzees live in a variety of habitats, from lowland tropical rain forests to open grasslands with only patches of trees. These habitats range across equatorial Africa from Gambia in the west to Lake Victoria in the east.

In some ways, chimpanzees strongly resemble people in their behavior, anatomy, and ways of life. For example, infant chimpanzees spend many years with their mother. Chimpanzees reach sexual maturity at about age 11. Females usually give birth for the first time in their midteen-age years and have a baby every four years for the rest of their life. Chimpanzees may live to about age 45 in the wild and may reach 60 in captivity.

Chimpanzees live in complex social groupings called *communities.* Males spend their entire life in the community in which they were born, while females typically immigrate at maturity to a neighboring group. Males of a community have strong social bonds, and they act together to defend their community boundaries against all outsiders. They attack and even kill chimpanzees from neighboring communities that wander into their area. Male chimpanzees spend a great deal of energy intimidating and fighting other males in an attempt to move up the chain of command, so to speak, in their community.

Males and females form temporary subgroups called *parties* that come together when trees are laden with ripe fruit or when females are ready to mate. Chimpanzees seem to relish the meat of other mammals and spend much time and energy hunting. However, they often get less energy from the meat they catch than the amount of energy they spend hunting. Most of the chimpanzee diet consists of ripe fruit.

Bonobos, also sometimes called *pygmy chimpanzees,* live in the rain forest south of the Congo River in the Democratic Republic of the Congo, often called Congo (Kinshasa). Bonobos look like chimpanzees, but their social behavior differs greatly. Although males dominate chimpanzee social life, female bonobos form alliances with other females to intimidate males and so try to prevent the males from dominating them. In addition, like human beings, bonobos do not use sexual contact solely for reproduction. Bonobos engage in sexual activity with members of their own gender as well as with members of the opposite sex as a way of reducing tensions, settling conflicts, and strengthening the bonds among members of a group.

The gorilla is the world's largest primate. Like chimpanzees and bonobos, gorillas live in tropical forests near the equator. Because of their size, gorillas spend more time on the ground and less time climbing trees than chimpanzees or bonobos do.

The name *gorilla* actually refers to two similar species. Western gorillas live in western and central Africa, primarily in lowland rain forests. Eastern gorillas live higher in mountain ranges. One *race* (subspecies) of eastern gorilla, the mountain gorilla, lives at elevations up to 4,000 meters (13,000 feet) in two small patches of forest near the border between Uganda, Rwanda, and Congo (Kinshasa). As males reach their midteenage years, the hair on their backs becomes silvery, earning them the common name of *silverback*. At about the same age, females tend to leave their home groups and join another group.

The orangutan is the only Asian great ape, and is, perhaps, still the least understood of the four great apes. These large red apes, which live in the tropical rain forests of the Indonesian islands of Sumatra and Borneo, are mostly solitary. As a result, scientific studies of orangutans have been able to produce only limited amounts of information. Adult male orangutans spend their lives alone, while adult females live in the company of their infants. Considering that all other great apes are highly social, this is strange behavior, which scientists have not been able to explain.

Like all the other great apes, orangutans grow slowly and reproduce infrequently; a female may go more than five years between the births of offspring. Orangutans spend most of their life high in trees, where they feed on ripe fruits. These apes live in complex societies that, when mapped out, resemble overlapping rings. Several females live alone or with their offspring on overlapping areas. One resident male, meanwhile, tries to control a territory that encompasses the areas of all his females. He constantly patrols his area in an attempt to keep other males away. At the same time, younger, "bachelor" males wander the forest hoping to find females when the resident male is not nearby.

Studying the great apes

Primatology emerged as a field of study in the early 1960's. Perhaps the best-known primatologist is Jane Goodall, a British chimpanzee researcher whose pioneering work opened the door to the indepth study of great apes in the wild. In 1960, Goodall traveled to Africa and landed a job as assistant to famed fossil hunter Louis

Leakey. The following year, Leakey sent her to Gombe, a forest along the Tanzanian shore of Lake Tanganyika that was home to a population of wild chimpanzees. At the time, scientists knew little about the lives of chimpanzees, and Leakey wondered whether scientists could learn something about the behavior of ancient human ancestors by studying modern living apes in the wild. Goodall spent months patiently working to make the chimpanzees comfortable in her presence. She would clear a patch of forest and lay out bananas to attract them. Then she would sit quietly near them. Eventually, the chimpanzees neither fled from her nor expected handouts of food, and Goodall could follow and observe them for hours.

By the mid-to-late 1960's, Goodall's discoveries about chimpanzee behavior had blurred the lines that, scientists thought, separated

Jane Goodall, one of the world's best-known primatologists, observes a chimpanzee at Gombe National Park in Tanzania. Goodall pioneered the in-depth study of great apes in the wild.

people from all other animals. She described the long and intense bond between chimpanzee mothers, their babies, and other relatives. She became the first to discover that chimpanzees fashion simple tools from sticks and blades of grass. Most amazing of all, she watched chimpanzees hunt and kill monkeys, antelope, and other animals, and share the meat. This discovery particularly shocked the public and the scientific world, which had long thought of all apes as *vegetarians* (nonmeat-eaters), chiefly because scientists had not witnessed chimpanzees killing other animals.

Goodall also documented that chimpanzee society values intelligence as much as it does physical strength. Members of a community remember the debts and favors they owe to other group members, as well as those owed to them. For example, if Frodo gives meat to Freud after a hunt, Freud will remember the favor and later repay Frodo by giving him meat from another hunt.

In the 1960's, Louis Leakey also sent other students off to study gorillas and orangutans. Dian Fossey, an American woman, became the pioneering researcher for gorillas. She conducted her research in the Virunga Volcanoes region of east-central Africa. There she documented the gentle nature of these giant apes, which, at that time, had a reputation for ferocity and aggression. She also opened the public's eyes to the threats to gorillas from poaching and loss of habitat.

In the early 1970's, Biruté Galdikas, a student from the University of California at Los Angeles, traveled to the rain forests of Indonesia and undertook the first long-term study of orangutans in the wild. She became the first scientist to document the unusual solitary nature of these apes and the often-violent relationships among males of the species.

Bonobos, which were unknown to scientists until the 1920's, were not studied in the wild until the 1980's, when Japanese primatologist Takayoshi Kano from Kyoto University established a research station in central Africa. Before Kano began studying bonobos, they were known mainly from studies carried out in zoos, where they appeared to be completely nonviolent. In the wild, however, female bonobos have less power, and males are more aggressive. Occasionally they even hunt and eat meat. Today, despite the work of Kano and others, the inaccessibility of the bonobos' habitat and the many political troubles in that part of the world have seriously interfered with primatologists' efforts to learn more about these fascinating apes.

Learning about apes

When I am in the field, I study particular aspects of great ape behavior that I have spent years reading about and preparing to observe. I follow chimpanzees, as well as some of the prey animals the chimpanzees like to hunt, and record the apes' behavior using notebooks, video, and still photography. Only by spending long periods in the field can one hope to see the amazing things chimpanzees and other primates do with their lives.

You might think that studying a particular group of animals for more than 30 years would be long enough to tell us all we need to know about it. But consider this. If extraterrestrial scientists came to Earth to study people, how long would they have to observe you and your family before they could say they had learned everything of importance about the whole human species? The answer is, of course, a very long time, and even then they would need to observe a variety of societies in a variety of places.

Each decade since the 1960's has brought new and exciting discoveries about the great apes. In the 1970's, after 15 years of closely observing wild chimpanzees, Goodall and her students first reported one of the most astonishing of all her discoveries about chimpanzee behavior—murder and warfare. Indeed, among primates, only chimpanzees and human beings engage in such brutal acts.

Field studies in the late 1970's—starting with those of Caroline Tutin of the Centre International de Recherches Médicales, a primate research center in Franceville, Gabon—revealed that gorilla social groups often have more than one male. This was a surprising develop-

A chimpanzee named Frodo holds a fawn he has killed while hunting. Jane Goodall discovered that chimpanzees, long thought to be vegetarians, sometimes hunt other animals.

Chimpanzees pass knowledge about tool use from generation to generation. In some communities (left), the apes use sticks to fish for termites. In others (above), chimpanzees use rocks to crack open nuts. Such differences between learned traits is evidence of chimpanzees' cultural diversity.

ment, as primatologists had previously thought that gorillas lived only in "harems" made up of one male and several females. Primatologists such as Tutin also witnessed gorillas in parts of Africa eating fruit rather than leaves, traveling long distances, and otherwise behaving quite differently from the gorillas Fossey had studied.

In the 1980's, scientists realized that chimpanzees in some parts of Africa use stone tools to crack open nuts. In the 1990's, researchers learned how frequent and intense chimpanzee hunting and meat-eating can be. And only in the early 2000's have we begun to appreciate the differences in *culture* in great ape societies. Culture is the learned beliefs and practices of a society.

One of the most fascinating examples of cultural *diversity* (differences) among chimpanzees involves their choice and use of tools. For example, in a forest in East Africa, a chimpanzee sits by a gigantic termite mound. He pokes a hole in the mound with his finger, then inserts a thin stick. Hundreds of huge-jawed soldier termites swarm over the stick to protect their nest. The chimpanzee gently withdraws his tool and swipes it through his mouth, licking off and chewing the insects. He endures the many termite bites he receives for the sake of a tasty snack rich in protein and fat.

Meanwhile, in a forest 3,200 kilometers (2,000 miles) away in western Africa, another chimpanzee sits under a nut tree pounding walnut-sized nuts open with a stone hammer. The meat inside is fatty and delicious. He has learned to do this by watching his mother and is now an expert nutcracker himself.

The termite-fishing chimpanzee in eastern Africa does not use stone tools, even though there are plenty of rocks and nuts in his forest. The stone-hammering chimp in western Africa does not fish for termites, even though there are many of the insects' huge mounds in his habitat. These behaviors are not, as far as we know, determined by the chimps' environment. If they were, then we would expect to see similar tools in similar forests, which we do not. These preferences for certain tools represent differences in chimpanzee culture, similar to the differences in styles of human homes, for example. Scientists have found some evidence for cultural diversity in the other three groups of great apes, though it appears to be much less common than among chimpanzees.

Apes under threat

Despite all the exciting recent discoveries about great apes, many dangers still threaten these amazing animals. The greatest threat to apes, as well as to all other tropical creatures, is *deforestation,* the destruction of their forest habitats. Faced with the intense pressure of a rapidly growing human population, many developing countries are doing little to protect what remains of their natural forests. People need land for farms and villages, and governments and companies want profits from timber sales.

All wild great apes live in poor nations—some of them among the poorest on Earth—where the populations are growing rapidly and governments have little incentive to protect wildlife or its habitats. For example, primatologist Carel van Schaik from Duke University in Durham, North Carolina, and his colleagues have estimated that since the early 1990's, timber-cutting operations have destroyed up to 80 percent of the orangutan habitat on Sumatra.

The trade in *bushmeat* (meat from wild animals) poses a second major threat to the survival of apes. People have been hunting and eating wild animals for hundreds of thousands of years. In Africa, the meat of chimpanzees, gorillas, and bonobos is considered a delicacy. This may sound gruesome, but it is no more strange than the popularity of turkey, lobster, or frogs' legs as food in many cultures. In March 2001, the United Nations Food and Agriculture Organization reported that the bushmeat trade was becoming an increasingly profitable industry. As logging roads are cut into the forests, local businesspeople

Rangers at Virunga National Park in the Democratic Republic of the Congo carry the body of a mountain gorilla killed by poachers to park headquarters for examination. *Poaching* (illegal hunting) is a major threat to great apes.

capitalize on the frequent truck traffic by setting up hunting businesses. Hunters ship the ape carcasses on trucks to nearby towns, where they are sold in the market at prices up to five times as high as that for beef. In addition, the logging companies sometimes provide their workers with shotguns to hunt for meat for themselves rather than supplying them with food.

In forests all across Africa, people set *snares* (leg traps) to catch antelope, wild pigs, and other animals for food. These snares also entrap great apes as they walk across the forest floor. Poachers used to make snares from natural fibers. If a chimpanzee stepped into one, the material usually rotted quickly and the snare would fall off, causing no major damage. However, metal wires have replaced fiber snares. These tighten around the ape's limb and continue to cut into the flesh until the hand or foot develops *gangrene* (a condition in which body tissues die from lack of oxygen), which can kill or maim the ape. More than one-third of all the chimpanzees living in some forests today, including Uganda's Budongo Forest, are either amputees or carry severe injuries from snares. In some parks, rangers collect snares—sometimes finding hundreds in a given area—but in unprotected areas, the danger from these traps is extremely high.

Because of their genetic similarity to us, great apes can catch nearly all infectious human diseases. And like us, apes lack any *immunity* (resistance) to diseases to which they have never been exposed. So when a chimpanzee contracts the common cold or other respiratory infection, the disease is often fatal. In particular danger are apes that

A logging company clears a section of forest in Gabon, Africa. Deforestation is one of the largest threats to all species of great apes. It destroys the apes' habitats and gives poachers easier access to the remaining forests.

come in contact with people, for example, in areas where farms and forests sit side by side.

Primatologists believe that thousands of gorillas and chimpanzees have died across Africa since the early 2000's in epidemics of the deadly Ebola virus, which may be transmitted between apes and human beings. A study published in 2004 by Eric M. Leroy of the Research Institute for Development in Gabon, Africa, linked five Ebola outbreaks in central Africa in the early 2000's to a 60-percent drop in gorilla populations and a 90-percent drop in chimpanzee populations. In 2004, Heinz Ellerbrock of the Robert Koch Institute in Berlin and Fabian Leendertz of the Max Planck Institute for Evolutionary Anthropology in Leipzig announced that they had discovered anthrax bacteria in chimpanzees that had died at Tai National Park in Côte d'Ivoire. Their findings represent the first time the disease had been identified in a wild ape population.

Can they survive?

The survival of the great apes, like that of all wildlife, is a human issue. When the living standards of people improve, their ability to preserve the natural environment and the creatures in it also increases. The question is, given the slow reproductive rate of the apes, whether they will be decimated before conservation efforts can succeed.

One of the most important steps is protecting their forest homes. Many African and Asian countries have set aside land as national parks and nature preserves. Unfortunately, that strategy is not always simple.

Protecting the land costs money and takes many dedicated people. Governments of poor countries are not eager to lock up natural resources, such as oil, gas, minerals, and timber, in national parks, when these areas could be exploited, at least in the short term, for profit. Developing nations must have economic incentives to set aside valuable land and protect its wildlife.

One such incentive, at least for gorillas and chimpanzees, is *ecotourism* (visiting rare and endangered species in their natural habitat). Dian Fossey felt the only way she could protect her gorillas was by threatening to shoot poachers. Today, ecotourism has dramatically reduced poaching of mountain gorillas. Tourists pay hundreds of dollars per hour to sit and watch a group of wild chimpanzees or gorillas. Revenue from such ecotourism goes mainly to the local government, giving it a strong economic incentive to protect the forest and its apes. Some ecotourism revenue also goes to local people, in the form of health clinics and dispensaries in villages near the forest.

Helping local people feel they have a stake in the future of the animals in their area goes a long way toward protecting them. Unfortunately, many of the countries where great apes live are not only poor but also politically unstable. Civil wars and terrorism can destroy a thriving tourist industry overnight. For example, in 1999, Rwandan rebels attacked an ecotourism center in Uganda's Bwindi Impenetrable National Park, taking 14 people hostage. Eight of the hostages were

Guards at Dzanga-Ndoki National Park in the Central African Republic hold a captured poacher. Guards patrol many national parks in Africa, capturing or killing poachers and removing the traps they set.

murdered, though the rest were released unharmed. Tourism plummeted for months as a result.

Ultimately, the fate of the great apes depends on the people of the nations where these magnificent and fascinating animals live. These days, as I work with scientists from African nations, I am impressed by their determination to save the natural heritage of their society, the apes with whom they share their land. We sit in tropical forests, watching gorillas and chimpanzees a few yards away as they go about their lives, unaware of the dangers they face from human beings. At the same time, only human beings can save them from extinction.

■ FOR ADDITIONAL INFORMATION

Books

Fossey, Dian. *Gorillas in the Mist.* 1983. Reprint. Mariner, 2000.
Galdikas, Biruté M. F. *Reflections of Eden: My Years with the Orangutans of Borneo.* 1995. Reprint. Back Bay, 1996.
Goodall, Jane. *In the Shadow of Man.* Rev. ed. Mariner, 2000.
Stanford, Craig. *Significant Others: The Ape-Human Continuum and the Quest for Human Nature.* Basic, 2001.

Web sites

Bushmeat Crisis Task Force—www.bushmeat.org
International Primate Protection League—www.ippl.org
The Jane Goodall Institute—www.janegoodall.org
Primate Info Net—pin.primate.wisc.edu

Tourists and guards watch a mountain gorilla in Virunga National Park in the Democratic Republic of the Congo. Revenues from ecotourism give local governments and people a strong economic incentive to protect great apes and other wild animals.

The future is only 3000 km away.

DAIMLER CHRYSLER BALLARD

CLEARING THE WAY FOR A
HYDROGEN ECONOMY

The Hysun3000, an experimental three-wheeled vehicle powered by a hydrogen fuel cell, passes through Marseilles, France, during a world-record-breaking trip across Europe in September 2004. The Hysun3000 traveled 3,000 kilometers (1,864 miles) from Berlin to Barcelona, Spain, on only 3.3 kilograms of hydrogen (the energy equivalent of 3.3 gallons of gasoline).

The hydrogen economy *seems* to be approaching fast, but is it really just around the corner?

By Jessica Gorman

The Shell filling station in northeast Washington, D.C., looks like any other gas station. Drivers are watching the dollars and cents add up while fuel runs through nozzles to their vehicles.

But this station, opened in October 2004, is the first retail hydrogen and gasoline station in North America. One of the pumps dispenses hydrogen fuel for a fleet of General Motors vehicles that do not depend on the gasoline that has powered nearly all vehicles since the invention of the automobile.

Welcome to the *hydrogen economy*, a world in which we get the power we need to move our vehicles, run our factories, and heat and light our homes from hydrogen—a highly efficient, virtually inexhaustible, and nonpolluting gas. (An economy is a system of managing the production, distribution, and consumption of goods and services.) Although the hydrogen economy is not here yet, in 2005 we were beginning to see its outline on the hazy horizon.

Since the 1990's, hydrogen has attracted a great deal of attention as an alternative to the *fossil fuels* upon which our energy-guzzling world depends. Fossil fuels—which include coal, oil, and natural gas—developed from the fossilized remains of prehistoric plants. Several automobile manufacturers

Biomass: Any organic material, including cornstalks, garbage, and waste paper, that can be converted into energy or a source of energy.

Catalyst: A substance that accelerates a chemical reaction while itself remaining practically unchanged.

Electrolysis: A process of producing hydrogen in which an electric current passes through a liquid, causing a chemical reaction. If the liquid is water, electrolysis splits the water molecules into hydrogen gas and oxygen gas.

Fossil fuels: Fuels such as coal, oil, and natural gas that developed from the fossilized remains of prehistoric plants.

Fuel cells: Pollution-free devices that convert chemical energy directly to electric energy.

Global warming: A gradual increase in the average temperature of Earth's surface that began in the 1800's.

Greenhouse gas: A gas that warms the atmosphere by trapping heat.

Hydrocarbons: Organic compounds made up of hydrogen and carbon; they are found in fossil fuels.

Hydrogen economy: A world in which we get the power we need to move our vehicles, run our factories, and heat and light our homes from hydrogen.

Organic: Containing carbon.

Steam reformation: A process of producing hydrogen using steam and vaporized fossil fuel.

The author:
Jessica Gorman is a freelance science writer.

have produced prototype cars whose internal-combustion engines run on hydrogen rather than gasoline. Some countries are operating buses powered by hydrogen. In addition, stationary hydrogen-run devices have found limited use as electric power generators. Meanwhile, hydrogen has emerged as the most promising fuel in the fast-developing field of *fuel cells* for use in vehicles and other power generators. Fuel cells are pollution-free devices that convert chemical energy directly to electric energy.

But many significant questions relating to technical, logistical, and financial roadblocks must be addressed before we will see highways teeming with hydrogen-powered cars and homes lit by personal fuel cell generators. How will we produce huge amounts of hydrogen without depending on the fossil fuels currently used for hydrogen production? How will we store this voluminous gas, which is 14 times as light as air? How will we transport hydrogen long distances, the way we currently transport natural gas and petroleum? Who will pay for a nationwide hydrogen-vehicle refueling network whose cost would likely reach tens of billions of dollars?

Fossil fuels have their drawbacks, but they also offer significant benefits. For instance, they are relatively easy to extract, produce, and transport. Their relatively low cost also makes them widely available to consumers.

But burning fossil fuels releases many unwanted chemicals into the atmosphere. For example, emissions from gasoline-burning cars contribute to *smog* (created by the action of sunlight on exhaust gases) and *acid rain* (precipitation polluted mainly by chemicals released during the burning of coal and oil).

Burning fossil fuels also creates carbon dioxide, a so-called *greenhouse gas* that traps heat in the atmosphere. Most scientists believe carbon dioxide emissions are contributing to *global warming* (a gradual increase in the average temperature of Earth's surface that began in the 1800's). Continued global warming could disrupt weather patterns and ocean circulation, shift agricultural zones, severely affect animal habitats, and cause other damaging environmental consequences. Finally, although fossil fuels are plentiful, the world does not have an endless supply of them. And creating new fossil fuel deposits takes millions of years.

Hydrogen, in contrast, is the most plentiful element in the universe. Earth holds an abundance of hydrogen, though it rarely exists in the gaseous form found in the sun and many other stars. On Earth, hydrogen is bound up with other elements in numerous compounds, most notably water. In fact, the word *hydrogen* comes from two Greek words meaning *water-former.* Hydrogen exists in nearly all *organic* matter (substances containing carbon), including sugars

WHAT IS THE HYDROGEN ECONOMY?

A *hydrogen economy* is a world in which hydrogen would be used as a source of energy for our cars, homes, and businesses. This new economy would require advances in production, storage, transportation, and uses of hydrogen as a fuel.

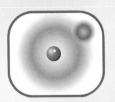

Production

Hydrogen can be produced from water using *electrolysis* (splitting water molecules into hydrogen and oxygen). Other methods of extracting hydrogen include *reformation* (splitting hydrocarbon molecules found in natural gas, methanol, or propane) and *photoelectrolysis* (using sunlight to split water molecules).

Storage

Hydrogen can be stored as a compressed gas or a cooled and compressed liquid. Hydrogen may also be stored by physically attaching it to the surfaces of metallic solids. Other storage methods may include *carbon nanotubes* (microscopic tubes made of carbon) and crystals with large amounts of interior space.

Transportation

Hydrogen can be transported by vehicles or pipelines. Consumers could fill up their hydrogen-powered vehicles at gas stations.

Uses

Hydrogen could be used directly in vehicles. It could also be used in fuel cells to produce electric power for cars, trucks, buses, locomotives, and ships. Fuel cells could also produce electric power for buildings.

and proteins found in plant and animal tissue. In addition, hydrogen is an essential component of *hydrocarbons,* which are organic compounds found in the fossil fuels that hydrogen may someday replace.

A hydrogen economy promises tantalizing advantages over an economy dominated by fossil fuels. A significant reduction in environmental pollution ranks as one of the most notable benefits of a hydrogen economy. For example, hydrogen fuel cells emit only one by-product, and it is a usable one—clean water. In fact, the astronauts' water supply on the United States space shuttle comes from hydrogen fuel cells used to power that craft's electric systems.

ENERGY PRODUCTION

Hydrogen accounts for an insignificant percentage of the electric energy produced in the United States each year. In a summary of energy production published by the U.S. Energy Information Administration, hydrogen falls into the "Other" category—along with batteries and miscellaneous technologies—totaling less than 1 percent of electric energy produced in 2003 (the latest year for which data are available).

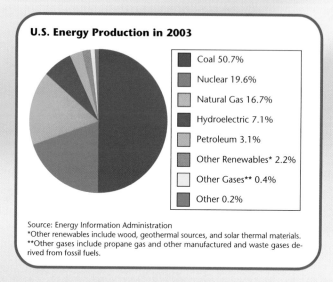

U.S. Energy Production in 2003

- Coal 50.7%
- Nuclear 19.6%
- Natural Gas 16.7%
- Hydroelectric 7.1%
- Petroleum 3.1%
- Other Renewables* 2.2%
- Other Gases** 0.4%
- Other 0.2%

Source: Energy Information Administration
*Other renewables include wood, geothermal sources, and solar thermal materials.
**Other gases include propane gas and other manufactured and waste gases derived from fossil fuels.

A switch to a hydrogen economy would also reduce or even eliminate U.S. reliance on foreign sources of petroleum and other fuels, especially from politically unstable regions. In addition, hydrogen can be obtained from many sources. As a result, a shortage of one source would not damage the hydrogen economy in the same way that a petroleum shortage can hurt a fossil fuel economy.

Finally, the widespread use of hydrogen fuel cells, especially in homes and businesses, could improve the reliability and security of the U.S. electric power system. Nearly all the electric power used in the United States is produced in large, centralized plants and then distributed to users. A spread-out system of electric power production would lower Americans' vulnerability to accidental blackouts as well as to terrorist attacks on electric power plants.

Strictly speaking, hydrogen is not an *energy source*—that is, a naturally occurring, unprocessed form of direct energy, such as natural gas, coal, and petroleum. Instead, hydrogen, like electric current or gasoline, is an *energy carrier,* a means of storing, moving, and delivering energy in an easy-to-use form. To serve as a source of energy, hydrogen must be produced (from water, hydrocarbons, or another source); stored (as a gas or liquid or in a chemical compound); distributed (as a pressurized gas or cooled liquid); and then converted (by *combustion* [burning] or processing in a fuel cell).

Producing hydrogen

The United States produces 45 million metric tons (50 million tons) of commercial hydrogen gas each year, which is used to create ammonia for fertilizers, remove sulfur from gasoline, and *hydrogenate* (solidify) liquid vegetable oils. All this hydrogen, however, is only a small percentage of the amount the United States would need in a hydrogen economy.

About 95 percent of the commercial hydrogen gas produced in 2005 resulted from the chemical conversion of hydrocarbons in a process called *steam reformation.* This process involves combining steam and vaporized fossil fuel—usually natural gas—at high temperatures and pressures with a *catalyst* (a substance that accelerates a chemical reaction while itself remaining practically unchanged). In the process, hydrogen gas splits off from the hydrocarbons in the natural gas.

Unfortunately, steam reformation requires a great deal of fossil fuel, which reduces the overall *efficiency* of the process to about 65 percent. (Efficiency compares the amount of energy obtained from a process with the amount used. A process that is 65-percent efficient, for example, converts 65 percent of the energy in the hydrogen to electric energy.) In addition, steam reformation plants currently depend on nonrenewable fossil fuels for power. By-products of the reforming process include the pollutant sulfur and the greenhouse gases carbon monoxide and carbon dioxide.

The remaining 5 percent of commercial hydrogen used in the United States is produced by *electrolysis.* In this process, an electric current passes through a liquid, causing a chemical reaction. If the liquid is water, electrolysis splits the water molecules into hydrogen gas and oxygen gas. The result is a pure product that is used mainly in manufacturing electronics. Electrolysis-based hydrogen is expensive—about 10 times as expensive as natural gas and 3 times as costly as gasoline per *British thermal unit* (Btu). (One Btu is the quantity of heat needed to raise the temperature of 0.454 kilogram [1 pound] of water 0.556 °C [1 °F].)

Nevertheless, some energy experts believe that electrolysis could play a much greater role in future hydrogen production. Because it relies on electric current—an energy carrier that can store power for later use—electrolysis plants could use electric power that might otherwise go to waste. In addition, electrolysis is about 80-percent efficient. However, researchers would have to figure out ways to produce hydrogen on a much larger, more cost-effective scale, without the need for so much electric power. If these larger plants relied on fossil fuels, they would need ways of *sequestering* the increased amounts of carbon dioxide

HYDROGEN STEPPING STONE

A recent application of hydrogen power is Ford's Model U Concept internal-combustion engine, which burns hydrogen instead of gasoline. Such low-emission engines could be an important step toward a hydrogen economy.

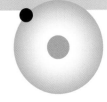

ELECTROLYSIS OF WATER

Electrolysis is one process for producing hydrogen gas. An electric current is passed through a liquid containing an *electrolyte* (water and a chemical that conducts electric current). The current produces hydrogen at the *cathode* (negative terminal) and oxygen at the *anode* (positive terminal). The arrows show the direction in which the electric current flows.

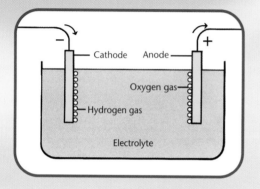

they would produce. Sequestering involves preventing carbon dioxide from entering the atmosphere, by storing it underground, underwater, or in living plants.

In the future, homes, businesses, and fuel stations might produce their own hydrogen using fossil fuels, electrolysis, or *biomass.* (Biomass is any organic material, including cornstalks, garbage, and waste paper, that can be converted into energy or into a source of energy.) The sun, wind, or fossil fuels could generate power for the *power grid* (electric power distribution system) that might be used during night-time, off-peak hours to produce hydrogen through the electrolysis of water.

In 2005, scientists were experimenting with other methods of producing hydrogen efficiently and economically in ways that eliminate the need for fossil fuels. Among these methods is *photoelectrolysis,* a process that uses sunlight to coax hydrogen from water or biomass. Other methods under investigation include splitting water molecules using high-temperature solar or nuclear energy, chemicals, heat, and sunlight. Some researchers are even exploring the use of algae, bacteria, and other microorganisms—some genetically altered for greater efficiency—to convert sunlight to hydrogen.

Storing hydrogen

Devising more efficient, safe, and cost-effective methods of storing hydrogen is one of the biggest challenges facing the creation of a hydrogen economy. Hydrogen gas has the lowest *density* (amount of mass per unit volume) of any known substance. As a result, the gas takes up significantly more space than gasoline or even natural gas with the same energy content. Hydrogen cannot become a widely used power source until scientists find new ways to squeeze useful amounts of this voluminous gas into automobile fuel tanks and other small containers.

In 2005, hydrogen storage mainly involved two processes—*compression* and *cooling.* In compression, hydrogen is stored in cylinders and tanks under high pressure, about 700 kilograms per square centimeter (10,000 pounds per square inch)—680 times the normal pressure of the air at Earth's surface. Even when compressed, however, hydrogen contains only about 3 percent of the energy found in the same volume of gasoline. In addition, the compression process requires a great deal of electric energy, a significant fraction of the total energy value of the hydrogen itself. Moreover, the energy for producing that electric power comes from fossil fuels.

To improve the compression process, scientists are investigating ways to reduce the amount of energy needed and to safely increase storage pressures. Researchers are also working to develop stronger, lighter materials for storage cylinders and tanks.

Hydrogen can be stored as a liquid by cooling it to the very low temperature of -253 °C (-423.4 °F). Liquid hydrogen must be stored at low temperatures to prevent it from returning to a gas. Like compression, however, liquid conversion requires a great deal of energy—about one-third of the energy value of the hydrogen.

In addition, hydrogen can be stored in a solid form, by physically attaching hydrogen atoms or molecules to the surfaces of metallic solids or by incorporating hydrogen atoms into the chemical structure of the solids. The advantage of storing hydrogen in solid form is that the solid can remain at temperatures close to room temperature. When needed, the hydrogen can be released by adjusting the temperature and pressure level of the solid or by mixing it with water or other compounds.

Unfortunately, none of these methods meets one of the main requirements of a hydrogen economy—the ability to pack a fuel tank with enough hydrogen to power a vehicle for at least 480 kilometers (300 miles). To reach this goal, researchers are investigating substances filled with microscopic pores or channels that offer ample storage space.

For instance, chemist Omar M. Yaghi and colleagues at the University of Michigan in Ann Arbor have created a new family of porous crystals that act like sponges by soaking up hydrogen molecules into their networks of empty spaces. These three-dimensional structures have a huge *internal surface area* (the sum of

An experimental device built around an automobile *fuel injector* may provide a portable method of extracting hydrogen gas from *ethanol*, an alcohol produced from corn. (A fuel injector squirts fuel into the cylinders of gas or diesel engines.) The device produces its own heat (glowing plug) and so could produce hydrogen at fueling stations or in cars.

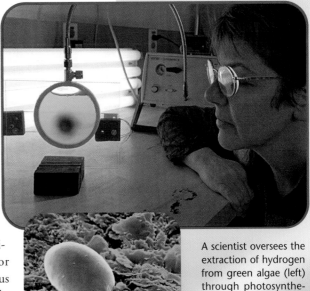

A scientist oversees the extraction of hydrogen from green algae (left) through photosynthesis in a laboratory. Researchers are studying the possibility of using green algae to produce hydrogen commercially.

all internal flat spaces). In fact, if 1 gram (0.035 ounce) of one of these crystals could be disassembled and laid out flat, its internal surface area could cover 4,500 square meters (48,400 square feet), almost the size of a football field. In 2003 and 2004, Yaghi and his colleagues reported developing new materials that store hydrogen and other gases at room temperature and at atmospheric pressures near normal—though they still don't hold as much hydrogen as a car would need to travel 480 kilometers.

Carbon nanotubes that collect hydrogen are also attracting researchers' attention. Carbon nanotubes are tubular structures made of carbon atoms several *nanometers* in diameter and several thousand nanometers in length. (A nanometer is 0.000000001 meter [1/25,400,000 inch]—approximately 1/10,000 the width of a human hair.) As hydrogen collects on the nanotubes' surfaces, it becomes absorbed into the tubes.

Distributing hydrogen

Before the hydrogen economy can take off, government and industry must devise safe, efficient, and economical ways to get hydrogen from centrally located production plants to the people who want to use it in their automobiles, homes, and businesses. In 2005, the United States had about 3.6 million kilometers (2.2 million miles) of pipeline for carrying petroleum and natural gas. In contrast, the United States had less than 720 kilometers (420 miles) of transmission pipelines for gaseous hydrogen. In fact, at least 80 percent of the hydrogen produced in the United States is not transported anywhere—it is used exactly where it is produced. The remaining hydrogen travels in gaseous form in high-pressure cylinders or along pipelines or as a liquid in supercooled, highly insulated tankers.

In a hydrogen economy, hydrogen would be transported to high-demand areas by transmission pipelines for distribution through service lines, like those used to carry natural gas to homes and businesses. Areas with a lower need would receive their hydrogen from tankers traveling by highway or rail. Researchers are currently working to improve the strength, capacity, and safety of tankers. They are also working to alleviate other transportation problems. For instance, because hydrogen is the smallest atom, it diffuses easily through pipeline metal alloys. Heavier pipes will be needed to prevent leakage. Hydrogen also speeds the cracking of pipelines and has a tendency to leak through junctions in the pipes.

Using hydrogen

Even if you could find a source of hydrogen for your fuel cell car, you wouldn't be able to drive the vehicle until it had converted the fuel into energy. One conversion method is combustion. Like natural gas or gasoline, hydrogen burns. Some automakers, for example, BMW and

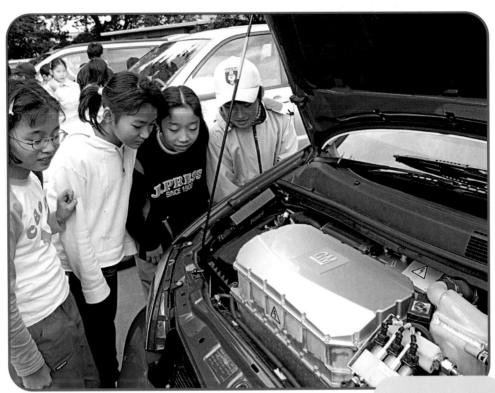

Japanese children in Tokyo examine the engine of a General Motors fuel cell vehicle called HydroGen3. The HydroGen3 was the first hydrogen-powered vehicle permitted on Japan's public roads.

Ford, have introduced prototype cars that burn liquid hydrogen instead of gasoline in an internal-combustion engine.

Hydrogen used as an additive to gasoline and other fossil fuels may serve as a transition to a hydrogen economy, according to some energy experts. Combining hydrogen with gasoline, methanol, ethanol, and natural gas can increase an engine's fuel efficiency and reduce the pollution it emits. For example, adding just 4 percent hydrogen to gasoline can reduce nitrogen oxide emissions by 30 to 40 percent in today's engines, according to the Energy Information Administration, an agency of the Department of Energy.

Most energy experts, however, believe fuel cells will play the starring role in the hydrogen economy. Like a battery, a fuel cell is a device that converts chemical energy directly to electric energy. Like a battery, a fuel cell has positive and negative *electrodes* (conductors). Unlike a battery, however, a fuel cell's electrodes remain largely unchanged during operation and so are not used up, making fuel cells virtually inexhaustible. Fuel cells are also from 40- to 60-percent efficient, significantly more efficient than batteries, electric power generators, and internal-combustion engines.

That efficiency is only one of the cell's many advantages. Fuel cells are also "clean," emitting only water, heat, and, depending on their fuel, a small amount of carbon dioxide. Fuel cells are quiet, partly because they have no moving parts. Another major advantage of fuel cells is that they can be made larger—for powering electric generators—or smaller—for powering cars and computers—using the same basic design. Individual fuel cells can also be stacked together to increase a device's *voltage* (strength of its electric force).

The main disadvantage of fuel cells is expense. Until the mid-1990's, the cost of the average fuel cell greatly exceeded the value of the electric power it could produce. However, the development of more efficient catalysts has lowered the cells' cost. (In fuel cells, the catalyst promotes the chemical reaction that produces the electric power.)

The most common type of fuel cell, developed in the 1830's, runs on hydrogen gas and oxygen gas. Hydrogen fuel cells actually reverse the electrolysis process by turning hydrogen and oxygen into water, producing electric power in the process.

Most hydrogen fuel cells use an *electrolyte* consisting of potassium hydroxide dissolved in water. (An electrolyte is a substance that conducts electric current.) Another electrolyte, called the *proton exchange membrane* (PEM), may be one of the most promising for future applications because of the simplicity of its design and function. Invented in the early 1960's, the PEM fuel cell was used in U.S. spacecraft, though it did not operate quite as reliably as engineers had hoped. In the

HYDROGEN FUEL CELL

A fuel cell converts chemical energy directly to electric energy. In this polymer electrolyte membrane (PEM) fuel cell, hydrogen gas is fed to a negative *electrode* (conductor) called an *anode*. At the anode, the hydrogen goes through a process that separates it into hydrogen ions and electrons. The electrons flow to the positive electrode called a *cathode*, producing an electric current. The hydrogen ions pass through the PEM to the cathode. At the cathode, oxygen reacts with the electrons and hydrogen ions, producing water and some heat as by-products.

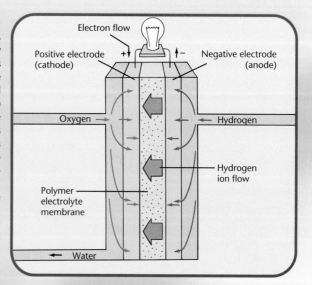

Electron flow

Positive electrode (cathode)

Negative electrode (anode)

Oxygen →

← Hydrogen

Hydrogen ion flow

Polymer electrolyte membrane

← Water

HYDROGEN'S BENEFITS AND CHALLENGES

A hydrogen economy offers many advantages over an economy based on the *fossil fuels* of coal, natural gas, and oil. For example, hydrogen-powered vehicles, like the German submarine launched in September 2004 (below), give off almost no pollutants. However, the establishment of a hydrogen economy poses numerous challenges because hydrogen gas usually exists only in combination with other elements. As a result, most hydrogen used today is extracted from fossil fuels (bottom).

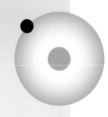

Benefits

- Hydrogen is the most common element in the universe.

- Hydrogen fuel cells do not emit the greenhouse gas carbon dioxide or pollutants.

- Hydrogen fuel cells are significantly more efficient than gasoline-powered engines.

- Hydrogen can be extracted anywhere water and electricity exist.

- Hydrogen fuel cells could generate electricity for homes and businesses.

- Widespread use of hydrogen could reduce U.S. dependence on foreign oil.

Challenges

- The process of extracting hydrogen requires another source of energy.

- Extracting hydrogen using *renewable* energy sources (sun, wind, and water) would require the construction of more wind turbines and solar panels and the increased use of water. Creating these structures would not be cost-effective in most parts of the world.

- Fuel cells are relatively expensive.

- Hydrogen will require new methods of storage and distribution.

- Hydrogen is 14 times as light as air and so must be compressed or cooled to a liquid before it can be transported.

Fuel cell buses carry passengers through Amsterdam, the Netherlands. The buses represent two of three participating in the Clean Urban Transport for Europe demonstration project to promote the use of low-pollution vehicles and alternative fuels.

1990's, the lightweight, compact PEM fuel cell began attracting renewed attention, this time from automakers. The PEM's ability to operate at a relatively low temperature—about 80 °C (176 °F)—offers both advantages and disadvantages. Most solid-state electrolytes require temperatures as high as 1000 °C (1832 °F) and so would be difficult to use in laptop computers and other household appliances. On the other hand, a low operating temperature reduces the PEM fuel cell's ability to produce electric current. (In general, catalysts are more productive at higher temperatures.)

A handful of PEM fuel cell vehicles are already on the road. For example, three hydrogen fuel cell buses move passengers in Reykjavik, Iceland. The buses fill up on hydrogen at a fueling station equipped with an electrolysis system powered by geothermal heat and hydropower. In 2004, the U.S. Postal Service began using a fuel cell minivan developed by General Motors to deliver mail in the Washington, D.C., area. About 14 of Honda's FCX fuel cell models are in use in several U.S. cities.

However, commercialization of hydrogen-powered vehicles is limited for numerous reasons. One main hurdle is the lack of fueling stations. Another problem is cold. In areas with cold winters, the water emitted from fuel cell vehicles can freeze when the vehicle is turned off. Yet another is expense. As of May 2005, hydrogen cost roughly twice as much as gasoline in the United States.

Fuel cells are also in limited use as power generators for buildings, including hospitals and factories. In 2005, these systems were generally expensive, unreliable, and short-lived, however.

Despite these developments, widespread adoption of fuel cell vehicles and generators is unlikely until hydrogen's many challenges are met. To meet those challenges, scientists are rethinking nearly every fuel cell component to increase efficiency and lower cost. One active area of research is the development of renewable sources of hydrogen that don't involve fossil fuels. Other research focuses on finding new catalysts for electrodes and new materials for electrolytes.

If these challenges are met, hydrogen fuel cells may eventually become clean, efficient, secure ways to power homes, businesses, and cars. They may also become useful devices for capturing excess energy from renewable—but variable—energy sources, including the sun and wind. Eventually, energy from sunlight or wind may be harnessed regularly to isolate hydrogen from water through electrolysis. People could store that hydrogen for later use when they need power, even on a windless night.

Tail pipe dreams

A hydrogen economy isn't just around the corner. Developments at university and industry laboratories will have to demonstrate that hydrogen fuel cells are reliable, cost-effective replacements for power generators and auto fuel. Production of hydrogen from renewable sources must become economical and efficient. Researchers will need to find safe ways to store the gas in small compartments. And countries must figure out how to get hydrogen to the people who will use it. The challenges are enormous, but the payoff could be a really clear view into the future.

■ FOR ADDITIONAL INFORMATION:

Books and periodicals

Behar, Michael. "Warning: The Hydrogen Economy May Be More Distant than It Appears." *Popular Science,* January 2005, pp. 65–68.

Coontz, Robert, and others. "Toward a Hydrogen Economy." *Science,* August 13, 2004, pp. 957–967.

Romm, Joseph J. *The Hype About Hydrogen: Fact and Fiction in the Race to Save the Climate.* Island Press 2004.

Web sites

Energy Information Administration home page—http://www.eia.doe.gov

How Stuff Works—http://people.howstuffworks.com/hydrogen-economy.htm

U.S. Department of Energy Hydrogen Program—http://www.hydrogen.energy.gov/

U.S. Fuel Cell Council—http://www.usfcc.com

Rising asthma rates are
puzzling researchers, while
new treatments are helping
people with asthma
breathe easier.

Advances in
Understanding
Asthma

By Siri J. Carpenter

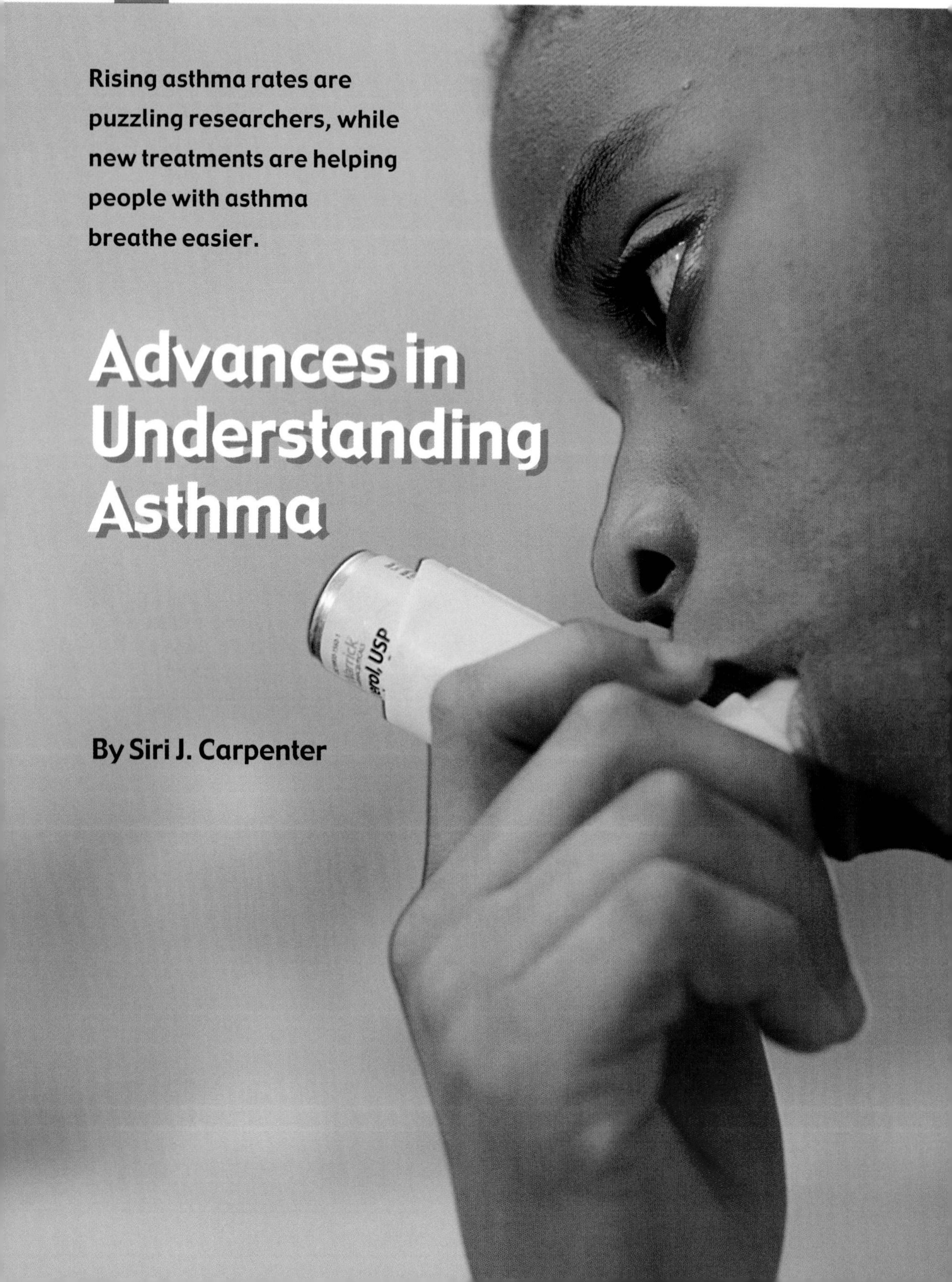

A 15-year-old in Nebraska divides much of her free time between two passions: working in her mother's pet store and taking part in such physical activities as horseback riding, dancing, and jogging. When she was younger, her severe asthma, which she's had since infancy, prevented her from enjoying any of these interests. Being in the store aggravated her allergies to animals, triggering bouts of wheezing and labored breathing. And just a few minutes of jogging or other physical activities left her exhausted and short of breath. The medications she took were not effective enough to keep her off the sidelines. Several times, asthma attacks sent her to the emergency room.

A few years ago, she participated in a research study evaluating the safety and effectiveness of a new type of asthma medication called omalizumab (a version is now available on the market as Xolair). Omalizumab is the first asthma drug created through *genetic engineering,* a technique in which human and animal *genes* (hereditary material) are manipulated in the laboratory to produce a specific biological product. Omalizumab, which is designed to be taken in addition to standard asthma medications, may reduce the occurrence of asthma symptoms in patients whose asthma cannot be controlled by these other medications alone. The Nebraska teen receives two injections of the medication every other week. Although omalizumab may have potentially serious side effects, it is generally well tolerated by most patients, including the Nebraska teen. Her asthma still flares up from time to time. However, the illness is finally under control and she can be much more active.

The number of people in the United States who reported having asthma rose steeply from 1980 to 1996, according to the Centers for Disease Control and Prevention (CDC) in Atlanta, Georgia. Since then, asthma rates have continued to climb, though at a slower pace. Researchers are uncertain about the reasons for either the jump or the slowdown in the rates.

In 2002 (the latest year for which data are available), 30.8 million people in the United States reported that they had, at some time, been diagnosed with asthma. About 12 million people, including 4 million children, reported that they had an *asthma episode* (also called an *asthma attack*) in the previous year. Asthma was responsible for almost 2 million emergency room visits and about 5,000 deaths. Hospitalizations and deaths from asthma are especially high among inner-city African American and Hispanic children.

Asthma has plagued humanity for thousands of years. The English word *asthma* comes from an ancient Greek term that means *breathlessness* or *panting.* By the 1800's, physicians using a newly invented instrument called a stethoscope had confirmed that asthma is a lung disease. By the early 1900's, scientists had realized that asthma tends to run in families and so has a genetic component.

The author:
Siri J. Carpenter is a free-lance science writer in Madison, Wisconsin.

Since the 1990's, a growing body of scientific evidence has supported the theory that asthma is not a single disease but a group of interrelated conditions. That is, there appears to be wide variation in the causes and course of the disease for different people and even across different socioeconomic or ethnic groups. For example, asthma rates are particularly high for Puerto Ricans and African Americans. In addition, though some people develop asthma as adults, the disease commonly emerges during childhood, typically before age 5. Some children who have asthma may experience temporary remission of their symptoms. In some cases, asthma symptoms may return years later. People who develop asthma during childhood typically also have allergies. About half of all children who develop asthma had *eczema* (an allergic skin disease) as infants or toddlers. Researchers at National Jewish Medical and Research Center in Denver, Colorado, are investigating whether eczema may set off a chain of allergic symptoms that ends in asthma. In contrast, in people who develop asthma as adults, the condition is more often linked to a recent upper respiratory infection or to gastroesophageal reflux disease (GERD), a condition in which stomach acids flow into the *esophagus* (passageway from the throat to the stomach).

Also in the 1990's, researchers opened a new front in their efforts to identify a cause and a cure for asthma—genetic research. By 2005, they had identified about two dozen genes that seem to play a role in the disease, though the precise roles of these genes are still unclear. Nor is it clear why some people who have genes related to asthma develop the disease while others with the same genes do not.

How an asthma attack begins

During an asthma attack, the airways that connect the *trachea* (windpipe) to the lungs become inflamed and swollen. The larger airways are called *bronchi* and the smaller ones, *bronchioles*. The muscles that encircle the bronchi contract, and the lining of both the bronchi and bronchioles releases a thick mucus that blocks the flow of air to and from the lungs. Together, these events cause the wheezing, coughing, breathlessness, and chest tightness that are the hallmarks of asthma. During severe attacks, the airways can *spasm* (constrict suddenly), which further interferes with breathing and can be life threatening.

Throughout the early 1900's, scientists believed that episodes of airway constriction were the primary cause of breathing difficulties in asthma. By the 1960's, however, they had recognized the important role that inflammation plays in asthma attacks, though most scientists still thought that the airways returned to normal after attacks abated. In 1992, researchers led by Jean Bousquet at the University of

Montpellier I in France found that airway inflammation may not be just an intermittent symptom of asthma but a chronic and more fundamental problem. In some people, Bousquet's team found, airway inflammation causes permanent scarring and thickening of the airway walls. They dubbed this process *airway remodeling.* By 2005, some researchers who had found evidence of airway remodeling in young children were suggesting that remodeling may begin early in the course of asthma, setting the stage for more frequent and severe attacks.

Triggering a chain reaction

People have asthma attacks because they are overly sensitive to certain substances or environmental conditions known as *triggers.* For about half of all people with asthma, the most common triggers are *allergens,* ordinarily harmless substances that cause the immune system of susceptible people to overreact. Common environmental allergens include pollens from trees, grasses, and weeds; molds and *fungi* (mold spores); pet *dander* (shed skin); dust mite feces; and cockroaches.

Normally, the immune system defends us against disease-causing viruses and bacteria and other foreign invaders. Exposure to such invaders,

DRAMATIC RISE IN ASTHMA RATES

The number of people in the United States with asthma increased significantly from 1980 to 1996, though researchers do not understand why. A revised method of counting people with asthma, developed by government researchers in 1997, resulted in a decrease in rates in the late 1990's and early 2000's. Nevertheless, the number of people with asthma has continued to rise. For reasons that are still unclear, teen-agers ages 15 to 19 have the highest prevalence of asthma.

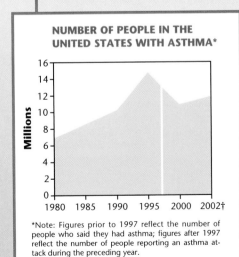

NUMBER OF PEOPLE IN THE UNITED STATES WITH ASTHMA*

*Note: Figures prior to 1997 reflect the number of people who said they had asthma; figures after 1997 reflect the number of people reporting an asthma attack during the preceding year.

†Most recent data available.

Source: Air Pollution and Respiratory Health Branch, National Center for Environmental Health, U.S. Centers for Disease Control and Prevention.

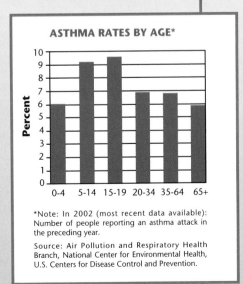

ASTHMA RATES BY AGE*

*Note: In 2002 (most recent data available): Number of people reporting an asthma attack in the preceding year.

Source: Air Pollution and Respiratory Health Branch, National Center for Environmental Health, U.S. Centers for Disease Control and Prevention.

WHAT HAPPENS DURING AN ASTHMA ATTACK?

When a person with asthma encounters a trigger—such as cat dander, tobacco smoke, or a sudden drop in temperature—a series of reactions causes air passages called *bronchi* and *bronchioles* to constrict and become inflamed. The constricted air passages make breathing harder. Long-term inflammation may lead to permanent damage to the lungs.

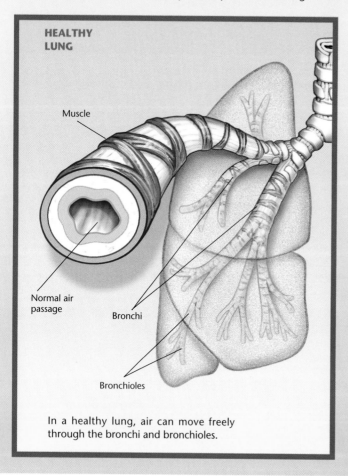

HEALTHY LUNG

Muscle

Normal air passage

Bronchi

Bronchioles

In a healthy lung, air can move freely through the bronchi and bronchioles.

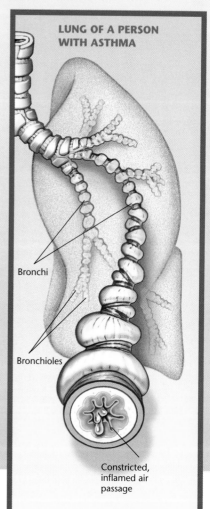

LUNG OF A PERSON WITH ASTHMA

Bronchi

Bronchioles

Constricted, inflamed air passage

In the lung of a person with asthma, an asthma attack causes the muscles around the air passages to constrict and the lining of the bronchi and bronchioles to become inflamed. The lining produces thick mucus that further clogs the passages. The restricted air passages make it difficult for the person to breathe.

called *antigens,* triggers an immune response. A specialized type of white blood cells, particularly a subtype called *T helper 2* (Th2) cells, coordinates the production of *antibodies* by white blood cells called *plasma cells.* Antibodies are proteins that can recognize and attack the antigens. The plasma cells produce a particular type of antibody, called *immunoglobulin E* (IgE). IgE antibodies attach to various types of cells, including *mast cells,* which may be found in the skin, lungs, and gastrointestinal tract. The mast cells then release a chemical called *histamine,* which elicits a range of allergy symptoms, including runny nose, nasal congestion, watery eyes, and sneezing. For people with asthma, the allergic response goes further and may lead to inflammation, mucus secretion, and constriction of the airways.

Medications to treat asthma

Researchers used the knowledge of how IgE works to develop the new asthma medication omalizumab. Omalizumab mops up IgE antibodies in the bloodstream, preventing them from staging an allergic response. The medication, which was approved for people over age 12 by the United States Food and Drug Administration (FDA) in 2003, is administered by injection once or twice a month to an asthma sufferer and may cost as much as $12,000 per year.

Standard asthma medications work by either relaxing the muscles around the airways or by controlling inflammation. Patients with mild intermittent asthma—for example, those who experience symptoms twice a week or less—are usually prescribed a drug called a *bronchodilator,* such as albuterol. Patients use the medication only when they are experiencing symptoms. Bronchodilators work by relaxing airway muscles.

AIRWAY REMODELING

Many researchers now believe that the inflammation caused by repeated asthma attacks results in permanent changes to the lungs. Air passages thicken, narrowing the channel and making it more difficult for air to pass through. In 1992, researchers at the University of Montpellier I in France dubbed these changes *airway remodeling.* The process is illustrated below in false-color images magnified 400 times.

NORMAL LUNG

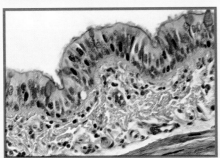

LUNG OF A PERSON WITH ASTHMA

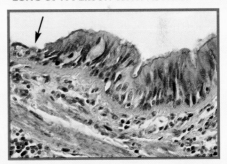

In a normal lung, the *epithelium*, which makes up the inner lining (shown in purple), is intact. It contains a limited number of mucus-producing goblet cells (blue). Below the *basement membrane* (green band) is another layer containing *collagen* (protein) cells and small bands of smooth muscle (lower right corner) that make up the flexible structure of the airway. Normal numbers of immune cells (red to black ovals) protect against infection.

In an asthmatic lung, the epithelium is often damaged and rough and may even be broken down (arrow, above). There are many more goblet cells, which fill the airway with thick mucus during each attack. The collagen below the basement membrane (green) is thicker, and the layer below it contains many more immune system cells, which contribute to inflammation. The smooth muscle bands are also larger, making airways smaller and less able to relax.

People who experience more frequent or more persistent symptoms of asthma usually use a bronchodilator during symptoms and take a daily medication for long-term control of inflammation. That daily medication is often an inhaled *steroid,* which is considered the gold standard therapy to treat inflammation in people with persistent asthma. Additional medications doctors may prescribe to treat persistent asthma include cromolyn sodium, antileukotrienes, or theophylline. All these medications work by preventing the body from releasing into the lungs chemicals that contribute to allergic reactions.

Short courses of oral steroids are used to treat severe asthma episodes. Omalizumab was developed, in part, so that patients taking oral steroids or high-dose inhaled steroids could reduce the amount of these medications needed to control their asthma.

Regardless of the type of medication an asthma patient is taking, doctors develop an individual action plan for each person with asthma. Such a plan allows patients to monitor their own condition and indicates how

Allergens such as pollen (pink), magnified thousands of times in this false-color image, are inhaled into the *trachea* (windpipe). *Cilia* (hairlike cells, yellow) trap the allergens and, by beating upward, try to remove them from the lungs. Allergens may cause breathing difficulties in asthma patients.

ASTHMA TRIGGERS

Asthma triggers are substances, environmental conditions, or behaviors that can set off an asthma attack in susceptible individuals. For about half of all people with asthma, the most common triggers are *allergens,* ordinarily harmless substances that cause the immune system to overreact. People with nonallergic asthma react to such triggers as irritants, certain medications, and environmental conditions.

Allergens	▪ animal dander (from the skin, hair, or feathers of animals) ▪ dust mites ▪ cockroaches ▪ pollen from trees and grasses ▪ mold (indoor and outdoor)
Irritants	▪ cigarette smoke ▪ air pollution ▪ cold air or changes in weather ▪ strong odors, such as those from painting or cooking ▪ scented products ▪ strong expressions of emotion, including crying, laughing hard, and angry behavior
Other triggers	▪ infections ▪ strenuous exercise ▪ gastroesophageal reflux disease (GERD—a condition, more common in adults, in which stomach acids flow into the esophagus) ▪ medications (such as aspirin and heart medications called beta-blockers) ▪ chemical preservatives called sulfites, which may be found in food and such alcoholic beverages as wine ▪ such irritants or allergens as chemicals found in the workplace

Critically reviewed by Giselle Mosnaim, Instructor, Section of Allergy and Immunology, Rush Medical College.

they must increase medications if their symptoms reach a certain threshold. Children with asthma are often required to have an action plan on file at the school nurse's office, so that school personnel know what kind of help to give a child during an asthma attack.

Environmental irritants as triggers

Irritants in the environment may also trigger an immune system overreaction. Tobacco smoke is the most common indoor irritant. It can provoke asthma symptoms not only in smokers but also in people who are exposed to secondhand smoke. Irritants also include air pollutants, such as diesel exhaust, wood smoke, and *ozone* (a gas that is poisonous at Earth's surface but that in the upper atmosphere protects Earth from harmful solar rays). Other irritants include certain chemicals or dust found in the workplace; substances with strong odors, such as perfumes, paints, and cooking fumes; and foods or beverages such as wine that contain preservatives called *sulfites.* Colds and other viral infections may also set off an asthma attack, as can exposure to cold air or changing weather conditions. Finally, certain medications, including beta-blockers—used to treat heart conditions—and aspirin may provoke an attack.

For some people, asthma symptoms occur during or, more commonly, just after exercise, a condition known as *exercise-induced asthma.* Prolonged exercise; exercising in cold, dry air; breathing through the mouth; and exercising when pollen counts or air pollution levels are high may all irritate the airways, increasing the chance of an asthma attack. For these reasons, people with asthma sometimes avoid physical activity. However, health experts caution that exercise is crucial for maintaining a healthy heart and lungs. People with asthma can usually prevent attacks by taking a prescribed short-acting bronchodilator before exercising and warming up properly.

Some people's asthma symptoms worsen at night, a phenomenon known as *nocturnal asthma.* Many factors may contribute to nocturnal asthma, including exposure to dust mites in the bedding, chronic sinus problems, postnasal drip from *allergic rhinitis* (an allergic reaction that causes sneezing and itchy, watery eyes), GERD, and a drop in airway temperatures during sleep. In addition, *cortisol* levels are naturally lowest in the early morning hours. This drop may cause asthmatics to wake from sleep with symptoms. (Cortisol is a hormone secreted by the body that has anti-inflammatory properties.)

Rising asthma rates

Researchers have proposed a number of theories in an effort to understand why asthma rates have increased. One theory links increases in air pollution—such as diesel exhaust particles and ozone—to an increase in asthma. Research supporting such a link was published in 2002 by Rob

McConnell, an associate professor of preventive medicine at the University of Southern California in Los Angeles. McConnell's study involved 12 communities in southern California. He reported that children who lived in communities with high ozone levels and who played at least three outdoor sports—exposing themselves to more air pollution—were three times more likely to develop asthma than were similarly active children in low-ozone communities.

According to the Environmental Protection Agency (EPA), people in the United States spend about 90 percent of their time indoors. Many experts believe that poor indoor air quality—created, in part, by increasingly airtight homes—may contribute to the development of asthma. Lack of exercise and an alarming rise in the number of people who are overweight may also be partly to blame for escalating asthma rates. A 1998 study conducted by Carlos Camargo, assistant professor of medicine at Harvard Medical School in Cambridge, Massachusetts, found that obese adults were three times as likely to develop asthma as people of normal weight. Camargo speculated that excess weight may compress the airways, making them more reactive to asthma triggers.

The hygiene hypothesis

In the 1990's, another theory called the "hygiene hypothesis" began to attract attention as an explanation for rising asthma rates. The theory, which became highly controversial, was introduced in 1989 by epidemiologist David Strachan at St. George's Hospital in London. Strachan proposed that increased sanitation, antibiotic use, and vaccination in Western countries have created an imbalance between two aspects of the immune system. In newborns, Th2 immune cells, which are involved in allergic responses, dominate the immune system. Over time, another arm of the immune system, composed of Th1 cells, gains strength. Like Th2 cells, Th1 cells repel such infectious organisms as viruses and bacteria. But unlike Th2 cells, Th1 cells do not use antibodies to fight infection. Instead, they activate immune cells that can directly attack infected cells. Supporters of the hygiene hypothesis argue that by reducing people's exposure to germs, modern hygiene practices prevent the Th1 arm from gaining strength and so skew the immune system toward allergic responses.

Several avenues of research support the hygiene hypothesis. For example, some studies have shown that children who have older siblings or who go to a day-care center during infancy are less likely to have allergies. These findings, some researchers argue, suggest that children who have been exposed to numerous viral infections are less likely to react strongly to allergens. A 1999 study led by pediatric pulmonologist Josef Riedler at the Children's Hospital in Salzburg, Austria, found a lower incidence of allergies and asthma among children who were exposed early in life to farm animals. And in 2003, an experiment conducted by

Richard Martin of the National Jewish Medical and Research Center showed that mice that were infected at a young age with a bacterium that causes pneumonia were less likely to develop allergies than mice that were not.

Despite these and other findings supporting the hygiene hypothesis, many questions remain. Some critics note that many of the studies supporting the hypothesis were not controlled scientific experiments. Rather, the scientists drew conclusions based on trends they had observed—such as the fact that children with older brothers and sisters tend to have fewer allergies and have asthma less often. When research is conducted in this way, scientists have a more difficult time distinguishing causes and effects.

Some researchers also argue that evidence linking an immune system imbalance and asthma is not as strong as the evidence linking allergies and asthma. Others observe that the hygiene hypothesis does not explain why U.S. asthma rates are highest in inner cities. Children living in such areas are no less likely than children living elsewhere to be exposed to infectious agents and harmless microbes that "exercise" the Th1 system.

Finally, some scientists point out that if the hygiene hypothesis were correct, rates of lupus and other *autoimmune diseases* (conditions in which the body's immune system attacks its own organs) should be dropping, because these diseases appear to involve the Th1 system. Instead, the rate of autoimmune diseases is increasing.

Finding a cause

Most asthma experts suspect that there is no single cause of asthma. Ultimately, efforts to explain why some people develop asthma but others do not may be a matter of weighing many different environmental, ethnic, socioeconomic, and genetic factors.

At the same time, a number of factors are complicating researchers' efforts to identify genetic susceptibility to asthma. First, asthma is what is known as a "complex" heritable disease, meaning

TESTING FOR ALLERGIES

Allergens serve as triggers for asthma attacks in about 50 percent of all people who have asthma. Learning what they are allergic to can help people with asthma avoid those triggers and avert an asthma attack.

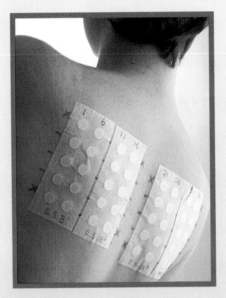

A woman is tested for allergies with a method called the *patch test*. Four patches, each containing small amounts of 10 different allergens, such as pet hair and house dust, are applied to her back. In some cases, the patient's back is pricked before applying the patches.

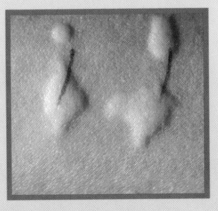

Any substance to which the patient is allergic will cause a skin reaction. The area around the patch becomes inflamed.

SEARCHING FOR THE RIGHT SNP

SNP's (single nucleotide polymorphisms—pronounced SNIPS) are tiny variations in an individual's DNA (deoxyribonucleic acid—the molecule genes are
made of). Researchers hope that finding SNP's will enable them to identify
the genes associated with asthma. SNP's may also help physicians determine
which medication will be most effective for a particular individual.

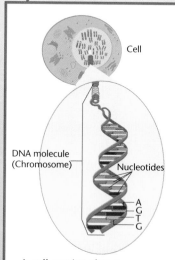

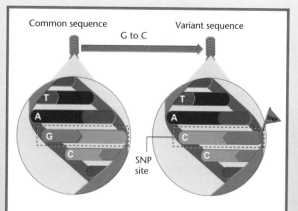

A cell carries chromosomes,
which are made up of DNA
molecules. DNA molecules consist of two intertwined strands
that carry four nucleotides, the
chemicals adenine, thymine,
cytosine, and guanine. The nucleotides always pair up in the
same way, A with T and C with
G, and so the order of one
strand requires a complementary ordering of the other.

Occasionally, one of the nucleotides in a sequence is
replaced with another. The variation—if it occurs in
more than 1 percent of the human population—is
called a SNP. Many SNP's have no effect on an individual's health. But some variations increase the likelihood that a person will develop a particular disease.

that it involves interactions between a number of genes.
Second, many environmental factors, none of which are fully understood, appear to influence the development and
severity of the disease. Finally, clinical symptoms of asthma
can vary widely. Doctors must rely on a thorough patient
history, detailed physical examination, skin tests, and *spirometry* (the
measurement of lung capacity) to aid in making a diagnosis.

Focusing on genes one at a time

In 2005, researchers working on asthma genetics were focused primarily on determining which genes play a role in the disease. The researchers
were using two distinct but complementary approaches—the *candidate-
gene approach* and the *genome-screen approach.*

With the candidate-gene approach, researchers focus on one gene at a
time. Scientists use their knowledge of the biological processes involved in
a disease to identify a gene that might logically affect that condition. Then
they try to determine whether that gene takes a different form in people
who have the disease and those who do not. For example, scientists know
that the interleukin-4 gene, located on *chromosome* 5, is involved in pro-

ducing IgE antibodies, and so it is a good candidate for asthma studies. (Chromosomes, which are found in the nucleus of a cell, carry genes.)

The development of *DNA* microarray technology has greatly enhanced the usefulness of the candidate-gene approach for such complex genetic diseases as asthma. (DNA—*deoxyribonucleic acid*—is the molecule that makes up genes.) DNA microarray technology speeds the identification of genes involved in a particular disease by allowing scientists to screen a large number of genes simultaneously. Using microarrays, scientists can analyze subtle variations in the arrangement of chemicals called *nucleotides* within candidate genes. Nucleotides are the building blocks of the genetic code and are sometimes referred to by the letters A, C, G, and T, for adenine, cytosine, guanine, and thymine, respectively. Each nucleotide has a chemical partner with which it always pairs, forming the typical double strand of a DNA molecule. Adenine, for example, pairs with thymine, and cytosine, with guanine.

Variations in nucleotides are called *polymorphisms.* The most common variations, *single nucleotide polymorphisms,* also known as SNP's (pronounced *SNIPS*), involve the substitution of just a single nucleotide. For example, a majority of individuals may have a gene that contains DNA with the sequence GTCCTA. If a small group of people has that same gene with a DNA sequence of GTCCAA, the variation is called a SNP. SNP's can be used to track inherited traits—including diseases—within families or larger populations.

To prepare a microarray (also called a gene or *genome* chip), researchers use a robot to apply short, single strands of DNA whose sequence they already know onto glass slides in an orderly arrangement. (A genome is the complete collection of genes possessed by an organism.) The strands in the microarray are called *probes.* Researchers then introduce DNA samples whose composition and identity they do not know. The samples contain a fluorescent dye. If a sample encounters a probe that contains its complementary pairs, it will bind with the probe and *fluoresce* (light up). Researchers can then determine the composition of the sample, and thus, its identity.

Gene screens

Because many genes may cause or contribute to complex genetic diseases, identifying individual asthma genes using only the candidate-gene approach may be inefficient and may miss previously unknown genes. A second approach, *genome screening,* takes a different tack. In this approach, scientists simultaneously screen the entire genome of family members with a particular disease, such as asthma, and search for regions of a chromosome that are shared by people with the disease. With asthma, for example, researchers may link a positive response on allergy tests or bronchial sensitivity with particular chromosomes. Those regions can then be tested further. Genome screens require no previous knowledge of—or even hypotheses about—particular genes or their function. However, such screens are expensive and require large numbers of patients from the same family in order to be effective. In addition, they typically identify broad chromosomal regions containing hundreds of genes.

Since the first genome-wide screen for asthma susceptibility was published in 1996, scientists have performed more than a dozen screens of the human genome and identified at least 20 chromosomal regions with links to asthma. There may be more. In 2003, researchers at the Cincinnati (Ohio) Children's Hospital Medical Center used microarray technology to identify some 300 genes that may be involved in asthma in mice.

Another technique called *positional cloning* has enabled researchers to advance beyond simply identifying broad chromosomal regions that may contain asthma genes. After such a region has been found, researchers identify candidate genes found there for further testing. Cloning the candidate genes then allows researchers to study the candidates more closely. By 2004, researchers using positional cloning had discovered five possible asthma genes.

How genes affect asthma

One of the five genes, ADAM33, may be involved in airway remodeling, according to studies by researchers in the United States and the United Kingdom in 2002. Other studies, however, have failed to confirm these results. Still others have found only a weak association between the gene and airway remodeling, showing an effect only within certain ethnic groups.

Two asthma genes identified in 2003, named PHF11 and DPP10, may be involved in allergic responses and airway inflammation, respectively. William Cookson, director of the Asthma Genetics Group at the University of Oxford in England, and his colleagues showed that PHF11 influences asthma severity by affecting allergic responses (specifically, IgE levels). Cookson also led a team of researchers from the United Kingdom, Germany, and France who found that DPP10 appears to be involved in airway inflammation.

Finally, in 2004, scientists led by molecular geneticist Juha Kere of the Karolinska Institute

HOW A NEW TYPE OF ASTHMA DRUG WORKS

Omalizumab, a new kind of asthma medication, blocks an asthma attack at one of its earliest stages. Omalizumab is intended for people who have moderate to severe asthma that is allergy related. The medication works by preventing IgE antibodies from attaching themselves to the receptors of mast cells.

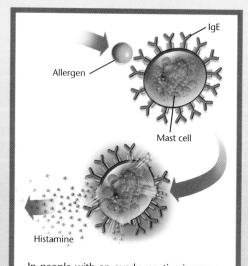

In people with an overly reactive immune system, normally harmless substances called *allergens* cause an allergic reaction. During such a reaction, immune system cells called *IgE antibodies* bind to *mast cells*, which store an allergy-causing substance called *histamine*. The release of histamine can trigger an attack in people who have asthma.

in Stockholm, Sweden, reported discovering two asthma genes common among groups of Finns and Canadians with the disease. One gene, called GPRA, is associated with a susceptibility to asthma. The other gene's effects on asthma remain unknown.

In addition to searching for genes involved in asthma, researchers in 2005 continued to explore how genetic makeup might affect the way that a person responds—or doesn't respond—to a particular asthma medication. Researchers in the field of *pharmacogenetics* (the study of how genetic variations are linked to drug responses) are examining genetic effects on the effectiveness of asthma medications and on the side effects that people experience. Some research, for example, has identified a genetic variation that affects the way an individual responds to albuterol, one of the most common asthma drugs. Such research is especially important because asthma drugs vary widely in how they affect different patients.

In 2005, experts regarded the discovery of asthma-related genes as a foothold in the effort to understand the complex genetics underlying asthma. They expected that many more asthma genes will be identified in the coming years. But the greater task—necessary before determining how this knowledge can have any practical use—will be to understand exactly what the genes do and how they interact with one another and with environmental factors. As research on asthma genetics matures, another important undertaking will be to untangle the genes that specifically affect asthma from those that are involved in a broader range of inflammatory conditions and immune disorders.

Scientists were also working in 2005 to develop new medications for asthma and even foresaw a day when people with a known genetic vulnerability to the disease could receive an asthma "vaccine" to prevent its development. However, such advances are likely far off and will require a much more thorough understanding of the disease's genetic and environmental underpinnings. Unfortunately, the disease that has afflicted people at least since the time of the ancient Greeks remains shrouded in mystery today.

■ FOR ADDITIONAL INFORMATION

Books and periodicals

Fanta, Christopher H., and others. *The Harvard Medical School Guide to Taking Control of Asthma.* Free Press, 2003.

Brown, Phyllida, "Take a Deep Breath," *New Scientist*, March 2004, pp. 36+.

Web sites

Breath of Life (National Library of Medicine online exhibition)—
    http://www.nlm.nih.gov/hmd/breath/breathhome.html
National Heart, Lung and Blood Institute Asthma Page—
    http://www.nhlbi.nih.gov/health/dci/Diseases/Asthma/Asthma_WhatIs.html
The American Academy of Allergy, Asthma & Immunology—http://www.aaaai.org

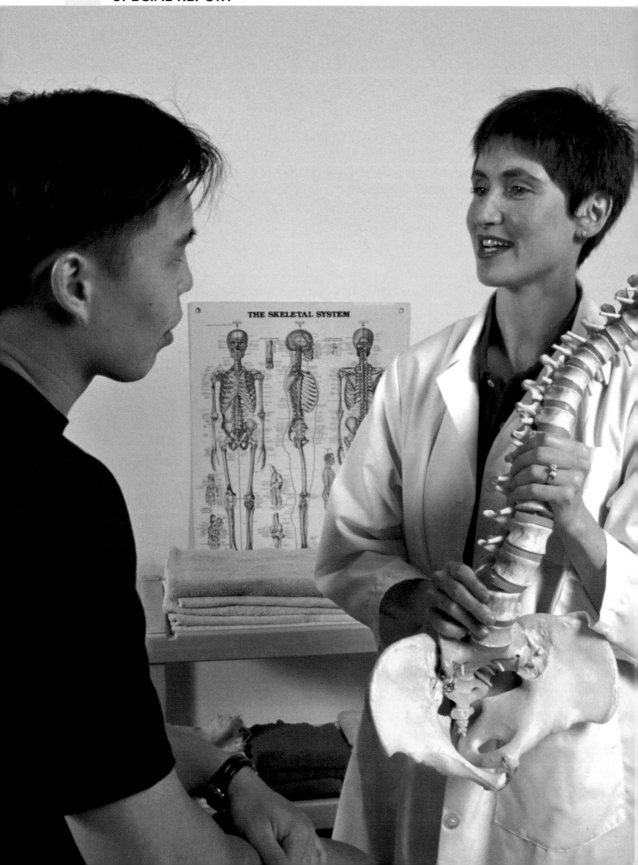

Straight Talk About
Back Health

Your back is a complex structure that is surprisingly prone to injury. Understanding how the back works can help you keep it healthy and free from pain.

By Daniel Hurley

The spine is such a symbol of strength that accusing someone of "being spineless" or "not having a backbone" is a serious insult. For such an essential support structure, however, the spine—and the ligaments, muscles, and nerves that surround it—are remarkably vulnerable to injury as well as to wear and tear.

Complaints about back pain, especially in the lower back, send people to their physician more often than any other health problem, except colds and similar respiratory illnesses. Back pain can be excruciating, and it can seriously interfere with daily life. One out of every six people in the United States suffers back pain, according to the North American Spine Society, a spine-health advocacy organization in LaGrange, Illinois. Adults under age 45 rank back pain as the most common reason for stopping or limiting their participation in various activities. Back pain is also the third most common cause of disability in people over age 45. By 2005, people in the United States were spending approximately $50 billion annually on low-back pain treatments, according to the U.S. National Institutes of Health. Although nearly all of us will experience

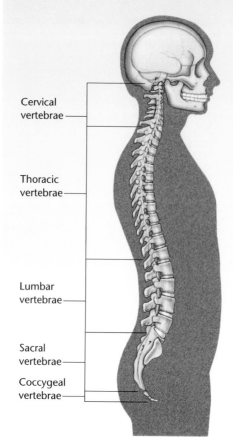

Cervical vertebrae

Thoracic vertebrae

Lumbar vertebrae

Sacral vertebrae

Coccygeal vertebrae

The spine helps support our body's weight and protect the spinal cord. The spine consists of 33 *vertebrae* (bones) divided into five segments. There are 7 *cervical* (neck), 12 *thoracic* (chest region), 5 *lumbar* (lower back), 5 *sacral* (hip region), and 4 *coccygeal* (tailbone region) vertebrae. Between most vertebrae are *intervertebral disks,* which absorb shock and protect the vertebrae.

back pain at some point in our life, understanding how to protect the spine and the back's muscles and nerves can help us avoid injury and make life a bit more pain-free.

Building blocks and soft spots

A backache is a pain that begins in or near the spine. The spine—also known as the *backbone, spinal column,* or *vertebral column*—gives human beings membership in a relatively small group of animals—the vertebrates. Animals with a spine make up only about 2 percent of all animal species. Many vertebrates walk on four limbs, with a horizontal backbone that runs parallel to the ground. Like birds, however, people have a vertical backbone and walk upright. Unfortunately, gravity is always pulling us downward, putting stress on our spine.

Your spine consists of rigid parts that provide the strength needed to support your weight and flexible parts that provide the elasticity needed for bending and twisting. In the neck, the spine permits a wide range of motion, allowing you to turn your head for maximum vision. The middle of the spine cannot twist much, and so it helps protect the heart and lungs in the chest. The lower backbone allows some twisting and enables us to lean forward and reach for things by stretching out our arms.

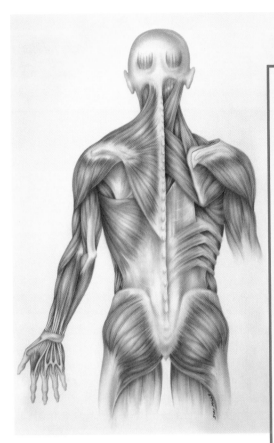

Risk factors for back pain

- Age—in older people, muscles and ligaments are more likely to become weakened or strained.
- Pregnancy—carrying the extra weight of pregnancy adds strain to the lower back.
- Homemaking—picking up children, carrying groceries, and twisting while cleaning or cooking can strain the lower back.
- Body weight—being more than 9 kilograms (20 pounds) overweight increases strain on the back.
- Heavy physical work, including frequent lifting, pushing, pulling, or other forceful movements.
- Bending, twisting, or working in an awkward posture.
- Standing or sitting in the same position for long periods.
- Frequent whole-body vibration, such as that caused by riding in trucks or other vehicles.
- Psychological stress and anxiety—may tense back muscles, increasing the risk of damage.
- Smoking—nicotine narrows blood vessels, reducing the supply of oxygen and nutrients going to the disks.

Source: United States Department of Health and Human Services.

The four main components of this engineering marvel are the vertebrae-disk complex, nerves, muscles, and ligaments. The spine consists of 33 stiff bones called *vertebrae*. Each vertebra is a different size, with the smallest vertebrae lying in the neck. The bigger the vertebrae, the more weight they can support. The vertebrae are connected by tiny joints called *facets*, in much the same way that train cars are joined by interlocking clasps. These facet joints limit the direction and degree of the vertebrae's motion.

Each vertebra has an arch in the back. Together, these form a tunnel called the *spinal canal*, which holds the *spinal cord* (the large cable of nerves that carries electrical signals between the brain and the nerves serving the rest of the body). Tiny openings at the sides of the vertebrae allow nerves to exit the spinal canal. The 30 pairs of nerve roots that lead to either the left or right side of your body carry sensory impulses from and motor impulses to different parts of your body.

Between the vertebrae are flat, round, rubbery disks called *intervertebral disks*. These disks—the largest of which are about 5 centimeters (2 inches) in diameter—serve as biological shock absorbers for the spine, absorbing the energy produced when you move. They also prevent your vertebrae from grinding against each other.

Muscles in the back help keep the spine properly aligned. Stretched or torn muscles, called *strains*, can cause back pain.

The author:
Daniel Hurley, M.D., is a board-certified physiatrist at the Chicago Institute of Neurosurgery and Neuroresearch.

The outside wall of the disk, called the *annulus fibrosus*, consists of thick, strong tissue. The annulus fibrosus surrounds a jellylike core called the *nucleus pulposus*, which has a high water content. Each of these fluid-filled disks loses a small portion of its water over the course of a day. As a result, you are almost ½ centimeter (¼ inch) shorter at the end of a day than you were when you awoke. When you lie down and reduce the pressure on your disks, they *rehydrate*. Over your lifetime, however, your disks will gradually lose more water than they reabsorb each day. As a result, at age 80, people are, on average, about 6 centimeters (2 ½ inches) shorter than they were at age 20.

Although the annulus fibrosus can withstand great pressure, poor posture or improper bending and twisting can weaken the disk wall over time. If too much stress is placed on the disk—by sudden jarring movements or by awkwardly twisting, for example—the jellylike nucleus pulposus can burst through the strained disk wall. This may result in what is known as a *herniated disk*, commonly called a *slipped disk*. Even a jerking movement from coughing, laughing, or sneezing can cause a disk to rupture if the annulus fibrosus is already weak.

Common causes of back pain

- Strain or sprain of back muscles or ligaments.
- *Herniated* (ruptured) intervertebral disk.
- Segmental instability, in which two adjacent vertebrae become unstable and shift in position.
- Spinal stenosis, a narrowing of the *spinal canal* (the canal through which the spinal cord passes).
- Degenerative disk disease, in which the disks deteriorate.
- Osteoporosis, a disease in which vertebrae and other bones lose their strength.
- Disease, including cancer and infections affecting the spine or body organs.

SPINAL INJURIES UP CLOSE

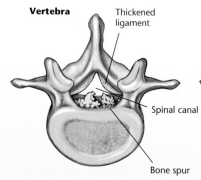

Vertebra   Thickened ligament
Spinal canal
Bone spur

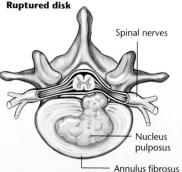

Ruptured disk
Spinal nerves
Nucleus pulposus
Annulus fibrosus

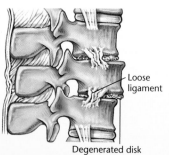

Misaligned vertebrae
Loose ligament
Degenerated disk

Thickened ligaments or *bone spurs* (small bone growths) can narrow the spinal canal, which houses the spinal cord. These conditions can compress spinal nerves and cause back or neck pain.

Intervertebral disks can rupture, causing the jellylike *nucleus pulposus* to burst through the *annulus fibrosus* (disk wall). The protruding material can pinch spinal nerves.

Ligaments that connect the vertebrae may become loose, causing the vertebrae to *misalign* (shift out of place). Over time, intervertebral disks can lose some of their jellylike interior and become *degenerated disks*.

A protruding nucleus pulposus often pinches one of the three nerve roots in the lower back that form the *sciatic nerve*, the large nerve that travels down the back of each leg. This pinching may cause a condition called *sciatica*, which results in lower back and leg pain and may also cause weakness, tingling, numbness, or a complete loss of feeling. The nerves in the back may also be damaged by *bone spurs* (bony projections that form along the facets), sprained *ligaments* (fibrous tissues that connect bones), or by poor alignment of the vertebrae. Because nerves do not heal as well as most other tissues in the body, a physician may find it difficult to predict how fast they will return to normal—or if at all. Nerve damage requires early, proper treatment.

Muscles and ligaments bind the vertebrae and help keep the spine properly aligned. Without them, the spinal column would be as unstable as a stack of children's building blocks. In addition, the spine serves as an anchor for muscles that wrap around the ribs or the abdomen, protecting internal organs and adding stability. Having weak muscles increases the risk of injury or wear and tear on the vertebrae and nerves. Such activities as raking leaves, shoveling snow, or performing household chores may stretch or tear muscles (*strains*) or ligaments (*sprains*). Slouching in front of a computer may also cause backache. Even too much exercise can make your back muscles hurt.

Stress hurts

Stress can be as harmful to back health as physical activity. Stress causes muscles to tense. When you are under stress, an area of the brain called the *hypothalamus* sends signals to the adrenal glands. These nerve signals stimulate the glands to release adrenaline and other hormones that raise the heart rate, breathing rate, blood pressure, and the amount of sugar in the blood. This reaction increases alertness and stimulates muscles in preparation for some type of action.

Muscles absorb and store some of the energy created by stress. If the muscles stay tight for long periods, they cannot function normally. Tight muscles can distort your posture, cause your joints to stiffen, and make your muscles sore. Tight muscles are also more prone to injury from tearing. These tears are usually microscopic and can occur from a sudden overload or overuse of the muscle. When muscles remain contracted, blood flow is blocked and *lactic acid* (a type of acid produced in the blood during muscular activity) builds up. In the process, oxygen levels in the muscles fall, further increasing soreness and the risk of injury.

Another common cause of back pain is muscle *spasm* (contraction). Back spasms may occur during or after strenuous exercise or when a heavy object is lifted incorrectly. Spasms may occur even after a cough or a sneeze or after lifting something as light as a sock off the floor. Most muscle spasms improve on their own over time, though medication containing

Tips to prevent back pain and injury

- When sitting, keep your back straight with your lumbar spine supported by the chair back. Prop your feet on a stool if your feet don't reach the floor.
- Do not sit for long periods. Stand or walk at every opportunity.
- Stand straight, with your spine centered over your pelvis.
- Avoid excessive overhead and low-level reaching.
- Wear comfortable, low-heeled shoes.
- Do not lift by bending over an object. Lift objects by bending knees to a squatting position while maintaining the natural curve of the spine.
- When carrying objects, distribute the weight evenly.
- Do not twist your body while holding a heavy load. Turn your entire body in the direction you want to move.
- Push heavy objects instead of pulling them toward you.
- Maintain proper body weight and exercise regularly.

Sources: Chicago Institute of Neurosurgery and Neuroresearch; United States Department of Health and Human Services.

acetaminophen or such nonsteroidal anti-inflammatory drugs as aspirin and ibuprofen can ease the discomfort they cause.

The ligaments are the fourth major component of the back. These fibrous tissues cross each of the facet joints of the spine. Larger ligaments, which look like big straps, run the length of the spinal column from front to back, holding the vertebrae and disks in place. Without strong muscular support, ligaments can tear, weakening the spine. In severe cases of neck injury, damaged ligaments may allow the vertebrae to collapse into one another or into the spinal cord.

Fortunately, most back pain is just a nuisance and will go away on its own over time. If your back pain is severe or *chronic*, however, you should consult a physician. (Medical experts define chronic pain as pain that lasts three or more weeks.) You should also see a physician if you have numbness, tingling, weakness, or bladder or bowel problems, as these are signs of potentially serious nerve damage. Back pain may be an indicator of something else going on in an organ deeper in the body, so a physician may explore a patient's overall health if the initial back evaluation seems normal. Backaches may result from infections, kidney disease (including kidney stones), diseases of the pancreas, tumors, and (in women) gynecological diseases.

Treatment options for back pain

Various types of physicians can diagnose back pain. *Physiatrists*, for example, are physicians trained in comprehensive diagnostic assessment, nonsurgical care, and rehabilitation medicine. *Orthopedic surgeons* specialize in disorders of the bones and muscles and their associated tissues. *Neurosurgeons* specialize in the brain and spinal cord. A physician may order you to get an X ray or undergo another imaging procedure, such as a magnetic resonance imaging (MRI) or computed tomography (CT) scan, to get a detailed picture of the spine. Unless serious injury or disease underlies back pain, surgery is usually the last option in treating a backache.

Other specialists treat back pain. *Acupuncturists* practice an ancient Chinese method of relieving pain and treating disease by inserting needles into specific places on the body. *Chiropractors* treat back pain by manually manipulating the spine and other body parts. *Physical therapists* use many

THE WRONG WAY AND THE RIGHT WAY

  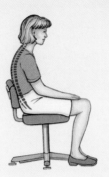 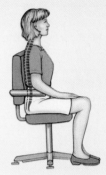

When standing, do not lean back from your hips or extend your neck forward.

Stand with your ears, shoulders, hips, and ankles aligned.

Do not slouch while sitting.

Sit straight with your spine supported by a chair with a tall back.

Never lift by bending over an object with your legs straight.

When lifting, try to maintain the natural curve of the spine, keeping your knees bent to shift the burden from your back to your legs.

Do not pull objects toward you or lean over when moving objects.

Push objects with your back straight and knees bent.

 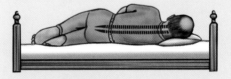

Do not sleep on a mattress that is soft or sagging.

Sleep on a supportive mattress that keeps your body—ears, shoulders, and hips—aligned.

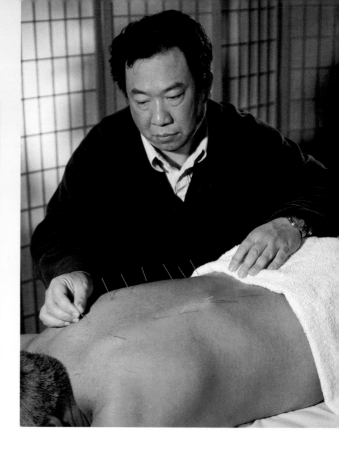

Treating back pain

Patients who suffer from back pain have a wide range of treatment options. Common types of treatment include:

- Cold compresses soon after the onset of pain.
- Hot compresses if pain continues.
- Over-the-counter or prescription medication.
- Physical therapy to mobilize joints and to stretch and strengthen muscles.
- Occupational therapy to address body mechanics, posture, and ergonomics.
- Spinal injections or surgery.
- Acupuncture, chiropractic adjustment, massage, Pilates, or yoga.
- Physical rehabilitation.
- Nutrition, exercise, aerobic conditioning, and relaxation.
- Reinjury prevention.

Critically reviewed by Dr. Daniel Hurley, Chicago Institute of Neurosurgery and Neuroresearch.

An *acupuncturist* inserts needles into a patient's back to relieve pain. Acupuncturists practice an ancient Chinese method of treating pain and illness by inserting needles in specific places on the body.

kinds of equipment and exercises to help people reduce pain and improve body function and posture.

If your muscles or ligaments are aching, sometimes simply relaxing the back will help. If your physician orders bed rest, lie on your side and place a pillow between your knees to align the spine and reduce pressure. You can also lie flat on your back with a pillow under your knees. Most back experts caution against remaining in bed for more than two to three days after an episode of back pain or spasm, unless you are advised to do so by a physician. Prolonged bed rest can weaken muscles, which can aggravate an existing condition.

Hot and cold compresses help reduce pain and inflammation in some patients. Hot compresses relax muscles by increasing blow flow, while cold compresses reduce pain caused by spasms or minor strains or sprains.

It may sound like old advice, but good posture is the first step toward keeping your back healthy. Proper posture helps prevent disks from being flattened or strained, facets and vertebrae from wearing down, and muscles and ligaments from being torn or suffering a spasm. Regular exercise can strengthen the lower back and support the spine. Specific types of exercise, such as yoga and Pilates, can help with stretching and strengthening muscles, maintaining proper balance and posture, and keeping the abdomen toned. Before beginning an exercise regimen, however, you should consult a certified trainer and, if you have bothersome back pain, speak with a physician.

Sitting for long periods can tighten the muscles leading from the spine to your hips. When you stand, these muscles act like tight straps, restricting your range of motion and often causing discomfort or pain. To avoid this problem, occasionally stand and gently lean back to stretch the front of the hips and thighs.

Being overweight also strains back muscles, increasing the chances for back pain. A general exercise program can help you control your weight and strengthen your back muscles.

Even shoes can impact back health. Good shoes with arch supports help you stand straight and balanced. Being off-balance can affect your posture—and the health of your back—by altering the position of your hipbones, pelvis, and base of the spine.

Working for a healthy back

Your workplace may also be hard on your back. This is where *ergonomics*—arranging your work environment to fit your body—helps. By 2005, many companies in the United States were stressing the importance of ergonomics. The National Institute for Occupational Safety and Health, an agency of the U.S. Centers for Disease Control and Prevention in Atlanta, Georgia, has identified five workplace risk factors for low-back pain. These factors are: doing heavy physical work; doing work that involves frequent lifting, pushing, pulling, or other forceful movement; bending, twisting, or working in an awkward position; working in the same position for an extended period; and experiencing whole-body vibrations—by riding in a truck, for example. Such whole-body vibrations force the muscles in your body to tighten.

Sitting at a computer is horrible for your back if you constantly lean forward, crunching your head into the top of your neck, stretching out your arms to reach the computer mouse, and rounding the rest of your back into a "C" shape. You should try to maintain a gentle backward curve in your neck, and keep your head sitting evenly above the center of your spine. You should never allow your head to slide or droop forward because this position puts unnecessary pressure on the spine.

As a general rule, when you are sitting on an office chair, the *lumbar region* (lower back) of your spine should curve inward. Your knees should be bent at a 90-degree angle, and your feet should be flat on the floor. The head and eyes should be about the same height as your computer screen, which should be close enough so you don't have to lean forward and squint. "Computer glasses," which are designed for mid-distance work, can help reduce neck strain for people who normally wear bifocals. Such glasses eliminate the need for you to lift your head upward to peer out of the bottom portion of your bifocals.

Driving can also be harmful to your back's health. A vehicle's seat should be adjusted so that the driver's knees are slightly bent and the back is arched. If you are driving for a long distance, you should stop frequently and stretch to relax your muscles.

Working around the house carries its own risks, too. When cleaning, carrying children, or lifting heavy bags of groceries, you can strain disks and muscles in the spine. Even when lifting, you should try to maintain the natural curve of the spine. To avoid injury, refrain from twisting when reaching for objects, carry objects close to your body, and use the muscles in your legs and not your back to help lift heavy objects.

Sometimes helping your back may be as simple as purchasing a new mattress. In general, you should not sleep on a mattress that is soft or sagging, because the lack of support causes the spine to fall out of alignment. Likewise, a mattress that is too firm will not adjust to the spine's natural curve. One study, reported in 2003 by researchers in Spain, found that a firm mattress placed too much pressure on the spine, while a medium-firm mattress gave patients a balance between back support and comfort.

Sports are a major cause of back injuries. Most contact sports have special gear—such as helmets and pads—designed to protect athletes from injury. Athletes should also learn proper techniques to protect themselves while on the field. For example, football players should never tackle an opposing player with their head down, as this position makes the neck more susceptible to injury.

Backpack safety

You may not have to look farther than the closet to find one of the biggest causes of a sore back in children—backpacks. Because they are typically crammed with heavy textbooks, they add extra weight to a child's frame. If they are flung over one shoulder, they can strain the muscles or vertebrae. Children frequently take backpacks off with a twisting motion and yank them up off the floor when in a hurry.

A study published in September 2004 by researchers at the University of California at Riverside found that 64 percent of the students surveyed reported having some pain as the result of carrying a backpack, and 21 percent of the students reported having pain that lasted for more than six months. The researchers had questioned 3,498 students between the ages of 11 and 15. The study found that the average backpack weighed 4.5 kilograms (10 pounds), though some weighed nearly 17 kilograms (37 pounds). According to the U.S. Consumer Product Safety Commission, about 21,000 Americans—mostly young people—were treated for backpack-related injuries in 2002.

Backpack users can take simple steps to help avoid a backache. First, keep your backpack light and limit the number of items you carry. Second, use proper techniques when wearing your pack. If the backpack is heavy, squat down first, keeping your back straight, before picking it up or taking it off. If the pack is not heavy, lean over with one leg extended

Selecting a safe backpack for a child

The American Academy of Pediatrics recommends that adults look for the following features when selecting a backpack for a child:

- A lightweight material that does not add to the child's load.

- Two wide, padded shoulder straps to lower the risk of pain and reduced blood circulation in the shoulders.

- A padded back to provide increased comfort and added protection from sharp objects or edges inside the pack.

- A waist belt to help distribute the weight more evenly across the body.

- Multiple compartments, which can be used to distribute weight. Heavier items should be packed in the center of the pack to distribute the load more evenly.

Children who carry heavy packs can ruin their posture and suffer back injuries. Some students use backpacks with wheels to reduce the strain on their backs. In some states, lawmakers are trying to limit textbook weights to help lighten the load.

backward—like a golfer leaning over to pick up a ball. This motion keeps the spine straight as you reach to the ground. You should wear your backpack on both shoulders to avoid neck strain. Snugly strap the pack to your back so it does not bounce around, which can cause muscles to tighten.

Leaning a little forward while walking with a backpack will also put some of the weight on the flat of your back rather than having the weight hang from your shoulders. Keep your neck in an upright position and keep your *hamstrings* (the muscles in the back of your thighs) and the muscles in your hips, back, and buttocks stretched and limber.

Understanding how to protect your back and avoid injury can go a long way in promoting proper back health. A little knowledge and care can keep you standing tall for years to come.

■ FOR ADDITIONAL INFORMATION

Books and periodicals

Burn, Loic. *Back and Neck Pain: The Facts.* Oxford, 2000.
Fehrsen-Du Toit, Renita. *The Good Back Book: A Practical Guide to Alleviating & Preventing Back Pain.* Firefly Bks., 2003.
Sutton, Amy L., ed. *Back and Neck Sourcebook.* 2nd ed. Omnigraphics, 2004.

Web sites

KidsHealth BackPack Safety—kidshealth.org/parent/firstaid_safe/home/backpack.html
MedlinePlus Back Injuries—www.nlm.nih.gov/medlineplus/backinjuries.html
Spine Health Back Pain and Neck Pain Information—www.spine-health.com
Spine School—www.spineuniversity.com/public/spineschool.asp

Marine mosaic from ancient Pompeii

FISHING POLL:
THE CENSUS OF
MARINE LIFE

By Ron O'Dor and Darlene Trew Crist

...larco, a type of jellyfish

Lobate ctenophore

An international team of scientists is now halfway through the largest survey ever taken of life in Earth's final frontier, the oceans.

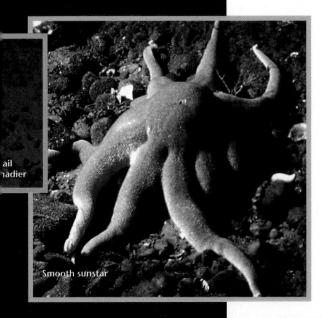

...ail ...nadier

Smooth sunstar

W hat creatures live in Earth's oceans? Which are likely to survive into the future? What sorts of sea animals have inhabited the oceans in the past? Finding answers to these questions is the goal of the Census of Marine Life (CoML), a 10-year, $1-billion research project that reached its halfway point in 2005. This quest by at least 1,000 scientists from 70 countries may be the first great voyage of discovery of the 2000's.

Oceans cover nearly 71 percent of Earth's surface, and yet oceanographers have explored less than 5 percent of this volume. We don't know how numerous marine species are—estimates vary wildly from 1 million to 10 million—or exactly where most species live.

A census of marine life is timely, even urgent. Few countries have a reliable base of information about their marine resources, including their *fisheries* (areas where fish are caught commercially or recreationally). Such information is needed to help governments develop successful strategies for protecting and managing these resources. Accurate information about the distribution, abundance, and variety of marine species can also help scientists determine how marine *ecosystems* have changed over time and help predict future changes. (An ecosystem consists of an area's biological and physical environments.)

Finally, basic information about the condition of the oceans is essential for tackling such pressing global issues as the loss of habitat, pollution control, and climate change.

The CoML has four main components, the largest of which consists of 14 field projects exploring ocean life from both a biological and geographic perspective. That is, scientists working on these projects are cataloging marine species ranging from the smallest microbes to the largest predators in ecosystems ranging from shallow coastal waters

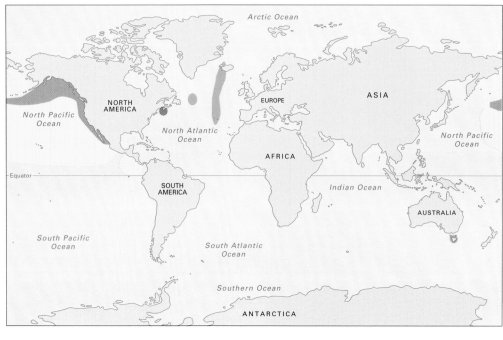

GoMA—Gulf of Maine Area Program	**MAR-ECO**—Mid-Atlantic Ridge Ecosystem Project	**POST**—Pacific Ocean Shelf Tracking Project	**TOPP**—Tagging of Pacific Pelagics

One of the four components of the Census of Marine Life (CoML) consists of 14 field projects covering all regions of the world's oceans. This Special Report includes information on four projects: GoMA, MAR-ECO, POST, and TOPP.

CENSUS OF MARINE LIFE PROJECTS

Census of Marine Life International Web Portal
http://www.coml.org

Arctic Ocean Biodiversity (ArcOD): Studies life in the sea ice, water column, and sea floor of the Arctic Ocean.
http://www.sfos.uaf.edu/ research/arcdiv/index.html

Biogeography of Chemosynthetic Ecosystems (ChEss): Studies ecosystems near deep-water heat vents and cold chemical seeps.
http://www.noc.soton.ac.uk /chess/

Census of the Diversity of Abyssal Marine Life (CeDAMar): Explores life in, on, and above the deep-sea floor.
http://www.cedamar.org

Census of Marine Zooplankton (CMarZ): Explores the diversity of the world's animal plankton—tiny organisms that drift in the ocean.
http://www.CMarZ.org

Future of Marine Animal Populations (FMAP): Creates models to predict changes in marine ecosystems, focusing on impacts from the fishing industry and global climate change.
http://as01.ucis.dal.ca/ fmap/index.php

Gulf of Maine Area Program (GoMA): Collects information on a single ecosystem to enable the establishment of ecosystem-based management.
http://www.usm.maine.edu/ gulfofmaine-census/

History of Marine Animal Populations (HMAP): Analyzes data from historical and environmental records to understand the relationship between marine life and human activities.
http://www.hmapcoml.org

International Census of Marine Microbes (ICoMM): Studies the biodiversity of marine microorganisms from all over the world.
http://icomm.mbl.edu

Mid-Atlantic Ridge Ecosystem Project (MAR-ECO): Exploratory study of the animals inhabiting the North Atlantic Ocean.
http://www.mar-eco.no

Natural Geography in Shore Areas (NaGISA): Monitors marine life near the shores of the oceans,

at depths of less than 20 meters (67 feet).
http://www.nagisa.coml.org

Ocean Biogeographic Information System (OBIS): An Internet-based provider of information on marine species collected by CoML projects.
http://www.iobis.org

Pacific Ocean Shelf Tracking Project (POST): Monitors the movement of marine animals through listening stations set along the west coast of North America.
http://www.postcoml.org

Tagging of Pacific Pelagics (TOPP): Tracks the movements of certain marine animals to learn more about Pacific Ocean ecosystems.
http://www.toppcensus.org

to the deep sea. By 2005, census scientists had recorded 15,300 new species of fish and thousands more new plants and other marine animals. By the time researchers conclude in 2010, they expect the number of new fish species to be closer to 20,000. They also expect to have identified hundreds of thousands more marine life forms.

The CoML would not be possible without exciting technological advances in marine research. These include robotic vehicles that can penetrate previously inaccessible depths and *hydroacoustic* (underwater sound) devices that can "hear" small fish 100 kilometers (60 miles) away. Census scientists are using new optical sensors and cameras to record animals' appearance and behavior with greater clarity. Smaller, lighter tracking tags that don't interfere with animals' normal behavior are providing more accurate information about habitats and migration routes.

This *Science Year* Special Report focuses on four CoML field projects that were well underway by 2005. They are the Mid-Atlantic Ridge Ecosystems (MAR-ECO) Project; the Tagging of Pacific Pelagics (TOPP) Project; the Pacific Ocean Shelf Tracking (POST) Project; and the Gulf of Maine Area (GoMA) Program.

Census researchers working on the History of Marine Animal Populations (HMAP) Project, a second CoML component, are compiling information on the numbers and *diversity* (variety of different marine species) of sea life since 1500. Researchers with the Future of Marine Animal Populations (FMAP) project, the third CoML component, are using the historical and field data to develop mathematical models to predict future changes in marine ecosystems. Finally, much of the information from all these projects is being collected into a fourth CoML component, a publicly accessible, interactive online database called the Ocean Biogeographic Information System (OBIS). By mid-2005, OBIS held more than 5 million records, including data on about 40,000 marine species. Both OBIS and HMAP are discussed in depth at the end of this article.

Coordinating all the work of the census is a secretariat based at the Consortium of Oceanographic Research and Education in Washington, D.C., an association of U.S. oceanographic research organizations. Financial support is coming from an international group of government agencies as well as from such private sources as the Alfred P. Sloan Foundation, a nonprofit philanthropic organization in New York City.

A Cod-End Aquarium (above, left), a net system that captures live marine animals from deep water, is pulled aboard a ship working with the Mid-Atlantic Ridge Ecosystem Project. Scientists on the ship (above) then sort and process specimens in an on-board laboratory.

The authors:
Ron O'Dor is the Senior Scientist at the Census of Marine Life in the Consortium for Oceanographic Research and Education. Darlene Trew Crist is a science writer and coordinates the Education and Outreach Network of the census.

MAR-ECO

In June 2004, an international team of scientists set sail from Norway aboard the *G. O. Sars,* a Norwegian research vessel, to explore one of the most remote regions on Earth. Their destination was the Mid-Atlantic Ridge, a vast underwater mountain range that stretches along the floor of the Atlantic Ocean for about 10,000 kilometers (6,200 miles) from a point north of Iceland to the Azores. Their quest was to observe and sample life in a rugged landscape that exists in near-total darkness thousands of meters below the surface. When the research ship returned to port two months later, its scientists brought back an abundance of data and an astonishing specimen collection. Like the great voyages of the 1800's and 1900's that pioneered ocean research, the expedition of the *G. O Sars* returned with enough material to keep marine scientists busy for years.

The *G. O. Sars* is one of several major research vessels working with the MAR-ECO Project, each committed by a different country, including Iceland, Germany, Portugal, the United Kingdom, and the United States. These ships are state-of-the-art, ocean-going laboratories that provide launching platforms for deep-sea exploration instruments and vehicles as well as facilities where scientists can study the samples and data they collect. In 2004, MAR-ECO scientists also chartered a Norwegian fishing vessel to sample bottom-living fishes.

As the *G. O. Sars* sailed along the northern part of the Mid-Atlantic Ridge, it stopped at about 40 locations called *stations.* At each station, the scientists sampled the water using a device that consists of a circular frame capable of carrying up to 36 bottles. Scientists can program the instrument to open the bottles, which each hold from 1 to 30 liters

A ceratoid anglerfish, a deep-sea fish caught by MAR-ECO scientists in 2004, may represent an entirely new species. The fish's unusual head structure and uniquely formed lure, which is used to attract prey, set it apart from other types of anglerfish.

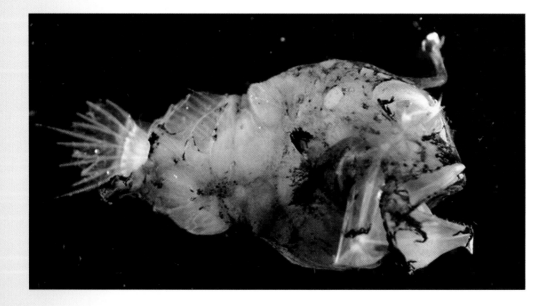

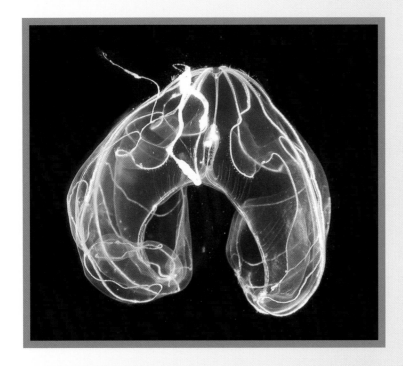

A ctenophore called *Bathocyroe fosteri* is one of many sea cretures caught by MAR-ECO scientists. Ctenophores look like jellyfish, but they are known by the eight bands of comblike organs on the sides of their bodies. These combs beat in a wave pattern, moving the animal through the water. Faintly glowing digestive canals lie under the comb rows, lighting up the transparent body.

(0.26 to 8 gallons), at specific depths. At the heart of the device, called a CTD instrument, is a sensor that measures the water's *conductivity* (ease with which it conducts electric current), temperature, and density. Conductivity measurements help scientists determine the water's *salinity* (saltiness). The greater the water's conductivity, the greater is its level of salinity. The data are sent continuously to a computer aboard the ship. Information from different areas help oceanographers plot the location and movement of ocean currents and other water masses. The data also help scientists chart the distribution of species.

The movement of ocean currents may explain one of the most interesting discoveries made by scientists aboard the *G. O. Sars*—surprisingly large rings of *plankton*. (Plankton is the mass of tiny organisms that drift in the ocean.) To "count" plankton or other small fish that live at middle depths and to track their movement, scientists use *sonar* to record the sounds reflected by the animals as they move through the water. (A sonar is a device that uses sound energy to locate objects; measure their distance, direction, and speed; and even produce pictures of the objects.) In one area east of the Mid-Atlantic Ridge, MAR-ECO's echosounders discovered four enormous, donutlike rings of ocean plankton hundreds of meters in diameter. Although scientists had observed plankton rings before, they had never seen any so large. Scientists suggested that the rings may have formed from plankton communities caught up in eddies that were created as ocean currents collided. The rings may also have

A new species of squid found by MAR-ECO scientists has a slightly *opaque cornea* (non-transparent outer layer) on its one eye. Most oceanic squid have no cornea at all. The squid measures 62 millimeters (2.4 inches) long. The squid was not weighed to avoid damaging its delicate parts.

been created in eddies formed as currents were swept off course by their passage over a *seamount* (underwater mountain) or other undersea feature.

Among the many specimens brought back by scientists aboard the *G. O. Sars* was a major collection of *zooplankton,* small free-floating organisms that include such tiny crustaceans as water fleas and shrimps and many *gelatinous* (jellylike) forms. Interestingly, some of the gelatinous species had never been documented before. Scientists expect the collection to provide new insights into the zooplankton's range and the structure of their communities.

To collect the zooplankton and other ridge inhabitants, MAR-ECO scientists are employing a variety of instruments, including *trawls* and other traditional fishing gear adapted for scientific use. (Trawls are funnel-shaped nets that are open at the mouth and closed off at the tail end, where the fish or other marine life collects.) Some of the *G. O. Sars's* trawls could reach a depth of at least 3,000 meters (10,000 feet). Some trawls were also equipped with video and hydroacoustic equipment to help scientists control nets operating behind and below the ship.

Trawls and nets provide a "snapshot" of the creatures living in a particular *water column,* a top-to-bottom cross section of a body of water. Net samplers operated vertically provide another means of studying life in a water column. These devices contain a number of mesh nets, each designed to catch animals of a different size. After the scientists haul their catch aboard, they identify, count, measure, and weigh the specimens. Most specimens are frozen or preserved in formalin or another chemical solution for later study.

To photograph creatures living in a particular water column, MAR-ECO scientists rely on *optical profilers.* These instruments are essentially advanced video cameras. As the devices descend, they photograph the organisms that swim or float by at various levels or capture the flashes of bioluminescence the animals may produce. The MAR-ECO scientists also use *free-fall photographic landers,* which are metal frames containing cameras and other optical equipment that fall to the sea floor and photograph scavenging animals as they pass by.

To photograph and sample marine life at depths to 4,000 meters (13,000 feet), MAR-ECO scientists employ *remotely operated vehicles* (ROV's). These small, submarinelike "robots" are tethered by cable to a research ship. Although ROV's carry no crew, the video cameras and sensors they transport allow scientists to observe and record the appearance and behavior of sea life at lower depths. Mechanical arms attached to an ROV can be used to collect samples.

During their voyage, scientists aboard the *G. O. Sars* observed or collected at least 90 different fish species that live near the sea floor, another 200 species that live at a variety of other depths, and 50 species of squids or octopods. Scientists were surprised to find many of these species living in certain areas, and so the discoveries have increased our knowledge about the animals' habitats.

In addition to providing scientists with a treasure trove of data, the ROV dives left *G. O. Sars* scientists with at least one mystery. North of the Azores, an ROV's camera revealed a strange line of burrows on a seamount about 2,000 meters (6,500 feet) down. The burrows, which extended for several meters in different directions, consisted of an odd grouping of circular and irregularly shaped holes about 5 centimeters (2 inches) wide. The holes were so evenly spaced that one scientist compared them to lines of stitching made by a sewing machine. The intrigued scientists watched the burrows for some time, hoping to catch sight of the digger and trying to figure out if the holes represented many burrows or only one burrow with many entrances. But the animal and the nature of the burrows remained a secret.

MAR-ECO researchers in the Russian submersible MIR (below, left) prepare to drop into the Atlantic Ocean for a 3-kilometers (2-mile) descent into the deep. Project scientists also use unpiloted landers (below), metal frames that carry cameras and a variety of other scientific instruments to the sea floor.

TOPP/ POST

Mapping the "highways" in the North Pacific Ocean that *pelagic* animals travel to feed, breed, and migrate is a focus of two census projects—the Tagging of Pacific Pelagics (TOPP) project and the Pacific Ocean Shelf Tracking Project (POST). (Pelagic means *of the open ocean*). Thanks to sophisticated electronic tags—which are implanted or attached to the animals without causing harm—the animals themselves are helping to provide the most detailed information ever collected about their movement and behavior in the open ocean. By 2005, TOPP scientists had tagged about 1,250 animals representing 20 species. POST had tagged or detected 3,000 members of the 7 species of salmon and sturgeon.

One type of tag, called an archival tag, can collect and store a variety of data over periods lasting two years or more. Implanted archival tags, for example, can record and store information on the internal temperature of tuna and swordfish as well as the temperature of the surrounding water. Such tags can help scientists track the animals' feeding behavior. Because a tuna is warmer than the fish it preys on, its internal temperature drops when it eats. Both implanted and attached archival tags also track an animal's depth—to learn about its diving behavior—and light levels in the surrounding water, which can be used to estimate location.

Archival tags, however, can reveal their data only if the tagged animal is caught. As a result, TOPP scientists are implanting these tags only in tuna and other commercial fish that are caught in large numbers or attaching the tags to sea turtles and other animals that regularly return to certain locations.

A more sophisticated form of archival tag contains a satellite transmitter and a "pop-up" device. TOPP scientists are using these pop-up tags with sharks, swordfish, ocean sunfish, and other animals that live below the surface, where the antenna would not be able to transmit properly. After collecting data for a predetermined period, these tags separate from the animal and pop to the surface. The tags then transmit their data to a system of remote-sensing satellites, which, in turn, send the information to TOPP scientists.

Some TOPP scientists are tracking several species of air-breathing sea animals daily with tags that communicate with satellites while still attached to the animals. The data transmitted by the tags, relayed to scientists by the satellites every 24 hours, are helping the scientists create maps showing exactly where the animals have traveled since being tagged.

By 2005, TOPP researchers had made fascinating discoveries about some of these movements. One of the most interesting finds involved a surprisingly well-traveled bluefin tuna.

A leatherback turtle, a critically endangered species, leaves a beach after being tagged by scientists from the Tagging of Pacific Pelagics (TOPP) Project. Researchers use the tag to track the turtle's movements by satellite.

Scientists had known that bluefin tuna, the most commercially valuable fish in the ocean, *spawn* (reproduce) only in Asian waters. They had thought that a year or two after hatching, the young tuna traveled eastward across the Pacific to North America, returning westward some years later to spawn and die. To their surprise, however, TOPP scientists tracked one young bluefin tuna as it crossed the Pacific Ocean three times and traveled up and down the West Coast several times—all within about 600 days. Scientists are unsure whether a search for food motivated the tuna's journey. But the findings have provided new data on tuna habitats and migratory highways that may one day be used to help shape the management of tuna fisheries in the Pacific.

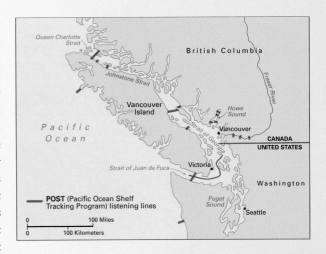

Learning more about the behavior of salmon, another commercially valuable fish, is the focus of the POST project. POST scientists use implanted acoustic tags that transmit coded signals unique to each fish. To receive the signals, the scientists have established a network of underwater listening stations. When a tagged fish swims by, tracking sensors in the stations pick up its signal, storing it along with the date and time in its memory.

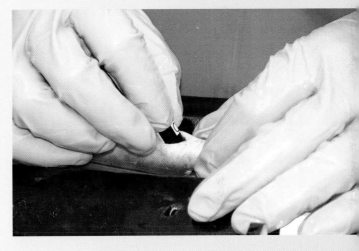

A scientist with the (POST) project outfits a young salmon with an acoustic tag (above). These tags transmit sounds that are picked up by listening devices (red bars on map, above, top) placed along the Pacific Coast.

In 2004, POST scientists made a surprising discovery about the dangers salmon face as they try to leave their hatching grounds in rivers for the open ocean. Before the study, scientists believed young salmon were most vulnerable while swimming through rivers and *estuaries* (coastal river valleys flooded by an ocean). Scientists thought that the dangers in these areas—human-related pollution, predators, and the stress of moving from a freshwater to saltwater environment—outweighed the perils awaiting them in the open ocean. In fact, POST scientists found that the salmon they tracked died at about the same rate along their entire migration path. This finding suggests that salmon conservation measures, which currently focus on rivers and estuaries, should include ocean habitats as well.

GoMA

The Gulf of Maine Area Program (GoMA) taking place off the coast of New England is the census demonstration project focusing entirely on a single ecosystem. Long famous as one of the world's richest fishing grounds, the Gulf of Maine has suffered since the early 1990's from the collapse of many of its fisheries, particularly the cod fishery, because of overfishing and improper management of fish stocks.

GoMA's first goal is to gain enough knowledge to help the governments of the United States and Canada establish *ecosystem-based management* within the region. Ecosystem-based management means regulating the activities of human beings so that we do not disrupt the web of relationships that exist among the organisms of the ecosystem and between the organisms and their environment. To implement such a system, however, scientists need an adequate knowledge of the diversity and distribution of life in the ecosystem and of the ecological processes that govern that life. GoMA's second goal is to make available, to areas with similar bodies of water around the world, information about how biodiversity can aid in ecosystem-based management.

The Gulf of Maine Area, which is bounded by land to the west and *banks* (underwater plateaus) to the east, is often called a "sea within a sea." It extends from Cape Cod (a peninsula on the coast of Massachusetts) in the south to the Bay of Fundy (which divides the Canadian provinces of New Brunswick and Nova Scotia) in the north. It also extends seaward to the rich fishing regions of Georges Bank and Browns Bank, which divide the Gulf of Maine from the rest of the Atlantic Ocean. The area also includes a section of the continental slope, which begins at the outer edge of North America's *continental shelf,* the submerged land at the continent's edge.

An unusual combination of geographic factors accounts for this ecosystem's staggering diversity. For example, the gulf includes both subarctic and temperate climate zones. This makes it the southernmost range for some Atlantic sea life and the northernmost range for others. Such temperature differences make the Gulf of Maine an excellent laboratory for studying the effects of climate change on the ocean. The gulf also encompasses a wide variety of habitats, including salt marshes, mudflats, and rocky coastlines as well as banks, deep basins, and seamounts. In addition, the gulf has the highest tides in the world, which help churn up and distribute nutrients through the water.

Because of these features, the area supports rich communities of marine life. It offers a bounty of zooplankton, which draws many species of fish and other larger animals, including endangered right whales. Thanks to the abundance of sea life, the gulf is also a migratory corridor for both sea birds and songbirds. The area is, perhaps, most renowned for its formerly rich fisheries of cod, haddock, herring, Atlantic salmon, flounder, and hake as well as shrimp, lobster, and other shellfish.

Census scientists working in the Gulf of Maine have two main tasks. The first is to collect data on the physical and biological characteristics of the region. To accomplish this, scientists go into the field—and sometimes into the water—to collect samples and learn more about the interaction of the area's species. Sometimes, scientists take a basic approach to collecting their samples. Along the shoreline, for example, they may crawl along on their hands and knees in *intertidal zones* to identify and count the number of the types of animals that reside there. (The intertidal zone is that part of the shoreline between the high-water mark and the low-water mark.)

Observing marine life at sea, however, requires a more complex and sophisticated approach. For that, scientists use a variety of remote-sensing devices. These include the video plankton recorder, for example, an underwater video microscope that captures images of small organisms and other particles. Another device, the laser-optical plankton counter, detects, sizes, and counts individual particles based on light measurements, usually as it is towed behind a boat. In this device, plankton particles passing through a light beam block the light falling on an array of sensors, registering the outlines of the particles.

To locate schools of larger fish, GoMA scientists use a number of acoustic devices, including Doppler-based sonars. These devices send out sound waves, which travel through the water until they hit a fish or other object. The signals reflect off the object and then return to a receiver, which analyzes the signals. Scientists can then use the signals to identify the location of the fish and determine the direction in which they are traveling.

A blood star feeding on palmate sponge (above, left) and a herd of northern sea stars feeding on a patch of mussels (above) are among the animals under study in the coastal waters of the Gulf of Maine. GoMA is the leading census project focusing on a single ecosystem.

Two male ocean pout (above) compete to mate with a female in the Gulf of Maine. During cold New England winters, these fish survive the frigid North Atlantic waters because of high concentrations of a chemical that prevents their blood from freezing.

GoMA scientists are also using instruments commonly employed by other CoML scientists to capture specimens. These devices include trawls, *dredges* (nets dragged along the sea floor), and plankton nets. ROV's and computer-controlled autonomous underwater vehicles carry cameras and other video equipment to deep waters. Piloted submersibles carry scientists there.

By 2005, GoMA scientists had accomplished a great deal. While most of the research is still preliminary and will require additional analysis and confirmation, scientists have made some exciting discoveries. For

Burrowing anemones in the Gulf of Maine extend their tentacles to capture food. The tentacles have stinging cells that paralyze and entangle small marine animals. Anemones then pass the food into their central mouth.

example, by closely studying data from past trawl surveys, GoMA scientists have found that nearly half of every sample load collected in their nets includes species previously unknown on the continental slope.

Scientists have also confirmed that fish diversity is widespread across different regions of the gulf. For example, fish are most diverse in regions near the shore and around the edge of Georges Bank. In these areas, different types of habitat converge to create overlapping areas where many types of species congregate to feed and breed.

Along the northern edge of the New England Seamounts, researchers have identified 30 new species of coral. GoMA scientists using *multibeam sonar* have also mapped enough of the gulf's sea floor to develop a reasonably complete atlas of the northern part of the chain. (Multibeam sonar records the travel time of acoustic signals from a transmitting device to an object and back again.) One group of GoMA scientists has theorized that the seamounts serve as "stepping stones" for some organisms to spread their offspring across the Atlantic Ocean. That is, they have found that certain species known to inhabit the eastern side of the Atlantic have unexpectedly taken up residence on the western side.

GoMA researchers haul in a set of *bongo* nets. These nets are often used to capture floating or suspended fish eggs or newly hatched *larvae* (immature fish).

At the other edge of the gulf, at the intertidal zone, preliminary data suggest that the number of species has dropped significantly. Scientists speculate that one cause may be the Asian shore crab, an omnivorous (plant- and animal-eating) crustacean first identified along the eastern coast of North America in 1988. The crab may be crowding other species out of its new territory.

These data and additional studies will enhance our understanding of how various parts of the Gulf of Maine fit together to form an ecosystem. By 2010, researchers hope to be using these data to develop more effective ways to protect the various parts of the gulf without harming the ecosystem as a whole. If they are successful, their plan will serve as a model for water bodies worldwide.

HMAP/ OBIS

Some of the world's oldest documents record human efforts to harvest the bounty of the sea. Scientists working on the History of Marine Animal Populations (HMAP) project are gathering historical records about 12 ocean ecosystems in order to chart the changes in the abundance and diversity of marine life there for the past 500 years. In particular, HMAP aims to document the effects of human activities and climate change on ocean ecosystems.

The HMAP project employs what may, at first, seem to be an unusual combination of researchers that includes ecologists, biologists, oceanographers, historians, archaeologists, and mathematicians. The records being analyzed are equally varied. These include modern fishery statistics as well as ships' logs and records kept by *monasteries*. These religious communities of men, which often served as trading places, kept accurate records of fish brought in, sold, and taxed. HMAP scientists are also examining environmental records for clues about changes in marine ecosystems. *Sediment cores* (cylindrical samples of material from various layers of the ocean floor), for example, can reveal how marine life has changed in a given area over time.

In 2005, HMAP scientists were expressing surprise at the change in marine life in every region under study. For example, in March, HMAP scientists reported that the volume of North Atlantic cod living on the heavily fished Scotian Shelf, which surrounds the Canadian province of Nova Scotia, had declined by 96 percent since the 1850's. HMAP researchers found that the waters of the shelf contained 1.26 million metric tons (1.38 million tons) of cod in 1852. By 2000, the total had fallen to less than 50,000 metric tons (55,000 tons), chiefly because of overfishing.

Another HMAP study, released in April 2005, linked the decline of coral reefs in the Caribbean Sea, in part, to the overfishing of that region's sharks. Researchers found that fewer sharks led to a rise in the number of smaller carnivo-

A ship's log, dated January 1828, discusses the presence of whales. CoML scientists are collecting historical records of fish and other marine life to compare present and past populations in the world's oceans. The History of Marine Animal Populations (HMAP) Project seeks to understand how and why marine biodiversity has changed over time.

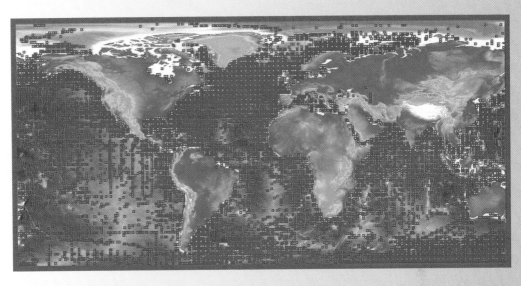

rous fish and a corresponding drop in the number of plant-eating fish that feed on the algae often found on coral reefs. The overabundant algae are, in turn, smothering the coral.

What is happening to the flood of information coming from CoML scientists? After all field projects conclude in 2010, the census will publish an in-depth report on its activities. It will examine how the diversity, distribution, and abundance of marine species in the oceans have changed since the 1500's and provide forecasts about the future of ocean life. It will also include descriptions of new species discovered by CoML scientists and discuss how these creatures fit into their ecosystems.

In the meantime, the data emerging from several census projects is being entered into the Ocean Biogeographic Information System (OBIS). Established by the CoML in 1999, OBIS is an Internet *portal* (gateway) to data on the distribution of marine species contained in many databases around the world. OBIS is freely available on the World Wide Web to researchers, students, or any other interested person. OBIS data from its many sources can be used interactively for such purposes as finding a species' scientific or common name, predicting a species' geographic range and distribution, and generating new hypotheses about marine ecosystems and then proving or disproving them. By mid-2005, OBIS users could access 4 million records from 45 databases on the distribution of 40,000 species, including at least 240,000 records dating from 1611 to 2000.

Another census legacy will be innovative technology for studying marine life. In addition, the census has created scientific connections that cross political boundaries. These links will make future studies of the oceans easier and more complete. Finally, this collaboration is strengthening our appreciation of Earth's oceans as a global resource.

Red dots on a page from the Ocean Biogeographic Information System (OBIS) Web site show the location of marine species found in, on, or above the seabed, from microscopic plankton to whales, recorded over several hundred years. OBIS includes records on the distribution of 40,000 marine species. Blue areas show unstudied areas where research is needed.

THE DARK SIDE OF THE UNIVERSE

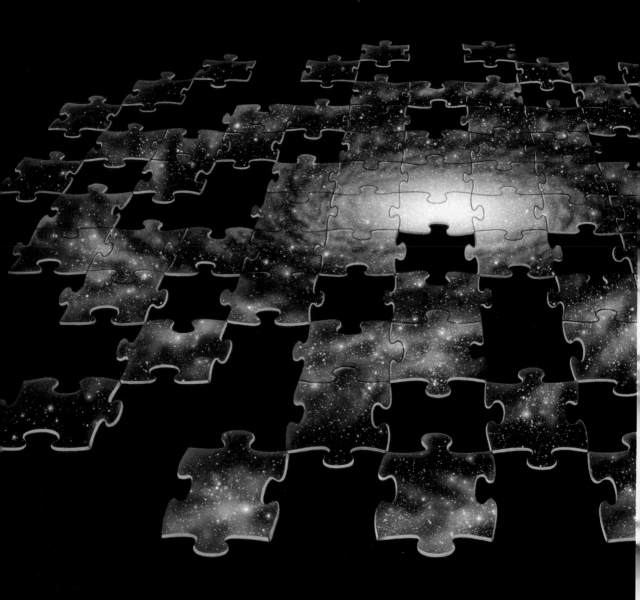

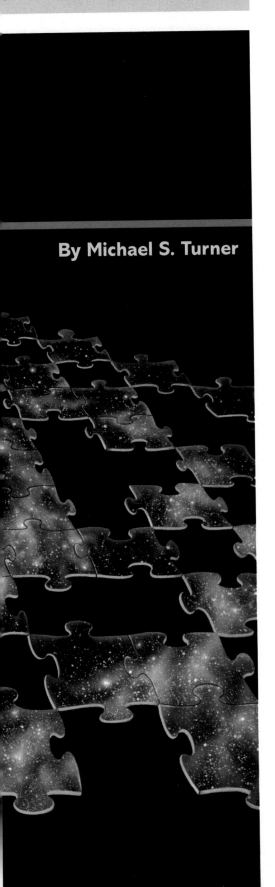

By Michael S. Turner

LIKE THE MISSING PIECES OF A COSMIC PUZZLE, DARK MATTER AND DARK ENERGY CANNOT BE SEEN. YET SCIENTISTS BELIEVE THAT THESE MYSTERIOUS FORMS MAKE UP ALMOST ALL OF THE UNIVERSE.

The night sky is filled with light—tens of thousands of stars that we can see with the unaided eye, and billions more that become visible with the aid of a modest-sized telescope. With the Hubble Space Telescope, we can see hundreds of billions of other galaxies like our own Milky Way. Yet in all these dazzling views of the heavens, we are actually seeing only a tiny fraction of the material that makes up the universe—about 0.5 percent. The other 99.5 percent of the universe does not emit or absorb light, and almost all of this cosmic darkness is a complete mystery to scientists.

In 2005, physicists around the world were searching for information about the "dark side" of the universe. Understanding unseen forms of matter and energy, these scientists believe, is essential to understanding the fundamental nature of the cosmos. How do scientists know that there is more to the universe than meets the eye? What does this mysterious matter and energy—which scientists have named *dark matter* and *dark energy*—consist of? And how will forces associated with dark matter and dark energy determine the fate of the universe?

In the exploration of the dark side of the universe, images made by two telescopic surveys, both released in 2003, have played a crucial role. These images—produced by the Wilkinson Microwave Anisotropy Probe (WMAP) and the Sloan Digital Sky Survey (SDSS)—have allowed scientists to estimate accurately the percentages of dark matter, dark energy, and regular light-emitting matter in the universe.

The author:
Michael S. Turner is the Rauner Distinguished Service Professor of Astrophysics at the University of Chicago.

TERMS AND CONCEPTS

Axion: A theoretical particle that has a mass trillions of times as small as that of an electron.

Dark energy: An unknown form of energy that has a gravitational force that is repulsive; it makes up about 70 percent of the universe.

Dark matter: An invisible form of matter that exerts a gravitational effect that holds galaxies together; it makes up about 26 percent of the universe.

Gravitational lensing: A phenomenon in which the gravity of a nearer massive object causes light rays from a more distant object to bend, distorting the way the distant object appears.

Neutralino: A theoretical particle that has a mass hundreds of times as large as the mass of a proton.

Quantum mechanics: The field of physics that describes the structure and behavior of atoms and subatomic particles.

Spectrograph: A device that spreads light into a spectrum of its component colors.

Supernova: An exploding star that can become billions of times as bright as the sun.

WIMP (weakly interacting massive particle): A theoretical particle that is hundreds of times as massive as a proton but interacts very weakly with atoms.

WMAP, an orbiting telescope launched by the National Aeronautics and Space Administration (NASA), produced images of the universe when the cosmos was only 380,000 years old—before there were stars or galaxies. The light captured in these images was the oldest—and most distant—light ever seen. This light is the "echo of the big bang," the enormous explosion that most scientists believe gave birth to the universe approximately 14 billion years ago. According to the big bang theory, the universe has been expanding ever since.

The WMAP images showed tiny *ripples* (variations) in the intensity of the microwave radiation left over from the big bang. The microwave ripples, explained the WMAP scientists, represented the gravitational effects of matter as it collected and condensed in certain regions of the hot, expanding gas cloud created by the big bang. Careful analyses of these ripples allowed the scientists to estimate how much matter and energy are in the universe.

The SDSS survey, created by a ground-based telescope at the Apache Point Observatory in New Mexico, revealed the distribution of hundreds of millions of galaxies out to a distance of 2 billion *light-years* from Earth. A light-year is the distance that light travels in one year—9.46 trillion kilometers (5.88 trillion miles). The survey revealed how gravity has caused galaxies to clump together in certain regions of space. By analyzing the distribution of these clumps, scientists were able to determine how gravity created the structure of the universe that we observe today.

Matter and energy estimates from telescopes

Scientists have used the data from WMAP and SDSS—as well as supporting data from measurements of certain chemical elements in the universe—to make the following estimates of the composition of the cosmos. Approximately 4 percent of the universe consists of ordinary atoms of matter, such as hydrogen, helium, carbon, nitrogen, and oxygen. Only about ⅛ of this 4 percent—or about 0.5 percent of the total amount of matter and energy in the universe—exists in forms we can see with visible light, such as stars and planets. The remaining ⅞ of this material exists in forms that can be detected only with special telescopes. Among these forms are giant clouds of hot gas that emit X rays. In addition, visible light, X rays, and other forms of electromagnetic energy account for just 0.01 percent of the universe.

About 26 percent of the universe exists in the form of mysterious, invisible dark matter. Scientists believe that the gravitational effects of dark matter hold together our galaxy and all the other galaxies in the universe.

WHAT MAKES UP THE UNIVERSE?

About 96 percent of the universe consists of material that scientists can neither see nor even detect directly with instruments. Scientists believe about 70 percent of the universe is made up of *dark energy,* a mysterious form of energy that pushes galaxies apart. About 26 percent of the universe consists of an unknown form of matter, called *dark matter,* that neither emits nor absorbs electromagnetic radiation. Only about 0.5 percent of the universe, including the stars and planets, consists of ordinary atoms that can be seen in visible light. Another 3.5 percent consists of atoms that emit forms of energy that can be detected only with special telescopes.

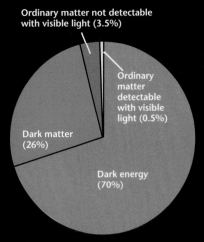

Ordinary matter not detectable with visible light (3.5%)

Ordinary matter detectable with visible light (0.5%)

Dark matter (26%)

Dark energy (70%)

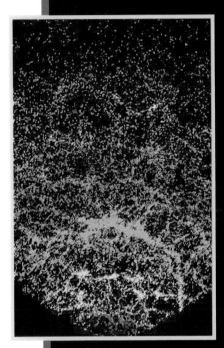

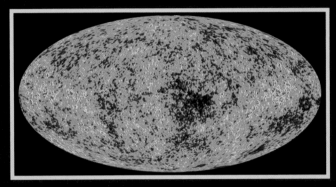

Scientists arrived at the figures in the graph by analyzing data from the Wilkinson Microwave Anisotropy Probe (WMAP) and the Sloan Digital Sky Survey (SDSS). WMAP, an orbiting telescope, produced an image (above) of the varying intensity of microwave radiation left after the big bang, the explosion that gave birth to the universe about 14 billion years ago. SDSS used a ground telescope to show the distribution of hundreds of thousands of galaxies in a slice of the universe around us (left).

Roughly 70 percent of the universe exists in an unknown but weird form of energy called dark energy. The most remarkable feature of dark energy is that it has a gravitational force that is *repulsive*—that is, it causes galaxies to speed away from one another. In fact, scientists have found that dark energy is so repulsive that it is causing the universe to expand at an ever-faster rate.

How can scientists be sure that dark matter and dark energy exist if researchers cannot see them or even measure them directly? A number of scientific observations—some going back to the 1930's—support the reality of dark matter and dark energy.

Gravity gives clues to dark matter

Scientists concluded that dark matter exists by studying the way gravity affects the movement of visible matter in the universe. Gravity affects everything in the universe, from solar systems to galaxies. For example, the gravitational attraction of the sun holds Earth and the other planets of our solar system in orbit around the sun. The closer a planet is to the sun, the greater is the gravitational pull on that planet, and the faster that planet moves. Mercury, the innermost planet, orbits the sun at the breakneck speed of about 48 kilometers (30 miles) per second, while Pluto, the outermost planet, orbits at a comparatively sluggish 5 kilometers (3 miles) per second. So even if we could not see the sun, we could still infer its existence from its effects on the planets.

Gravitational effects of dark matter can also be observed in galaxies. In the 1930's, the Swiss-American astronomer Fritz Zwicky of the California Institute of Technology in Pasadena made many observations of *galaxy clusters.* These objects are large groups of hundreds or thousands of galaxies held close to one another by gravity. Zwicky measured the speeds at which galaxies within the clusters are moving. He made his measurements with a *spectrograph,* a device that spreads the light from galaxies (and other light sources) into a spectrum of its component colors—like the colors of a rainbow—ranging from red to blue. When objects in space that are moving away from Earth are observed with a spectrograph, their light is *red-shifted*—that is, their light displays more colors toward the red end of the spectrum. In contrast, the light of objects moving toward Earth is shifted toward the blue end of the spectrum.

Zwicky proposed that if the only gravity holding galaxies in place came from the visible stars within clusters, then the speedier galaxies in a cluster should have been able to escape the cluster's gravitational bonds. Zwicky deduced that because these galaxies remain in place, there must be a huge amount of gravity unaccounted for. He coined the term *dark matter* to describe the unseen material producing this gravitational influence. Today, scientists believe that dark matter accounts for almost 100 times as much *mass* (quantity of matter) as stars do.

At the time of Zwicky's observation, the idea that the universe contains large amounts of dark matter was too radical for most scientists to take seriously. It would take researchers several more decades to collect enough evidence to convince the scientific community that dark matter was real.

The individual galaxies in a cluster (below) move so fast that some unseen matter must be exerting a gravitational influence that holds them within the cluster. An X-ray image of the same galaxy (below, bottom) shows hot gas spreading throughout the cluster. Even with this hot gas, the galaxy cluster does not have enough gravity to hold together. This indicates that an additional unseen material—dark matter—is exerting a gravitational influence.

Beginning in the 1980's, X-ray telescopes revealed that some of Zwicky's dark matter actually consists of ordinary matter in the form of a hot gas that spreads throughout galaxies. However, this hot gas, which accounts for about seven times as much mass as the stars of the galaxies, still fails by a wide margin to produce enough gravity to hold galaxy clusters together.

Zwicky had suggested that some of the dark matter might consist of unusual stars and starlike objects that emit forms of electromagnetic radiation other than visible light, such as *white dwarfs* (small stars that have run out of fuel) or *neutron stars* (the spinning cores of exploded stars). Later, other scientists estimated the total mass of these objects, along with that of *brown dwarfs* (dim objects with more mass than a planet but less than a star) and *black holes* (regions where the gravitational force is so strong that nothing can escape). The researchers concluded that the total mass of all these strange objects does not amount to much—it is even less than that of ordinary stars. Therefore, there must be more to the dark matter mystery.

Scientists have discovered additional clues for solving this mystery since the 1980's. Some of these clues have come from the work of

Unusual stars and star-like objects that emit forms of electromagnetic radiation other than visible light may account for a small amount of dark matter. Such objects include neutron stars, white dwarfs, black holes, and brown dwarfs.

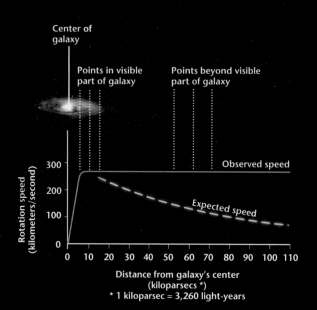

Center of galaxy

Points in visible part of galaxy

Points beyond visible part of galaxy

Observed speed

Expected speed

Rotation speed (kilometers/second)

300
200
100
0

0   10   20   30   40   50   60   70   80   90   100   110

Distance from galaxy's center (kiloparsecs *)

* 1 kiloparsec = 3,260 light-years

The discovery that the outermost stars and gas clouds of a typical galaxy rotate at the same speed as the stars and gas clouds closer to the galactic center has provided additional evidence for the existence of dark matter. The rotation speed of an object depends on the force of gravity acting on it. If all of a galaxy's mass were associated with the stars and clouds that emit visible light or other forms of electromagnetic radiation, the force of gravity would be very weak in the outer regions. These regions would then rotate very slowly ("Expected speed," left). However, the outer stars and gas clouds as well as the inner regions rotate rapidly ("Observed speed," left). Therefore, additional mass—in the form of dark matter—must exist beyond the visible part of the galaxy.

American astronomer Vera Rubin of the Carnegie Institution of Washington (D.C.) and others who have studied the speeds of stars within galaxies. By carefully measuring the motions of stars and clouds of gas within thousands of spiral galaxies like our own Milky Way, Rubin and the others demonstrated how dark matter holds the galaxies together. In spiral galaxies, stars move in almost circular orbits around the galactic center, much like a giant version of the solar system. However, in the solar system, the inner planets travel faster than the outer planets. In contrast, the stars and gas clouds far from the dense, star-rich center of a galaxy move at about the same speed as do the stars close in. This finding implied that the outlying stars and clouds must be influenced by gravity from unseen matter.

In the 1990's, more evidence for dark matter came from research into a phenomenon called *gravitational lensing,* which affects some light waves traveling to Earth from such distant objects as *quasars* (objects at the center of some galaxies that give off enormous amounts of radiation). The gravity of nearer massive objects, such as galaxies or galaxy clusters, causes these light rays to bend. As a result, the distant object appears as an arc, a ring, or even as multiple images. A team led by American astronomer J. Anthony Tyson, then of Lucent Technology's Bell Labs in Murray Hill, New Jersey, used gravitational lensing to map the distribution of dark matter in galaxy clusters. Tyson demonstrated how dark matter is responsible for the large amount of light bending observed through telescopes. Other astronomers have reported similar conclusions.

By 2000, the evidence was overwhelming that gravity from some form of mysterious dark matter holds galaxies and clusters of galaxies together. However, scientists still do not know what this mysterious matter is.

Exotic leftovers from the big bang

In 2005, the leading ideas for the makeup of dark matter involved certain exotic forms of matter that were created in the high temperatures and enormous energies that existed shortly after the big bang. Physicists who study the elementary particles of the universe believe that not all of these particles have been observed in the laboratory. And scientists think that one or more of the particles may turn out to be the stuff of dark matter.

Two of the main candidates for dark matter particles are *axions* and *neutralinos*. Axions are theoretical particles that have a mass a trillion times as small as that of an *electron*. Electrons are negatively charged parti-

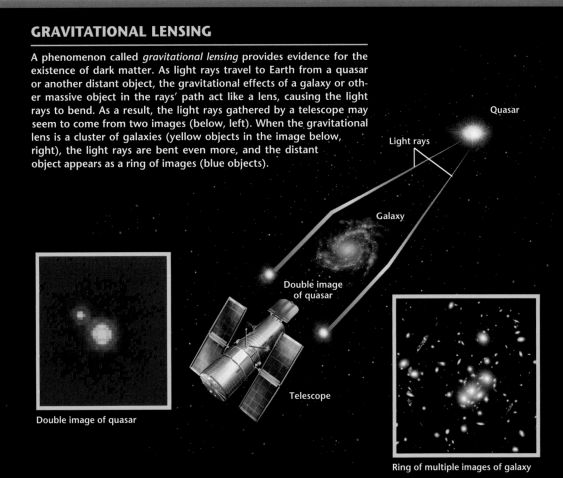

GRAVITATIONAL LENSING

A phenomenon called *gravitational lensing* provides evidence for the existence of dark matter. As light rays travel to Earth from a quasar or another distant object, the gravitational effects of a galaxy or other massive object in the rays' path act like a lens, causing the light rays to bend. As a result, the light rays gathered by a telescope may seem to come from two images (below, left). When the gravitational lens is a cluster of galaxies (yellow objects in the image below, right), the light rays are bent even more, and the distant object appears as a ring of images (blue objects).

Quasar

Light rays

Galaxy

Double image
of quasar

Telescope

Double image of quasar

Ring of multiple images of galaxy

An enormous halo made of theoretical particles called *WIMPs* (weakly interacting massive particles) surrounds a galaxy in an artist's illustration. WIMPs, which rarely react with particles of ordinary matter, are one of the leading candidates for dark matter.

cles that orbit the *nucleus* (center part) of an atom; they are the lightest known particle with an electric charge. Neutralinos are theoretical particles predicted to be hundreds of times as massive as *protons,* the positively charged particles inside the nucleus. Neutralinos belong to a general class of theoretical particles known as *WIMPs* (weakly interacting massive particles). Despite their great mass, neutralinos and other WIMPs interact very weakly with the atoms of ordinary matter. As a result, scientists believe that out of billions of WIMPs passing through your body every few seconds, only one interacts with any of the atoms that make up your body.

The tiny mass of axions and the weakly interacting nature of WIMPs make these particles difficult to detect. In fact, as of 2005, scientists had observed neither WIMPs nor axions—though they were carrying out ever more sensitive experiments to find these elusive particles.

One type of exotic particle that has been observed and identified as a small component of dark matter is the *neutrino*. Neutrinos—which are different from neutralinos—are electrically neutral particles produced in nuclear reactions inside stars, in the interaction of cosmic rays with the atmosphere, and in the decay of radioactive elements. Special detectors on Earth can sometimes measure the effects of neutrinos. In 1998, scientists using the Super-Kamiokande (Super-K) neutrino detector in Japan studied neutrinos produced in the atmosphere to show that neutrinos have a tiny mass—less than one-millionth that of an electron. This finding suggests that neutrinos left over from the big bang could account for about the same amount of cosmic mass as stars do. The Super-K experiment did not solve the riddle of dark matter, but it established that at least some dark matter consists of exotic particles rather than ordinary atoms.

Dark energy and accelerating expansion

Although much remains unknown about dark matter, dark energy is an even deeper mystery. Research that would eventually lead to the idea of dark energy had its roots in 1929, when American astronomer Edwin Hubble, making measurements at Mount Wilson Observatory in California, observed that other galaxies are moving away from ours. This observation provided the first evidence that the universe is expanding. Before Hubble's discovery, most scientists had believed that the size of the universe was unchanging. After the discovery, astronomers began to wonder if the universe would keep expanding forever.

The answer to this question, astronomers believed, lay in the *general theory of relativity,* the theory of gravity proposed in 1915 by the German-born scientist Albert Einstein. Most scientists familiar with Einstein's theory assumed that the gravitational attraction of all the matter in the universe would cause the expansion of the universe to slow down over time. They theorized that the future of the universe would depend only on the amount of matter it contained. If the amount of matter was great, the universe might eventually stop expanding—and then it could begin to contract. If the amount of matter was not so great, the expansion could continue forever. For almost 70 years after Hubble's discovery, these appeared to be the only two possibilities.

Then, in the late 1990's, a startling new understanding of cosmic expansion arose from the work of two groups of astronomers. One group was led by Saul Perlmutter of the Lawrence Berkeley National Laboratory in Berkeley, California. The other group was directed by Brian Schmidt of the Mount Stromlo and Siding Spring observatories in Australia. Each of these groups independently reached the totally unexpected conclusion that the universe is expanding at a rate faster than it had been in the past. Additional observations by these and other researchers confirmed this discovery and placed the beginning of the speed-up at approximately 5 billion years ago. Observations by astronomer Adam Riess of the Space Telescope Science Institute in Baltimore, Maryland, showed that before that time, the expansion rate of the universe had been slowing down.

The surprising discovery of an accelerating expansion rate was based on careful analyses of the brightness levels of exploding stars called *type Ia supernovae* in galaxies between 4 billion and 7 billion light-years away. Soon after they explode, these supernovae become as bright as an entire galaxy and can be seen over vast cosmic distances. And because they are

Observations of exploding stars called *type Ia supernovae* have provided evidence for the existence of dark energy. Scientists have found that type Ia supernovae that are from 4 billion to 7 billion light-years from Earth are dimmer—and, thus, farther away—than they would be if the expansion rate of the universe was slowing. This finding suggests that about 5 billion years ago, the universe began to expand at a faster rate. Many scientists believe that dark energy caused the speed-up.

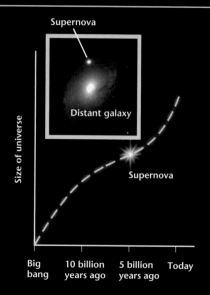

Supernova

Distant galaxy

Size of universe

Supernova

| Big bang | 10 billion years ago | 5 billion years ago | Today |

all similar to one another, they serve as cosmic "yardsticks" for astronomers attempting precise measurements of distance. The dimmer the supernova appears, the farther away it is. The astronomers measured the distances to numerous supernovae, as well as the rates at which their galaxies are moving away from us. They discovered that supernovae roughly 4 billion to 7 billion light-years away are dimmer—and thus farther away—than would be expected if the universe had been slowing down. Therefore, the researchers concluded, the universe has been expanding at an accelerating pace over the past 5 billion or so years.

A repulsive force of gravity?

However, if gravity is an attractive force, how can the universe's expansion be accelerating? To answer this question, astronomers turned again to the general theory of relativity. General relativity actually allows for the possibility of a repulsive form of gravity operating in the cosmos. Dark energy is the unusual form of energy whose gravitational force is repulsive.

The nature of dark energy is one of the most profound mysteries in science. Some physicists note that the simplest explanation for dark energy is that it consists of the energy associated with the *vacuum* (space with no matter in it)—a type of energy predicted by the theory of *quantum mechanics*. Physicists use the theory of quantum mechanics, also called *quantum theory*, to describe the often-bizarre behavior of the microscopic world of atoms and subatomic particles.

According to the laws of quantum mechanics, even a vacuum is not entirely empty. It is full of "virtual" particles that suddenly pop into existence and then rapidly disappear. The existence of such particles in a vacuum was demonstrated in the 1940's by physicist Willis Lamb at Columbia University in New York City. Lamb measured slight shifts in the radiation that hydrogen atoms give off when they are heated. He attributed these shifts to the effects of invisible particles that materialize for brief periods. According to the general theory of relativity, the gravity associated with such virtual vacuum particles is repulsive.

Also according to quantum theory, the degree to which this vacuum force repels objects in the universe is directly proportional to the energy of the virtual particles in the vacuum. In other words, the greater the energy of the vacuum particles, the more repellent is the vacuum force. Since the birth of quantum mechanics in the early 1900's, theoretical physicists have tried to use mathematical calculations to estimate the energy of these particles. But these energy estimates, based on quantum theory, are absurdly large. If the vacuum of space weighed as much as the estimates imply, the universe would be expanding billions and billions of times as fast as it appears to be. In 2005, this problem continued to bedevil theorists who favored the energy of the vacuum as an explanation for dark energy.

Some theoretical physicists are pursuing other ideas about the nature of dark energy. Among these ideas is the possibility that dark energy is a tangle of invisible, elastic "sheets" of energy that fill the universe. Another idea is that dark energy is an indirect influence on the universe caused by hidden, extra dimensions of space—dimensions beyond the three familiar spatial dimensions of height, width, and depth. These and other ideas are based on the mathematical calculations of theorists. As of 2005, physicists had discovered no hard evidence for any of these ideas.

A great cosmic battle

The true nature of dark energy will determine the outcome of the continuing battle between the attractive gravitational force of dark matter and the repulsive gravitational force of dark energy. For approximately the universe's first 9 billion years, the gravity of dark matter dominated the struggle. During this period, the expansion of the universe gradually slowed, and as dark matter came together, its gravity swept up atoms into galaxies. Then, approximately 5 billion years ago, there was a big change. The repulsive gravity of dark energy overcame attractive gravity, and the expansion of the cosmos began to speed up.

Depending on how this battle between dark matter and dark energy plays out, the universe will have one of at least three possible—and very different—futures. If the *density* of dark energy—that is, if the amount of dark energy in a given area of space—remains constant the expansion

Until scientists determine the nature of dark energy, the future of the universe will remain uncertain. Depending on the actual nature of dark energy, the universe has at least three possible—and very different—futures.

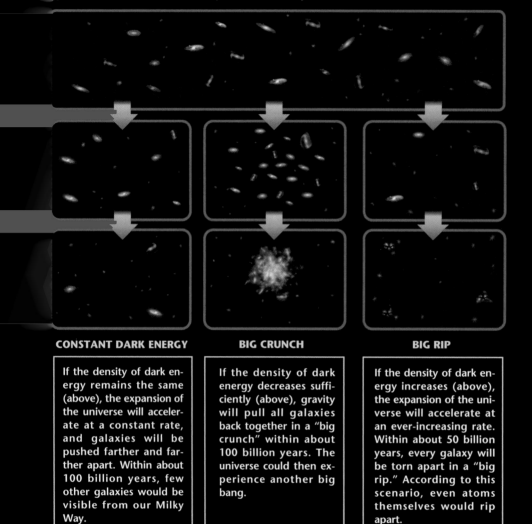

CONSTANT DARK ENERGY

If the density of dark energy remains the same (above), the expansion of the universe will accelerate at a constant rate, and galaxies will be pushed farther and farther apart. Within about 100 billion years, few other galaxies would be visible from our Milky Way.

BIG CRUNCH

If the density of dark energy decreases sufficiently (above), gravity will pull all galaxies back together in a "big crunch" within about 100 billion years. The universe could then experience another big bang.

BIG RIP

If the density of dark energy increases (above), the expansion of the universe will accelerate at an ever-increasing rate. Within about 50 billion years, every galaxy will be torn apart in a "big rip." According to this scenario, even atoms themselves would rip apart.

of the universe will accelerate at a steady rate. The expansion would eventually push almost all galaxies so far away that each galaxy would become a far-flung, isolated island. Today, hundreds of billions of galaxies can be seen from our Milky Way, but in another 100 billion years, only a few hundred galaxies would be visible from the Milky Way.

If the density of dark energy decreases sufficiently, the expansion could begin to slow, and then reverse, with galaxies moving closer and closer over time. In 100 billion years, all the galaxies could squeeze together in a "big crunch." This crunch might be followed by another big bang—and a brand-new universe. If the density of dark energy increases over time, the expansion of the universe will accelerate at an ever-increasing rate. Galaxies, stars, and planets will spread farther apart at a rapidly accelerating pace. In approximately 50 billion years, they will be torn apart in a violent "big rip." Even individual atoms will be torn apart under this scenario.

Daring to explore the dark side

Although scientists may still be in the dark regarding many questions about the universe's dark side, they are not without the means to solve some of the remaining riddles. Many ongoing and planned projects around the world are exploring the nature of dark matter and dark energy.

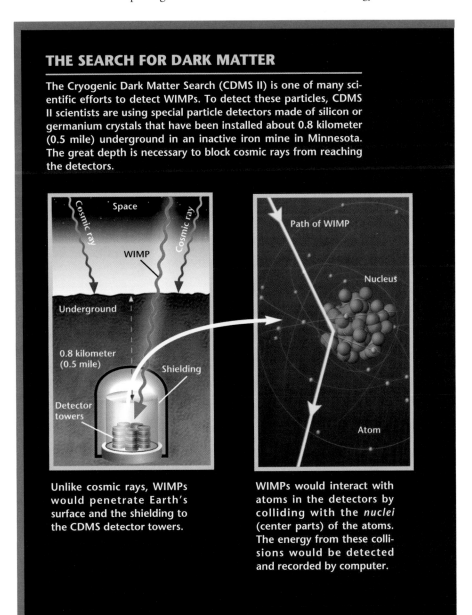

THE SEARCH FOR DARK MATTER

The Cryogenic Dark Matter Search (CDMS II) is one of many scientific efforts to detect WIMPs. To detect these particles, CDMS II scientists are using special particle detectors made of silicon or germanium crystals that have been installed about 0.8 kilometer (0.5 mile) underground in an inactive iron mine in Minnesota. The great depth is necessary to block cosmic rays from reaching the detectors.

Unlike cosmic rays, WIMPs would penetrate Earth's surface and the shielding to the CDMS detector towers.

WIMPs would interact with atoms in the detectors by colliding with the *nuclei* (center parts) of the atoms. The energy from these collisions would be detected and recorded by computer.

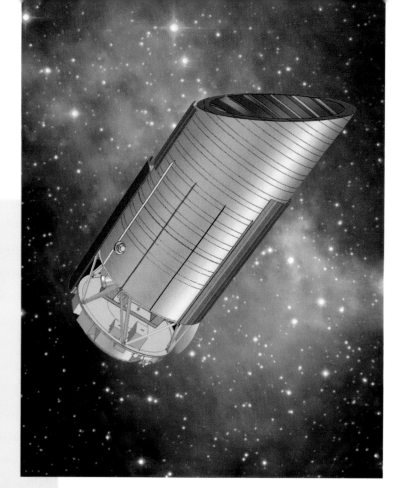

An orbiting telescope that detects light from type IA supernovae up to 10 billion light-years away, shown in an artist's illustration, is one proposal for the Joint Dark Energy Mission. Scientists expect that detailed analyses of these distant stellar explosions will help them determine the true nature of dark energy.

Powerful *particle accelerators* as well as various kinds of specialized detectors and new types of telescopes are all pointing the way to a better understanding of dark matter and dark energy.

Particle accelerators are large machines that allow physicists to briefly duplicate the intense temperatures, pressures, and energies of the universe shortly after the big bang. These machines force subatomic particles to collide at high speeds, causing them to either break apart into new particles or join together to form other types of particles. Some of the resulting particles may be similar to the exotic dark matter that was created in the early universe. At Fermi National Accelerator Laboratory (Fermilab) near Batavia, Illinois, physicists were using the world's most powerful accelerator in 2005 to try to create such theoretical dark matter particles as the neutralino. An even more powerful accelerator—the Large Hadron Collider near Geneva, Switzerland—was scheduled to begin operation in 2007. The detection of dark matter particles would go a long way toward answering questions about the nature of dark matter.

Another dark matter project is the Cryogenic Dark Matter Search (CDMS II), a collaboration involving several institutions, including Fermilab and Brown University in Providence, Rhode Island. This project, which seeks to detect WIMPs, consists of special crystal detectors buried about 0.8 kilometer (0.5 mile) underground in an inactive iron mine in Minnesota. The depth of the detectors as well as protective shielding around them block cosmic rays and most other unwanted particles from reaching the detectors. By contrast, WIMPs would be able to penetrate the layers of earth and shielding and make it to the detectors because they interact so weakly with ordinary matter. In the detectors, they would produce telltale electronic signals that scientists could identify to verify the existence of these theoretical bits of dark matter.

The Joint Dark Energy Mission (JDEM) is a plan for an orbiting telescope that NASA and the Department of Energy hope to launch on a three-year mission to learn more about dark energy. The telescope, which would contain the largest digital camera ever constructed, would be able to find thousands of type Ia supernovae by looking back in time some 10 billion years. Precise measurements of the distances to these stellar explosions and the rates at which they are moving away from us would help scientists clarify the nature of dark energy.

Another telescope in the works is the Large Synoptic Survey Telescope, a ground-based telescope that might begin operating by 2012. This project, directed by J. Anthony Tyson of the University of California at Davis, is being designed to map and measure dark energy and dark matter through various kinds of detailed sky surveys.

These are just a few of the many projects that astronomers, physicists, and other scientists hope will increase their understanding of the mysterious, invisible matter and energy that make up most of the universe. In 2005, it was hard to believe that scientists once thought the universe consisted of only the stars and other shining objects they could see in the night sky. Now we know that an unseen dark side holds more secrets than those scientists ever imagined.

■ FOR ADDITIONAL INFORMATION

Books and periodicals

Kirshner, Robert P. *The Extravagant Universe: Exploding Stars, Dark Energy, and the Accelerating Cosmos.* Princeton University Press, 2002.
Rees, Martin, and Natarajan, Priyamvada. "A Field Guide to the Invisible Universe." *Discover,* December 2003, pp. 42–49.

Web sites

Cosmology Primer: The Dark Universe—
pancake.uchicago.edu/~carroll/cfcp/primer/dark.html
Cryogenic Dark Matter Search, Brown University—
cdms.brown.edu
Dark Energy: An Introduction, Goddard Space Flight Center—
imagine.gsfc.nasa.gov/docs/science/mysteries_l1/dark_energy.html
Sloan Digital Sky Survey—www.sdss.org
Supernova Cosmology Project—http://panisse.lbl.gov

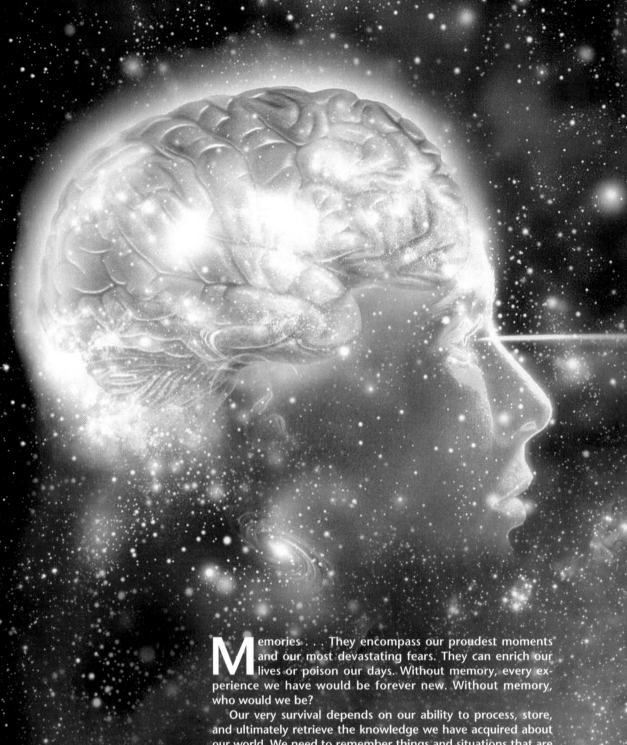

Memories . . . They encompass our proudest moments and our most devastating fears. They can enrich our lives or poison our days. Without memory, every experience we have would be forever new. Without memory, who would we be?

Our very survival depends on our ability to process, store, and ultimately retrieve the knowledge we have acquired about our world. We need to remember things and situations that are safe and those that are dangerous. We must recognize the people who take care of us and those for whom we are responsible. We need to remember such basic things as how to find food and other necessities and where we live. We need to remember how to perform tasks in our job or in the classroom. We also need to remember certain physical skills, from the most basic—such as walking and talking—to the more complicated, such as driving a car or throwing a baseball straight over home plate.

REMEMBERING AND FORGETTING:

The Science of Human Memory

Since the time of the ancient Greek philosopher Plato (427?-347? B.C.), who compared memory to a wax tablet, scientists have sought to discover the physical basis of memory and to understand how it works. Where in the body does memory dwell? How are memories formed and stored? How does emotion affect memory? Why do some people develop disabling memory problems while others astonish us with their sharp recall? How is it that two people can experience the same event—a traffic accident, for example—but report such different versions of it? Why do we sometimes remember incorrectly, or even think that we remember events that never actually occurred?

Scientists have begun to find the answers to many of these questions. They have succeeded thus far only because, as the ancient Greek dramatist Aeschylus (525-456 B.C.) wrote, "Memory is the mother of all wisdom."

The authors:
Thomas A. M. Kramer is an associate professor of psychiatry and associate dean and director of the Student Counseling and Resource Service at the University of Chicago.

Alison Winter is an associate professor of history at the University of Chicago.

John F. Disterhoft is a professor of physiology and a member of the Institute for Neuroscience at the Feinberg School of Medicine at Northwestern University in Chicago.

WHAT IS MEMORY?

By Thomas A. M. Kramer

The human memory system is a lot like an Internet search engine. If you want to look online for information about a particular subject—the Empire State Building, for example—you enter that name and the search engine calls up links to numerous Web sites mentioning it. In the same way, we remember because a *cue*—an experience, an emotion, a sensation—links us to something that happened in the past.

Sometimes, the cues are obvious. We see a photo of the Empire State Building, and we may remember a vacation in New York City. Sometimes, the cues are more mysterious. What made us think of the Empire State Building when we smelled the aroma of hot pretzels? Perhaps we recall the connection later. Perhaps we never do.

Like terms keyed into a computer search engine, memory cues can lead us in more than one direction. For example, our Internet search on the Empire State Building may lead to sites on New York City, Art Deco architecture, or famous skyscrapers. In the same way, seeing a photo of the Empire State Building may call up memories of not only a summer vacation or hot pretzels but also the movie *King Kong* or the feeling of being afraid of heights. Memories may vary, depending on where we are, what we are doing, or what we have been thinking about.

In essence, all recalled information is *associative*—that is, linked to information previously processed and stored in our brain, the seat of memory. Even when faced with new and very different experiences, our mind looks for something in the past to which it can relate those experiences. As a result, most—if not all—of our understanding of the world comes from relating a lifetime of experience to our current situation.

Collective memory

The role and importance of memory have changed dramatically through time. In the Middle Ages (a period lasting from about the 400's through the 1400's), a powerful memory ranked as one of the most highly prized of all mental attributes, more valued than a vivid imagination or reasoning skills. If people with an excellent memory could read and had access to the handwritten books of that time, they could accumulate knowledge to an extent that others could only envy.

Reading gave them access not only to their own individual memory—their personal experiences and knowledge—but also to an external *collective* memory—the collected experiences and knowledge of others.

Today, collective memory is available to a much larger number of us on a much bigger scale. When we need to know about the beliefs, history, lifestyles, science, and technology of other individuals or groups—whether past or present—we can read about them. We can also listen to audio recordings or watch films or videos. Once we learn the information, we can build on it. As a result, we need not, for example, reinvent the coffeemaker or figure out the ingredients for headache remedies. Over the centuries, the availability of collective memory and its effect on science and technology have improved the quality of life for countless people in the world.

The growth in collective memory that resulted from the development of writing and, later, the printing press laid the foundation for the development of *information technology*. This term refers to the use of computers and computer applications to process huge amounts of information. Today, at the touch of a button or the click of a mouse, we have access to an almost unlimited amount of information. Has this abundance decreased our dependence on our internal memory? Will internal memory grow increasingly less important as information technology grows?

Research into memory

At the same time, scientific advances have dramatically increased our knowledge of the brain in general and memory in particular. For example, researchers have learned that we have different types of memory. Memories may last for just a short time or for a lifetime. They may be linked to the senses—what something sounded or tasted like. Memories may also involve other information about the world, such as the names of the United States presidents, or physical skills, such as tying shoes or riding a bicycle.

Until the late 1990's, most *neuroscientists* (scientists who specialize in the study of the brain) believed that we were born with all the *neurons* (brain cells) that we were ever going to have. These scientists thought that neurons could not *re-*

generate (grow back) the way skin cells and some other body cells can. We now know that the brain grows neurons throughout our life. This finding has opened new doors in brain research as scientists expanded their focus from studying how to preserve existing neurons to how to encourage the growth of new ones.

At the same time, researchers have been working to identify the *genes* (basic units of heredity) involved in the memory system. Genes carry the instructions for assembling the proteins used to build cells, tissues, and organs. Researchers have begun to explore the role of proteins and their related genes in processing, storing, and recalling memories. In some cases, scientists have found that the failure of such genes to function properly may result in developmental disorders and mental retardation. Scientists are also studying Alzheimer's disease and other conditions that damage or destroy memory. These efforts are pointing the way to more effective treatments for preventing or slowing memory loss.

Finally, researchers have also made great strides in learning how and where the brain stores certain types of information. Particularly useful to this line of research has been the development of various *neuroimaging* techniques. This technology allows researchers to view the brain and nervous system in action. For example, one form of neuroimaging, *functional magnetic resonance imaging* (fMRI), shows which parts of the brain are active as various tasks are performed. Researchers using fMRI have discovered that different parts of the brain become active when we remember a visual image—a car, for example—than when we remember the sound a car makes.

Much about memory remains unknown. Neuroscientists are still exploring, for example, how one neuron communicates with another and how that communication creates a pathway that becomes a memory. Work has barely begun on understanding the opposite process—how memories are recalled. Nevertheless, researchers have made considerable progress in understanding how we gather our memories and what we can do to keep them.

Ancient Greek philosophers and scientists, including Plato and Aristotle (center, left, and center, right, respectively), exchange ideas in a painting by Italian Renaissance artist Raphael (1483-1520). By exchanging ideas and experiences and recording them, a group of people can know and remember more than a single individual ever could. This group knowledge is called *collective memory*.

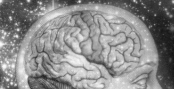

MODELS OF MEMORY

By Alison Winter

Scientists and philosophers attempting to explain the nature of memory have always struggled with the problem of describing something we know is there but which cannot be directly observed in action. Over the centuries, therefore, memory researchers have looked for more readily observable processes in the everyday world that seem to work in a similar way. They have then used these processes as models for their understanding of how memory itself works. These comparisons have usually drawn upon the latest technologies for recording information to model memory processes. Advances in neurosciences and medical technology, however, have developed new ways of accounting for human memory. As a result, scientists have come to consider previous accounts obsolete.

Early theories

The ancient Greek philosopher Plato (427?-347? B.C.) said our minds contain something resembling a wax tablet, which was commonly used in his time for making notes. When we want to remember something, we "stamp the impression" of that idea or perception on the tablet.

Plato's student Aristotle (384-322 B.C.) also used the wax-tablet analogy for his theories about memory, though his comparison was more literal. Aristotle proposed that the process of storing a memory produces an actual physical change in the body. This *memory trace,* he claimed, enables us to recall memories later.

In the Middle Ages (the period from about the A.D. 400's through the 1400's), scholars described memory as a "book" that was lodged in the heart. The pages of this book become filled with text as the mind collects new information, according to this explanation.

Scholars also developed special techniques called *mnemonics* (memory aids) for strengthening the memory. These "arts of memory" originated in the writings of such ancient Roman orators as Cicero (106-43 B.C.) and Seneca (4 B.C.?-65 A.D.). Later writers during the Middle Ages and Renaissance (the period from about the 1300's through the 1600's) greatly expanded these mnemonics. These writers suggested that people should create imaginary *memory palaces* or *memory theaters*. Then they should place objects representing ideas that they wanted to remember into the various niches of these imaginary buildings. Later, they could imagine walking around the palace, and the objects would still be there, ready to be recalled in sequence. One of the most remarkable adaptations of this technique was created by the Jesuit missionary Matteo Ricci (1522-1610). Ricci used the memory palace, a technique still practiced today, extensively in his efforts to communicate with and educate people in China in the 1600's.

In the 1600's and early 1700's, a new emphasis on scientific experimentation provided fresh ideas for the understanding of memory. The discovery of *phosphors* inspired Robert Hooke (1635-1703), an English *natural philosopher* (physicist), to describe memory as a chemical event in the brain. Phosphors are substances that *emit* (give off) visible light after absorbing certain types of *radiation* (energy). In contrast, most substances emit light while being burned. Hooke argued that the brain used a phosphorlike substance to store and recall information gathered by the senses.

During the 1800's, scientists seized on new recording technologies as models for understanding how the brain stores information. Photography became an especially popular model because photographs capture a moment in time. Toward the end of the 1800's, the development of the phonograph and motion picture had an even greater impact on memory studies. These technologies symbolized the storage and recall of a series of actions rather than just still images.

Experimental psychology yields clues

A new approach to understanding the creation and storage of memories arrived with the techniques of *experimental psychology* in the late 1800's. Experimental psychologists devised laboratory studies using people, as well as rats, primates, and other animals, to investigate the processes by which memories are made, stored, and recalled. German psychologist Hermann Ebbinghaus (1850-1909), for example, learned sequences of nonsense words and tracked the rate at which he forgot the words. Ebbinghaus thought that the creation of a memory involved the formation of new associations and that the work of forming these associations could be studied in a laboratory. He found that subjects quickly forgot a sequence of nonsense syllables unless it was repeated several times. The more times the sequence was repeated (up to a certain number of repetitions), the slower the subject was to forget it. The rate of forgetting decreased rapidly at first, and then more slowly. This change was known as the *forgetting curve.* The increasing rate of recall correspondingly came to be known as the *learning curve.*

Other experimental psychologists, such as German-born psychologist Hugo Munsterberg (1863-1916) of Harvard University in Cambridge, Massachusetts, studied how memories of an actual event change over time among a particular group of people. In numerous studies, Munsterberg demonstrated that eyewitness memories of a crime were far less reliable than juries tended to assume. Such experiments led experimental psychologists to conclude that the mind has a *reconstructive* nature—that is, it actively changes memories over time.

Some researchers, however, believed that memory was a perfect record. For example, Wilder Penfield (1891-1976), a prominent Canadian neurosurgeon, became a powerful advocate of the theory that memories were both reliable and re-

playable. While attempting to find a surgical cure for epilepsy, Penfield discovered that, in some cases, stimulating the temporal lobe (part of the cerebrum) seemed to cause his patients to relive or replay past events. He concluded that the brain stores experiences much like a motion-picture film, and that under certain circumstances the past can be replayed. Penfield persuaded few other psychologists, but his characterization of memory as perfect and replayable had a great impact on popular beliefs about memory.

In the early 1920's, physician Robert House (1875-1930) announced that he had discovered that a commonly used anesthetic, *scopolamine hydrobromide,* could be used as a "truth serum." He believed that a patient under the influence of this anesthetic was physically unable to lie. His claim assumed that memories are both permanent and recoverable—that they exist as records in the brain like files within a filing cabinet. House used the analogy of a telephone system to express the idea that memories can be tapped and extracted through reliable lines of communication.

House's controversial claim was an early exploration into the use of drugs and other "trance" techniques (such as hypnotism) used for extracting memory. During World War II (1939-1945), such techniques were used as a means of trying to help soldiers relive and recover from traumatic memories of war. After the war, the same techniques were used to help witnesses "refresh" their memories of a crime in the hope of catching the culprit. However, the United States Supreme Court ruled in 1963 that testimonies given under the influence of scopolamine and similar "truth serums" were unconstitutional.

Memory and the brain

For hundreds of years, physicians have studied the physical basis of memory by examining people with brain injuries. They tried to match the site of the injury with the type of memory problem the patient was experiencing. Advances in *neuroscience* (the study of the structure and biology of

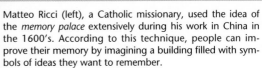

Matteo Ricci (left), a Catholic missionary, used the idea of the *memory palace* extensively during his work in China in the 1600's. According to this technique, people can improve their memory by imagining a building filled with symbols of ideas they want to remember.

the brain) also contributed to the understanding of memory.

One famous study, involving a patient with epilepsy, occurred in the 1950's. The patient, known by the initials H. M., experienced such severe seizures that he agreed to have a substantial part of his brain—the medial temporal lobes—removed. After the surgery, H. M.'s seizures became less severe, but he developed memory problems. Although his short-term memory remained intact, H. M. could not form long-term memories. Each time he visited the doctor studying his condition, H. M. behaved as though he had never met the doctor before.

A mouse navigates a radial arm maze during a memory experiment. Such devices allow scientists to learn about the nature of memory in animals, which they can apply to human beings.

By studying H. M. and similar cases, neuroscientists learned that the process of converting short-term memories to long-term ones takes place in the medial temporal lobes. Further research revealed that this process involves other structures in the brain as well, including the hippocampus.

In the 1970's, *cognitive psychologists* (psychologists who study thinking and learning) conducted numerous investigations of individuals' memories of particular events. Their studies identified specific ways in which the first memory of an event differs from the elements of the event itself. They also showed how the method used to call forth a memory—such as the phrasing of a question—could itself change the nature of a memory. These findings suggested that the practices widely used at that time to recover memories were actually likely to change these memories or even promote the creation of new memories, leading people to "remember" events that never occurred.

Recent developments

In the late 1900's and early 2000's, cognitive psychologists continued to design studies aimed at developing a more specific understanding of the ways in which different kinds of memories are stored, retained, altered, and recalled. They have found that memories are deeply affected by several factors, including the context in which they are created as well as events relevant to the memory that occur between the event and the act of recall.

In the 1990's, neurophysiological research began to provide more evidence for the reconstructive nature of memory. This research showed that each act of remembering changes the structures involved in storing memory.

Such findings led researchers to devise a new model for memory. Remembering, according to this model, is like editing a document on your computer. Each time you recall a memory—each time you save your document—you produce a new version.

The development of functional brain imaging technology, such as *fMRI* (functional magnetic resonance imaging), has revealed that the neurophysiology of personal memory is different from and more complex than earlier neuroscientific accounts, such as Penfield's. For instance, the recall of different kinds of personal memories involves activity in different regions of the brain. This is true even for autobiographical memories with the same content. The recall of a memory of a specific event (last week I missed the bus) stimulates activity in a different area of the brain than a memory of a habitual act (I take the bus every week and often miss it).

From the wax tablet to the photograph to the computer file, developing technologies have influenced the way scientists study and describe memory. No doubt the tools we reach for to describe memory will change as our understanding of the memory process—and our development of information technology—change.

THE MANY KINDS OF MEMORY

By Thomas A. M. Kramer

All animals with a nervous system have some sort of memory. Even roundworms, whose brain consists of only a few hundred neurons, can remember certain things, such as what they eat and what they do not eat. Human memory is different from the memory of all other animals because our brain is particularly good at processing large amounts of information. Human memory has developed to allow us to retain and recall the complex information we need to survive and thrive. It isn't just that we can remember more than other animals can—we probably can, though capacity is difficult to measure. What really separates our memory from that of other animals is the complicated nature of what we remember.

How we form memories and where we store them depend on what we are trying to remember and how long we need or want to remember it. The most widely accepted *model* (diagram used to explain a system) of human memory is the model first published in 1968 by mathematical psychologists Richard C. Atkinson and Richard M. Shiffrin of Stanford University in Palo Alto, California. This model identifies three basic types of memory: *sensory memory, short-term memory,* and *long-term memory.* Many neuroscientists also recognize a fourth type called *working memory.*

Sensory memory is the most fleeting of the four types. It stores perceptions gathered by our senses—sights, sounds, touches, tastes, and smells. Sensory memories last just long enough for our brain to register them, and then fade quickly, usually within less than one second. They pass into short-term memory, the second level of memory, only if we pay attention to them. For example, you may see a garden with many types of flowers but remember only that you saw roses, your favorite kind of flower.

Short-term memory consists of information you are thinking about at any particular moment, such as a phone number you are about to dial. Short-term memory can hold only a little information at one time. How many numbers do you think you can remember as you hear them spoken one after another? Most people remember seven, give or take one or two. Short-term memory usually lasts only about 20 seconds, just as long as the information holds your attention.

PARTS OF THE BRAIN INVOLVED IN MEMORY

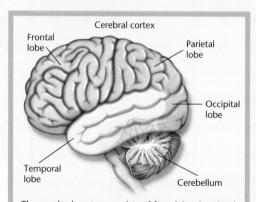

The cerebral cortex consists of four *lobes* (sections) that, along with several of the structures deep within them, are involved in forming and storing various kinds of memories. The cerebellum, which lies below the cerebral cortex, stores memories of motor skills.

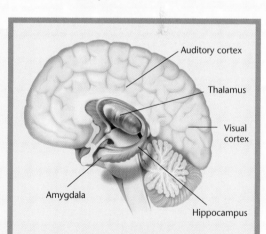

Various structures deep within the brain also play a role in memory. The hippocampus prepares information to be stored. The auditory and visual cortices store memories that involve sights and sounds, respectively. The amygdala holds memories involving emotions. When a memory is recalled, the thalamus collects the information from various parts of the brain and sends it to the cerebral cortex, which reassembles it.

Long-term memory contains information we have stored over a lifetime. Short-term memories become long-term ones when we repeat or review the information at regular intervals. Long-term memory stores information even after we quit thinking about it. Neuroscientists have not yet determined how long long-term memories last, though some researchers believe that nothing we have committed to memory is ever lost. We simply are not always able to retrieve it.

Many researchers consider working memory to be a combination of short-term and long-term memory. Working memory involves using both kinds of memory to solve a problem. For example, you want to remember where in the parking lot of a shopping mall you have left your car. So you must use the knowledge of the layout of the parking lot stored in your long-term memory and clues to the current location of your car that are in your short-term memory.

Long-term memory

Even before Atkinson and Shiffrin's model was developed, neuroscientists had concluded that we have two kinds of long-term memory: *explicit* and *implicit*. Explicit memory consists of information that we are aware of remembering. It consists of *semantic memory* and *episodic memory*. Semantic memory includes such facts and ideas as the information we learn at school. Episodic memory includes what we consider personal memories or experiences in our life, such as winning a soccer championship or celebrating our 16th birthday.

Implicit memory includes information that seems to come to us without our conscious awareness. This includes our knowledge of activities that include movement, such as riding a bike, whistling, or typing. These activities become a part of our implicit memory by being repeated over and over again. Eventually we can do these things without thinking about them in a step-by-step fashion. For example, the first time we drive a car, we concentrate on each move we make. The more we drive, however, the better we get at such tasks as judging the distance to another car or executing a smooth turn and the less we consciously think about how we are going to perform these maneuvers.

Implicit memory also includes emotion. We become frightened when we encounter a dark street

TYPES OF MEMORY

Neuroscientists have developed several different *models* (diagrams used to explain a system) to describe various types of memory. One of the most widely accepted of these is the model developed by mathematical psychologists Richard C. Atkinson and Richard M. Shiffrin of Stanford University in Palo Alto, California.

Short-term memory
Information you are thinking about at any particular moment, such as a telephone number you are about to dial.

Long-term memory
Information you remember even when you are not thinking about it, including facts you learn through your studies, past events in your personal life, or motor skills you have developed.

Explicit memory
Information you are aware of remembering.

Implicit memory
Information you are not aware of remembering, including emotional reactions to places and situations.

Episodic memory
Experiences that you have had, including particularly important moments in your life—both good and bad—such as graduating from school or visiting the emergency room after an accident.

Semantic memory
Facts that you have committed to memory, such as the multiplication tables or the name of the current president of the United States.

Procedural memory
The knowledge of certain skills, such as riding a bike or throwing a ball.

Perceptual-representational memory
Sensory information, such as the aroma of coffee or the feel of velvet, that allows you to recognize these stimuli when you encounter them again.

late at night, or we feel happy when we become aware of the touch of someone we love. We do this without necessarily remembering a similar event. Rather, we have learned from an earlier situation to react automatically in a certain way. This type of automatic memory—particularly in the case of fear—plays a critical role in keeping us safe by warning us to avoid situations that, we have learned, may be dangerous.

The stages of memory

The different types of memory are based on distinct processes that involve various parts of the brain. To explain these processes, we can compare the stages of memory to the steps we might take to record a new telephone number on a piece of paper.

All memories—whether facts, experiences, skills, or emotions—begin with information perceived through our senses. For example, we may see the phone number we wish to record written in a phone book, or someone may tell us the number. These sensory data then travel to the specific part of the brain that processes those particular kinds of information. For example, when we see something, the information travels as chemical and electrical impulses along networks of neurons running from our eyes to the *visual cortex,* a region in the back of the brain. When we hear something, the sound information travels from our ears to the *auditory cortex,* on the left side of the brain.

Most memories, however, involve information from multiple senses—you see someone, listen to her talk, smell her perfume, and experience feelings about your encounter. The sensory information then travels from the various sensory processing areas and is collected in a part of the brain called the *thalamus.*

If an explicit memory is being formed, the thalamus routes it to the front part of the *cerebral cortex,* a thin sheet of tissue that forms the outer layer of the brain. Initially, the memory enters the short-term memory system. There, if we think it is important enough to retain, it goes through one of two "rehearsal systems," one for language and one for vision and action. The language rehearsal system might be used to hold onto a phone number as you prepare to dial it; the visual rehearsal system might be used to remember someone

The sight of a dark street often elicits fear even if we do not consciously remember a frightening occurrence in a similar place. Such a reaction is based on emotional memory, a type of implicit memory in which we react in a particular way without the conscious awareness that we are remembering.

whom you've just met. Neuroscientists believe these systems are probably centered farther back in the brain. They hold the memory briefly, increasing its chances of entering long-term memory.

The process of converting explicit short-term memories to long-term ones takes place deep within the brain. Such processing involves a number of structures, particularly one called the *hippocampus.* In the brain, this step is called *encoding.* When the brain encodes information, it organizes the data so that the information can be recalled later. In the case of the phone number, we may encode the information by finding a numerical or visual pattern in the numbers or by associating it with similar numbers. The encoding stage is comparable to writing the number down on a piece of paper.

The next step would be to figure out where to put the piece of paper so we can find it when we need it. In memory, this process is called *consolidation.* During consolidation, the information undergoes several steps in the hippocampus before it is sent on for final storage. Networks of neurons are established and then strengthened to preserve the new memory. Some neuroscientists believe that a significant amount of consolidation occurs as we sleep. Perhaps that is why teachers have often found that students do better on an exam after a good night's sleep than after spending the whole night cramming.

We may worry that we don't have room to store even one more piece of paper, but scientists assume that our brain has an unlimited capacity for long-term storage. After long-term explicit memories leave the hippocampus, they seem to be stored in the areas of the brain that originally received the sensory information.

Finally, when we need the phone number again, we get the paper from the storage location. In the brain, this process is called *retrieval*. When an explicit memory is recalled, the thalamus retrieves the information from various storage sites and the cerebral cortex reassembles it into a mental image. Imaging research, for example, has found that the visual cortex of the brain becomes most active when someone is remembering a par-

A western scrub jay hides its food to prevent other birds from stealing it. Scientists believe that such behavior shows that scrub jays have a type of episodic memory. The birds remember what happened in the past—another bird stole their food—and take action to prevent it from happening in the future. Until experiments such as those with scrub jays proved otherwise, researchers had always assumed that only human beings are capable of episodic memory.

ticular visual image. Similarly, the auditory cortex becomes active when a person is remembering sounds, such as the melody of a song. When people remember doing something with their hands, such as using a tool, those memories elicit brain activity near the area that receives sensory information from the hands.

Implicit memories of physical activities are usually stored in the regions that encode a particular function. Motor skills—such as riding a bike—are stored in an area of the brain called the *cerebellum,* which seems to coordinate repetitive movements.

Another brain structure, called the *amygdala,* encodes and stores implicit memories involving emotion. One crucial function of the amygdala is to identify facial expressions. The facial expressions that convey emotion—happiness, sadness, or anger—are remarkably similar across cultures. Because we have no conscious awareness of implicit memories, they do not move from their initial sensory processing areas to a short-term holding area.

How reliable is memory?

Certain memories are more likely to be forgotten than others. Because memories go through stages as they are being stored—from sensory memory to short-term memory to long-term memory—the newer, or more recent, the memory is, the more likely it is not to have been processed sufficiently or consolidated firmly.

In addition, human memory is not always accurate. Memory depends upon our senses to take in information about the world. From that information, our brain constructs a "best guess" of what reality is. If our sensory information is inaccurate or incomplete, a particular memory will be as well. Sometimes, strong emotions or other distractions interfere with our ability to understand what is going on. As a result, what we recall may be based on flaws in our construction.

Distortions of memory can take other forms, too. Researchers have learned that we remember things more effectively when we can associate them with things already well established in our memories. As a result, our brain may distort a new perception to make it resemble something that we already know. When looking at an optical illusion, for example, we tend to see the object in the form that is most familiar to us. That is why two people looking at the same illusion can see two completely different things.

Even after a memory is stored, later experiences or new information may change the way we recall the original fact or incident. For example, a victim who looks at photos of people who may have committed a crime in a book of mug shots may be influenced by the photos in recalling the criminal's face.

The more that researchers learn about different types of memory, the clearer the fact becomes: Although it may all feel like "remembering," the process is considerably more complicated.

FROM NEURONS TO MEMORIES

By John F. Disterhoft

Memories are formed in the brain's 1 trillion neurons, the information-processing units of the nervous system. Each neuron consists of a cell body, an *axon,* and a number of *dendrites.* The cell body handles all the normal cell functions, such as taking in food and oxygen, eliminating waste, and reproducing. In addition, each cell body carries genes that define the specific purpose of that cell, such as making a particular protein. The axon, which often has several branches, transmits the electrical *impulses* (signals) that travel to and from the brain. The dendrites, which may also be branched, receive signals from the axons.

Neurons come in many different sizes. The cell body of a human neuron can be anywhere from 4 microns to 100 microns wide (1 micron equals 0.0001 millimeter [0.000003 inch]). Some axons, such as those that extend from the spinal cord down the legs to the feet, may be from 75 to 100 centimeters (30 to 40 inches) long.

Neurons also come in many different types. *Sensory neurons,* for example, pass along information gathered through the senses, including sight, smell, sound, touch, and taste. *Motor neurons* carry information from the brain and spinal cord to muscles and glands.

Neurons communicate with one another and with other cells *electrochemically.* When a *stimulus* (a sound or other sensory perception) triggers a reaction in a neuron, the *membrane* (outer skin) of the cell body opens at points called *channels.* The channels are proteins that change their structure in order to allow positively charged *ions* in the fluid that surrounds the neuron to flow into the cell body. (Ions are atoms or molecules that carry an electric charge.) Each cell body has a *threshold* (level) below which it will not *fire* (transmit a signal). If the collective electric charge of the ions entering the cell body exceeds the threshold, the neuron fires, releasing a signal called an *action potential.*

The action potential travels down the length of the axon. At the end of the axon, the impulse prompts the axon to release chemicals called *neurotransmitters.* The neurotransmitters cross a gap between neurons called a *synapse* and attach to sites called *receptors* on another neuron. The neuron that sends the signal is called the *presynaptic* neuron; the neuron that receives the signal is called the *postsynaptic* neuron. Usually, the axon of one neuron passes the signal to the dendrites of another neuron. Because axons can have many branches and a neuron may have dozens of dendrites, a neuron can communicate with thousands of other neurons at the same time.

The postsynaptic neuron passes the signal along to another neuron if the signal it received is strong enough to set off the postsynaptic neuron's own action potential. The electrical impulse then travels from cell to cell creating a *neural circuit,* a pathway made up of many neurons. If the signal received by the postsynaptic neuron is too weak to trigger its action potential, the impulse is not passed along and no pathway is established.

Forming a memory

A memory is formed when neurons establish a circuit. Some neural circuits remain connected briefly, creating short-term memories. Others are strong enough to last for a long time, creating long-term memories. Whether a memory will last depends on the strength of the connections between neurons in the circuit. Researchers have found that when a neuron fires an action potential, a protein called CREB is activated within the cell. (CREB stands for cyclic adenosine monophosphate responsive element binding.) CREB is sent to

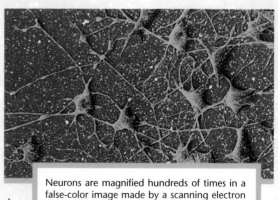

Neurons are magnified hundreds of times in a false-color image made by a scanning electron microscope. Memories form when many neurons establish a pathway called a *neural circuit.*

all the neuron's synapses. At synapses that have been stimulated by the neurotransmitters of another neuron, CREB activates genes that release synapse-strengthening proteins. Those strengthened synapses then form a circuit that stores a memory. Synapses that are not strengthened do not become part of a circuit. Brief stimulation of a synapse forms a short-term memory. Repeated stimulation, which results in frequent strengthening of the synapse, forms a long-term memory.

New information can change or re-form a memory by forming new synapses or weakening old ones. The brain's ability to change in the presence of new information is called *neuroplasticity.*

Animal models reveal how we learn

Neuroscientists began to understand how memories are formed as early as the late 1800's. However, the pace of discovery increased considerably in the 1950's through studies of *model systems.* Model systems include simple organisms, such as fruit flies or rats, as well as simple behaviors that can be observed closely. Researchers then apply their understanding of such organisms and processes to more complex systems, such as the human brain. One advantage of using simple animals to study learning and memory is that these animals can be trained and their nervous system analyzed in detail at the cellular and molecular level. For ethical reasons, these types of experiments cannot be done in human beings.

Through repeated experiments, scientists have found that the mechanisms of simple learning in animals form the components of more complex learning in people. In addition, learning takes place in similar brain regions in both animals and people. Finally, memories are stored through similar cellular processes in both groups.

In the 1960's, neurobiologist Eric Kandel and his colleagues at Columbia University in New York City made tremendous advances in understanding learning and memory through their studies of a relatively unusual model, the giant marine snail—or sea slug—called *Aplysia californica. Aplysia* has only 20,000 nerve cells. The cells are so large that they are easily visible under a microscope, and

HOW MEMORIES ARE FORMED

Memories are formed when neurons are able to pass signals from one to another, creating *circuits* (pathways). These signals consist of both electrical impulses and chemicals called *neurotransmitters.*

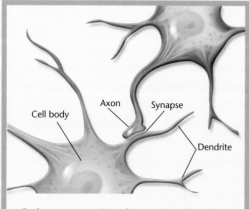

Each neuron consists of many signal-receiving branches called *dendrites,* a cell body, and a signal-sending extension called an *axon.* A stimulus, such as a sound, produces an electrical impulse that causes a neuron to *fire* (transmit an impulse).

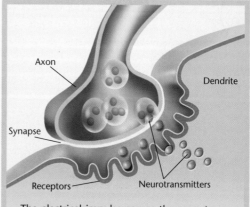

The electrical impulse causes the axon to release neurotransmitters that travel across a gap called a *synapse* to another cell. The neurotransmitters attach to receptors on the other cell's dendrites. If the signal is strong enough, the second cell fires and passes the signal along. Memories are formed when the connection between neurons at the synapses grows strong enough to link the neurons together in a circuit.

they appear in the same patterns in every slug. These characteristics allowed Kandel and his group to easily insert glass pipettes or electrodes into *Aplysia's* neurons and then watch how the neurons responded as the snail learned to react to various stimuli—that is, as it acquired memory.

Kandel studied three forms of memory formation in the snails: *sensitization, habituation,* and *classical conditioning.* Sensitization is the process of learning to react strongly to a stimulus. The behavior continues even when the stimulus becomes nonthreatening. Soldiers who are exposed to frequent gunshots in battle, for example, learn to react with fear at the sound of explosions. Later, they may react the same way to the sound of firecrackers in their own backyard.

The animal that Kandel chose to study, *Aplysia,* breathes through a gill on the upper side of its body. Near the gill is a fleshy part called a *siphon* through which the snail expels water. When either the gill or siphon is touched, *Aplysia* pulls it into a cavity in a defensive *reflex* (action performed without conscious thought). Kandel repeatedly applied painful shocks to *Aplysia's* tail, causing it to reflexively withdraw the gill. He soon found that whenever he touched any part of the snail's body—even gently—it quickly withdrew its gill. The snail had become sensitized.

On the cellular level, Kandel found that, after repeated painful shocks, certain synapses between *Aplysia's* neurons had grown stronger. He also noted that the axons of presynaptic sensory neurons had grown more branches, allowing them to send the pain signal to even more motor neurons and elicit a quicker gill-withdrawing reaction. The animal's sensitivity to touch lasted for several weeks, leading Kandel to conclude that a long-term memory of the shock had been formed. When Kandel's team administered only one shock to the animal, the slug was sensitive to all touches for only a few hours.

Habituation is the process of learning to ignore a repeated, unimportant stimulus. People living near a busy highway, for example, learn to ignore the noise of speeding cars without even being aware that they are learning anything. Kandel found that the axons of the snail's sensory neurons that had become accustomed to a nonthreatening touch of the siphon had fewer branches. The level of neurotransmitters released by *Aplysia's* sensory neurons also decreased, as did the intensity and frequency of the snail's reflex response.

Classical conditioning

Sensitization and habituation represent the simplest forms of learning. In both, an organism learns to respond to a single stimulus. Toddlers are capable of such simple learning when, for example, the painful touch of a hot stove teaches them to avoid this appliance. Classical conditioning is a more complex type of learning, in which the organism is presented with two stimuli and learns to associate one stimulus with the other. Eventually, the second stim-

The sea slug *Aplysia californica* has large neurons that can be seen under a simple microscope. Scientists studying *Aplysia* have learned how neurons communicate as they form memories.

ulus evokes the response all by itself. The first stimulus is called the unconditioned stimulus (US). For an animal, an effective US is food. The US produces a particular unconditioned response (UR), such as *salivation* (drooling) in the animal. If a second stimulus, such as the sound of a bell, is repeatedly paired with the presentation of the US, eventually the second stimulus—called the conditioned stimulus (CS)—evokes the response by itself. The response is then called a conditioned response (CR).

The most famous classical conditioning experiment was the work of Russian physiologist Ivan Pavlov (1849-1936). Pavlov discovered that a dog that salivates (UR) when it is given meat powder (US) can be taught to salivate (CR) at the sound of a bell (CS) when the sound is paired with the presentation of meat powder.

In the decades that followed Pavlov's experiment, psychologists and neuroscientists alike have used classical conditioning to gain a greater understanding of learning and memory. Kandel, for example, gently touched *Aplysia's* siphon (CS) at the same time that he applied a shock to its tail (US). He found that *Aplysia* began to withdraw its gill (CR) at the gentle touch of the siphon alone. When Kandel's team examined the neurons in

Aplysia's brain, they found that the siphon touch had created the same synapse pattern as the tail shock had.

In the 1960's, psychologist Isidore Gomerzano, then of Indiana University at Bloomington, conducted classical conditioning experiments with rabbits. Gomerzano paired a weak tone CS with a strong US—an airpuff to the *cornea* (the transparent outer coat of the eye). After a number of pairings, the tone began to elicit the eyeblink by itself.

Researchers began using eyeblink conditioning, which has also been used to study learning in human beings, to study the mechanisms for associative learning in other animals, such as rats and mice. Neuroscientists Theodore Bergen and Richard Thompson, then at Harvard University in Cambridge, Massachusetts, found in 1976 that neurons in the hippocampus increase their firing rate in response to a tone very early in the learning process, often in a manner that mimics their response to an eyeblink. In 1986, neuroscientist John Disterhoft of Northwestern University in Chicago observed that after the learning process has been completed, hippocampal neurons show signs of increased excitability, making it easier for the neuron to fire a series of action potentials. In addition, researchers have found a changed pattern in the synapses between hippocampal neurons after the conditioning.

The role of long-term potentiation

In addition to sensitization, habituation, and classical conditioning, another model that has helped scientists understand memory formation is *long-term potentiation* (LTP). LTP is a strengthening of synapses that occurs when presynaptic neurons are exposed to frequent bursts of intense stimulation. After such strengthening, the postsynaptic cell reacts much more quickly and strongly to a stimulus. The effect lasts for hours or even days.

The fact that LTP may be an important model for learning was first noted by Terje Lomo and Timothy Bliss at the University of Oslo in Norway. In 1973, the neuroscientists described this short-term memory in the hippocampus of rabbits. The hippocampus is in the *temporal lobe*, a critical region for learning in mammals. Other researchers later observed LTP in other brain structures, including the cerebral cortex, cerebellum, and amygdala.

To strengthen the synapse and prime the postsynaptic neuron to react, LTP depends on a neurotransmitter called *glutamate.* The presynaptic cell releases glutamate from its axon, and the neurotransmitter attaches to receptors called NMDA (N-methyl-D-asparate) on the postsynaptic

cell. Many researchers believe that LTP and stable memory formation are established with the same processes.

Neuroscientists Richard Morris at the University of Edinburgh in Scotland and Gary Lynch at the University of California at Irvine explored the role that LTP plays in *spatial learning tasks* in mice and rats. Spatial learning, which takes place in the hippocampus, is the process by which animals get their bearings in a new environment. When a mouse or rat is placed in an unfamiliar location, such as a maze, it quickly orients itself to the new area and learns, for example, where food is placed.

In 1981, Morris developed a new type of maze to test spatial learning. He built a platform that stood just below the surface in a murky pool of water and then placed a series of rats into the water. (Rats are by nature good swimmers; though they prefer not to be in water, swimming does not distress them.) The rats learned to swim to the invisible platform using only visual cues that they picked up from pictures on the walls and the placement of furniture in the laboratory.

In 1986, Morris and Lynch reported that when they blocked the NMDA receptors in rats, the rats had difficulty finding the platform in the water maze. Since then, other researchers have found that any forms of conditioning that depend upon the hippocampus cannot take place if drugs block the NMDA receptors. Hippocampus-associated forms of learning are enhanced by drugs that make the NMDA receptors work more effectively. In this sense, the hippocampus appears to react the same way during eyeblink conditioning, water maze spatial learning, and LTP.

Morris and Lynch's findings helped put into perspective the research of John O'Keefe, a neuroscientist at University College London. Earlier, O'Keefe and his colleagues had observed that, as rats learn to navigate in a new location, single neurons in the hippocampus fire vigorously when the animal is in a specific place. In fact, different neurons fire when the rats are in different areas. O'Keefe's group concluded that the rats are creating in their hippocampus a mental map of the maze. The researchers theorized that the human brain uses the same mapping technique during spatial learning tasks, such as finding one's way home from school or work.

By the early 2000's, neuroscientists had made tremendous progress in understanding how memories are initially formed. For the years ahead, an equally challenging task remains: discovering how and where memories are stored more permanently.

PROBLEMS WITH MEMORY

By Thomas A. M. Kramer

A s anyone who has ever taken a test knows, memory is a less-than-perfect ability. We tend to forget much of the information and many of the experiences to which we are exposed. Forgetting is a natural and frequent part of the memory process. That is why people throughout the ages have developed techniques and technology to back up what they know. The process accelerated with the advent of written language, became widespread with the invention of the printing press, and continues today with the ongoing development of computer-based information technology.

Why do we forget? Despite years of research, psychologists and neuroscientists in 2005 still had no definitive explanation for either simple memory loss among otherwise healthy people or severe loss among people with memory-robbing diseases. For researchers, the crucial issue is not whether people will forget, but how much they are going to forget.

One factor that scientists have ruled out as a possible reason for memory loss is brain capacity. Neuroscientists have found no evidence for a limit to the human capacity for long-term memory, as long as people are healthy, able to focus on what they are learning, and have the opportunity to organize and associate the information their senses take in.

The fact that we tend to remember things by associating them with something we know works both for and against us. If we can find a relationship between something we already know and something that we wish to learn, we will remem-

A daughter (below, right) sits with her mother, who has Alzheimer's disease. Alzheimer's disease causes brain cells to die, resulting in memory loss and problems in judgment, decision making, orientation (finding one's way to the store or home), and language. A computer graphic of part of the brain of a patient with Alzheimer's disease (far left) demonstrates the degree of neuron loss associated with the disease. A brain section from a person who does not have Alzheimer's (left) has many more neurons.

ber the new material considerably better. For example, it is easier to remember details about your favorite television program than it is to remember information about a new show.

But sometimes memory can complicate our efforts to learn—and remember—something new. For example, throughout January, many people persist in writing the previous year's date on their personal checks. The memory of the previous year's date has already been formed in the brain and interferes with the formation of a memory recording the current year's date. This phenomenon is called *interference*. The brain has already laid down specific neural pathways to store the old memory. Now it must create new pathways or re-form the old ones. That process requires time and some effort on the part of the person learning the new material, such as the check writer remembering that it is a new year.

Freud's ideas about forgetting

Some of the best-known theories about why we forget were developed by the Austrian physician Sigmund Freud (1856-1939). Freud believed that the mind consists of two distinct and sometimes competing areas that he called the *conscious* and *unconscious.* According to his theory—which remains widely accepted by psychologists—unconscious thought processes rule most of our behavior. For instance, in the morning, when we dress, eat breakfast, and drive to work, we rarely think about what we are doing in detail. Our conscious mind is elsewhere, perhaps thinking about a meeting we planned for later in the day or wondering what we will eat for dinner that night. Rarely are we thinking about the steps involved in buttoning a shirt or even steering the car. These things seem to happen automatically.

Forgetting, according to Freud, is not an error of mental process but a purposeful decision of our unconscious that sneaks past conscious decision making. For example, you need to pick up your best suit at the dry cleaner on your way home from work for an important meeting the next day. However, you forget about this errand until you are already home. According to Freud's theory, your unconscious mind did not want to stop. You were tired and just wanted to go home, and your unconscious won out.

Various kinds of memory problems

Some memory problems are related to learning disabilities. Learning disabilities are not specifically categorized as memory disorders. But we cannot recall something that we never learned in the first place. Thus, anything that interferes with the process of learning also interferes with the process of memory. People with dyslexia, for example, see some letters backward and have a difficult time processing written material. Thus, they have difficulty memorizing something they have read. (Such people, however, are often able to efficiently memorize information that they have heard.)

Some developmental disorders, including *autism,* affect learning and recall because of their impact on a specific part of the memory process. People with autism have, among other challenges, difficulty understanding social cues, such as the meaning of an expression on another person's face. In numerous studies, researchers have used neuroimaging techniques to compare the brains of people with autism with those of people without autism while the participants viewed pictures depicting different facial expressions. The researchers found that when people without autism viewed faces that expressed fear, the amygdala—which is involved in processing emotion—showed increased activity. The amygdala of people with autism did not become active.

The phenomenon of *amnesia* (loss of memory) is one of the best-known memory problems. People usually develop amnesia because of injury to an area of the brain involved in memory. The patient H. M., for example, whose medial temporal lobes were removed in an attempt to control epilepsy, could no longer process new information from short-term to long-term memory.

People who receive a blow to the head, in a car accident or a fall, for example, develop different types of memory problems. Neurons in the areas of the brain that strike the hard, bony shell of the skull may die or suffer damage. If the neurons die, memory stored in the affected portion of the brain will disappear. The memory functions they governed cannot be restored. If the cells are merely damaged, the injured person may regain memory.

Other types of memory loss do not involve permanent damage to the brain. Often, people who have an epileptic seizure have a loss of memory for a short period around the time of the seizure. Patients experience seizures when receiving electroconvulsive therapy (ECT) for depression or other severe mental illnesses. Such people often have amnesia for the period right before and during their treatments.

Finally, some medications and high doses of alcohol can cause amnesia. Studies have found that certain medications intended to help people sleep may cause memory problems the next day. People who drink too much alcohol may have so-called blackouts, long periods for which they have no memory.

Delirium and dementia

Medical disorders that can cause memory loss fall into two broad categories. The first is *delirium,* a condition in which the brain malfunctions and the person becomes disoriented and confused. Delirium often results from a high fever caused by an infection or from an overdose of or bad reaction to medication. Stress and lack of sleep can increase the effects of delirium. Older people —particularly if they are hospitalized—are especially vulnerable to delirium. Scientists do not understand why this is.

Researchers also cannot fully explain why delirium occurs. However, they have found, in studies of both animals and people, that during delirium, levels of the neurotransmitters dopamine and serotonin increase while levels of the neurotransmitter acetylcholine decrease. How these brain chemicals, which transmit messages between neurons, contribute to delirium is not yet clear. After a patient's delirium passes, both the brain and memory return to normal. In other words, delirium is reversible.

In contrast, *dementia,* the second broad category of disorders that cause memory loss, is not reversible. In dementia, brain cells die, affecting memory and behavior.

The most common forms of dementia

The two most common forms of dementia are Alzheimer's disease and *multi-infarct dementia.* Scientists are working particularly hard to get a better understanding of Alzheimer's disease. In 2005, researchers at Rush University Medical Center in Chicago estimated that almost 5 million people in the United States have Alzheimer's. One in 10 people over age 65 have the condition, as do half of all people over age 85. As the large group of people known as *baby boomers* (those born in

A U.S. soldier is overcome with the stress of battle in Iraq. People who are exposed to extremely stressful or traumatic events may develop a condition known as *post-traumatic stress disorder* (PTSD). Instead of having trouble remembering, people with PTSD have trouble forgetting painful memories. Such memories intrude on their everyday lives, leading them to respond inappropriately to even minor stresses.

the United States from 1946 to 1964) enter their 60's, public health officials are concerned that the health care system may not be equipped to handle the number of patients expected to develop Alzheimer's.

Alzheimer's disease involves the gradual death of brain cells. At first, its effects are mild. But as the disease continues over a number of years, people with Alzheimer's become so severely impaired that they can no longer handle the most basic personal care tasks.

Memory processing areas around the temporal lobes of the brain are often affected early in the progression of Alzheimer's disease, so the first symptoms to appear are memory difficulties. Although people with Alzheimer's can still recall memories from the distant past, they have increasing difficulties storing new memories. They continually lose familiar objects or forget names they once knew well. These difficulties are followed by problems in judgment, decision making, orientation (finding one's way to the store or home), and language.

Cognitive (knowledge and problem-solving) tests are an important tool in diagnosing Alzheimer's disease. The physician asks the patient questions designed to show whether the individual's brain can still transfer new information into long-term memory. A physician may ask such questions as "What day is it today?" or "Who is the president of the United States?"

Multi-infarct dementia is the result of multiple *cerebrovascular accidents* that are sometimes called brain attacks because of their similarity to heart attacks. When blood vessels get clogged, the tissue to which they deliver oxygen-rich blood is starved and dies, becoming an *infarct*. A heart attack, also called a myocardial infarction, occurs when the heart is deprived of oxygen. In the brain, this event is called a stroke or a cerebrovascular accident.

Strokes tend to occur in areas close to big blood vessels, because these vessels sometimes carry pieces of clotted blood or *cholesterol,* a fatty substance found in blood and body tissues and also in such foods as eggs and meat. The pieces circulate through the blood system until they reach a blood vessel that is too small for them to pass through. If they block the vessel long enough, the area beyond it becomes deprived of blood, causing a stroke. Individuals who have numerous strokes may lose so much tissue in the brain that they develop dementia, losing part or all of their memory, depending on the location and number of strokes.

Stress and memory

Stress may have a profound effect on memory as well. According to Freud's theory of repression, we unconsciously decide to avoid thinking about unpleasant things. As a result, we recall unpleasant memories in less detail and with less frequency. For example, we may think fondly about our grammar school years, even though they may have been full of unpleasant and humiliating experiences. Freud argued that the stress we experienced at the time of the original event affected our ability to remember. Many psychologists believe that repression may help us to adapt to a difficult situation. We function much better when we can forget unpleasant experiences and move on.

Some people, however, cannot stop remembering. People exposed to extremely stressful or traumatic experiences may develop *post-traumatic stress disorder* (PTSD). Symptoms of PTSD include painful, unpleasant, and unwanted memories of those events. This playback of traumatic events can take place in dreams or in sensory *flashbacks* while the patient is awake. For example, someone who developed PTSD after being in combat might recall a painful, vivid memory of battle after hearing a car backfire or a firecracker go off. This recall involves not only the brain but also the body. Researchers have found that in people experiencing flashbacks, the heart rate increases, muscles tense, and the body goes through all of the other physical preparations it needs to react.

During a flashback, a trigger—the explosive sound—that had once served a life-saving function and set off such an appropriate response as seeking cover continues to send danger signals through the brain's neural pathways. However, in a noncombat situation, the learned response—seeking cover—causes the person to react in ways that are inappropriate to the current situation, interfering with a return to normal life until the condition is treated.

Perhaps the biggest enemy of memory is time. As we get older, most of us struggle more with our memory. In addition, our chances of developing a condition that interferes with memory increase. Nevertheless, there are many individuals who live well into their 90's with a strong, accurate memory. Although scientists still do not understand why, several ongoing studies are focusing on such individuals, hoping to unravel the secrets of their memory and find ways to benefit us all.

PROTECTING OUR MEMORY

By Thomas A. M. Kramer

The ability to remember, like artistic ability or any other personal trait, varies considerably from person to person. In addition, some of us are better than others at remembering certain kinds of information, such as telephone numbers. Individual memory skills also vary throughout our life. They are not a relatively constant quality, such as eye color or height. In addition, various factors, such as illnesses and injuries, can interfere with, damage, or impair memory.

Memory also changes with age. According to conventional wisdom, memory deteriorates as we get older, but studies suggest this is not universally true or inevitable. We can take steps to strengthen our memory and to protect it—at least to a certain degree—from age-related declines. By 2005, many researchers also believed that taking certain steps may lessen an individual's risk of developing Alzheimer's disease, or at least delay its onset. For individuals with a family history of early onset Alzheimer's (before about age 70), genetics may play a greater role in the development of the disease.

In general, good memory depends on good health. Memory involves multiple complex systems in the brain. For all these to work well, the systems that support them with nutrients and oxygen must also be in good working order. Proper nutrition and adequate exercise may help prevent such conditions as cardiovascular disease, which can increase the risk of delirium and dementia.

Recent studies have suggested an even more direct link between physical health and memory. Even light exercise, including walking, can help us preserve our memory, according to a 2004 study of more than 18,000 nurses led by Jennifer Weuve at the Harvard School of Public Health in Boston. The nurses participated in the study for a period of from 8 to 15 years. When they reached the age of 70 or older, those who had either walked or jogged several hours a week performed better on *cognitive tests* than the women who had not exercised. (Cognitive tests measure memory and problem-solving skills.)

Other studies have also shown that exercise can significantly slow age-related memory decline. For example, an international group of researchers studied 295 healthy men in Finland, Italy, and the Netherlands for 10 years. The men were all 70 to 90 years old. The group reported in August 2004 that men who increased both the time spent on and the intensity of such activities as walking, bicycling, swimming, and gardening experienced no decline in memory.

Exercise also appears to offer some protection against dementia-causing illnesses, such as Alzheimer's disease. In a study reported by Canadian researchers in 2001, inactive individuals were twice as likely to develop Alzheimer's as those who exercised vigorously three times a week. Rene Verreault and her colleagues at the Geriatric Research Unit of Laval University in Canada and other insti-

WAYS TO PROTECT MEMORY

Although there are currently no foolproof ways to prevent memory decline, researchers have found that certain activities may slow down memory loss. These activities include:

- Physical exercise, such as walking, biking, low-impact aerobic exercise, or yoga;

- Mental exercise, such as working a crossword puzzle; playing chess; or joining a book discussion group;

- Travel, which provides the mind with such challenges as new languages, cultures, and currencies;

- Music, either making music oneself or listening to it.

tutions based their findings on a study of 5,000 men and women over age 65 for five years.

In June 2002, researchers at the University of California at Irvine reported that they had discovered a reason why exercise may help slow the onset and progression of Alzheimer's. In experiments with rats, Carl Cotman, director of the Institute for Brain Aging and Dementia, and researcher Nicole Berchtold found for the first time that exercise—running on a cage wheel—stimulated genes that control growth hormones and other important molecules in the rats' hippocampus. The researchers had expected to find an increase in brain stimulation in areas related to motor activity. The hippocampus, however, is associated with higher reasoning and memory. The researchers theorized that this increase in gene activity may improve those higher functions.

Exercise your brain

Mental exercise may be even more important than physical exercise for protecting and strengthening memory. Many researchers have concluded that the brain, like a muscle, functions better if it is exercised. Until the late 1990's, researchers believed that we are born with all the neurons that we are ever going to have. They thought that, unlike the skin and other organs in the body, the brain could not grow new cells. In November 1998, neuroscientists Fred Gage of the Salk Institute in La Jolla, California, and Peter Eriksson of Göteborg University Institute of Clinical Neuroscience in Göteborg, Sweden, demonstrated that this is not true. New neurons develop in certain areas of the brain, such as the hippocampus, throughout life. In addition, existing neurons constantly make new connections with one another as they process new information.

Brain stimulation helps new cells and connections grow. In 1956, psychologist K. Warner Schaie and other researchers at the University of Washington in Seattle began to monitor the cognitive abilities of several hundred people from ages 20 to 90. By the late 1990's, the researchers had also evaluated the study participants' children and grandchildren, bringing the number of participants to more than 5,000 people. In 1998, Schaie and his colleagues reported on their use of training sessions geared toward improving reasoning and spatial orientation with participants who were beginning to experience cognitive decline. They found that at least half these participants improved significantly. In other words, keeping your brain active may help limit memory loss in old age.

Researchers believe that almost any kind of mental stimulation is good for your brain as long as it requires active participation. Watching television is probably not beneficial because it requires virtually no thought. Solving puzzles or playing games that make you think are much better for strengthening memory.

Music is a beneficial stimulant for the brain as well. Music therapists who work with Alzheimer's patients report that music relaxes patients and reduces the number of aggressive interactions between patients. In addition, even patients who no longer speak because they cannot remember words are often able to sing along to familiar songs. Some researchers speculate that such a response is possible because the various elements of music—including rhythm, pitch, and melody—are processed in different areas of the brain, including the brain stem, the most primitive part of the brain. Therapists have found that participation in music therapy—in which patients sing, listen to music, or beat out a rhythm—often improves patients' short-term and long-term memories to the point that they begin to remember the names of other group members.

Helping the brain repair itself

Stimulating the brain does more than simply protect and strengthen memories by forming new connections and producing neurons. Stimulation can also help repair the brain when it is damaged. If the brain is injured because of a head injury, a stroke, or brain disease, it may attempt to *rewire* itself (form new connections between neurons) to compensate for the injury. This capability is called *injury-induced plasticity.*

Exactly how the brain reshapes itself depends on the site of the injury. For example, the middle of the left side of the brain controls speech. If that area is damaged and the damage is not too extensive, the brain can rewire itself so that it processes speech in another, undamaged part of the brain. With training, the new area can learn this task, just as an undamaged brain would learn a new skill.

Although crossword puzzles and other mental exercises can help people sustain their memory, they are not much help to people who begin to lose their memory because of Alzheimer's disease. In 2005, researchers were working on specific mental exercises that may help people with early Alzheimer's or other memory disorders regain some of their memory, or, at least, slow the loss.

One group of researchers, psychiatrist David A. Loewenstein and his colleagues at the University of

A patient with Alzheimer's disease counts money using a new technique that relies on a region of his memory not yet ravaged by the disease. By 2005, researchers had made significant advances in understanding how we store, process, and recall memories, offering some hope to people with memory disorders.

Miami School of Medicine in Miami, Florida, reported in July 2004 that they had developed a cognitive rehabilitation program for people who were mildly impaired by Alzheimer's disease. The researchers tested their program with two groups of participants. The 19 participants in the first group received mental stimulation by playing computer games that stressed concentration, memory, and problem-solving skills. Twenty-five other participants, however, were trained in such tasks as face-name association, object recall, functional tasks—including making change and paying bills—and using a notebook to jot down things they needed to remember.

This more intensive cognitive training was designed to activate parts of the participants' brain that were unaffected by Alzheimer's. For example, the frontal cortex of the brain, which we use to reason and make decisions, can become more involved in the process of learning and memory. To encourage this transition, trainers had the patients in the cognitive training group make up their own associations for things they were trying to remember or had them categorize the things they were trying to remember in some way.

After 12 weeks, the patients who had received cognitive training improved their ability to associate names with faces by 170 percent compared with the patients in the mental stimulation group. They also improved their ability to make change by 71 percent. Three months later, the researchers found that the trained participants had maintained their improved ability. (All the study participants were also taking donepezil hydrochloride, a medication sold under the brand name Aricept that slows memory loss for a time in some people with Alzheimer's. However, the researchers believed the medication did not affect the results, because all of the study participants used the medication.)

Medications that improve brain function

In 2005, mental and physical exercise remained the main treatments for protecting and strengthening memory. However, medications that may improve mental abilities are attracting interest among researchers as well as the public. Researchers used the term *nootropics* (from the Greek words *noos*, which means *mind,* and *tropos,* which means *changed*) to describe this group of so-called smart drugs. The potential effects of nootropics are known as *cognitive enhancements,* which include improvement of memory, learning, attention, concentration, problem-solving, reasoning, social skills, decision making, and planning.

In 2005, some nootropics were targeted for people with specific neurological disorders. Medications designed for people with Alzheimer's, for example, such as donepezil hydrochloride and galantamine (Reminyl), can slow the progress of the disease. Such drugs work by enhancing the activity of a neurotransmitter called *acetylcholine,* which appears to play a role in memory and reasoning. However, the drugs work only in some patients and only to a degree for a limited period.

Other medications are used to treat *attention-deficit/hyperactivity disorder* (ADHD), a behavior problem in which people have unusual difficulty paying attention or controlling their impulses. One such medication, atomoxetine (Strattera), blocks the reabsorption of *norepinephrine* in the brain, making it more available for use by brain cells. Norepinephrine is a neurotransmitter that aids in concentration and organization, and, therefore, aids memory. Other medications, such as methylphenidate (sold as Ritalin or Concerta), are stimulants. Researchers are still not sure how they help control symptoms of ADHD, but they believe the medications may help balance the levels of the neurotransmitters *dopamine* and norepinephrine in the brain. Dopamine also plays a role in the ability to pay attention. In several studies, researchers have found that healthy people who took Ritalin experienced mental gains. Nevertheless, the medication has not been approved for such a purpose.

Smart drugs?

Although medications to improve memory were developed to treat people with specific neurological disorders, increasingly, some people with no such problems have become interested in using nootropics to increase their energy level and improve their memory and intelligence. In addition, they were using over-the-counter (OTC) products promoted as cognitive enhancers. These products are sold as drinks, power bars, and diet supplements and may be purchased in health food stores or over the Internet. Many are imported.

Researchers know little about the long-term effect of OTC enhancers on neurological function and behavior. According to the U.S. Food and Drug Administration, researchers have found no scientific evidence that such products actually work. In addition, many of them are associated with such undesirable side effects as insomnia, nausea, and abdominal cramps.

Because testing medications that affect people's thinking can be dangerous, researchers have performed some studies of smart drugs with rats. For example, researchers have trained rats to run in a maze. They then gave the rats a smart drug and tested the animals' performance. Such studies have generally found an improvement in the rats' ability to get through the maze.

It is difficult, however, to apply these results to human learning and memory. What if the smart drug just made the rats hungrier? The drugged rats may have run faster in the maze to collect the food reward, not because of increased cognitive ability.

What does the future hold? The greatest threat to memory is dementing diseases. In addition to researching medications, scientists are exploring the changes in brains affected by a disease of memory such as Alzheimer's. Some researchers believe that *peptides* (protein fragments) called amyloid-beta peptides (Aß) cause Alzheimer's symptoms. These peptides build up in the brain, forming clumps called *plaques* that clog synapses and prevent them from transmitting messages. Just as our body makes antibodies to fight off viruses, scientists think it may be possible to make antibodies that neutralize and remove Aß.

In April 2005, researchers at New York-Presbyterian Hospital/Weill Cornell Medical Center in New York City experimented with just such an antibody, called *immunoglobulin* (IVIg), in a group of people with Alzheimer's. The scientists administered IVIg to eight patients. After six months, cognitive function improved in six of those patients and stopped declining in another one.

Another type of cognitive enhancer under development in 2005 was based on drugs called *ampakines*, developed by neuropharmacologist Gary Lynch at the University of California at Irvine in the mid-1990's. Ampakines increase the sensitivity of receptors in the brain to glutamate, the neurotransmitter that strengthens synapses. Preliminary experiments conducted with Swedish medical students in 1997 indicated that ampakines may improve short-term memory.

Finally, researchers were also working to develop gene therapy for such diseases as Alzheimer's. Neurologist Mark H. Tuszynski and his colleagues at the University of California at San Diego reported the results of the first gene therapy trial for Alzheimer's in April 2005. The researchers had injected a gene that prompts neurons to produce their own *nerve growth factor* into the brains of eight people with early-stage Alzheimer's disease. Nerve growth factor is a protein that keeps neurons alive and stimulates communication between them. Of the eight patients who received the therapy, six experienced measurably slower cognitive decline in the 22 months after treatment than they had in the 14 months before treatment began. (One patient died as a result of the treatment, however.)

Further research may indeed develop safe and effective medications for cognitive enhancement. For the time being, however, the best way to protect memory, researchers say, is to maintain good physical health—especially cardiovascular health—and to remain mentally fit.

CONSUMER SCIENCE

Topics selected for their current interest provide information that the reader as a consumer can use in understanding everyday technology or in making decisions—from buying products to caring for personal health.

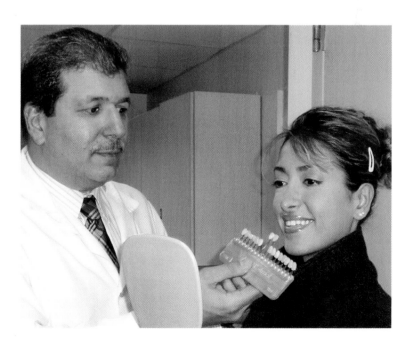

Shifting Gears to Hybrid Cars

Hybrid cars, such as the Lexus RX400 H (above, top) and Honda's Accord Hybrid (above), have become increasingly popular since hybrids were introduced in 2000. Hybrid cars run on both gasoline and electric power. They use less gasoline and release fewer emissions than standard gasoline-powered cars.

Skyrocketing gasoline prices, concerns about environmental pollution, and efforts to conserve natural resources have prompted many motorists in the United States to look beyond the standard gasoline-powered vehicle. Many consumers are now seeking out hybrid cars—cars powered by more than one energy source. The most common of these are gas-electric hybrids, which combine an internal-combustion engine that burns a mixture of gasoline and air with a battery-powered electric motor. The electric motor shares some of the burden of the gasoline engine. The less work the gas engine does, the less fuel it burns, and the fewer pollutants it releases into the atmosphere.

Hybrids accounted for about 100,000 of the 17 million vehicles sold in the United States in 2004. Industry analysts predicted that hybrid sales would double in 2005 and climb to at least 500,000 vehicles by 2010. The Toyota Prius—introduced to the U.S. market in 2000—ranked first among hybrid cars in 2004, with sales of 54,000 vehicles. This figure was more than double the combined sales of the next three most popular hybrids: the

Honda Insight, introduced in 1999, and the Honda Civic and Accord. Other hybrids available to the U.S. public in mid-2005 included the Ford Escape and the GMC Sierra.

Hybrid cars emerged as an intermediate step in auto companies' efforts to introduce the electric car as an alternative to gasoline-powered vehicles. Electric cars appeared to offer Americans a solution to problems plaguing the gas-powered engine, including pollution, overconsumption of natural resources, and U.S. reliance on foreign petroleum.

In the mid-1990's, several companies—most notably General Motors (GM)—tried to popularize electric cars, which had first appeared in Europe in the 1880's. However, these newer versions had serious drawbacks. The lead-acid batteries used for power gave the cars a driving range of only about 80 kilometers (50 miles). In addition, the batteries took up to 10 hours to recharge.

The nickel metal hydride batteries used in later prototypes improved the driving range somewhat, to about 160 kilometers (100 miles) before the need for a recharge, which might take from six to eight hours. However, many gas-powered cars can travel more than 500 kilometers (300 miles) before they need to be refueled. In addition, the nickel metal batteries were twice as expensive as lead-acid batteries and did not work well in cold climates.

The most popular of the available electric cars was GM's EV-1, which the company began leasing in 1996. But by 2000, GM had leased only 800 of the cars and removed the model from the market. In 1997, Toyota rolled out the Prius, the first mass-produced hybrid car, for the Japanese market.

Gas/electric hybrids come in two different *power train* designs—parallel and series. In standard cars, the power train transmits power from the engine to the driving wheels. In most *parallel hybrids*, both the gas engine and the electric motor are connected to the car's *transmission*, a device that carries power from the engine to other parts of a vehicle. The engine and motor can turn the transmission separately or together.

In a *series hybrid*, only the electric motor powers the transmission. The gas engine is connected to the *alternator*. This device produces power for the car's electrical system and recharges the batteries. As a result, the gas engine never supplies power directly to the vehicle.

Although most of the consumer-model hybrids available in 2005 were parallel hybrids, the cars featured two slightly different engine styles. Like conventional vehicles, hybrids can be designed to produce fewer emissions or to improve *fuel efficiency* (how much energy is created per unit of fuel). The Prius, for example, was designed to reduce

emissions. It combines elements of both series and parallel design systems. Other hybrids, including Honda's models, were designed to increase mileage and fuel efficiency.

The benefits of a gas/electric hybrid kick in at start-up. In most hybrids, the electric motor starts the *drive shaft,* which delivers power to the wheels. This process eliminates the need for the large amounts of gas required to start a gasoline-powered car and reduces the amount of hydrocarbons and other pollutants emitted during ignition, particularly when the engine is cold.

In some hybrids, the electric motor shuts off once the car reaches a speed of from 30 to 50 kilometers (20 to 30 miles) per hour. At that point, the car needs more power than the batteries can provide, so the gas engine takes over. The electric mode starts again when the driver needs additional acceleration for passing, merging, or climbing hills. This boost eases the burden on the gas engine, again saving fuel and reducing emissions.

Hybrids really come into their own in stop-and-go city driving. Instead of wasting fuel while idling at a stoplight

Parts of a hybrid car

A hybrid's gasoline engine powers an alternator, which produces electric current. An inverter converts the alternator's alternating current to direct current to be stored in a pack of batteries. The batteries supply electric power to the car's motor as needed. Braking the car charges the batteries. The electric motor can also act as a generator to produce electric power for storage in the batteries.

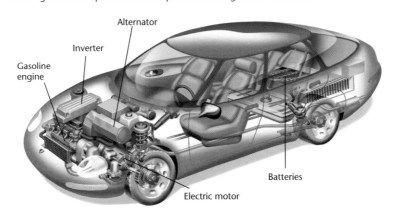

Alternator

Inverter

Gasoline engine

Batteries

Electric motor

Gasoline-powered cars v. hybrid cars

Gasoline-powered cars and hybrid cars differ in significant ways. Among these are their *fuel economy* (how far the car can travel on one unit of fuel), their *fuel energy use* (how much energy it takes to travel one kilometer), and their *fuel efficiency* (how much energy is created per unit of fuel).

	Gasoline-powered car	**Hybrid car**
Fuel source	Gasoline	Gasoline and electricity
Fuel economy		
in miles per gallon	21	44
in kilometers per liter	8.93	18.71
Fuel energy use		
(in kilojoules per kilometer)	3,282	1,536
Acceleration		
0-60 miles per hour		
(0-97 kilometers per hour)	18 seconds	10 seconds
Engine efficiency		
(average)	21%	30%
Types of emissions produced	Water vapor, carbon dioxide, carbon monoxide, hydrocarbons, nitrogen oxides	Carbon monoxide*, hydrocarbons*, nitrogen oxides*

*Trace amounts.

Sources: Demirdöven, Nurettin, and John Deutch. "Hybrid Cars Now, Fuel Cell Cars Later." *Science,* Aug. 13, 2004, pp. 974-976; "Fuel Cells in Transportation." *Fuel Cells 2000.* http://www.fuelcells.org.

Critically reviewed by Panos Y. Papalambros, Ph.D., Department of Mechanical Engineering, University of Michigan.

or in traffic, hybrids shut down their gas engine and then use the electric motor to start up again. As a result, drivers need not keep a foot on the brake pedal to avoid rolling forward. In addition, hybrids at a stop are virtually silent. Delivery trucks and buses are, therefore, a good application for hybrid technology.

Hybrid cars use several other design characteristics that further increase their efficiency, though some of these features can also be used for conventional vehicles. For example, some hybrids are designed to offer less air resistance when moving. Most hybrids are made of lightweight materials and so require less energy for propulsion. Hybrid cars also use special tires that cause less *drag* (resistance) than standard tires and, therefore, travel over the road more easily and require less energy to move. When a hybrid's electric motor is not needed for propulsion, it charges the batteries. Also, hybrids employ a unique process known as *regenerative braking.* In regenerative braking, the wheels power the alternator (thus slowing the car down) and convert the energy of motion to electric power, which is stored in the batteries.

Hybrids, however, are saddled with some drawbacks. Chief among these is their price. Because of increased engineering complexity, hybrids generally cost about $3,000 more than an equivalent vehicle model with a gas engine. Replacement batteries may also pose a problem. Battery packs usually come with a warranty good for from 8 to 10 years or up to 161,000 kilometers (100,000 miles). However, hybrids have been on the market for only a few years, so auto companies have borne the cost of replacing any batteries. Battery technology and production costs remain a challenge. Some industry analysts estimate that replacing a hybrid's battery pack could cost customers several thousand dollars.

Most major auto companies are either producing or developing hybrid cars, and many of these companies are diversifying into the hybrid truck and sport-utility vehicle market. GM, for example, is developing a *dual mode* hybrid, a car with a gas-powered engine and two electric motors. According to GM, the second electric motor will allow the vehicle to reach speeds of up to 80 kilometers (50 miles) per hour in electric-only mode. The second motor will also provide additional power for going up hills or towing a heavy load. Executives at GM say the car will conserve fuel at highway speeds as well as in stop-and-go traffic. At high speeds, half the gas engine's *cylinders* (chambers where fuel and air mix) will shut down and the electric motor will boost the vehicle's power, conserving fuel but still providing propulsion.

Despite the advantages of gas/electric hybrids, some auto industry experts believe that hybrids are simply an intermediate step until *fuel cell vehicles* become widely available. Fuel cells are devices that convert chemical energy directly to electric power. In regular batteries, the *electrodes* (conductors through which current enters and leaves) wear down relatively quickly. In fuel cells, however, energy-producing reactions continue as long as fuel is being supplied to them. Therefore, they last much longer than batteries.

A fuel cell can use any combustible material to produce the electric power to propel a vehicle. The automotive industry, however, is most interested in hydrogen, the most abundant element in the universe. A shift to hydrogen-powered vehicles would eliminate the need for petroleum-based fuels for transportation and so reduce U.S. reliance on energy from foreign countries.

When hydrogen is burned to produce electric power, the only by-products are heat and a few drops of water. Using hydrogen as the main energy source for vehicles would also mean a sharp reduction in air pollution.

While the advantages of fuel cell automobiles would be tremendous, the challenges are monumental. Hydrogen costs approximately 5 times as much to produce as gasoline. In addition, fuel cells now cost roughly 100 times as much as gasoline per unit of power. The cost to equip a vehicle with a hydrogen fuel cell is estimated at about $50,000. It costs only about $5,000 to build a car with a V-6 gas engine and 5-speed automatic transmission. Additionally, current methods of producing hydrogen create pollution, offsetting the environmental advantages of using hydrogen.

A bigger roadblock in the way of hydrogen fuel cells becoming the power source of the future is the need to build hydrogen refueling stations for fuel cell cars. Executives at GM estimate that it would cost $12-billion to create 12,000 hydrogen refueling stations across the country. It is unclear, however, who would pay for this hydrogen refueling network. Experimental fueling stations are being introduced with support from the U.S. government.

Some industry experts estimate fuel cell vehicles will be available in limited numbers by 2010. Others expect that fuel cells may not appear in significant numbers until 2020.

Because of the prohibitive costs of the hydrogen fuel cell infrastructure, auto industry experts predict continuing growth in the hybrid market. Many people within the automotive industry feel hybrids will maintain a strong market presence because they offer better mileage than conventional gas engines while requiring no special infrastructure.

Moreover, few industry experts think that gasoline-powered vehicles will disappear quickly. Millions of gas- or diesel-powered vehicles will still be running from 10 to 15 years from now. Given the popularity of gasoline-powered cars, it seems likely that, for some time, the auto-buying public will have a range of vehicle options.

■ Jim Mateja

Byte Back: Protecting Your Computer

Has your zippy broadband Internet connection slowed to a dial-up poke? Are pop-up advertisements for cut-rate mortgages or prescription drugs bombarding your browser? Has someone charged hundreds of dollars in fraudulent purchases to your credit cards?

You might encounter any or all of these problems if you fail to protect your computer from *malware* (*malicious software*), a general term for computer programs designed to damage or disrupt computer systems or perform certain tasks without their users' knowledge. A *hacker* can use certain types of malware to monitor everything you type, copy your passwords, break into your online bank account, and steal your savings. (The word *hacker* is used in this article to refer to a computer programmer who engages in criminal activities.) Malware sucks up a computer's memory and uses its Internet connection. These actions hijack re-

sources that other programs, including your computer's operating system, need to run smoothly. Other types of malware can slow your Internet connection or prevent your computer from operating properly.

Problems associated with malware affect both homes and businesses. A 2004 survey by *Consumer Reports* magazine found that 64 percent of those surveyed had detected a virus—one of the most common forms of malware—on their home computer during the previous two years. The Federal Bureau of Investigation reported that in 2004 viruses attacked 78 percent of U.S. corporations (down slightly from 82 percent in 2003). Viruses managed to penetrate 4 out of 5 corporate *networks* (groups of computers that are connected to share information and resources), bypassing the antivirus software that corporations had installed.

There is hope, however. Taking a few simple steps, such as installing antivirus software and being conscientious about where you use your computer, can protect you from most types of malware.

The most common types of malware include *viruses, worms, Trojan programs* (also called *Trojan horses*), and *spyware*. A virus is a *self-reproducing* program designed to invade computers, damage files, and spread to other machines. Viruses usually copy themselves secretly to other computers—sometimes thousands of other computers.

Many viruses are disguised as legitimate e-mail attachments that activate when you open them. Some viruses infect specific types of files, such as Microsoft Word documents. Some viruses create minor problems, such as causing a silly or obscene image to pop up on your monitor. Other viruses, however, can significantly damage your system by deleting all data from your hard drive. Even more disturbing, viruses may alter themselves as they spread, making them more difficult to detect. Regardless of their actions, viruses are always *parasitic*—that is, they need another program to survive.

Worms, in contrast, are *self-replicating* and *self-propagating.* That means they can reproduce and spread quickly on their own. Instead of piggybacking on another program, they take advantage of features that can transport files or information from one computer to another. Worms can clog networks and make entire corporate systems crash.

In January 2004, MyDoom became the world's fastest-spreading computer worm. When it first struck, on January 26, the worm was infecting up to 12,000 computers per hour. Within three days, 1 out of every 10 e-mails on the Internet contained the worm, which entered many users' e-mail address books and sent itself to every address listed. The worm slowed computer networks worldwide.

On February 1, MyDoom caused 50,000 infected computers to simultaneously try to access a software company's Web site. This overload, known as a *denial-of-service attack,* forced the company to take down its Web site and then temporarily relocate it for several weeks. Variants of MyDoom continued to appear into 2005.

A Trojan program is software that appears to be useful or nonthreatening but actually has a harmful purpose. A user might download such a program not knowing it contained extra, hidden code that causes trouble—possibly allowing a hacker to gather, falsify, or destroy data. For example, a Trojan might appear to be a game but instead may forward a user's passwords to a hacker.

When bad things happen to good computers

- **Malware** (*mal*icious soft*ware*): Includes adware, spyware, viruses, worms, Trojan programs (horses), and any other computer program that is designed to damage or disrupt computer systems or perform any task without their users' knowledge.

- **Adware:** A program, usually created by an advertising agency or company, that secretly monitors a user's computer habits and provides the user with unrequested advertisements, sometimes in the form of pop-up windows. Adware is generally not harmful but can be a nuisance.

- **Spyware:** Like adware, spyware programs secretly monitor a user's computer habits and transmit that information to an outside source. However, unlike adware, spyware is designed to steal passwords and other sensitive information, such as bank account numbers, from a user.

- **Virus:** A general term for any self-reproducing program that can infect other programs and files on a computer and damage them. Viruses spread from computer to computer after a user innocently opens an infected file.

- **Worm:** A program that infests computer networks, usually through e-mails, copying itself over and over and filling up storage space. Unlike viruses, worms operate on their own by taking control of features that can transport files or information.

- **Trojan program (horse):** A program that appears to be harmless, such as a game, but actually has a harmful purpose. Trojans secretly transmit a user's keystrokes to an outside source to permit the source to steal passwords, financial information, and other personal information.

Critically reviewed by Frederick F. Sears, Jr., computer security consultant.

Many Trojan horses are *nonreplicating,* meaning that they don't automatically spread to other machines.

Trojans are named after the Trojan horse of Greek mythology. This giant wooden horse appeared to be a gift from the Greeks to their Trojan enemies but actually hid Greek soldiers. After the Trojans wheeled the horse into their city, the Greeks sneaked out of the horse and opened the city gates to the rest of their army, which massacred the Trojans.

Spyware is software that monitors your activities on the computer, such as online purchasing or banking, without your knowledge. Spyware programs may come secretly bundled with other programs available for

How a virus infects a computer

A computer virus (represented in these illustrations by a red string of computer code) is a program that can infect and damage files and programs. Many viruses are sent in e-mail attachments and remain inactive until a computer user opens the attachment.

E-mail attachment

When the virus is activated, it may infect other programs on the computer's hard drive by copying itself onto them.

E-mail attachment   Program on hard drive

Some viruses place messages called *virus markers* inside the programs they infect. Virus markers help manage the virus's activities. After a virus marks all the files of a program, it can begin to damage the data on the computer.

Virus marker

Viruses corrupt programs or data files, causing them to work abnormally or not at all. In some cases, a virus can destroy all the files on a computer's hard drive.

Corrupted program

download from the Internet. Some spyware programs send your passwords to a hacker. Others may monitor computer use in an effort to gather marketing information. In its 2004 survey, *Consumer Reports* magazine also found that 36 percent of home computers in the United States showed signs of being infected with spyware. One sign, for example, is a change in a Web browser's home page made without the user's input. The same study found that only 41 percent of surveyed households said they actively try to protect their computers with special antispyware programs.

Some advertising companies are experimenting with their own kinds of spyware—sometimes called *adware*— to gather data about their customers. For example, a company might want to monitor your actions on its Web site to see if you go to a competitor's site to shop for the same product. Adware programs can provide users with unrequested advertisements in their Web browser.

Fortunately, there are plenty of warning signs to let you know if you've been hit by malware. Telltale signs include strange noises—indicating that your computer is acting without your input—and frequent crashes. Some forms of malware will cause strange images or advertisements to pop up on your monitor or unfamiliar icons to suddenly appear on your desktop.

Guarding your machine against malware is not difficult. Being careful about what programs you allow onto your computer offers the best protection. Because many malware programs are transmitted as e-mail attachments, you should open attachments only from people you know and only when the e-mails are expected.

Another important measure is to install and run antivirus and antispyware software. Such programs scan e-mail, attachments, and other incoming data that may be infected and then remove any malware from your computer. Some antivirus programs can be purchased at your local software store, while others are available for downloading from the Internet.

Simply installing the software isn't enough, however. Software companies continually update their antivirus programs to defend against new viruses. Out-of-date antivirus software won't be able to detect the newest creation from a clever hacker. Additionally, companies that produce system and application software vulnerable to hackers issue *patches,* software fixes for security holes. Updates and patches can be downloaded from a company's Web site.

Computer users can also protect against unauthorized access by installing *firewalls*—the digital equivalent of a medieval moat that protected a castle from invaders. A firewall is software or hardware that forbids unauthorized users from entering a private computer network. Firewall software examines all incoming data and screens out anything that appears to be an attack being launched against your computer network. Firewalls are often built into *routers,* hardware that connects computers in a network and links them to the Internet.

Some routers must be connected to a network's computers with cables.

How a firewall protects a network

A firewall is a hardware or software barrier that protects computer networks from unauthorized access. Many corporations and other organizations that have private computer networks install firewalls to prevent unauthorized users from stealing sensitive information. If a firewall doesn't recognize you as a legitimate user of that network, you will be denied access.

Internet connection

STOP

Firewall

Private computer network

Unauthorized user

Newer models may connect wirelessly using radio signals. However, hackers lurking nearby can pick up those radio signals and intercept passwords or other private information that you key into Web sites or send by e-mail. Wireless networks can be protected using *encryption* software, which scrambles the data you send. That way, even if hackers do intercept your data, they will be unable to read them.

Laptop computers are especially vulnerable to malware and unauthorized access because users often connect to wireless networks in places with low computer security. Airports, coffee shops, convention centers, and hotels often provide the perfect places for a criminal to tap into your computer.

In 2005, hackers were using *evil twins*—malicious wireless networks that pretend to be trustworthy public networks. The hackers can use these networks to steal users' login information from sites the users visit while connected to the evil twin. Evil twins tend to be a risk for large public wireless networks. They don't appear to pose a threat to wireless networks in users' homes.

Before you connect to a new wireless network, try to determine if the public Internet access point is encrypted by asking someone who works there. If your computer doesn't have encryption software and you're on an unprotected wireless network, don't read or write anything that you wouldn't mind showing to the entire world. Additionally, turn your computer's wireless connection off when not in use to avoid accidentally connecting to an evil twin.

Another fast-growing threat to computer security is *phishing*. In a classic phishing scam, a hacker sends you an e-mail that looks as though it has come from a reputable company and attempts to trick you into revealing private data. The e-mail usually asks you to visit a Web site that looks similar to that of the legitimate company. On the site, you are asked to supply your name and password, along with such information as credit card numbers, Social Security numbers, and bank account information. Of course, the site is a bogus site created to steal data. Using those data, identity thieves may establish new credit card accounts and ring up debt or plunder your bank account.

Because it's relatively quick and easy to create a professional-looking Web site, phishing scams are one of the fastest-growing means of stealing identities. Phishing scams increased by 50 percent from 2003 to 2004, according to a 2004 study by Gartner Inc., a research and consulting firm in Stamford, Connecticut. Major companies *spoofed* (impersonated) in the scams included America Online, Bank of America, Citibank, and eBay.

The easiest way to combat phishing, of course, is to refuse to get suckered into providing information to fake Web sites. Companies concerned about computer security never e-mail their customers asking them to visit sites requesting sensitive data. If you receive an e-mail from a company you've done business with but are unsure of the e-mail's authenticity, don't click on any of its links and don't provide any personal information. Instead, go to that company's Web site independently, using your browser's address bar. Log in to your account on the site to check for any real problems with your account.

A type of hacking becoming more common in early 2005 was *pharming*. In pharming, hackers redirect users to an imposter Web page even if users type a Web address directly into their browser. One way to verify that you are connected to a genuine Web site is to make sure that the site uses encryption before you submit any personal information. Some Web browsers use a special symbol, such as a lock, to show that you are connected to a secure page. Also, most secure Web sites have an address that begins with *https* instead of the standard *http*.

The Internet is a valuable resource. If you are careful about which e-mail attachments you open, which programs you download, and which links you follow, and if you maintain updated virus-protection software, you should be able to surf safely.

■ Rachel Konrad

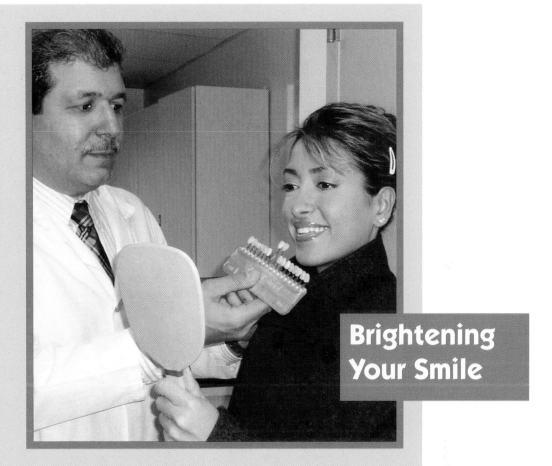

Brightening Your Smile

Our smile is often one of the first things other people notice about us. Many people believe that having dazzling teeth will improve their chances at everything from landing that big job to attracting the attention of a potential love interest.

A desire for a whiter, brighter smile led people in the United States to spend about $2.3 billion on tooth-whitening products and services in 2003 alone (the last year for which data are available). Tooth-whitening products and services ranked as the second fastest growing area of U.S. dental practices—after restoring teeth with natural-colored fillings—according to a 2003 survey by the Chicago-based American Dental Association (ADA). The same survey found that tooth whitening was the most request-

ed procedure by people between ages 40 and 60. In 2004, the American Academy of Pediatric Dentistry reported an increase in whitening procedures for children and adolescents.

Tooth-whitening products work on both *enamel* and *dentin*. Enamel is the hard, white covering on teeth that enables a tooth to withstand the pressure created by chewing. Beneath the enamel lies the dentin, a hard, yellow substance that makes up the bulk of a tooth.

Over time, particles from the food we eat and the beverages we drink can work their way into the enamel and dentin, causing visible stains. For example, such drinks as coffee, tea, and red wine contain substances that can darken enamel and dentin, as do smokeless (chewing) tobacco,

A doctor shows a patient the difference between her newly whitened teeth and the color of her teeth before treatment with an in-office whitening procedure.

Hard parts

A layer of *enamel,* the hardest tissue in the body, forms the outermost covering of a tooth. Another type of tissue called *dentin* makes up most of the rest of the tooth. Some beverages, foods, tobacco products, and antibiotics can stain enamel and dentin.

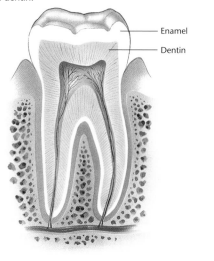

Enamel

Dentin

cigarettes, and other tobacco products. Particles can also cause some of the enamel to wear away, allowing the dentin to show through. In addition, dentin can become stained from *antibiotics* (drugs used to fight disease-causing bacteria), especially tetracycline.

An interest in white teeth is not a modern phenomenon. Egyptians from as long ago as 5000 B.C. made a toothpowder of ox hoofs' ashes, myrrh, eggshells, and pumice. In 2003, researchers from the National Library in Vienna, Austria, found a recipe on a piece of papyrus for a toothpaste made of rock salt, mint, pepper, and dried iris flowers used by ancient Egyptians in about the A.D. 300's. Other ancient peoples, including the Greeks and Romans, used abrasives, such as crushed bones and oyster shells, to clean their teeth. *Dentrifice* (tooth powder) made from such abrasives as brick dust and crushed china could be purchased from doctors, dentists, and chemists in the 1700's in Great Britain (now the United Kingdom). The first commercial

toothpaste was introduced in 1873 by New York City-based Colgate & Company, now Colgate-Palmolive Limited of the United Kingdom.

In 2005, people seeking a whiter smile—beyond that resulting from brushing teeth with regular toothpaste—had three main options: products applied in a dentist's office by a professional; products dispensed by a dentist for use in the home; and products for home use available at a wide variety of retail outlets. Professionally applied or dispensed products as well as many home-use whitening products contain the same basic ingredient—peroxide. This chemical lifts stained molecules out of teeth. Most tooth-whitening products, especially those intended for home use, contain relatively low levels of peroxide.

ADA studies have confirmed the safety and effectiveness of peroxide. Tooth-whitening procedures may cause minor side effects, however. For example, they may temporarily increase teeth's sensitivity to hot and cold as well as irritate the gums and other soft tissue in the mouth. Also, patients can damage tooth enamel and irritate gum tissue if they fail to use whitening systems as directed.

Dentists recommend that patients who are thinking of having their teeth whitened have a dental checkup beforehand. The dentist will clean the teeth, fill cavities, and perform other work needed to get teeth as healthy as possible.

Dentists also recommend patients begin their treatment with realistic expectations of how their teeth will look after treatment. Whiteners remove stains, but the color left behind is the original color of the tooth. As a result, people who have naturally whiter teeth will see better results.

Tooth-whitening products have almost no effect on decayed or extremely discolored teeth. In addition, whiteners will not lighten the white flecks or patches that may result from taking in high levels of fluoride, a chemical added to drinking water to help teeth resist decay. But because whiteners lighten the teeth, the flecks become less noticeable. In addition, whiteners will not brighten fillings, crowns, and other dental work. Finally, tooth whiteners are likely to have a more dramatic effect on acquired stains (like those from tobacco or coffee) than permanent stains (like those from antibiotics).

An in-office bleaching treatment begins with the dentist placing a rubber *dam* (protective barrier) or protective gel over the gums and other soft tissues to protect them from becoming irritated during the procedure. The dentist or dental assistant then applies a solution containing from 15 to 35 percent peroxide to the teeth. To speed up the bleaching process, he or she may apply heat—sometimes from a laser—to the teeth. A single in-office treatment, which generally lasts from 40 to 60 minutes, costs from $300 to $1,000. Dentists may recommend more than one treatment, depending on the condition of the patient's teeth.

Take-home tooth-whitening systems are products that dentists provide to patients for home use. These systems use concentrations of peroxide that are usually from 10 to 20 percent lower than professionally applied products.

The dentist first creates molds of the patient's teeth, then uses the molds to make soft mouth trays that fit snugly against the teeth. At home, patients place a small amount of peroxide solution in the trays and then fit them against their teeth. The trays should be worn for at least two hours daily for two to four weeks, depending on the dentist's instructions. They can also be worn at night, while sleeping. Take-home treatments usually cost less than in-office treatments, though they are still in the $300 to $1,000 range.

Although professional products tend to work faster and better than over-the-counter (OTC) products, you do not need a dentist to get whiter teeth. Like professionally applied or dispensed whitening products, most OTC products use peroxide-based bleaching solutions, though concentrations are lower. In general, OTC whiteners cost much less than in-office or dentist-supplied systems—from $1 for gum to $30 for whitening kits.

At-home versions of dentist-supplied trays are one OTC option. Instead of using trays custom-fitted by a dentist, the consumer soaks the plastic mouthguards in boiling water and then bites down to form an impression. Although these trays hold the peroxide against the teeth longer than other OTC products, they leak more often than the dentist-dispensed ver-

Whitening ways

Various products containing peroxide, a bleaching agent, can be used to whiten teeth. These include liquids applied directly to the teeth, solutions in trays custom-fitted to the teeth, and strips worn against the teeth.

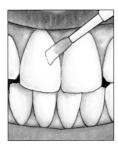

Liquid whitener

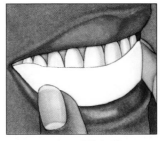

Mouthguard filled with whitening solution

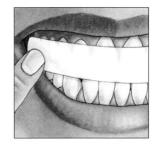

Whitening strip

Kinds of tooth whiteners

Type	Time	Whitening agent	Approximate cost
Dentist-supplied products			
In-office treatment	40 to 60 minutes	15 to 35 percent peroxide	$300 to $1,000
Take-home bleaching kits	2 or more hours daily for 2 to 4 weeks	5 to 25 percent peroxide	$300 to $1,000
Whitening strips	30 minutes twice daily for 2 weeks	14 percent peroxide	$45 to $100
Over-the-counter products			
Mouthguards	20 to 30 minutes twice daily for 1 week	peroxide solution	$30
Whitening strips	30 minutes twice daily for 2 weeks	6 to 10 percent peroxide	$20 to $30
Paint-on products	varies	peroxide solution polishing	$10 to $15
Whitening toothpastes	2 minutes twice daily	mild abrasives and agents; may contain peroxide	$1 to $10
Whitening gums	2 pieces after eating and drinking for 4 weeks	chemicals intended to remove surface stains	$1

Critically reviewed by Paul Schoenbeck, D.M.D. Dr. Schoenbeck is a member of the American Academy of Cosmetic Dentistry, the American Dental Association, the American Association of Hospital Dentists, and the Androscoggin Valley (N.H.) Hospital medical staff.

sions, which fit teeth more precisely. Three or four kits may be necessary to achieve maximum results, however, raising the total cost of treatment to as much as $175.

Tooth-whitening strips are a second OTC option. (Strips with higher concentrations of peroxide, costing from $45 to $100, are also available through dentists.) To use these products, consumers place an adhesive strip over the teeth and leave it in place for about 30 minutes. Strips, which are normally used twice a day, leave teeth slightly whiter.

Paint-on products containing peroxide are also available over the counter. They are applied with a pen or brush.

Whitening toothpastes contain special chemicals and polishing agents designed to remove stains; they sometimes also contain peroxide. Manufac-turers recommend that consumers brush their teeth with whitening toothpastes for two minutes twice a day.

Whitening chewing gum is another option for at-home use. Manufacturers recommend chewing two pieces for about 20 minutes four times a day to lighten teeth.

The effects of tooth-whitening procedures last from six months to three years, depending on diet, habits such as smoking, and dental care. Dentists recommend that patients avoid beverages and foods that may stain teeth, such as coffee, tea, and blueberries, to maximize their investment in a whiter smile.

Perhaps the most effective means of keeping those pearly whites pearly is to follow your dentist's advice: Brush your teeth twice a day, floss after meals, and visit the dentist regularly.
■ Dan Blunk

The Power of Tea

since the early 1990's, both in the United States and worldwide. Tea is the second most widely consumed beverage in the world—after water. According to the Tea Council of the USA, Incorporated, Americans in 2004 drank at least 8.5 billion liters (2.25 billion gallons) of tea and spent $5.5 billion on the beverage. Grocery stores boast shelves filled with teas, specialty tea shops have sprung up around the United States, and online tea merchants are ready to ship gourmet teas at the click of a button.

According to legend, the Chinese Emperor Shen Nong was boiling some drinking water in 2737 B.C., when the leaves of a nearby plant fell into his pot. He drank the resulting brew and supposedly became the first to experience the pleasant taste and stimulant effect of tea.

For centuries, people who believe that tea possesses healing qualities have used it in folk medicines. Many modern scientific studies suggest that certain kinds of tea may play a role in preventing and controlling cancer, reducing the risk of heart and blood vessel disease, preventing dental cavities, and more.

Health experts caution that much research on tea's benefits still needs to be done. Most studies on the effects of tea have not been performed under controlled conditions. Instead, scientists have drawn conclusions from trends they have observed. According to the National Cancer Institute (NCI), such factors as diet and environment could contribute to the conclusions drawn by tea researchers.

Partly because of the increased interest in tea's potential health benefits, sales of tea have increased steadily

True tea comes from the tea plant, *Camellia sinensis,* an evergreen plant that thrives in warm, wet weather. So-called *herbal teas,* which come from a variety of plants, are more correctly called *infusions,* as they do not contain *C. sinensis.*

The four main types of tea—black, oolong, green, and white—all come from *C. sinensis.* Processing helps determine tea's taste, color, and other characteristics.

At least 95 percent of the tea consumed in the United States is black tea. Black tea is made by first *withering* fresh tea leaves—that is, blowing air over the leaves to remove excess moisture. Then the leaves are crushed under rollers or sliced into pieces. Rolling releases *enzymes* (proteins) that help give tea its taste. The enzymes react with oxygen in the air in a process called *oxidation.* The leaves are spread out until oxidation is complete, which can take from one to five hours. The leaves are then *fired,* placed in large hot pans or a large dryer. During firing, the leaves turn black.

Oolong tea is created when the tea leaves are only partially oxidized before firing. Green tea is made by firing the leaves immediately after they are picked, which destroys the enzymes that allow oxidation, and then drying the leaves. Green tea retains its color because it is not oxidized. White tea is made of only the developing leaves of the tea plant, which are covered in fine white hairlike parts. The young buds are steamed and then dried immediately, so that no oxidation occurs.

Scientists' research into the health benefits of tea have focused mainly on *antioxidants,* molecules that neutralize *oxidants.* Oxidants, also called *free radicals,* are molecules produced when the body burns oxygen for energy. When this happens, oxidants lose *electrons* (negatively charged particles), becoming unstable. They then "steal" electrons from other molecules. This process causes damage to cell proteins and genetic material. The damaged cells may render people vulnerable to cancer, heart disease, and other chronic diseases. Free radicals may also play a role in the aging process.

Antioxidants protect cells by giving an electron to the oxidant molecules, neutralizing them. As much as 40 percent of a dried tea leaf may consist of these antioxidants.

Tea contains natural plant antioxidants called *polyphenols,* which, according to the NCI, may prevent cell damage and reduce inflammation. Green tea is especially rich in polyphenols called *catechins.* One catechin, called epigallocatechin-3-gallate (EGCG), makes up 40 percent of the total polyphenol content of green tea extract (GTE). According to the American Institute for Cancer Research, a 235-milliliter (8-ounce) cup of green tea may contain up to 300 milligrams of EGCG. Green tea may contain higher levels of polyphenols because it undergoes less processing than black or oolong teas. Oxidation transforms most of the catechins to color pigments. White tea appears to be even higher in polyphenols and other antioxidants. However, some researchers believe that black and oolong teas contain other antioxidants similar to EGCG. In addition, some evidence suggests that the body may be able to break down the larger catechin molecules in black tea more easily than the catechins in green and white tea.

Researchers suggest drinking tea throughout the day—rather than many cups at once—to keep catechins in the bloodstream. Blood levels of catechins start to drop about five hours after being ingested, according to a 2001 study by researchers at the U.S. Department of Agriculture's (USDA) Agricultural Research Service and a number of universities. The researchers also found that study participants absorbed less than 2 percent of the catechins in the tea they drank. Bottled ready-to-drink teas and instant teas have fewer polyphenols, or none at all, according to a 1998 study by the USDA's Human Nutrition Research Center on Aging at Tufts University in Boston. This decrease occurs because these teas are generally stored longer and undergo more processing than freshly steeped tea made from tea leaves.

A growing body of research suggests that the polyphenols in tea may play a role in reducing the risk of developing cancer and in slowing the growth of cancer. EGCG, for example, may prevent *dioxin,* a widespread contaminant that may pose serious human health threats, from attaching to cells.

The NCI cautions that most studies of tea's antioxidant effects on cancer have been conducted using test-tube experimentation or laboratory animals. Studies in human beings have reported contradictory results.

In February 2005, researchers at the Jonsson Cancer Center at the University of California at Los Angeles reported that GTE (which is available at health food stores) interrupts a process crucial to bladder cancer's ability to spread to other areas of the body. In the lab, the researchers demonstrated that GTE made cancer cells mature more quickly and bind together closely. Both of these processes slowed the movement of the cancer cells. The researchers believe GTE may also inhibit the growth of other types of cancer as well.

Several clinical studies have suggested that drinking black tea may reduce "bad" cholesterol levels and other cardiovascular disease risk factors. Drinking tea may also increase the survival rate of people who have suffered a heart attack. A 2002 study by researchers from Harvard University in Cambridge, Massachusetts, followed 1,900 people who had suffered one heart attack. The researchers found that people who routinely drank more than 14 cups of tea per week were 44-percent less likely to die during the four years following their attack than those who drank fewer than 14 cups per week.

Some research suggests that drinking tea may stimulate the immune system, helping to ward off certain infectious diseases. A 2004 study conducted by researchers at Pace University in New York City suggested that white tea may help to destroy bacteria that cause *Staphylococcus* and *Streptococcus* infections.

Several studies have shown that drinking tea may also help to reduce the chance of tooth decay and bad breath. For example, a 2001 study by researchers at the College of Dentistry at the University of Illinois at Chicago showed that black tea suppresses or kills harmful bacteria that cause cavities and gum disease.

Tea may also produce undesired effects, however. In 2005, researchers from the University of Mississippi's National Center for Natural Products Research found that extremely high

How antioxidants work

Antioxidants are chemical compounds that prevent certain types of cell damage. They block the effects of *oxidation,* a chemical reaction in which a substance loses charged particles called *electrons.* Antioxidants stabilize *free radicals,* unstable molecules produced by oxidation, by giving them an electron. Free radicals may be involved in the aging process and a number of diseases.

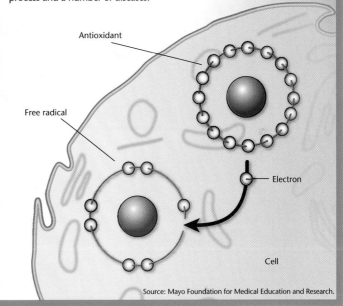

Antioxidant

Free radical

Electron

Cell

Source: Mayo Foundation for Medical Education and Research.

doses of GTE—which may contain the equivalent of hundreds of cups of tea—may stimulate, rather than inhibit, the development of tumors.

Tea plants absorb minerals and chemicals, including fluoride, from the soils where they grow. In a 2005 study, researchers from the Washington University School of Medicine in St. Louis, Missouri, discovered high levels of fluoride in a variety of brands of instant tea. Instant teas are made in factories using local water, which may be naturally high in fluoride. Taking in excess fluoride may make bones and teeth dry and brittle.

Additionally, the polyphenols in tea can interfere with the body's ability to absorb iron from plant foods. However, this effect seems to occur only when tea is consumed at the same time as food. Studies have shown that drinking tea between

Kinds of teas

Variety	Part of plant used	Process	How to steep*
Black	leaves	oxidized, fired	use boiling water steep for 3-5 minutes
Oolong	leaves	partially oxidized, fired	use boiling water steep for 3-5 minutes
Green	leaves	fired	boil water, let cool for 10 minutes, steep for 1
White	developing leaves	steamed, dried	boil water, let cool for 10 minutes, steep for 1

*These are suggestions. Altering the steeping time will change the flavor of the tea. (Longer steep times yield stronger tea.)
Source: Tea Association of the U.S.A., Inc.

meals, rather than with meals, does not inhibit iron absorption. Adding lemon—specifically, vitamin C—to a cup of tea can also help reduce this effect. This is because vitamin C reacts with the chemicals in tea that inhibit iron absorption.

All types of tea contain *caffeine,* a mild stimulant. Green and white teas, which undergo the least amount of processing, have the lowest levels of caffeine, approximately 25 milligrams per cup. (Americans consume an average of about 230 milligrams of caffeine a day.) Oolong tea has from 25 to 35 milligrams, and black tea has roughly 40 milligrams per cup. In comparison, coffee has an average of 85 milligrams of caffeine per cup.

You can reduce the caffeine in your tea while retaining most of the tea's polyphenols. About 85 percent of catechins are released within the first five minutes of brewing. In contrast, caffeine dissolves quickly in hot water. Pour boiling water over a teabag, wait 20 to 40 seconds, then discard the water. Most of the caffeine will be discarded with this first cup. Pour a second cup of hot water over the tea bag and allow it to steep for five minutes.

Although some tea studies have been contradictory or inconclusive, a growing body of research supports the idea that tea drinking offers a multitude of health benefits. Further research may provide more precise conclusions. One thing is certain—this 5,000-year-old drink shows no sign of losing its popularity. ■ Renée Despres

SCIENCE NEWS UPDATE

Contributors report on the year's most significant developments in their respective fields. The articles in this section are arranged alphabetically.

AGRICULTURE

The discovery of the first known case of highly destructive soybean rust in the United States was reported by the U.S. Department of Agriculture (USDA) on Nov. 10, 2004. Ray Schneider, a plant pathologist at Louisiana State University in Baton Rouge, discovered the rust at one of the school's research farms.

Soybean rust is a fungal disease that can destroy up to 80 percent of a field's crop. Until Schneider's discovery, the United States had been the only soybean-producing country to escape infection by the rust. The USDA estimates that the disease could cost U.S. farmers up to $2 billion annually in crop damage and control costs. The use of certain fungicide sprays could reduce this cost, however.

One possible explanation for Schneider's discovery is that the rust blew into Louisiana from South America when winds from Hurricane Ivan reached the U.S. Gulf Coast on Sept. 16, 2004. Wind-borne rust spores can travel hundreds of kilometers per day when temperatures range between 16 °C (60 °F) and 27 °C (80 °F).

Soybean rust infects a variety of plants, including peas, beans, and most other *legumes* (plants with seed pods). The fungus is especially harmful to soybeans. However, soybeans grown in fields infected with soybean rust are safe to eat. There are two known species of soybean rust fungus: *Phakopsora pachyrhizi* (Asian species) and *Phakopsora meibomiae* (New World species). Neither species is limited to Asia or the New World. The Asian species, which was found in Louisiana, is more harmful to soybeans.

Soybean rust infects all parts of the soybean plant but typically is found on the leaves. On the surface, rust appears as reddish-tan bumps called *lesions.* The spores begin to multiply, spreading inside the leaf tissue. After several days, the rust lesions erupt and spew the spores into the air. The wind carries the spores into new fields, infecting more plants. Soybean rust spores die in freezing weather, though they have reportedly survived cold snaps when temperatures dropped to 0 °C (32 °F). Scientists expect warm southerly winds will blow the disease north each year.

New genes mean resistant greens. A new process involving *genetic engineering* has enabled agricultural scientists to produce plants resistant to glyphosate, a common herbicide, according to a report published in January 2005. Researchers led by plant scientist Daniel L. Siehl of Verdia, Inc., a biotechnology company based in Redwood City, California, announced they had modified tobacco and maize to resist the herbicide. As a result, the genetically engineered plants remain unaffected when a field is sprayed with glyphosate.

Genetic engineering involves adding, changing, or removing a plant's *genes* (units of heredity) to alter specific traits. Scientists use genetic engineering to make some crops resistant to destructive insects or to herbicides used to control weeds. The challenge is to find a gene that gives plants a trait strong enough to be useful.

Siehl's study developed from research published in 2004 by a research team headed by plant scientist Linda Castle, also of Verdia. Castle's team discovered a process for strengthening a gene that can make plants resistant to glyphosate.

Verdia's process is called *DNA shuffling.* This process changes the combination of *DNA* molecules in genes, which alters their properties. DNA (deoxyribonucleic acid) is the molecule that directs development in all living things.

The DNA shuffling process begins when scientists discover a gene that gives plants a low level of resistance to a pest or chemical but is not strong enough to help farmers. Castle reported that scientists from Pioneer Hi-Bred International of Des Moines, Iowa, had found a bacterial gene that *encoded for* (carried the instructions for) a protein that could inactivate glyphosate. However, the encoded protein needed to be about 5,000 times stronger to work effectively in plants. Castle and her team discovered that the same gene taken from several bacteria had small differences in the DNA chain. By mixing and matching the slightly different sequences, scientists created thousands of new genes.

Each time the scientists mixed and matched the DNA chains in the set of similar genes, a few of the new genes gave plants a stronger resistance to glyphosate. Then the scientists mixed and matched the genes with a higher resistance to glyphosate again to create even stronger genes. After shuffling the DNA 11 times, the genes' level of glyphosate resistance was 10,000 times as strong.

Ideal weather makes record crops. Unusually beneficial weather helped farmers in Illinois and other parts of the central United

States produce record yields of corn, soybeans, grain sorghum, and alfalfa during the 2004 growing season. This conclusion, reported by the Midwestern Regional Climate Center, emerged from a study by Stanley A. Changnon, chief emeritus of the Illinois State Water Survey, and David Changnon, a geography professor at Northern Illinois University in DeKalb.

In 2004, Illinois cornfields produced an average of 445 bushels per hectare (180 bushels per acre), beating the record 2003 crop by 40 bushels per hectare (16 bushels per acre). Illinois soybeans yielded an average of 125 bushels per hectare (50 bushels per acre), 12.4 bushels per hectare (5 bushels per acre) more than the record set in 1994. In the United States, the national average corn yield was 395 bushels per hectare (160 bushels per acre) in 2004—44 bushels per acre (18 bushels per acre) more than the record set in 2003.

For their study, the Changnons analyzed weather patterns and crop yields in the central United States since 1888. They found that not only were yields in 2004 unusually good but also the weather that helped produce them was extremely rare. The study showed that 2004 had an unusually high number of clear, sunny days, which increase crop *photosynthesis* (the process of converting the sun's energy into food). Unlike other years with abundant sunny weather, however, temperatures stayed below average in June, July, and August. Plants need warm weather to grow, but hot weather can damage plants and make them stop growing to conserve moisture.

The summer of 2004 also benefited from

LOCUST SWARMS

Children run through a swarm of locusts in Dakar, Senegal, on Sept. 1, 2004, during Africa's worst locust invasion since 1989. The United Nations Food and Agriculture Organization estimated that as many as 500,000 locusts per hectare (200,000 per acre) infested much of northern Africa and the Middle East in late 2004, causing at least $100-million in damage.

AGRICULTURE continued

adequate rainfall throughout the season, another unusual feature. The Changnons concluded that 2004's beneficial crop-growing weather resulted mainly from 20 cold fronts sweeping into the Midwest from Canada. The fronts brought clear days with moderate temperatures.

Nutrition comes in different colors. A series of new studies in 2004 about the nutritional content of carrots may have farmers growing a rainbow of carrots in the near future. Carrots have a natural range of colors—from light yellow to dark purple—though most carrots sold in grocery stores are orange. Orange carrots are high in beta-carotene, which people need to make vitamin A.

In July 2004, plant geneticist Philipp Simon of the USDA's Agricultural Research Service and Sherry Tanumihardjo, assistant professor of nutritional sciences at the University of Wisconsin-Madison, reported that yellow carrots are rich in *lutein,* a pigment present in human retinas. Several studies have suggested that eating a diet high in lutein may decrease the risk of developing *macular degeneration,* a serious disorder of the retina that can result in loss of vision. Simon and Tanumihardjo measured lutein levels in the blood of people who obtained lutein from yellow carrots or got an equal amount of the nutrient from vitamin supplements. The scientists concluded that lutein from yellow carrots is 65 percent as *bioavailable* (useful to the body) as it is from the vitamin supplement.

Earlier in 2004, Simon and Tanumihardjo reported that the color pigment in red carrots contains *lycopene.* Lycopene is a nutrient that may help prevent heart disease and some types of cancer. Tomatoes also are a good source of lycopene. The scientists discovered that the lycopene in red carrots is 40 percent as bioavailable as the lycopene in tomatoes. Thus,

people who don't like tomatoes could substitute red carrots as a source of lycopene.

The researchers planned to conduct taste tests of the various colors of carrots. If consumers like the taste and look of multicolored carrots, farmers may begin to diversify the colors of their carrot crop. ■ Andrew Burchett

COLORFUL CARROTS

Rainbow-colored carrots and other foods rich in pigments called *flavonoids* may help reduce the risk of chronic illness, according to a report published in November 2004 by an international team of researchers. Flavonoids are *antioxidants,* chemical compounds that prevent damage to human cells. The study—the most recent confirming the benefits of flavonoids—reported that people who eat a variety of flavonoid-rich fruits and vegetables are less likely to develop Alzheimer's disease, heart disease, and other chronic illnesses.

ANTHROPOLOGY

The degree to which modern human beings differ from our prehistoric ancestors was the focus of several significant studies in 2004. The studies support the theory that modern people, *Homo sapiens sapiens,* differ from primitive human beings and our closest prehuman ancestors, collectively known as *hominids,* to a greater degree than these various species differ from one another. In particular, the studies, along with other research, support the belief that language and culture are unique to modern human beings.

A study charting the growth and development of wild chimpanzees suggests that the social life of *Homo erectus* may have resembled that of modern apes more closely than that of modern human beings. *H. erectus* was a species of primitive human beings who lived from about 1,900,000 to 400,000 years ago. Most anthropologists believe that the rates at which human beings and apes mature and their lifespan are closely related to differences in their intelligence as well as the complexity of their social lives.

The age at which chimpanzees get their first molar was the subject of a study by anthropologists Adrienne Zihlman and Debra Bolter of the University of California in Santa Cruz and primatologist Christophe Boesch of the Max Planck Institute for Evolutionary Anthropology in Leipzig, Germany. Their findings were published in the July 20, 2004, issue of the *Proceedings of the National Academy of Sciences of the United States of America* (PNAS). Human children get their first molars at about age 6. Zihlman, Bolter and Boesch found that wild chimps get their first molars at about age 4, about one-third faster than modern people. Most anthropologists believe that human beings need more time to mature because human social life is far more complex than that of chimps.

In 2001, anthropologist Christopher Dean and colleagues at University College in London found that *H. erectus* children got their first molars at about age 4. At that time, the only chimpanzee data available for comparison were those from captive chimps, who get their first molars between the ages of 3 and 3½. As a result, Dean and his colleagues had concluded that the growth rate of *H. erectus* fell between that of chimps and modern people. The new data on wild chimps provided by Zihlman and her colleagues show that, in fact, chimps and *H. erectus* matured at an almost identical rate. This finding

suggests that *H. erectus's* social life may have been more like that of apes than most anthropologists had assumed.

In another study, a team of researchers found that *H. erectus* matured considerably faster than modern people. Anthropologist Hélène Coqueugniot of the Université Bordeaux in Talence, France, and collaborators from France, Germany, and Indonesia studied the most complete skull of a *H. erectus* child ever found. Their results were published in the Sept. 16, 2004, issue of *Nature.* The fossil, called the Mojokerto skull, was discovered in 1936 on the Indonesian island of Java. Coqueugniot and her colleagues wanted to know how fast the brain of *H. erectus* grew compared with those of apes and modern people, but they first had to know how long ago the child died and how old the child was when death occurred.

Determining how long ago the Mojokerto child died was difficult because the fossil was removed from the ground long before the invention of modern dating techniques. In 1994, a team of archaeologists and physicists led by Carl Swisher of the Institute of Human Origins in Berkeley, California, had calculated that the Mojokerto child had died about 1.8 million years ago, based on an analysis of soil that matched bits of dirt that were stuck to the skull. After reviewing Swisher's work, Coqueugniot and her team accepted his estimate of 1.8 million years.

The scientists' next task was to determine how old the child was when he or she died. Because no teeth were found with the fossil, the scientists used high-resolution *computed tomography* (CT) scans to examine features in the skull that indicate age. (A CT scan is a kind of X-ray system.) Among these age-related features were the tympanic plate and the subarcuate fossa, both of which help make up the bony structure that contains the inner ear, and the bregmatic area on the top of the skull, where the frontal bone and the left and right parietal bones come together. For example, infants have a *fontanelle* (soft spot) at the bregmatic area. By comparing the tympanic plate, the subarcuate fossa, and the bregmatic area of the Mojokerto child with those of 159 modern human infants and 201 infant chimpanzees, the scientists concluded that the Mojokerto child was most likely between 6 and 18 months old when he or she died.

Having determined the geological and

ANTHROPOLOGY continued

chronological ages of the Mojokerto child, Coqueugniot and her colleagues turned to their central question: How fast did the brain of *H. erectus* grow? The brain of a newborn chimpanzee is about 40 percent as large as an adult chimp brain. By the time the chimp is 1 year old, its brain has grown to 80 percent of its adult size. Among newborn human beings, however, the brain is only 25 percent of its adult size. The brain reaches 50 percent of its adult size by the age of 1 and 95 percent of adult size by the age of 10. Compared with chimps, the human brain is relatively smaller at birth but grows much faster during the first year of life. This phenomenon—a small brain at birth but a rapid period of brain growth during the first year—is called *secondary altriciality*. (If the newborn human brain were 40 percent of its adult size at birth, like that of a chimp, the infant's head would be too large to pass through the birth canal.)

Using this comparative data for chimps and modern human beings, the researchers then compared the brain size of the Mojokerto child with the brain size of an adult *H. erectus.* The scientists measured the brain sizes of 13 adult *H. erectus* skulls from individuals who lived from 2 million to 800,000 years ago. The scientists then used CT scans of the Mojokerto fossil to estimate the size of its brain. They concluded that at age 6 to 18 months, the Mojokerto child's brain had grown from 72 percent to 84 percent the size of an adult brain. Clearly, the brain of *H. erectus* grew about as rapidly as that of an ape and more rapidly than that of modern people. Thus, it appears that secondary altriciality appeared late in human development, possibly at the same time as the appearance of modern human beings.

Tooth research. Even early modern people lived much longer than their premodern ancestors, according to a study led by anthropologists Rachel Caspari of the University of Michigan in Ann Arbor and Sang-Hee Lee of the University of California, Riverside. Caspari and Lee published their results in the July 27, 2004, issue of PNAS. The team studied a large sample of teeth and jaws from hominids that lived from approximately 2 million years ago to 50,000 years ago. By examining how much the tooth surfaces had worn down over a lifetime of chewing, the scientists were able to sort the teeth into those from younger adults and older adults. They found that among all of the premodern hominids, younger adults outnumbered older adults. They interpret-

ed these findings as suggesting that few individuals lived to be older than 35 or 40. Among all early modern people, however, older adults outnumbered younger adults, the same pattern found among people today. Anthropologists suspect that, among early modern people, those who lived long enough to pass on their group's wisdom and tradition and to help their children raise their grandchildren had a better chance of survival.

Also in 2004, anthropologists Fernando V. Ramirez Rozzi of the Dyamique de l'Evolution Humaine in Paris, and José Maria Bermudez de Castro of the Museo Nacional de Ciencias Naturales in Madrid, Spain, compared the growth rate of the tooth *crowns* from different hominid species. The crown is the section of a tooth covered with *enamel* (the outermost tissue) that lies above the gum line. Faint lines in the tooth enamel of incisors and canines, called *perikymata,* form roughly every nine days while the tooth is growing. By counting the lines, scientists can tell how long it took the tooth to grow. By measuring the amount of enamel between each pair of lines, they can tell how fast the enamel formed. For example, if a pair of lines lie close together, not much enamel formed during that nine-day period.

Ramirez Rozzi and Bermudez de Castro collected data on 246 teeth, including 146 teeth from the extinct hominid species *H. antecessor, H. heidelbergensis,* and *H. neanderthalensis*, and 100 teeth from prehistoric modern human beings. The scientists found that the prehistoric modern people grew up at exactly the same rate as people living today, but that *H. antecessor* and *H. heidelbergensis* grew up considerably more quickly. This finding supports Dean's findings about the social life of *H. erectus* and implies that the cultures of premodern hominids did not include the use of language and symbols.

The scientists were also surprised to discover that Neandertals grew up fastest of all hominid species studied—even faster than their more ancient ancestors. Neandertals became adults by age 15 and rarely lived past 35. The scientists said that this finding supported the idea that the Neandertals were a separate species of hominid not directly related to modern human beings.

All these studies indicate that modern people differ significantly from our premodern ancestors. Although some anthropologists think that even *H. erectus* might have possessed language, others argue that the apelike pattern of growth and development followed by *H. erectus* makes that extremely unlikely. These anthropologists also contend that the evidence indicating that Neandertals grew up more quickly than even earlier hominids effectively removes Neandertals from the ancestry of modern people. More and more, it seems that the appearance of modern human beings was one of the most significant events in the evolution of humanity.

Born to run. A 2004 report suggests that running, not walking, explains several modifications to the frame of our hominid ancestors. Hominids began walking upright several million years ago, and, over time, their skulls, backs, hips, knees, and feet changed so that walking became an energy-efficient way to move. With the appearance of our own genus, *Homo,* about 2 million years ago, hominids completely gave up life in the trees and acquired a more human body form. Anthropologists have long associated that change in body form with habitual walking. In 2004, however, biological anthropologists Dennis Bramble of the University of Utah in Salt Lake City and Daniel Lieberman of Harvard University in Cambridge, Massachusetts, suggested that running, not walking, was the reason.

Bramble and Lieberman studied physical evidence that although human beings aren't very fast or energy efficient as sprinters, they are remarkably good endurance runners. Jogging and running marathons are both examples of endurance running. People can trot or jog for long distances as efficiently as horses or hunting dogs. The researchers showed that changes that distinguish the body of early human beings—such as *H. habilis* and *H. erectus* — from that of their prede-

OLDEST MODERN HUMAN REMAINS

The reassessment of the skull (right) and bones (below) of an early *Homo sapiens* specimen known as Omo I has led researchers to conclude that the remains are the oldest human remains known, and much older than previously thought. Omo I was originally unearthed in Ethiopia in 1967, along with another partial skull known as Omo II. The Omo remains were thought to be 130,000 years old. Researchers announced in February 2005 that they had dated layers of sediment above and below the layer from which Omo I was extracted. They found that Omo I was much older than the 104,000-year-old layer above it and dated close to the 196,000-year-old layer beneath it. The researchers estimated that Omo I is about 195,000 years old, which would make the bones the oldest known modern human remains. This new date also suggests that *H. sapiens* lived in Africa 40,000 years earlier than scientists had previously thought.

ANTHROPOLOGY continued

cessor, *Australopithecus,* are little used when walking but esential to endurance running. Among these modifications is the Achilles' tendon.

Human beings are good endurance runners because the ligaments and muscles in the legs and feet act like springs, storing energy and then releasing it as the runner strides forward. This puts the "spring" in a runner's step and greatly reduces the amount of calories needed to maintain the pace. The energy is stored in the arch of the foot, in short leg muscles with long, elastic tendons, and in the muscles of the thighs and buttocks. Human beings have long, stout heel bones and long, strong Achilles' tendons to transfer the stored energy to the feet. Human beings also have a long neck and waist, which allows the torso to swivel back and forth to balance the swing of the legs. Our legs are unusually long, letting us cover more ground with each stride. All of these modifications and more are of comparatively little value when walking, but endurance running would be impossible without them.

Bramble and Lieberman concluded that the ability to jog long distances over the African savanna set early *Homo* apart from its australopithecine ancestors. The most likely reason for the development of this ability is that jogging enabled them to cover more ground in search of food. It may also have allowed *Homo* to catch small mammals, chasing them until they dropped from exhaustion. As Bramble and Lieberman observed, it seems that *Homo* was born to run.

He's a hominid after all. The discovery of new fossils and cranial reconstructions made with state-of-the-art computer software further support the theory that a controversial skull discovered in Chad in 2001 is a hominid and not an ape, as some anthropologists have argued. Anthropologist Michel Brunet of the Université de Poitiers in France announced the discovery of the oldest known hominid, 7-million-year-old *Sahelanthropus tchadensis,* by the Mission Paléoanthropologique Franco-Tchadienne, in 2001. Since then, Brunet's team has found more *S. tchadensis* fossils, including two lower jaw fragments, each with remains of some of the teeth, and the crown of a lower premolar. The new finds were reported in the April 7, 2005, issue of *Nature.* These additional fossils supported Brunet's claim that *S. tchadensis*—Toumaï, as he is called—really was a hominid and not an ancestor of the great apes.

The upper and lower canine teeth of apes shear past each other as the mouth opens and closes. A canine tooth in one of the new fossils shows that this was not the case with *S. tchadensis.* The enamel on the fossil teeth is thicker than it is on apes' teeth, though still thinner than that in later hominids. In these and other respects, *S. tchadensis* resembles later hominids more than he resembles apes.

CAN YOU HEAR ME NOW?

A computer reconstruction of the ear structures of *Homo heidelbergensis,* a human ancestor that lived more than 350,000 years ago, shows that human speech may have developed much earlier than previously thought. A group of Spanish scientists created the reconstruction from several fossilized *H. heidelbergensis* skulls and determined that their ear structures are similar to those of modern human beings. They interpreted this as evidence that *H. heidelbergensis* had the capacity for humanlike speech.

To make an even stronger case that *S. tchadensis* was a hominid, a team of anthropologists and other specialists led by Christoph Zollikofer of the University of Zurich in Switzerland used a high resolution CT scan of Toumaï's skull to produce a "virtual reconstruction." The fossil skull had been broken and deformed in the ground, but digitizing it let the scientists use known anatomical relationships in the skulls of apes and humans to put the fossil "back together." The reconstructed skull shows that Toumaï resembles later hominids but shares few characteristics with apes. ■ Richard G. Milo

See also **ARCHAEOLOGY.**

Tiny People Amaze Anthropologists

One of the most astonishing announcements in the history of anthropology came in October 2004, when paleoanthropologist Peter Brown of the University of New England in Armidale, Australia, reported the discovery of bones of a new human species that stood only 1 meter (3.3 feet) tall. This human species, which Brown's team named *Homo floresiensis,* may have existed from 90,000 to 13,000 years ago on the small Indonesian island of Flores, according to the scientists. Because anthropologists had long thought that modern human beings—*Homo sapiens sapiens*—have been the only human species on Earth during the past 30,000 years, this announcement came as a great shock to most scientists. Brown's team nicknamed the tiny species "Hobbits," after the little humanlike creatures in *The Lord of the Rings,* a series of novels by J. R. R. Tolkien.

The announcement immediately drew fire from several other anthropologists, including one of Indonesia's most prominent anthropologists, Teuku Jacob of Gajah Mada University in Yogyakarta, Java. These scientists noted that the small size of the creature did not necessarily mean that it was a new species. They said the bones might instead have come from *pathological* (diseased) members of *H. sapiens.*

Brown headed a joint Australian and Indonesian research team. The researchers discovered bones from as many as eight individuals in a limestone cave, named Liang Bua, hidden within the tropical rain forest of Flores. The remains included a single skull, which the scientists identified as belonging to a female—based on the shape of the specimen's *pelvic* (hip) bones. The pelvic and leg bones also indicated that the creature was *bipedal* (walked on two legs). The scientists dated the skull to about 18,000 years ago.

The skull was extremely small for a human species. In fact, it was chimpanzee-sized, with the capacity to hold a brain measuring only 417 cubic centimeters (25.5 cubic inches). By contrast, a modern human brain averages 1,350 cubic centimeters (82.4 cubic inches). The small brain size was especially puzzling because scientists working with Brown's team also found relatively sophisticated stone tools in the same cave as the human bones. These tools included small flakes, finely worked points, and blades of various sizes. Such tools are usually associated only with large-brained *H. sapiens.* However, the scientists believed that the tools were made by the tiny-brained *H. floresiensis.*

Brown speculated that *H. floresiensis* might have evolved from a population of *Homo erectus* that became isolated on Flores, perhaps more than 800,000 years ago. *H. erectus* was a human species that emerged approximately 1.9 million years ago in Africa and later migrated to other areas, including southeast Asia.

According to Brown, the small body and brain size of *H. floresiensis* could have been the result of a natural phenomenon known as *insular dwarfism.* In this process,

SMALL SKULL

A skull from what may be a previously unknown human species (below, left) that existed until about 13,000 years ago appears to be about half the size of a modern human skull. The skull was among a collection of bones named *Homo floresiensis* found on the Indonesian island of Flores. *H. floresiensis,* which stood only about 1 meter (3 feet) tall, apparently existed at the same time as *Homo sapiens sapiens,* the species to which all modern people belong.

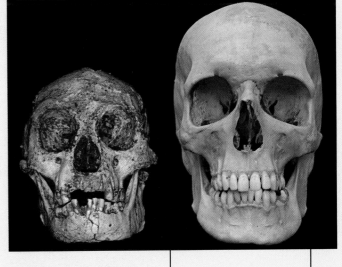

which has been documented in a number of mammal species, animals that become isolated on small islands tend to shrink over many generations. The smaller body size is favored by *natural selection* because of the limited food resources available on small islands. Natural selection is a process by which the organisms best suited to their environment are the ones most likely to leave offspring. Smaller animals require less food and are, therefore, more likely to survive in areas with scarce resources.

This scenario was met with skepticism by a number of scientists, who noted that the brain size of *H. floresiensis* was smaller than would be expected in the case of insular dwarfism. Typically, a dwarfed individual would have a much smaller body but only a slightly smaller brain than a normal-sized individual. These scientists proposed that the skull found by Brown's team might have been from a pygmy human who suffered from a developmental abnormality known as *microcephaly*. This genetic disorder results in a tiny head with an abnormally small skull and brain.

As for the tools, the critics insisted that a creature with a chimp-sized brain would simply be incapable of producing them. Thus, these scientists argued, the tools may have been left in the Flores cave by normal *H. sapiens* who occupied the site after the specimens identified by Brown.

One of the few scientists who gained access to the Flores bones—besides those affiliated with Brown's group—was Teuku Jacob. After examining the remains in late 2004, he argued that the skull represented a pygmy human with microcephaly.

TINY TOOLS

Small stone tools found along with the remains of *Homo floresiensis* suggest that this species may have been capable of advanced thought. Other scientists think the tiny human beings would not have been capable of producing such tools, which may have been left in the cave by later inhabitants.

In March 2005, however, anthropologist Dean Falk of Florida State University in Tallahassee reported that the skull was probably not from an individual with microcephaly. She led a team that produced three-dimensional, computer-generated images of the brain of *H. floresiensis* by examining the skull with *computed tomography* (an X-ray system that can be used to make three-dimensional images). Based on the bumpy impressions on the inside of the skull, Falk concluded that the corresponding areas of the brain were unusually complex for the brain's small size.

Falk found the hobbit's temporal lobe particularly interesting, noting that it is proportionally larger than the temporal lobe of *H. erectus*. In modern human beings, the temporal lobe is the area of the brain that processes speech. In addition, Falk noted that the frontal lobe was surprisingly complex. According to Falk, these results showed that even though the brain of the Flores specimen was small, it was capable of advanced thought processes.

Many anthropologists felt that the best conclusion regarding the Flores finds, as of mid-2005, was to withhold judgment on whether the bones truly represented a new species of human being. These scientists stressed that more specimens—with intact skulls—needed to be found before any firm conclusions were possible. Considering this point of view, it will likely be several years before scientists arrive at a consensus regarding the fossils found on Flores.

■ Alfred J. Smuskiewicz

ARCHAEOLOGY

The discovery of an area of tremendous archaeological potential in a remote area of east-central Utah was revealed in September 2004. Utah state archaeologist Kevin Jones announced that 300 prehistoric sites had been recorded in Range Creek Canyon. These range in function from *cliff dwellings* (homes built in canyon walls or under rocky overhangs) of stone and mud, *granaries* (grain storage bins) made of similar materials, villages of *pit houses* (dwellings dug into the ground) atop high elevations, and a variety of rock art. Remarkably, most of the sites had remained undisturbed since they were abandoned about 750 years ago. The sheer number of found sites is sure to increase, as archaeologists have surveyed only 5 percent of the canyon.

The sites lie in a 1,700-hectare (4,200-acre) ranch in remote, high desert country, characterized by deep, rugged canyons; steep cliffs; and high mesas overlooking Range Creek, a tributary of the Green River. The ranch owner, Waldo Wilcox, was familiar with the sites and worked for more than 50 years to protect them from vandals and artifact hunters. The U.S. Bureau of Land Management purchased the title to the land in 2001 and sold it to the state of Utah in 2004.

The state will fund a long-term plan to study and preserve the area.

Most of the ancient remains are from 800 to 1,000 years old and can be linked to what archaeologists call the *Fremont Culture.* Archaeologists know little about the Fremont Culture, which was concentrated in Utah. It probably consisted of loosely affiliated family groups that shared a way of life based both on agriculture and hunting and gathering. Distinctive artifacts include a form of gray pottery, human figurines made of clay, basketry, sandals made of mountain sheep or deer hide, and a specific style of rock art. At Range Creek, the Fremont people lived in small villages; farmed maize, squash, and beans; and relied heavily on the meat from mountain sheep, deer, and smaller mammals. The villages consisted of pit houses. The floors lay about a meter below the surface. Roofs of timbers rose about 2 meters (6½ feet) above the surface. They were covered with soil and mud for insulation against the cold.

BEAUTIFUL MUMMY

Archaeologists in Egypt unearthed in March 2005 what many believe to be the most beautiful mummy ever discovered . The 2,300-year-old mummy, which is decorated in vivid colors and intricate designs, was discovered in the *necropolis* (cemetery) of King Teti in the Saqqara pyramid complex, 20 kilometers (12 miles) south of Cairo.

ARCHAEOLOGY continued

Some buildings at Range Creek are located about 275 meters (900 feet) above the valley floor and in similarly inaccessible spots. Archaeologists suggest that the location of the buildings indicates that these ancient people felt a need to defend themselves.

Additional evidence supporting this scenario are the many remote granaries, made of red clay and sticks, tucked away in small overhangs and crevices high on the cliff faces. Maize, beans, and squash were stored there, with many small, dry corn cobs remaining today. The thick, sturdy walls of the round, flat-topped granaries kept mice and other rodents away from the stored food. The secretive locations made them difficult to find by outsiders.

Throughout Range Creek Canyon, archaeolo-gists have found rock panels with stunning Fremont art. Much of the art is *pictographic* (rock paintings), painted with red and yellow ocher. Others are *petroglyphs*, designs carved into the cliff faces. Common themes in both types of rock art are large human figures, which archaeologists sometimes call "shamans," with broad-shoul-dered, trapezoidal bodies; head gear that in-cludes horns and feathers; and ornaments that appear to be pendants made of turquoise, shell, and other materials. The art also shows mountain sheep, some with hunters nearby; triangular de-signs; and sticklike depictions of people with their arms outstretched.

Because the Range Creek sites have been so well preserved, they hold great promise for help-ing to unravel the secrets of the Fremont Culture,

TSUNAMI REVEALS ARCHAEOLOGICAL TREASURES

Visitors in southern India examine a monument in the shape of a lion's head that was revealed by a tsunami on Dec. 26, 2004. Receding tsunami waves re-vealed what archaeologists believe to be the remains of an ancient temple complex and a 1,300-year-old port city.

ranging from the details of daily life to the ultimate disappearance of these people. Archaeologists debate whether the Fremont were wiped out by invaders or were absorbed by other people who moved into the region from the west in about 1250.

Ruins revealed by tsunami waves. The tsunami waves that ravaged coastal areas of Asia on Dec. 26, 2004, may also have uncovered a large archaeological site on the southeastern coast of India. Archaeologists have been excavating in the town of Mahabalipuram since 2001. Most of the fieldwork was taking place at an ancient Hindu temple known as the "Shore Temple." Some underwater exploration was also underway, and archaeologists had found a number of large blocks of building stone offshore.

Archaeologist Alok Tripathi of the Archaeological Survey of India reported the new findings in March 2005. As the ocean waters receded from the shoreline before the tsunami waves hit, hundreds of stone blocks were exposed. The incoming sea covered most of the blocks. However, some of the ruins were left exposed, including statues of two lions, one seated and one about to attack; a statue of an elephant; and a series of boulders with carvings of servant girls, animals, and gods.

Mahabalipuram was a major seaport in ancient India, and the modern town has dozens of Hindu temples. The town was spared the massive destruction and death that resulted from the tsunami elsewhere in the region. Some Indian archaeologists have discounted the reports of the offshore "lost city," which have drawn thousands of tourists. These archaeologists contend that they have long known about a 1,300-year-old seaport at the site.

Origins of early agriculture. The earliest evidence of cereal grinding, human consumption of cereal grains, and the emergence of agriculture have been found in Israel, according to an August 2004 report. The findings were made by archaeologists Dolores Piperno of the Smithsonian Tropical Research Institute of Balboa, Panama, and Ehud Weiss of Harvard University in Cambridge, Massachusetts.

A long-term drought that began in 1989 and lowered water levels in the Sea of Galilee exposed the remains of a campsite of hunting and gathering people dating from the Upper Paleolithic (Stone Age), about 23,000 years ago. Lake sediments covered and sealed the campsite in an airtight environment that prevented normal rates of decay. Excavations revealed well-preserved plant remains from ancient cooking pits and food-grinding tools. These had been *charred* (lightly burned), which helped to preserve them.

At the site, named Ohalo II, archaeologists from the United States and Israel found remnants of six small, oval huts originally made of brush, cooking areas, stone tools, polished bone awls, shell beads, and animal bones, all scattered over an area of 2,000 square meters (21,500 square feet). A burial of an adult male, who died at about age 40, was also found within the campsite.

At one of the hut foundations, the excavators discovered a grinding stone, along with grass and cereal seeds. Such perishable items are extremely rare at campsites of this age. *Archaeobotanists* (archaeologists who specialize in the identification of ancient plants) conducted intensive studies of the approximately 90,000 charred plant remains that were retrieved through *flotation* (using water to separate delicate remains from soils). At the same time, *archaeozoologists* (archaeologists specializing in bone identification) identified the remains of mammal, fish, and waterfowl species as well as mollusk shells. Fish was the most common food in the Ohalo II diet, though the people there also ate such mammals as gazelle, fallow deer, wild cattle, and wild boar.

Plant analysis revealed that the people of Ohalo II ate at least 100 types of wild plants. There was no evidence of farming. Archaeologists found 2,600 grains of wild barley and wild wheat and 16,000 grass seeds.

The intensive use of wild grasses, wheat, and barley required a lot of work for the inhabitants of Ohalo II. After the plants were collected, the people had to separate the grass and cereal grains from their husks. The seeds and grains were crushed and powdered on a milling slab and used to make gruel and, perhaps, bread. One of the cooking areas was a stone-lined oven of the type that is usually linked to bread baking.

Since the site was discovered in 1989, archaeologists have established that farming began from 10,000 to 13,000 years ago in the Middle East. However, one still-unanswered question involves the processes through which farming was developed and widely adopted. The researchers believe that the discoveries at Ohalo II reflect the growth in human populations as the Pleistocene Epoch came to an end. People began to rely less on hunting and more on wild grasses and cereals, which became a routine part of the diet. This phenomenon is known as the *Broad Spectrum Revolution,* during which people began to focus

ARCHAEOLOGY continued

more and more on certain plants, including barley and wheat, that were eventually domesticated about 10,000 years ago.

Human sacrifice in ancient Mexico. In December 2004, Saburo Sugiyama, an archaeologist who teaches in Japan and at Arizona State University in Tempe, announced the discovery of a tomb at Teotihuacan's Pyramid of the Moon that seems to support the theory that human sacrifice has a long history in Central America.

Located 50 kilometers (30 miles) northeast of Mexico City, Teotihuacan was built and occupied by unknown people about 2,000 years ago, long before the Aztecs appeared in the region. The Aztecs themselves were puzzled by the pyramids and mounds within the 20 square kilometers (8 square miles) of the city. They honored Teotihuacan as a religious center and referred to it as "the City of the Gods." Sugiyama's excavators exposed a major tomb in the center of the Pryamid, in what was the fifth stage of construction. In all, seven construction stages took place before the Pyramid of the Moon took its final shape, rising to a height of 46 meters (151 feet).

Within the tomb were 12 human bodies, 10 of which had been decapitated. All had their hands tied behind their backs. Around the sides of the tomb were the skeletons of 5 canines (thought to be wolves or coyotes), 3 felines (thought to be pumas or jaguars), and 13 birds, (most of which were eagles).

The central part of the tomb was marked with rich offerings, including shell ornaments, pottery vessels, obsidian figurines, spear points, and 18 large obsidian knives arranged in a radial pattern. Nine of the large obsidian knives depict a feathered serpent, a symbol of political power. The archaeologists suspect that the 12 people and the animals who accompanied them were all sacrificed in a ritual marking the beginning of the fifth building stage. The excavations at Teotihuacan demonstrate that this was a practice that had been carried out at least 1,500 years before the Aztecs.

In a related discovery, in December 2004, Mexican archaeologist Nadia Velez Saldana reported more archaeological evidence of human sacrifice from the site of Ecatepec. Located about 16 kilometers (10 miles) northeast of Mexico City, the site dates to Aztec times. Excavations exposed a burial of eight children, all burned during a sacrifice to the Aztec god of death. The same area of the site yielded cooking dishes and human bones suggesting possible sacrifice or cannibalism as depicted in some of the Aztec picture-histories known as *codices*.

Early Egyptian ships. An archaeologist reported what may be the remains of one of the earliest seagoing ships in history. As Egyptian civilization developed through time, Egyptians developed seagoing ships. Kathryn Bard, an archaeologist at Boston University, reported her findings in March 2005.

Ancient depictions of ships traveling to the "Land of Punt" (thought to be on the east coast of Africa) are on the walls of the tomb of Queen Hatshepsut, who ruled in the 1400's B.C. Excavations in human-dug caves on Egypt's Red Sea coast led to the recovery of what Bard believes to be ship timbers and sail rigging. She also found two curved cedar planks that may have been parts of oars used to steer these ships.

If the findings are confirmed, these would be the first archaeological remains of ship fragments dating to the 1400's B.C. Bard and her team of Italian archaeologists plan to return to the caves in December 2005 for further research.

Egyptian tomb discovered. A joint Egyptian-American archaeological team uncovered the tomb of an ancient Egyptian ruler dating to about 5,600 years ago. Renée Friedman, an Egyptologist with the British Museum, reported in April 2005 on the excavation of a rectangular tomb enclosed by a wall of wooden posts in Hierankopolis, now known as Kom el-Ahmar. The earliest political capital of ancient Egypt, Hierankopolis lies along the Nile in southern Egypt, about 600 kilometers (370 miles) south of modern-day Cairo. At the time the tomb was constructed, Hierankopolis was Egypt's largest city.

Although the tomb had been plundered by grave robbers in ancient times, the researchers were still able to expose four burials at one end of the tomb. They are believed to be servants or prisoners who were sacrificed and placed at the foot of the ruler's body, who has not been identified. One remarkable funerary offering is a chipped-flint effigy of a cow's head; another is thought to represent an ibex. An adjacent tomb yielded three additional burials, wrapped in textiles and padding and covered with thick matting. Other architectural remains indicate that an offering chapel lay next to the tomb complex.

■ Thomas R. Hester

See also **ANTHROPOLOGY; GEOLOGY.**

ASTRONOMY

The Cassini–Huygens spacecraft completed its seven-year voyage to Saturn in 2004, entering into an orbit around the planet in July. The mission is a joint project of the United States National Aeronautics and Space Administration (NASA), the European Space Agency (ESA), and the Italian Space Agency, Agenzia Spaziale Italiana (ASI). On Jan. 14, 2005, the Huygens probe descended through Titan's atmosphere, becoming the first probe to land on that moon's surface. Huygens found streambeds—likely carved by liquid methane and ethane—as well as fields of rounded pebbles.

Does methane mean life on Mars? The discovery of methane on Mars was reported in December 2004 by a team led by planetary scientist Vittorio Formisano of the Institute of Physics of Interplanetary Space at Rome. The orbiting ESA spacecraft Mars Express detected the methane in trace amounts in the atmosphere.

SEE ALSO

THE SPECIAL REPORT,
CLOSE ENCOUNTERS WITH SATURN, PAGE 12.

THE SPECIAL REPORT,
THE DARK SIDE OF THE UNIVERSE, PAGE 112

The scientists found the methane using *spectroscopy*, a technique in which light is absorbed and broken apart into individual wavelengths—essentially bands of colors—and the intensity of light at each wavelength is measured. Different gases absorb light at various wavelengths to a greater or lesser extent and so provide definitive "fingerprints" that allow scientists to identify the gases. Methane absorbs

HOLDING UP THE SKY

The Farnese Atlas statue, which dates from about A.D. 150, may be the oldest surviving pictorial record of Western constellations. The statue depicts the god Atlas kneeling with a globe, after being sentenced by Zeus to hold up the sky. The statue at the National Archaeological Museum in Naples, Italy, shows the placement of the constellations from around 125 B.C. In January 2005, scientists reported that the statue may be the pictorial representation of the long-lost star catalog of Hipparchus (180 B.C.?–125 B.C.?), an ancient Greek astronomer.

ASTRONOMY continued

light in the *infrared* part of the spectrum. Also called *heat rays* or *thermal radiation,* infrared light resembles visible light but cannot be seen by the human eye. At one wavelength in particular, the Mars Express spectrometer detected methane as it passed over various parts of Mars.

The amount of methane in the Martian atmosphere is small, ranging from about 10 to 25 molecules for every billion molecules of carbon dioxide, the main gas. Furthermore, the amount of methane seems to vary over different parts of the Martian surface, suggesting that the methane comes from different places.

Methane consists of one atom of carbon and four atoms of hydrogen. It is considered an *organic* molecule because it contains carbon. Methane is unstable. In the presence of oxygen, such as that found in large amounts in Martian minerals, it reacts with the oxygen to form water and carbon dioxide. If Mars had no other source of methane, all the methane would have been transformed within several hundred years. Scientists theorize that an active source of methane must be present.

That source became the focus of intense discussion. Methane may be produced by living or nonliving sources. On Earth, methane is produced by living organisms ranging from cows to primitive bacteria and other microorganisms as well as by such nonliving sources as marshes, rice paddies, natural gas, lakes, and oceans.

Most scientists believed that nonliving methane-producing sources on Mars should be considered first. Some comets contain carbon and may have delivered it to the Martian atmosphere in a recent impact, within the last 100 years. However, this hypothesis does not explain the variation in methane over different regions of Mars. Methane could be coming from volcanic vents on the Martian surface, though no evidence for active volcanism has been found on Mars. Finally, deposits of water ice on the Martian surface at polar latitudes and beneath the surface near the equator could store large amounts of methane and release it as the angle at which Mars tilts on its axis changes over thousands to millions of years. This alters the amount of sunlight reaching the planet and so could affect the temperature at different locations. NASA's Phoenix spacecraft is to be launched to Mars in 2007 to search for methane in the polar regions.

Fragmentary impacts. Fragments of extraterrestrial debris slowed by Earth's atmosphere may have formed the famous Meteor Crater near Flagstaff, Arizona. Writing in the March 10, 2005, issue of *Nature,* planetary geologists H. Jay Melosh of the University of Arizona in Tucson and Gareth Collins of the Imperial College of London offer this explanation for the mysteriously small amount of melted rock seen around and within this well-known crater.

NEW VIEWS OF MARS

Spacecraft exploring Mars in 2004 and 2005 discovered interesting surface features. An approximate true-color photo (right) of a dune field near Endurance Crater was captured by the Opportunity rover and released in August 2004. Tendrils of sand extend less than 1 meter (3.3 feet) from the main dune field toward the rover. Opportunity is one of two rovers launched by the National Aeronautics and Space Administration that landed on Mars in January 2004. What may be a dust-covered frozen sea on Mars (far right) lying near the planet's equator appears in a photo taken by the Mars Express spacecraft and released in February 2005. This spacecraft, launched by the European Space Agency, has been orbiting Mars since December 2003.

Impact craters are formed when a rocky or icy body—an asteroid or comet—slams into the surface of a planetary body at high speed. Typical impact speeds for objects hitting the Earth range from 15 to 20 kilometers (roughly 8 to 12 miles) per second. At these speeds, the projectile may crash with enough force to blast holes in the ground many times its diameter. The *kinetic energy* (energy of motion) deposited in even a small impact, such as the Meteor Crater impact, rivals or exceeds that produced by typical nuclear warheads. If the kinetic energy is high, some of the rock within the crater is melted and ejected.

Meteor Crater, which is 1.2 kilometers (0.7 mile) in diameter, formed about 50,000 years ago. It has less melted rock in and around it than would be expected for a crater of its size, based on computer models of impacts and studies of other craters. Further, *meteorites* (small fragments of extraterrestrial rock) pepper the area around the crater; these, too, are not melted.

To explain why the rocks from Meteor Crater did not melt, Melosh and Collins turned to the Earth's dense atmosphere, which acts as a brake on incoming debris. For instance, spacecraft returning to Earth use the atmosphere to slow their descent. However, they must also use a heat shield to protect against the extreme heat encountered during descent.

The two planetary geologists theorized that the atmosphere would slow a swarm of small fragments of extraterrestrial material more effectively than it would a single object. For their study, they calculated that, if the swarm was made of iron, with the largest piece no more than 100 meters (roughly 300 feet) across, the debris would be slowed by the air to about 12 kilometers (7 miles) per second at impact. While still forceful enough to release the energy of a 2- or 3-megaton nuclear warhead, the impact would produce relatively little melt, consistent with conditions at Meteor Crater. Thus, one of the best-known craters shows the importance of our atmosphere in protecting life.

Icy observations. The discovery of ice crystals and an unusual mixed ice consisting of ammonia and water on the surface of one of the most distant objects that can be observed in our solar system was reported in December 2004. Astronomers David Jewitt from the University of Hawaii at Manoa and Jane Luu from the Massachusetts Institute of Technology's Lincoln Laboratory in Lexington reported that they had detected these materials on the surface of Quaoar, an object in the Kuiper belt, an area of debris beyond the orbit of Neptune that is thought to have been left over from the era of the formation of the planets. Quaoar, which is about 1,300 kilometers (800 miles) in diameter, is about 6.4 billion kilometers (4 billion miles) from Earth. Because of its great distance from the sun, Quaoar is very cold. Astronomers had speculated that it might contain large amounts of water ice.

For their study, Jewitt and Luu observed Quaoar using the giant Japanese telescope Subaru, located on the top of the dormant volcano Mauna Kea on the island of Hawaii. Subaru

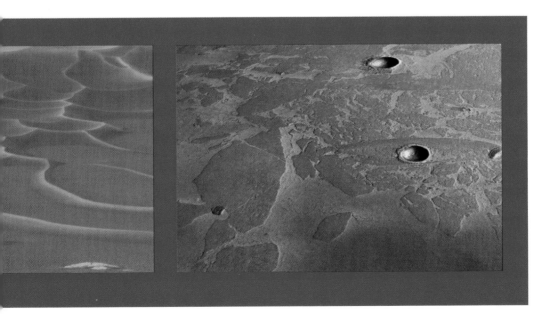

ASTRONOMY continued

has a main mirror with an opening some 8 meters (27 feet) in diameter, which allows it to gather large amounts of light from even distant and, therefore, faint solar system bodies. Jewitt and Luu then used spectroscopy to break up the light into its component wavelengths. They found that Quaoar absorbs light at wavelengths characteristic of water ice. Detailed study of the variation of light at these wavelengths revealed that the ice exists in the form of crystals. Such formations are typical at Earth temperatures but not at the very low temperatures in the Kuiper belt, where ice should have a glassy structure. The scientists speculated that the crystalline ice might have formed if Quaoar had sources of heat, perhaps radioactive elements bound in rock in its interior that melted the ice, which then refroze.

Jewitt and Luu also found evidence of ammonia hydrate, a frozen mixture that consists mainly of water and a small amount of ammonia. Ammonia is a very effective antifreeze for water ice, dropping the freezing point of liquid water as much as 100 Celsius degrees (210 Fahrenheit degrees). The ammonia might have reached Quaoar in comets, some of which contain small amounts of ammonia.

Ammonia is readily destroyed by ultraviolet light from the sun, however. Its existence on Quaoar suggests that this object has been geologically active in the recent past, expelling ammonia from its interior or shedding outer layers of ice and dust to reveal deposits of ammonia and water to an earthbound telescope.

Alien planets come out of hiding. In March 2005, NASA astronomers, using the Spitzer Space Telescope, saw light from two *extrasolar* (beyond the solar system) planets for the first time. Astronomers had previously found some 130 planets orbiting distant stars. All these extrasolar planets, including these two, were discovered by indirect methods, however.

The most common strategies used in the search for extrasolar planets are the Doppler shift and transit methods. In the Doppler shift method, scientists look for the tiny motions of a star that are caused by the gravitational tug of an orbiting planet, as the two orbit a point in space between them called the *center of mass.* The planet, which has far less mass than the star, moves through a large orbit at high speed. The more massive star orbits in a small path at low speed.

Because the planet is too dim and too close to the star to be seen directly from Earth, astronomers detect its presence by examining the orbital motion of the star. As the star alternately approaches us and recedes from us, the Doppler effect shifts the wavelengths of its light very slightly. (The Doppler effect is the change in frequency of sound, light, or radio waves caused by the relative motion of the sources of the waves and their observer.) When astronomers find a star whose spectral wavelengths are shifting back and forth, they conclude that the star has an unseen companion—that is, a planet.

Another indirect way to detect planets orbiting distant stars is to look for tiny dips in the star's brightness as the planet passes in front of it. These so-called planetary transits are rare, because the orbital plane of the planet must be aligned with our line of sight. So far, two extrasolar planets have been detected in this fashion.

Using the Spitzer Space Telescope, the scientists detected light from the two extrasolar planets directly. Spitzer measures infrared radiation from cosmic sources.

In a planetary system, both the planets and the star emit infrared radiation at intensities determined by their surface temperatures. The star, being much hotter, emits most of its radiation at visible wavelengths, with only a small fraction of its energy coming out in the infrared part of the spectrum. But a planet, being much cooler than the star, emits most of its radiation at infrared wavelengths. Because the star may be millions of times as bright as the planet in visible light, scientists cannot see the planet's visible light amid the glare from the star. In contrast, the star may be only a few hundred times as bright as the planet at infrared wavelengths. This makes the infrared emission from a planet easier to detect.

Two teams of astronomers, one led by David Charbonneau of the Harvard–Smithsonian Center for Astrophysics in Cambridge, Massachusetts, and the other by L. Drake Deming of NASA's Goddard Space Flight Center in Greenbelt, Maryland, jointly announced the detection of infrared radiation from the extrasolar planets. One of the planets orbits the star HD 209458; the other orbits a dim, unnamed star about 500 light-years from Earth. (A light-year is the distance traveled in one year by a pulse of light, about 9.46 trillion

YOUNGEST PLANET CLEARS THE WAY

A planet that may be the youngest ever found orbits the star CoKu Tau 4, in an artist's illustration based on an announcement made in mid-2004. The planet may be larger than Jupiter, whose diameter is 11 times as large as Earth's. Scientists used the Spitzer Space Telescope to detect a clearing in the cloud of gas and dust that surrounds CoKu Tau 4. According to the scientists, the clearing may have been created by a massive body orbiting through the cloud.

this discovery was not a surprise, as astronomers already knew that the planets are orbiting much closer to their parent stars than Jupiter or Saturn are to the sun.

Organic compounds in space. In 2004, astronomers reported the existence of organic materials in two unusual kinds of astronomical environments. In modern chemistry an organic compound is one that contains carbon, whether or not the material has a biological origin. Thus, organic molecules may include such simple molecules as carbon monoxide and carbon dioxide as well as such complex biological molecules as DNA (deoxyribonucleic acid, the material from which genes are made). Since the 1980's, astronomers have found evidence that organic compounds are common in interstellar space and in *circumstellar* environments (clouds of gas and dust closely surrounding some stars). The new discoveries, which included data from two of NASA's orbiting observatories, added to the impression that organic materials are everywhere.

kilometers [5.88 trillion miles].) Both planets are in orbits closely aligned with our line of sight from Earth. As a result, the planets periodically pass behind their stars. By carefully comparing the infrared intensity of light coming from each system when the planet was behind the star and when it was not, the astronomers were able to measure the slight additional infrared emissions coming from the planet. These emissions amounted to only about one-fourth of 1 percent of the total infrared radiation from each system and so required great accuracy in the Spitzer observations.

The detected infrared emission enabled the astronomers to determine the surface temperature of the planets, which was found to be around 830 °C (1,500 °F). These planets are much hotter than the gas giants in our solar system. However,

ASTRONOMY continued

One of the announcements was based, in part, on images obtained by the Hubble Space Telescope of a peculiar object called the Red Rectangle. This object is a *nebula* (cloud of dust particles and gas) that is shaped like a square and surrounds the star HD 44179. The nebula has an obvious red color because chemical compounds in its gas emit light in the red part of the visible spectrum. Astronomers analyzing these images determined that many of these chemical compounds are organic.

The Hubble images came from a study of the Red Rectangle by astronomers Hans Van Winckel of Catholic University in Leuven, Belgium, and Martin Cohen of the University of California, Berkeley. These detailed images revealed new structures in the Red Rectangle, indicating that the central star had ejected gas and dust in stages. Many stars, as they age, expand and release some of their outer layers into space. Apparently HD 44179 is now doing this, with the outflowing material forming the Red Rectangle.

In a separate analysis using data from a ground-based telescope, Lewis M. Hobbs of the University of Chicago and a team of collaborators identified *spectral lines* in the glowing gas of the Red Rectangle as simple organic compounds. Spectral lines are specific wavelengths at which an atom or molecule emits or absorbs light. The Hobbs team determined that the Red Rectangle contains mostly simple two- or three-atom molecules containing carbon.

Gas and dust may also be associated with newly forming stars. On May 27, 2004, a team of astronomers led by Dan Watson and William Forrest, both of the University of Rochester in New York, announced the discovery of organic materials in one star-forming region, the constellation Taurus. Using the Spitzer Space Telescope, the scientists discovered spectral lines in the infrared part of the spectrum, indicating the presence of ices of water, carbon dioxide, and ethanol in the dust.

Historic massive gamma ray flare. On Dec. 27, 2004, the most intense flash of radiation ever recorded from outside the solar system briefly illuminated Earth. The event was detected by several observatories. The burst of gamma rays, lasting less than 0.2 second, was so intense that it would take the sun more than 150,000 years to produce a comparable amount of energy. If the outburst had occurred nearer to Earth, our atmosphere could have been severely dam-

aged, with disastrous consequences for life. Some scientists have theorized that similar outbursts may have caused mass extinctions in the past.

Among the observatories recording the flash was NASA's newly operational Swift satellite, which was designed specifically to look for gamma ray bursts. Gamma ray bursts occur frequently, with most coming from distant galaxies. Physicist David Palmer of the Los Alamos National Laboratory in New Mexico headed the team of Swift scientists who analyzed the burst. Bryan Gaensler of the Harvard–Smithsonian Center for Astrophysics in Cambridge led a group of astronomers who used the Very Large Array radio observatory in New Mexico to detect and study radio emissions from the event. Another observation of the burst was obtained by the Reuven Ramatay High Energy Solar Spectroscopic Imager, another NASA satellite, which found a six-minute spike in X-ray emissions from the same source.

The source of the gamma ray outburst was quickly identified as the *neutron star* SGR 1806-20, which lies about 50,000 light-years from Earth. A neutron star is the collapsed core of a massive star that no longer produces nuclear energy. The mass of a neutron star may be two or three times that of the sun, yet its radius is only about 10 to 15 kilometers (6 to 10 miles).

Astronomers have detected many neutron stars, and a few of them—about a dozen—fall into a special class called *magnetars*. These have such a powerful magnetic field that magnetic forces dominate their behavior. A subgroup of the magnetars are soft gamma ray repeaters (SGR), which occasionally emit bursts of relatively low-energy gamma rays. Gamma rays have much shorter wavelengths and carry far more energy than other forms of electromagnetic radiation.

Astronomers do not yet understand why this particular event on SGR 1806-20 was so much more energetic than the typical gamma ray bursts from similar magnetars. Most scientists think that tangled magnetic field lines of the neutron star snapped and then quickly reconnected. This event is similar to the process that causes *solar flares,* energetic outbursts of X rays occasionally emitted by the sun. But given the enormous magnetic field strength of the neutron star, the snapping and reconnection of the magnetic field released far more energy than even the most powerful flares from the sun.

The detection of the rapid gamma ray flare from SGR 1806-20 may help resolve a long-standing question about the origin of some unusual gamma ray bursts from other galaxies. These bursts have been observed for years, occurring on approximately a daily basis, and most last longer than the December 27 event. Astronomers now believe that most of these bursts occur as stars collapse during supernova explosions in distant galaxies. A few of the bursts, specifically the very short ones, do not fit this model, however. Scientists can study the very brief December 27 gamma ray outburst in order to find an explanation for the rapid gamma ray bursts in other galaxies, where similar magnetars may occasionally undergo similar magnetic field disruptions.

Dwarf galaxies rule the universe. News of the discovery of a new companion to the Andromeda galaxy was published in September 2004 in the *Astrophysical Journal*. This discovery helped reveal how common dwarf galaxies may be in the universe.

Stars throughout the universe are concentrated in galaxies, which are huge conglomerations with as many as a trillion sunlike stars that

BENEATH THE DUST

The stars inside a *nebula* (a cloud of dust particles and gases in space) in the Milky Way are revealed in unprecedented detail in an image captured by NASA's Spitzer Space Telescope. The nebula, called RCW 49, is one of the most prolific sites of star formation in the galaxy. Researchers in 2004 announced that they had found *organic* (carbon-containing) compounds at such sites.

emit hundreds of billions times as much luminous energy as the sun. The galaxy we live in, the Milky Way, is a large, disk-shaped system with spiral arms, containing about 100 billion suns. About half the known bright galaxies are spirals similar to our own. The other half are rounded systems with no disk. These galaxies are called *elliptical galaxies* (or *ellipticals*). Some ellipticals are among the largest and most massive galaxies known. But other ellipticals are much smaller and fainter, and astronomers are finding that these so-called dwarf ellipsoidal galaxies may be the most common type of all.

ASTRONOMY continued

The Andromeda galaxy, also known as M31, is a large spiral galaxy about 2 million light-years from Earth. Both the Milky Way and M31 are among the largest and most luminous spiral galaxies known. Because of their large masses, these two galaxies have trapped a number of small, low-mass galaxies into orbit around them. The Milky Way has at least a dozen companions, ranging from the relatively bright Magellanic Clouds to a number of very dim, small dwarf ellipsoidal systems. A similar family of companions accompanies M31, including a new one discovered in 2004. This new member of M31's family, the ninth one discovered so far, is the dimmest galaxy ever detected by astronomers.

Daniel Zucker of the Max Planck Institute for Astronomy in Heidelberg, Germany, and a team of collaborators named the new galaxy Andromeda IX. The scientists discovered Andromeda IX in data obtained from an all-sky mapping project called the Sloan Digital Sky Survey (SDSS). The SDSS, now complete for the Northern Hemisphere, is providing astronomers with a wealth of new information on the distribution of faint objects all over the sky. Zucker, seeking to learn how many faint galaxies there might be in the universe, has been analyzing SDSS data in a search for nearby, faint galaxies.

An image of Andromeda IX is not very impressive, because the galaxy has a very low *surface brightness* (light emitted per square degree on the sky). Only by noting a slight concentration of stars in one area on the sky near the Andromeda galaxy was Zucker able to find the new dwarf. Andromeda IX is not even as luminous as the brightest individual stars in the Milky Way.

Adding such small, dim systems to the known family of galaxies changes the traditional view of galaxies as massive, large, bright collections of stars. Now astronomers are finding that the vast majority of galaxies are small and dim, which makes them difficult to detect at large distances. Because astronomers cannot see dwarf galaxies at far distances from Earth, the only method they have for determining how many of these dim systems populate the universe is to count nearby ones and then assume that similar stellar systems exist everywhere in comparable numbers. The addition of Andromeda IX to the list of nearby dwarfs indicates that galaxies can be even fainter than previously thought, adding to the estimated total number of dwarf systems in the universe. The discovery suggests that dwarf galaxies, small and dim as they are, contribute significantly to the overall star and galaxy content of the universe and must be included in models of the formation of galaxies and the distribution of matter in space.

■ Jonathan Lunine and Theodore P. Snow

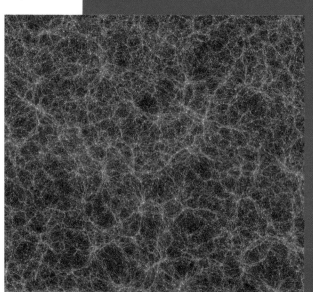

EXPANDED UNDERSTANDING

Galaxies appear as bright dots clumping to form a mesh of matter within a sea of *dark energy* in a computer-generated image created with data from the Hubble Space Telescope. Dark energy, an unexplained antigravity force, pushes the galaxies outward at an ever-faster rate. An international group of researchers announced in February 2005 that their computer model has provided evidence of the existence of dark energy in our part of the universe.

ATMOSPHERIC SCIENCE

The midwestern United States may be a relative cool spot in a world increasingly affected by *global warming*, according to research reported in September 2004. A team of atmospheric scientists at St. Louis University in Missouri and Iowa State University in Ames found strong evidence that one region in the Midwest is warming at a much slower rate than the rest of the country. The scientists were led by Zaitao Pan of St. Louis University.

Global warming is an increase in the average temperature of Earth's surface that has occurred since the late 1800's. A majority of climatologists believe that human activities are responsible for most of the warming.

Although Earth is slowly warming overall, the warming is not occurring at a uniform rate around the world. Scientific models and experiments show that some regions are warming more than others. For example, the Arctic region is heating up dramatically.

Using a computer model they created, Pan and his colleagues concluded that, by 2040, a "warming hole" would form near the border of Kansas and Missouri, in the Farm-Belt region of the United States. They predicted the hole would also include parts of Iowa, Nebraska, and Oklahoma. The scientists estimate that, in the future, the region's daytime-high temperatures in summer would not increase as much as they would in the rest of the United States.

To confirm the accuracy of their model, the researchers looked at temperature data from 1975 through 2000. They found evidence that the hole is already developing. The temperature records showed that the central United States warmed only slightly, in contrast with the rest of the country. During this period, the region's daytime-high temperature increase in summer was less than 0.5 °C (0.9 °F), compared with an average increase of about 3 °C (5 °F) over the rest of the United States. Since the late 1800's, the global average temperature has increased about 0.4 to 0.8 °C (0.7 to 1.4 °F).

The scientists presented an explanation for the formation of the hole. Their model predicts that, due to global warming across the United States, more warm air will flow over the Midwest. Warm air holds more water than cool air, so the region would have more rainfall and wetter soil. More of the sun's energy would go into evaporating the water than heating the air,

which would lower daytime-high temperatures.

Gene Takle, an atmospheric scientist at Iowa State University and member of the research team, predicted several changes in the region's future weather patterns. He said the area would probably have a slightly longer growing season, milder winters, and warmer nights. The region may also get heavier rainfalls in late summer.

The prediction may be good news for Midwestern farmers, because more late-summer moisture is generally good for crops. However, Takle said that the region would probably get heavier rains during more extreme events, such as thunderstorms, instead of more overall rainfall. This increase in extreme events could mean more runoff from the heavier rainfalls, more flooding problems, and higher water levels along the Upper Mississippi River.

Pan and his team say that their results stress the need to examine global warming on a region-by-region basis. Further careful monitoring of the Midwest's climate is necessary to confirm their results. Future research may reveal whether the predicted hole is a temporary effect that could disappear as global warming becomes more severe in the second half of the 2000's.

Sweeping hurricane predictions. Two major scientific forecasts about the 2004 hurricane season in the Atlantic Ocean accurately predicted the continuation of a 10-year trend toward increased activity. (The Atlantic hurricane season runs from June 1 to November 30.) According to a forecast issued in May 2005 by the National Oceanic and Atmospheric Administration (NOAA) in Washington, D.C., this trend is likely to continue through the 2005 hurricane season.

The 2004 season ranked as one of the most active and destructive as well as the costliest hurricane season in history. In the United States alone, hurricanes caused 59 deaths and led to $42 billion in property damage. Eight storms swept inland, including one hurricane that made two landfalls. The forecasts came from NOAA and from the Tropical Meteorology Project (TMP) at Colorado State University in Fort Collins.

In April 2004, meteorologist William M. Gray and atmospheric researcher Philip J. Klotzbach of the TMP predicted eight hurricanes for the season. In their report, Gray and Klotzbach said: "The recent upturn in Atlantic basin hurricane activity which began in 1995 is

ATMOSPHERIC SCIENCE continued

expected to continue in 2004. We anticipate an above-average number of Atlantic basin tropical cyclones and an above-average probability of U.S. hurricane landfall."

A tropical cyclone is a violent, swirling storm. If the cyclone's wind speeds exceed 63 kilometers (39 miles) per hour, it becomes a *tropical storm* and receives a name. Hurricanes are cyclones with wind speeds of greater than 119 kilometers (74 miles) per hour.

The TMP also predicted that three of the eight storms would be major hurricanes—Category 3 or higher on the Saffir-Simpson Hurricane Scale. This scale designates five categories of hurricanes, ranging from Category 1—described as weak—to Category 5, which can be devastating. A Category 3 hurricane has wind speeds from 178 to 209 kilometers (111 to 130 miles) per hour.

The NOAA forecast, issued in May 2004, predicted from 12 to 15 tropical storms. Researchers forecast that from 6 to 8 of these storms would develop into hurricanes, with 2 to 4 becoming major hurricanes.

The hurricane season started late in 2004, with the first hurricane forming in late July. However, by the end of the season, forecasters' worst predictions had come true. The season included 15 storms, with names ranging from Alex (a Category 3 hurricane lasting from July 31 to August 6) to Otto (a tropical storm lasting from November 30 to December 3).

Nine storms hit the United States during the six-month season—three as tropical storms (Bonnie, Hermine, and Matthew) and six as hurricanes (Alex, Charley, Frances, Gaston, Ivan, and Jeanne). Every storm except Alex swept onto land. Typically, two to three hurricanes make landfall in the United States each season.

Florida suffered the most damage during the 2004 hurricane season. Four hurricanes (Charley, Frances, Ivan, and Jeanne) and one tropical storm (Bonnie) hit the state from mid-August through late September. Four hurricanes had not hit the state in one season since official record-keeping of landfalling hurricanes began in 1851.

The hurricanes struck major human and economic blows to Florida. Throughout the season, about 9.4 million Florida residents evacuated their homes. The Insurance Information Institute, a nonprofit public education organization based in New York City, estimated that hurricanes affected 1 in every 5 Florida homes. Hurricanes Charley and Ivan caused $14 billion and $13 billion in damages, respectively. They ranked as the second and third costliest hurri-

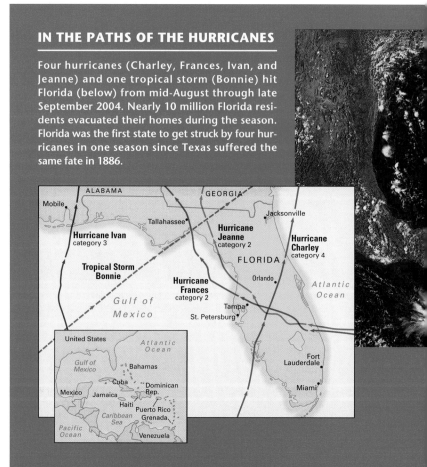

IN THE PATHS OF THE HURRICANES

Four hurricanes (Charley, Frances, Ivan, and Jeanne) and one tropical storm (Bonnie) hit Florida (below) from mid-August through late September 2004. Nearly 10 million Florida residents evacuated their homes during the season. Florida was the first state to get struck by four hurricanes in one season since Texas suffered the same fate in 1886.

ALABAMA

Mobile

Tallahassee

Hurricane Ivan
category 3

Tropical Storm Bonnie

Gulf of Mexico

GEORGIA

Jacksonville

Hurricane Jeanne
category 2

Hurricane Charley
category 4

FLORIDA

Orlando

Atlantic Ocean

Hurricane Frances
category 2

Tampa

St. Petersburg

Fort Lauderdale

Miami

United States

Atlantic Ocean

Gulf of Mexico

Bahamas

Cuba

Dominican Rep.

Mexico

Jamaica

Haiti

Puerto Rico

Caribbean Sea

Grenada

Pacific Ocean

Venezuela

canes on record, after Hurricane Andrew in 1992. Most of the damage from Charley and Ivan occurred in Florida.

Many hurricanes in the 2004 season also affected the Caribbean. Charley crossed western Cuba, and Frances and Jeanne swept through the Bahamas, all as major hurricanes. Ivan hit Grenada and battered Jamaica, Grand Cayman, and western Cuba. Jeanne also swept by Puerto Rico as a strong tropical storm and then hit the Dominican Republic and Haiti as a hurricane. Severe floods, caused by heavy rain from Jeanne, led to at least 3,000 deaths in Haiti.

A number of long-term climate patterns contributed to the active 2004 season, according to meteorologists at NOAA. One factor was the lack of El Niño activity in the Pacific Ocean. An El Niño is a weather event caused by the interaction between Earth's atmosphere and the tropical waters of the Pacific Ocean. When an El Niño is active in the Pacific, the Atlantic has fewer hurricanes. During the El Niño years of 1997 and 2002, for example, the Atlantic had relatively quiet hurricane seasons. Except for these

two years, the Atlantic hurricane seasons have been very active since 1995.

A second factor was a continuation of warmer-than-normal temperatures across the tropical Atlantic. Warmer waters can produce atmospheric circulation patterns that favor active hurricane seasons.

In reviewing the season, NOAA scientists pointed to a strong region of high pressure in the middle levels of the atmosphere over the western Atlantic. The clockwise winds that formed around this region helped to steer hurricanes toward the United States rather than out to sea.

Fierce winds. Wind farms, which harvest energy from the wind, can cause environmental changes to nearby areas, according to a study published in October 2004. The study was conducted by meteorologist Somnath Baidya Roy of Princeton University in New Jersey (now at Duke University in Durham, North Carolina) and his colleagues at Duke. The researchers created the first detailed computer simulation of the effects a large wind farm would have on its surroundings.

A wind farm is a collection of *wind turbines*, devices that extract energy from the wind using large, fanlike rotors (typically with three blades) connected to electric power generators. Wind farms can produce large amounts of energy. For example, the Top of Iowa Wind Farm in Kensett generates enough electric current to power 24,000 homes. Unlike such fossil fuels as oil and coal, wind power has a reputation for providing clean, nonpolluting energy.

For their study, the researchers examined the effects of the turbulent *wakes* (streams of disturbed air) created as wind turbines take energy from the wind. The wakes, which are initially the size of the circle cut by the spinning blades, expand upward and downward as they flow away from the rotor.

Baidya Roy and his colleagues created a computer simulation of a wind farm with 10,000 wind turbines, arranged on a square array of 100 by 100 turbines, each spaced 1 kilometer (0.6 mile) apart. They designed the model using observations of wind speed, temperature, and ground-level evaporation in north-central Oklahoma over a two-week period in 1995.

Hurricane Ivan roars by Jamaica and western Cuba in a satellite image (above) taken on Sept. 13, 2004. At this point on its path, Ivan had maximum sustained wind speeds of about 260 kilometers (160 miles) per hour, making it a Category 5 storm, the most destructive level on the Saffir-Simpson Hurricane Scale.

ATMOSPHERIC SCIENCE continued

The turbines in the simulation were 100 meters (330 feet) tall, with blades that were 50 meters (165 feet) long. These devices are similar to modern wind turbines, which are typically about 75 meters (245 feet) tall, with rotor blades 25 meters (80 feet) in length. For example, the Top of Iowa Wind Farm has 89 turbines, each standing 72 meters (236 feet) tall with blades 26 meters (85 feet) long. Although the simulation used many more turbines than are found on existing wind farms, the model could represent the future of wind power technology.

The simulation predicted that the turbulence from large wind farms would increase local wind speeds and air temperatures at ground level, causing an increase in the soil moisture evaporation rate. The model showed that, averaged over a day, wind speeds at ground level would increase by about 0.6 meter (2 feet) per second and surface temperature would rise by 0.7 °C (1.3 °F). Soil evaporation would jump by as much as 0.3 millimeter (0.01 inch) per day, a potentially harmful rate for agriculture in dry regions.

The researchers also concluded that the strength of these effects depended on the time of day. During the daytime, sunlight causes strong mixing of the lowers layers of the atmosphere, so the wake turbulence would have a relatively small impact. In the predawn hours, however, when the atmosphere is calmer, the wakes from the wind turbines would cause large boosts in surface-level wind speeds and temperatures.

In addition, in the simulation, the wind speed at 3 a.m. at the turbine height was about 30-percent lower than the wind speed would have been with no farm present. Because wind turbines extract much more power from faster-moving winds, these slow winds would reduce the power generated by turbines located farther downwind.

According to Baidya Roy, the turbines' wakes force some of the energetic, high-speed winds typically found at turbine heights down to the ground. The wakes also carry hot air down and cool, moist air up, which causes more evaporation. The computer simulation suggested that reducing the turbulence would reduce the environmental impact and increase the efficiency of the turbines. ■ John Snow

BIOLOGY

An African elephant that makes noises like a truck has helped change the way scientists think about elephant communication. The truck imitator and another African elephant that imitates sounds made by Asian elephants have shown that elephants can learn to copy sounds or calls made using their voice, an international research team reported in March 2005.

Such a talent interests scientists because people are among the few animals that learn to speak by imitating the voices of people around them. Other animals that practice vocal imitation include some birds, bats, and marine mammals (whales and their relatives) as well as apes and other primates.

Many of these other voice imitators have social lives similar to those of elephants', said research director Joyce Poole of the Amboseli Elephant Research Project in Sandefjord, Norway. These animals form strong bonds with others of their kind and live in groups that often

SEE ALSO THE SPECIAL REPORT, **GREAT APES: CULTURE AND CONSERVATION,** PAGE 40.

separate and then reunite. Perhaps voice imitation offers advantages for animals with such active social lives.

Poole found out about the first elephant from a friend with an elephant orphanage. The friend reported that a young female elephant there made odd sounds. The orphanage lies about 3 kilometers (2 miles) from the major highway connecting the African cities of Nairobi and Mombasa. Poole wondered if the elephant's noises could be imitations of distant traffic. When Poole set up recording equipment and listened through her earphones, she sometimes couldn't tell which noises were being made by traffic and which by the elephant.

The second elephant was an African male that had spent 18 years in a Swiss zoo where he could hear Asian elephants. Most of the sounds he made resembled the chirplike calls made by Asian elephants instead of the sounds usual for his own species.

Poole and her colleagues worked with biologist Peter Tyack of Woods Hole Oceanographic Institution in Massachusetts to analyze the *spectrograms* (visual records of sound waves) of the elephants and trucks. Tyack studies sound learning in marine mammals. After comparing the durations and frequencies of all the noises, the researchers concluded that the elephants really were mimicking the noises they heard.

Sleepless but smart. During certain times of the year, white-crowned sparrows show a remarkable ability to cheat on sleep, according to a report published in July 2004. Researchers led by psychiatrist Ruth Benca of the University of Wisconsin in Madison found that captured wild birds living in their laboratory made do with less sleep during the spring and fall, when the members of this species living in the wild naturally migrate. Moreover, the birds were able to accomplish this with no apparent effect on their mental skills. During other times of the year, however, birds whose sleep was restricted were slower to respond and were not as accurate on tests the day following a night of limited sleep.

Just how much migratory birds sleep has interested scientists for many years. Many of these birds seem to fly mostly at night, though they are active during the day, too. During the rest of the year, these birds sleep at night like other creatures that are active during the day.

During the migration season, the researchers studied sleep patterns in sparrows that would normally fly at night, migrating some 4,000 kilometers (2,500 miles) between Alaska and southern California. Benca's group brought some sparrows into the lab and attached sensors to them to monitor their sleep. Although birds in laboratories could not migrate, these birds slept only a third as much as usual during the normal migration time.

In daytime, the researchers tested the sleep-deprived birds on their skill at pecking three keys in the correct order (left, right, center, for example). Although the birds slept less, they still scored well. If the researchers kept the birds awake for much of the night during the summer or winter, the birds did not do as well on the tests the next morning.

Such research might help scientists answer one of the most puzzling questions in science:

HEATED FIGHTS

A California ground squirrel harasses a rattlesnake by kicking sand at it, nipping at its tail, and whipping its tail back and forth. Animal behaviorist Aaron Rundus at the University of California, Davis and colleagues reported in June 2004 that the squirrels' tails heat up so much when the squirrels are harassing rattlesnakes that they broadcast an infrared signal. California ground squirrels are the first animals known to produce such a signal. Researchers believe the infrared signals enhance the taunting, which the squirrels use to get the rattlesnakes to go away.

What is the purpose of sleep? In addition, these studies may help researchers develop ways to help people whose sleep and moods suffer at certain seasons or to help people with sleep problems stay mentally sharp.

Long primate sleep. The discovery of the first tropical animal that hibernates has broken the long-observed pattern that animals hibernate only in cold climates. Animal physiologist Kathrin Dausmann and her colleagues at Phillips University in Marburg, Germany, reported in June 2004 that dwarf lemurs, which live on the island of Madagascar off the African coast, hibernate because of a scarcity of food.

BIOLOGY continued

Hibernating is common among bears, groundhogs, and other animals that live in places with cold winters. However, winter temperatures in the dwarf lemurs' habitats often reach 30 °C (86 °F).

The dwarf lemur is the first known *primate* to hibernate. (Primates include human beings and other animals that closely resemble them, including apes, monkeys, and lemurs.) The fat-tailed dwarf lemurs look a little like monkeys with dark eye circles and fat tails. Because the lemurs are hard to find during the dry season, Dausmann and her colleagues fitted 53 of the animals with special collars that let the researchers track their location and temperature.

Dwarf lemurs disappear into holes in trees and hibernate there for at least seven months between March and November, when food for them is scarce. Before lemurs hibernate, their tails grow as much as 40 percent bigger because of increased feeding. During hibernation, the lemurs live off the fat in their enlarged tails.

The body temperatures of animals hibernating in cold climates often increase at intervals to preserve life. The heat-ups, however, require the animals to expend a lot of energy. In contrast, some of the lemurs seem to have found a way to save themselves the energy. Most of them snuggle into trees with thin walls so their internal body temperatures rise and fall with the environmental temperature. In Madagascar, that meant the air temperature inside the lemur hideaway naturally rises during the warm part of the day. However, in the study, when Dausmann checked on lemurs in thick-walled trees, she found that lemurs did not warm each day from the increase in temperature in their tree hole because there wasn't an increase in the environment's temperature. In those instances, lemurs warmed themselves like other hibernating animals: by occasionally expending energy to increase their body temperature.

Dausmann said that because the hibernation patterns of tropical animals have not been studied in detail, she suspected more of them might hibernate. However, a scarcity of food—not a cold environment, as previously supposed—seems to be the reason animals hibernate.

New plant ideas. Scientists now know how the plant hormone *auxin* makes plants grow, according to reports published in May 2005 by botanists led by Mark Estelle of Indiana University in Bloomington and a separate group led by

Ottoline Leyser at the University of York in the United Kingdom. Since the mid-1920's, researchers had known that plants use the hormone auxin to grow but scientists have never before understood how it worked.

Plant embryos, young leaves, and the tips of stems and roots produce auxins that influence the growth of different parts of plants. Auxins play an important role in plant *tropisms* (bending movements). For example, the stems or leaves of many plants bend toward light. Such movement, called *positive phototropism,* occurs because auxins accumulate on the dark side of the stem or leaf stalk, causing the cells on that side to lengthen. This elongation gradually bends the stem or leaf toward the light.

Researchers found that when auxin combines with a protein called TIR1, the protein helps the plant cells to bring in other proteins it would not normally allow in. The plant then can break down those proteins and grow. The results could improve crop yields and genetically modified foods.

Piece songs. Young white-crowned song sparrows that hear only two-part pieces of songs or song phrases can still learn to sing entire songs. That finding was reported by biologist Gary Rose of the University of Utah in Salt Lake City and his colleagues in December 2004. The study results provided additional evidence for the theory that the brain responds particularly strongly to the way basic units are combined.

Rose and other scientists have been interested in how birds learn songs because birds share with people the need to train their voices instead of just being able to make the right sounds by instinct. Researchers theorized that teaching the birds to sing song phrases could help them figure out how the songs are stored in a bird's memory while it is learning.

For a songbird to learn to sing properly, it must hear songs at the right period early in its development. Then the young bird starts making a soft jumble of noises, a bird form of baby talk. As the youngster matures, it works out how to stop babbling and creates the songs it heard when it was younger.

The song Rose and his colleagues picked as a test for the young sparrows had five parts—including a whistle, a trill, a buzz, and several melodic note sequences—which they labeled A, B, C, D, E. The researchers kept the young birds from hearing the whole sequence straight through, instead playing it to them in bits. Those birds that heard the parts as separate units—such as E (pause), D (pause), C (pause), for example—were never able to sing the whole song correctly when they grew up. Yet when researchers played the same bits in pairs (for example, DE, CD, BC, AB) to other young birds, the youngsters strung them together correctly and created a song starting with A.

As an extra test, the researchers trained some young birds with bits paired in reverse order: ED, DC, CB, BA, for example. These birds were also able to link together the units to create a whole song in the sequence E, D, C, B, A.

Growing heart. A Burmese python may be the most extreme example of an animal that can increase the power of its heart muscle just by eating, according to research published in March 2005 by ecologist and evolutionary biologist James Hicks of the University of California, Irvine. To get food, Burmese pythons just sit and wait for prey to come by. This approach, however, involves the risk of a long wait. Pythons cope by slowing their body processes and letting unused organs shrink. When the moment comes to eat again, a python swallows the food, revs up its body, and restores its organs to their normal size for digestion. This is not an easy job because a Burmese python usually eats a dinner equal to its own weight. A big snake, therefore, tackles such prey as pigs.

To study what happens to the python's heart during this starve-binge cycle, Hicks and his colleagues checked the size of heart muscles in pythons that had been waiting days for dinner. Then they fed hungry snakes a feast of rats and checked the heart muscles afterward. Just two days after swallowing a big meal, the snakes' hearts were 40 percent larger than the hearts of snakes that were not fed. That is the fastest growth rate of a heart yet measured, Hicks said. The Burmese python could make a good study subject for scientists interested in human heart growth, especially in athletes or people with health problems, the researchers suggest.

Silent screams. For the first time researchers have found an animal that gives an alarm call using *ultrasound frequencies* (sound pitched above the range of human hearing). Zoologist James Hare at the University of Manitoba and his colleagues reported in August 2005 that when a ground squirrel becomes upset, it may squeak out a high-pitched alarm that many other creatures cannot hear. Other animals make ultrasonic calls. For example, many bats make very high sounds and use the

GREAT PRESSURES

A thin glass rod—taking the place of an insect—tickles the hairlike structures of a Venus's-flytrap, *Dionaea muscipula* (top), causing the leaves to shut quickly to capture its prey (bottom), in images from a high-speed video. In January 2005, researchers at the University of Cambridge in England suggested that the flytrap can move so fast because of the structure of its leaves. When an insect lands on a leaf, it stimulates hairlike structures that, in turn, cause cells along the outer side of the leaf to fill with fluid. This action causes the leaf to bend inward, creating mechanical pressure that the open leaf resists at first. Within about one second, however, the pressure grows too great and the leaf snaps shut.

BIOLOGY continued

echoes to navigate. However, this work, said Hare, has shown the first evidence for an ultrasonic alarm call.

Hare and his research team studied the alarm calls of a type of squirrel called a Richardson's ground squirrel. The researchers found that, occasionally, the ground squirrels' body language suggested that the animals were alarmed. The squirrels looked as if they were making some sort of alarm call, but the scientists could not hear them.

The researchers then turned to recording equipment used to study bats, well-known for their high-pitched sounds. To startle the squirrels enough to make them become alarmed, the researchers tossed a hat onto the ground.

The idea of high-pitched sounds makes evolutionary sense, Hare said. A ground squirrel could alert others of its kind of danger without advertising its position to dangerous predators, which couldn't hear the calls.

Acrobat ants. Some wingless ants that fall or are dropped from tall tropical trees survive by gliding in the air, according to insect ecologist Stephen Yanoviak of the University of Texas Medical Branch Galveston and University of Florida in Vero Beach. Yanoviak reported this finding in February 2005.

The ant *Cephalotes atratus* lives in trees as tall as a nine-story building. The worker ants in these colonies (like those of other ants) lack wings. When *C. atratus* ants fall off a tree branch, they guide themselves in a curve toward the trunk until they can catch hold.

Yanoviak was studying other aspects of how animals adapt to life in tropical treetops when he brushed ants off his arm and saw that they didn't fall straight down. Intrigued, he tested this behavior in a number of ant species. Some species just drop, but others—like the *C. atratus*—come close to gliding.

Ants of the treetops do not usually die if they fall, so jumping off branches is a standard way for them to escape getting eaten. Scientists refer to "ant rain" in these forests as little creatures routinely fall or jump down. However, Yanoviak said, falling still has risks. The ants must climb home, and they might get lost on the way. Also, hungry animals might find ants when they fall on unfamiliar territory.

To check Yanoviak's impression that the ants were controlling their fall, he dropped at least 100 of them from a tall tree. To make sure the dark ants falling into a dimly lit forest would show up in videos, he painted white nail polish on their bodies.

About 85 percent of the dropped *C. atratus* ants swooped close enough to the trunk to catch hold, he and his colleagues reported. Then the ants climbed back to the treetops. Some rejoined him only 10 minutes after he had dropped them.   ■ Susan Milius

See also **ECOLOGY.**

ATTRACTING DUNG BEETLES

A burrowing owl stands alongside pieces of dung that it may use as bait to attract dung beetles, a favorite prey, according to a report published in September 2004. Burrowing owls, which live throughout North and South America, commonly collect animal dung for deposit around the entrances to their underground burrows. Scientists from the University of Florida at Gainesville found that owls with dung scattered near their nest entrances ate 10 times as many beetles as the owls whose entrances the scientists had cleared of dung. The difference, they suggested, indicates that the owls used the dung to attract the beetles.

■ BOOKS ABOUT SCIENCE

These 11 important new books about science are suitable for the general reader. They have been selected from books published in 2004 and 2005.

Astronomy. *Big Bang: The Origin of the Universe* by Simon Singh presents the current state of our knowledge about the beginnings of the universe. In the 1920's, American astronomer Edwin Hubble discovered that virtually all the galaxies are moving away from our Milky Way Galaxy, with the more distant galaxies moving the fastest. British science journalist Singh explains how astronomers came to understand that this strange outward flight was the result of a primordial cosmic cataclysm known as the big bang. (Fourth Estate, 2005, 532 pp. $27.95)

Origins: Fourteen Billion Years of Cosmic Evolution by Neal deGrasse Tyson and Donald Goldsmith explains the most recent discoveries about the universe's distant past. Tyson, director of New York City's Hayden Planetarium, and Goldsmith, a veteran science writer, cover the origin of the universe, the birth of stars and planets, and the beginnings of life on Earth. (W.W. Norton, 2004, 336 pp. $27.95)

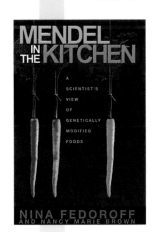

Biology. *Mendel in the Kitchen: A Scientist's View of Genetically Modified Foods* by Nina Fedoroff and Nancy Marie Brown addresses the highly controversial issue of using gene manipulation to enhance the *palatability* (taste), nutritional value, and disease resistance of crop plants. Fedoroff, a molecular biologist at Pennsylvania State University in University Park, and science writer Brown argue that the wise use of genetics will ultimately benefit plant breeders, farmers, and consumers alike. (National Academies Press, 2004, 370 pp. $24.95)

The Philosopher Fish: Sturgeon, Caviar, and the Geography of Desire by journalist Richard Adams Carey explores the biological, social, and commercial history of this remark-able creature and discusses the efforts being made to help it flourish once again. The sturgeon is one of the most sought-after fish in the world. It is prized for its tender meat and, even more, for its eggs, which make the finest caviar. Not surprisingly, it is an endangered species. Nevertheless, populations of sturgeon survive in several spots around the world, from the Suwannee River in Florida and the Hudson River in New York to the shores of the Caspian Sea in Azerbaijan. (Counterpoint Press, 2005, 300 pp. $26)

Ecology. *Collapse: How Societies Choose to Fail or Succeed* by Jared Diamond is a sequel to Diamond's Pulitzer Prize-winning *Guns, Germs, and Steel.* In *Guns,* Diamond, a professor of geography at the University of California at Los Angeles, described how geographical factors helped promote the rise of Europe's industrial civilization and hinder the growth of empires in other areas of the world. In *Collapse,* Diamond argues that geography also plays an essential role in the collapse of civilizations both great and small. Chance—in the form of climate change, for instance—can cause farms to fail and economies to crumble. But for many societies, mortal wounds are self-inflicted, caused by runaway population growth or reckless damage to the environment. (Viking Press, 2004, 592 pp. $29.95)

Geology. *Frozen Earth: The Once and Future Story of Ice Ages* by Doug Macdougall traces the frequent cooling periods experienced by our planet from the earliest known glaciation 3 billion years ago to the present. During those times, polar ice caps expanded and glaciers covered most of North America, Europe, and Asia. Macdougall, a professor of earth science at the University of California at San Diego, describes how scientists learned about these drastic changes in climate, what causes them, and what the future may hold. (University of California Press, 2004, 256 pp. illus. $24.95)

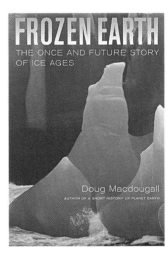

BOOKS ABOUT SCIENCE continued

Earthquakes in Human History: The Far-Reaching Effects of Seismic Disruptions by Jelle Zeilinga de Boer and Donald Theodore Sanders reviews some of the most notable earthquakes of the past. The earthquake that caused the Indian Ocean tsunami of December 2004 reminded people how devastating these events can be. Yet earthquakes are far more common than people might suppose, and their effects are more far-reaching. De Boer, a professor of earth sciences at Wesleyan University in Middletown, Connecticut, and Sanders, a writer and former student, describe how civilizations foundered, religions arose, and works of art were destroyed—and created—in the aftermath of earthquakes. (Princeton University Press, 2004, 278 pp. $24.95)

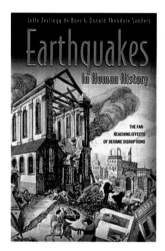

Meteorology. *Defining the Wind: The Beaufort Scale, and How a 19th-Century Admiral Turned Science into Poetry* by Scott Huler recounts how an observant young sailor devised a scale of numbers that has become the standard for measuring the wind. In 1805, Francis Beaufort, while commanding his first ship, wrote a table to describe the force of the wind. His entries began with "0—calm: smoke rises vertically" and ended with "12—hurricane: devastation occurs." Science historian Huler goes beyond biography to demonstrate how Beaufort employed scientific principles to unveil the complex wonders of the world around us. (Crown Publishers, 2004, 304 pp. $23)

Natural history. *The Remarkable Life of William Beebe: Explorer and Naturalist* by Carol Grant Gould tells the story of one of the best-known natural historians of the 1900's. Science writer Gould describes Beebe's work at the New York Zoological Society and his ground-breaking expeditions

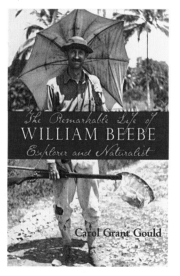

to the tropics, to the Himalaya, and even to the bottom of the ocean in a *bathysphere* (one of the earliest deep-sea exploration capsules). Beebe was an eloquent writer, a popular radio personality of the 1930's and 1940's, and a passionate ecologist who inspired a new generation of scientists. (Island Press, 2004, 447 pp. illus. $30)

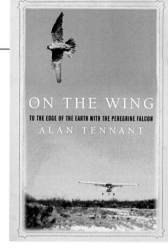

On the Wing: To the Edge of the Earth with the Peregrine Falcon by Alan Tennant is filled with detailed lore on the biology and ecology of birds of prey. Naturalist Tennant follows the migration of a radio-tagged falcon from Texas to its summer home in the Canadian Arctic and back to its winter home in the jungles of Central America. Describing his flight in a rickety, single-engine plane piloted by a feisty old barnstormer, Tennant provides both an informative natural history and an adventure story as he and his friend George Vose struggle to keep on course and in the air. (Knopf, 2004, 320 pp. $25)

Physics. *The Fly in the Cathedral: How a Group of Cambridge Scientists Won the International Race to Split the Atom* by Brian Cathcart, a science reporter, recounts this remarkable achievement and the people who made it happen. At the center of every atom, like a "fly in a cathedral," is the nucleus, a dense pinpoint of material whose inner structure remained a mystery until the 1930's. In 1932, at the Cavendish Laboratory in Cambridge, England, a team of scientists succeeded in splitting open the nucleus of an atom for the first time, revealing how tiny neutrons and protons combine to form the grand edifices of the elements. (Farrar, Strauss and Giroux, 2005, 320 pp. $25)

■ Laurence A. Marschall

BOOKS ABOUT SCIENCE FOR YOUNGER READERS

These five important new books about science are suitable for the younger reader. They have been selected from books published in 2004 and 2005.

Archaeology. *The Usborne Introduction to Archaeology: Internet-Linked* by Abigail Wheatley and Struan Reid presents a concise, continent-by-continent overview of archaeology, highlighting a wide range of discoveries (keyed to maps) that bind us to ancient civilizations. The oversized book is filled with excellent graphics, maps, photos, and charts. The publisher's dedicated Web site (www.usborne-quicklinks.com) supplements the book with additional links to print, audio, and video material. In addition, visitors to the site can unwrap a virtual mummy or attempt to decipher ancient writings. (Usborne, 2005, 128 pp. illus. $22.95)

Biology. *Guts: Our Digestive System* by Seymour Simon explores the inner workings of the human body. Simon, a long-time author of science books, introduces the complex processes that are involved in digestion from the time food enters the mouth until various organs transform it into energy, nutrients, and waste. Large, clearly labeled, full-color photos show the anatomy close up—everything from an X ray of the colon and a photo of a dissected pancreas to an image of what heartburn looks like inside the stomach. (HarperCollins, 2005, 32 pp. illus. $15.99)

Invisible Allies: Microbes that Shape our Lives by Jeanette Farrell explains how these tiny, invisible creatures that can make us sick or even kill us may be extremely beneficial as well. Farrell, a medical doctor, shows how human beings depend on microbes to perform such important tasks as digesting our food and training our immune responses. Outside the body, microbes help in the production of cheese, bread, and chocolate. They also help dispose of human waste in sewage plants and clean up oil spills and toxins. (Farrar, Strauss and Giroux, 2005, 165 pp. illus. $17)

Ecology. *The Race to Save the Lord God Bird* by Phillip Hoose recounts how the ivory-billed woodpecker lived and faced extinction and how a wide range of people—from artists to scientists to ordinary bird lovers—tried to save it. For thousands of years, the majestic bird was a distinctive inhabitant of the Southeast (with a related species in Cuba). The bird's nickname came from the exclamation of naturalists when they first saw it: "Lord God, what a bird!" By the 1800's, however, the numbers of these birds were dwindling. They had been killed for sport or for their feathers, or they were delivered to collectors who prized them for their rarity. (Scientists in April 2005 reported the first sighting of an ivory-billed woodpecker in more than 60 years, in Arkansas.) (Farrar, Strauss and Giroux, 2004, 208 pp. illus. $20)

Natural science. *Wild Science: Amazing Encounters Between Animals and the People Who Study Them* by Victoria Miles offers a detailed view of scientists at work in the wilderness. Miles begins each chapter with a profile of a wildlife biologist. Among them are a whale specialist who saves a beached blue whale off the coast of Newfoundland and a scientist who studies endangered marmots. The author includes information on what it's like to work outdoors, explores issues surrounding the scientists' research, and presents facts about the animals and their habitat. (Raincoast, 2004, 168 pp. illus. $18.95)

■ Ilene Cooper

CHEMISTRY

The discovery of the strongest acid ever created was reported by researchers in the United States and Russia in October 2004. Remarkably, the new acid, which is at least 1 million times as strong as concentrated sulfuric acid, is also one of the gentlest acids. The discovery of the super-strong acid, a type of *carborane acid,* was reported by chemists Christopher A. Reed and colleagues at the University of California at Riverside and Evgenii Stoyanov of the Boreskov Institute of Catalysis in Novosibirsk, Russia. (Carborane acid is a mixture of carbon, boron, and hydrogen.)

The strength of an acid is measured by how easily it gives up a *hydrogen ion* (a hydrogen atom with a single positive charge) to other chemicals or surfaces in its surroundings. The strongest acids shed their hydrogen ions with little effort, but weaker acids hold on to their hydrogen ions more strongly. Left behind after an acid gives up a positive hydrogen ion is a negative atom or group of negative atoms called an *anion.*

Most strong acids are also *corrosive* (tending to eat away substances gradually) because their anions react strongly with compounds or surfaces that have accepted the hydrogen ions. For example, hydrofluoric acid can eat away glass, which is made of a network of interconnected silicon and oxygen atoms. Hydrofluoric acid's anion attacks the silicon atoms in glass, while the acid's hydrogen ions attack the oxygen atoms. Together, these reactions weaken the silicon-oxygen bonds in glass and cause it to dissolve.

By contrast, after the carborane acid donates a hydrogen ion, it leaves behind an anion that is chemically unreactive. As a result, chemicals or surfaces that accept the hydrogen ions from the acid become positively charged but are not attacked by the acid's anion.

The new acid consists of 1 hydrogen atom bonded to an interlinked cluster of 11 boron atoms and 1 carbon atom, with various other atoms and chemical groups bonded to the borons. The carborane acid loses its hydrogen ion so easily that it is hundreds of times as strong as fluorosulfuric acid (which has the formula $HFSO_3$), the previous recordholder for high acidity.

Because it is a very strong acid but does not promote other reactions, the carborane acid could have many useful applications, its discoverers believe. The new acid, they say, might be able to raise the *yield* (amount) of high-octane gasoline produced from petroleum in a process called *hydrocarbon cracking.* (Hydrocarbon cracking uses acids to break down the hydrocarbon molecules in oil into smaller molecules.) The researchers also believe that pharmaceutical companies might be able to use the acid to produce drugs more cleanly and with higher yields.

Sniffing out trouble. Airport security officers may be able to instantly detect traces of explosives or illegal drugs on people or luggage using a new device for analyzing chemical samples, according to research reported in October 2004 by scientists at Purdue University in West Lafayette, Indiana. The device, developed by a team led by chemist R. Graham Cooks, consists of a wandlike detector connected to an instrument about the size of a backpack.

The new device employs a miniaturized and simplified version of a widely used method of chemical analysis called *mass spectroscopy.* Mass spectroscopy identifies chemicals by the way they break down into ions when they are bombarded with a stream of *electrons* (negatively charged subatomic particles). Scientists can determine the makeup of a compound by analyzing the unique set of ions produced in the process. Normally, however, mass spectroscopy is a slow and cumbersome process. A sample being analyzed must first be dissolved in a *solvent* (liquid that breaks up other substances) and then bombarded with electrons in a vacuum chamber.

To make mass spectroscopy useful for analysis outside a lab, the Purdue team developed an easier way to convert samples into ions. Their method, called *desorption electrospray ionization* (DESI), requires neither a solvent nor a vacuum.

The DESI method uses a long, needlelike wand to spray a high-pressure stream of tiny droplets of a solvent mixed with reactive chemicals onto a surface containing residues of an unknown chemical. (The solvent is typically water or a water-alcohol mixture.) In much the same way that wind kicks up dust particles, the solvent stream knocks off molecule-sized fragments of the unknown sample. These fragments then combine with the reactive chemicals to form ions. The same wand used to spray the solvent also sucks up the resulting ions and delivers them to a portable mass spectroscopy instrument that sorts out the ions for analysis.

By combining the DESI technique with a portable mass spectrometer, the Purdue scientists have detected traces of the explosive RDX (cyclotrimethylenetrinitramine) on a leather surface. They have also picked up evidence of a chemical warfare agent called DMMP (dimethyl methlyphosphonate) from a pair of rubber gloves that had been washed after a one-second exposure to the agent. In addition, they detected traces of an over-the-counter allergy medication on the finger of a person who had taken a 10-milligram tablet of the drug 40 minutes earlier. As promising as these results are, the Purdue researchers caution, further tests of their device are needed before it can be used for airport screening or in police field investigations.

A lobster of a different color. Scientists reported the discovery of pigments that cause 1 in 1 million lobsters to be a brilliant blue color naturally. The investigations were reported by chemists Harry A. Frank of the University of Connecticut in Storrs and Ronald L. Christensen of Bowdoin College in Brunswick, Maine, in March 2005.

All lobsters turn bright red when they are cooked. Scientists have long known that this is because their shells contain a red pigment called *astaxanthin*. This compound, which is made of carbon, hydrogen, and oxygen atoms, also gives shrimp and salmon their reddish and pinkish colors. The shells of live lobsters, however, contain not only astaxanthin but also a blue pigment called *crustacyanin*. Crustacyanin actually consists of several astaxanthin molecules bound tightly to a protein.

To find out the secrets of lobsters' color differences, the team first had to determine why red astaxanthin molecules turn blue when combined and bound to a protein. The researchers

WHY SO BLUE?

A lobster with a blue shell—a 1 in 1 million occurrence—owes its unusual color to a genetic mutation, according to research reported in March 2005. All lobster shells, which are normally brownish, have a mixture of blue *crustacyanin* and red *astaxanthin* pigments. Researchers from Connecticut and Maine determined that a few lobsters have a blue shell because they produce too much crustacyanin.

CHEMISTRY continued

used high-speed lasers to study how astaxanthin molecules absorb light as their environment changes.

They found that light absorbed by the molecules shifts to the red region of the *visible spectrum* as they become bound to proteins. (The visible spectrum is light that can be seen by the unaided eye.) They concluded that the protein in crustacyanin twists the astaxanthin molecules bound to it so that they overlap slightly. This overlap causes the protein-bound astaxanthin molecules to behave as if they were a single, much larger molecule. In general, the larger a pigment molecule is, the more red light it absorbs. When a molecule absorbs red light, the light reflected from it appears blue. Thus, crustacyanin has a blue tint.

In the wild, lobsters have shells that appear as a mottled brown because they contain roughly equal amounts of red astaxanthin and blue crustacyanin. But when lobsters are dunked into boiling water, according to the researchers, the heat causes the protein in the crustacyanin to loosen its grip on the astaxanthin molecules, freeing them to drift away. Each individual astaxanthin molecule then displays its normal red color and gives cooked lobster its typical red hue.

Blue lobsters exist, the researchers explained, because they have a genetic mutation that causes the production of excess amounts of crustacyanin. If a blue lobster is cooked, its crustacyanin pigment breaks apart and releases its astaxanthin. As a result, a cooked blue lobster is the same color as a normal cooked lobster—red.

First snapshot of a molecular orbital. The first three-dimensional image of a *molecular orbital* was reported in December 2004 by a research group from the National Research Council of Canada in Ottawa. A molecular orbital is a fuzzy, cloudlike region containing the paths of electrons that are shared by atoms linked together in dumbbell shapes by chemical bonds. The research team included physicists Jiro Itatani, David M. Villeneuve, Paul B. Corkum, and their colleagues at the National Research Council's Steacie Institute of Molecular Sciences, along with investigators at other Canadian institutions and the Japan Science and Technology Agency.

The scientists believe that their method of capturing these pictures will enable researchers to determine how the shapes of molecular orbitals change as bonds between atoms form and break during chemical reactions. The technique used to create the image is similar to *computed tomography* (CT) scanning, a common medical imaging technique. (A CT scan image is assembled by a computer using X-ray images of a patient taken at different angles.)

Electrons in atoms do not circle the *nuclei* (centers) of the atoms in fixed planetlike orbits but are actually spread out in *atomic orbitals*—regions in space where electrons have a high probability of being found. When two atoms bond to form a molecule, their outermost atomic orbitals—which have the highest level of energy—overlap to form a molecular orbital. Although many textbooks show pictures of molecular orbitals, these images are based on mathematical calculations. The new imaging technique now allows scientists to see a molecular orbital directly.

The orbital made visible by the NRC team belonged to a molecule of nitrogen, which consists of two nitrogen atoms bonded together. In their experiments, the scientists first beamed a brief flash of laser light into a chamber filled with nitrogen, which caused the nitrogen molecules to line up in the same direction. Once the molecules were aligned, the researchers exposed them to pulses of laser light lasting only a few millionths of a *nanosecond* (one billionth of a second). Each pulse threw an electron in the nitrogen bond to a position slightly outside the bonding molecular orbital. When the electron fell back into the orbital, it emitted a brief flash of light. That light gave the researchers information about the electron's atomic orbital before it was excited by the laser. By shifting the angles of the laser pulses and recording the emitted light at these angles, the researchers obtained a computer-generated three-dimensional picture of a complete molecular orbital.

Chemists immediately hailed the new molecular imaging technique as a potentially valuable research tool. In particular, they expressed the hope that it would allow them to view changes in orbitals while chemical reactions are in progress. Knowledge gained by such images could be used to predict new reactions and improve the yields of existing ones.

■ Gordon Graff

See also **ENGINEERING; PHYSICS.**

COMPUTERS AND ELECTRONICS

Software threats continued to plague computer users in 2004 and 2005. Although *worms* and *viruses* posed the greatest threat, other types of dangerous software also became common. Worms and viruses are small pieces of software that can damage computers and be forwarded to other computers.

Spyware, software that enters a computer without the user's knowledge and monitors certain patterns of use, became a major problem. Up to 90 percent of all Internet-connected computers were infected with spyware in 2004, according to a March 2005 report compiled by Earthlink, Inc., an Internet service provider based in Atlanta, Georgia, and Webroot Software of Boulder, Colorado.

Much spyware is legal and relatively harmless. For example, *cookies* are bits of software code used by many advertisers and Web sites to record such information as the identity and location of a user's computer. However, criminal spyware can track computer keystroke patterns in an attempt to capture credit card and bank account numbers, passwords, and other sensitive

| **SEE ALSO** | CONSUMER SCIENCE, **BYTE BACK: PROTECTING YOUR COMPUTER,** PAGE 156. |

and confidential information. The spyware then relays these stolen data to criminal networks.

With such private information in hand, criminals are able to access the accounts in question. In addition, they can create new accounts using the victim's identity. These kinds of crimes, called *identity theft,* ranked among the most rapidly growing types of computer crime in 2005.

Spyware is transmitted over the Internet. It can be embedded in e-mail attachments, Web sites, or pop-up advertisements. For these

MUSIC ON THE MOVE

The iPod Shuffle, released in January 2005, was the latest addition to the iPod family of portable digital music players. Apple Computer, Inc., of Cupertino, California, produced the iPod Shuffle as a smaller and less-expensive version of the original iPod. The iPod Shuffle could store up to 240 music files, compared with 5,000 files for the standard iPod. The device plays the music in a different order every time the user listens to it.

COMPUTERS AND ELECTRONICS continued

reasons, computer experts warn users to avoid opening unfamiliar e-mail attachments and to exercise caution when clicking on advertisements on the Web.

Many manufacturers of software designed to prevent virus and worm infections also offer antispyware and spyware-removal tools. Microsoft Corporation of Redmond, Washington, the world's largest software maker, released a free program called Microsoft Antispyware in January 2005. The program could be downloaded from Microsoft's Web site. Within weeks of the program's release, however, *hackers* (authors of viruses and other malicious software) created *Trojan horses* capable of disabling the antispyware program. A Trojan horse is a malicious program that enters a computer while appearing to be harmless software.

Computer hijackings. Another use of spyware is to "hijack" the infected computer, using the computer's resources and network connections to infect additional computers. Users often cannot tell that their computer has been hijacked, because the spyware may tamper with the computer's resources only when the user is not operating the machine.

Such hijacked computers are called *bots*, and networks of hijacked computers are called *botnets* or *zombie networks*. In March 2005, the Honeynet Project, an international organization working to improve Internet security, estimated that at least 1 million computers around the world had been hijacked. Some botnets had more than 50,000 hijacked computers in their ranks, according to the organization.

Hackers controlling botnets use the hijacked computers for various purposes, including launching virus, worm, and *phishing* attacks. In phishing, the computer user is presented with what appears to be a legitimate Web page from a bank or other major company. The Web page requests that the visitor provide such private information as credit card or account numbers. This information can then be used by the hackers for illicit purposes.

Users can detect possible computer hijackings by watching for declining computer performance, including noticeable slowdowns in operating speed. Most computer experts recommend that all computer users equip their devices with software designed to detect and eliminate spyware, viruses, and worms. Because hackers are constantly updating their criminal software, users should update their protective software on a regular basis. Updates are generally available from the software's developer over the Internet.

Phone viruses. Many cellular telephones and handheld personal organizers acquired more of the functions usually found in computers in 2004 and 2005. For example, these devices could send and receive text messages and find and display Web pages. As they became

SEE-THROUGH CIRCUITS

A transparent semiconductor material that can be deposited on thin, flexible sheets of plastic was developed by scientists at the Tokyo Institute of Technology in Japan, according to a November 2004 report. Researchers said transistors made from the see-through circuitry are 10 times as *conductive* (able to transmit electric current) as silicon transistors used in liquid-crystal displays. They noted that the new material might be used for a number of unique purposes, such as map displays on car windshields and roll-up computer displays.

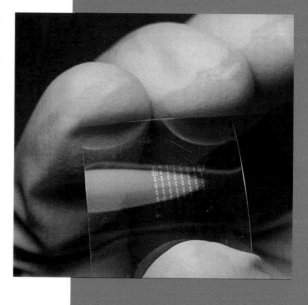

equipped with more sophisticated software, their *operating systems* (OS) also became more vulnerable to attack. The operating system controls the various electronic elements of the device. By infecting a cellular telephone's OS with a virus, hackers may be able to damage the phone or even cause it to stop working.

The first widespread cell phone worm, called Cabir, appeared in June 2004. Updated versions of this worm continued to appear for months afterward. Cabir did not directly damage the phones it infected. However, it served as a successful demonstration that phone worms could use the resources of the infected phones to copy themselves. These copies were then transmitted to other cellular phones. Cabir targeted phones using the Symbian OS, a widely used cellular phone OS, as well as phones using Bluetooth wireless technology.

Another Symbian-targeting virus was Commwarrior, which was identified in March 2005. Commwarrior caused little or no damage to the infected phones, but it demonstrated that phone viruses could spread through *multimedia files,* messages that can include graphics and sound.

The most serious attack on Symbian-equipped phones occurred in April 2005. A Trojan horse called Fontal.A destroyed all data in infected phones, including stored phone numbers, user settings, and other information. Attempting to restore the information by turning off and restarting the telephone resulted in the complete shutdown of the OS. Users could restart their phone only by reformatting its software and could not recover the phone's lost information.

Search engine expansion. Google, Inc., a well-known *search engine* company based in Mountain View, California, applied its popular search technology to information stored on the hard drives of personal computers in October 2004. Search engines are programs that maintain updated indexes of pages on the World Wide Web, enabling users to search quickly through tens of millions of pages in pursuit of a specific fact or bit of information.

Google Desktop Search, a program that could be downloaded from Google's Web site, tracks a computer's use in various applications, including Web browsing, word processing, and e-mailing. The program takes several hours to make an initial index of all this information. Information added later by the computer user is indexed as it is added.

When the computer searches for a topic or term, Google Desktop Search displays matching information from the Web, as well as from the computer's hard drive and e-mail system. These results are displayed side-by-side in the user's *Web browser,* a software program for navigating and displaying pages from the Web. The version of Google Desktop Search released in 2004 worked only with Microsoft's Internet Explorer Web browser and only for computers running Microsoft's Windows OS.

Google attracted further attention in April 2005, when it added satellite photos of Earth's surface to its popular map-search function. While searches for maps in Google's regular files return many familiar geographical maps, the new feature allowed users to search for satellite photographs of such specific locations as their own home.

Google acquired the satellite images through the purchase of a digital map company called Keyhole Corp., which was also based in Mountain View. Keyhole had charged users $29.95 for the satellite map software, but Google offered the service at no charge. Some observers raised questions about the widespread availability of the satellite images, arguing that it amounted to an invasion of privacy and confidentiality.

Miniature Mac. The Mac Mini, a smaller, less expensive version of the Macintosh computer, was introduced in January 2005 by Apple Computer, Inc., of Cupertino, California. The $499 Mac Mini marked Apple's first inexpensive Macintosh aimed at a large consumer audience.

The Mac Mini, which did not include a keyboard or monitor, measured 16 ½ centimeters (6 ½ inches) wide and 5 centimeters (2 inches) high. It included a combination DVD/CD-ROM drive, a 40-gigabyte hard disk, and a 1.25-gigahertz processor. It also featured a variety of ports to enable users to connect the machine to such devices as televisions and advanced sound systems. A $599 version of the Mac Mini offered a faster processor and larger hard disk.

Consumer excitement over the new Macintosh resulted in a brief shortage of the computers early in the year. By April 2005, however, Apple had increased production to meet demand.

iPod Shuffle. The success of the Mac Mini followed on Apple's successes with such portable music devices as the iPod and iPod mini. The standard 20-gigabyte iPod could store 5,000 songs, and the iPod mini, 1,500 songs. In January 2005, Apple released the latest addition

COMPUTERS AND ELECTRONICS continued

to the iPod family—the iPod Shuffle, a smaller and less expensive version of the popular digital music players.

With prices starting at $99, the iPod Shuffle provided users with the ability to store up to 120 songs. A $149 version offered a capacity of up to 240 songs. Both versions store music files using *flash memory,* a form of electronic memory, rather than the magnetic storage offered by disk-based devices. As with the Mac Mini, enthusiastic consumer demand for the iPod Shuffle resulted in temporary delays in filling orders.

Nanograss batteries. A potentially revolutionary approach to computer battery technology was announced in September 2004 by mPhase Technologies, Inc., of Norwalk, Connecticut, and Lucent Technologies of Murray Hill, New Jersey. The battery break-through emerged from cutting-edge research in *nanotechnology,* the manipulation and manufacture of materials at the molecular or even atomic level.

The batteries are made with a material called *nanograss,* which consists of tens of thousands of silicon posts, each a thousand times thinner than a human hair. The nanograss serves as a storage device for liquid *electrolytes,* nonmetallic substances that can conduct electricity. Applying heat or sound waves to the nanograss brings the electrolytes into contact with electrodes, which carry electric current into the liquid. This contact activates the battery.

Among the key advances offered by the batteries was a dramatic increase in *shelf life,* the amount of time an unused battery can remain usable. Conventional computer batteries have limited shelf life because they lose as much as 3 percent of their potential power for every month they remain unused. By contrast, the electrolytes in the nanograss-based batteries remain completely dormant until the nanograss posts are activated. This gives the batteries an estimated shelf life of up to 25 years.

The researchers noted that nanograss offered other potential applications. For example, the material might be made into tiny heat sinks, which would capture and dissipate the heat generated by electrical reactions in computer processors and other electronic equipment.

Blog mania. One of the most prominent computer-based trends in 2004 and 2005 was the dramatic growth in the popularity of Web logs, also known as *blogs.* Blogs are personal journals or diaries that their authors post on Web pages.

From October 2004 through February 2005, the number of blogs worldwide on the Web doubled, reaching 8 million, according to Technorati, Inc., a blog-tracking company based in San Francisco. Analysts expected this figure to continue growing at a rapid rate—perhaps doubling every five months for the near future.

Anyone with a computer and access to the Internet can start a blog. The most common method of creating a blog is to register with a *blogging service,* a software company that maintains a Web address where the blog will be posted. The service also provides software tools for writing and editing the blog. Some blog-creation software allows users to incorporate graphics, photographs, and even video into their blogs. Other services are text only. Many blog services charge bloggers a monthly fee, but readers can usually view blogs at no charge.

Because blogs are individual creations, the range of topics they cover is as varied as the range of people's interests. One type of blog that attracted particular attention during the second half of 2004 was the political blog. Many political bloggers commented on the United States presidential election, often questioning the accuracy of news reports by such traditional media outlets as newspapers and television. Traditional media outlets countered by expressing doubts about the overall accuracy of the commentary found in blogs.

Some political blogs had a significant impact on news coverage by the traditional media during the 2004 presidential election. For example, the CBS television news show "60 Minutes II" aired a report in September 2004 that cited Texas National Guard memos critical of President George W. Bush's service in the Guard. After bloggers noted that the memos appeared to be forgeries, CBS News admitted that it could not vouch for the authenticity of the documents.

Many observers noted that blogs served as a reminder of how quickly computer technology can affect our world. The word *blog* was virtually unknown in early 2004. By the end of that year, however, the term was used relatively frequently in news reports and everyday conversations. ■ Keith Ferrell

See also **ENGINEERING; PHYSICS.**

CONSERVATION

September 2004 marked the 40th anniversary of the enactment of the Wilderness Act, landmark conservation legislation that was signed into law by United States President Lyndon B. Johnson in 1964. The act designated 3.7 million hectares (9.1 million acres) in the United States as *wilderness areas,* which the legislation defined as areas "where the earth and its community of life are untrammeled by man, where man himself is a visitor who does not remain." Motorized vehicles and power tools, including chain saws, are banned in wilderness areas. Such potentially harmful activities as commercial logging, mining, road building, oil and gas development, and mountain biking are also prohibited. However, camping, fishing, hunting, hiking, canoeing, and horseback riding are allowed.

By 2005, the total area protected by the Wilderness Act had grown to 42.9 million hectares (106 million acres). Protected wilderness covers nearly 5 percent of the United States—an area approximately equal in size to the state of California. Every U.S. president since Johnson has added land to the wilderness system. President George W. Bush had added 214,490 hectares (529,604 acres) to the system since taking office in 2001.

Conservationists praised the act on its 40th anniversary by noting that wilderness areas protect breathtaking scenery as well as many undisturbed *ecosystems.* An ecosystem is a natural system made up of living organisms and their environment. Among the protected ecosystems were active volcanoes and lava fields in Hawaii; swamps and other wetlands in South Carolina; and alpine lakes and perennial snowfields in the evergreen forests of Wyoming. Altogether, as of 2005, 677 sites had been designated as part of the National Wilderness Preservation System. The sites range in size from a 2-hectare (5-acre) island in Florida to a 3.64-million-hectare (9-million-acre) scenic area in Alaska. Many of these sites are parts of national parks, wildlife refuges, national forests, or other federally owned lands.

Tasmanian devils and cancer. In 2005, an unusual form of cancer was threatening the survival of a well-known, important member of Australia's native wildlife—the Tasmanian devil. Up to two-thirds of the 150,000 Tasmanian devils that lived on the Australian island of Tasmania in the mid-1990's had disappeared by 2005, according to a January report by the

SEE ALSO THE SPECIAL REPORT, GREAT APES: CULTURE AND CONSERVATION, PAGE 40

Tasmanian government. Tasmanian conservation authorities attributed this population crash to the spread of a contagious type of cancer.

Tasmanian devils—like many Australian mammals—are *marsupials,* mammals whose young are born in an extremely immature state. Marsupial females usually carry their young in pouches. Tasmanian devils are fierce creatures that sometimes hunt smaller animals but get most of their food by scavenging the carcasses of dead animals. By helping to break down these remains, Tasmanian devils play a key role in the ecology of wildlife communities.

The cancer, which was first reported in the mid-1990's, causes disfiguring tumors and open *abscesses* (sores) to grow on the mouth, face, and muzzle of Tasmanian devils. These tumors can eventually become serious enough to prevent the animals from feeding. The illness can kill an animal within six months. Adults seem more at risk than juveniles do. As a result, the disease affects the animals' birth rate.

Although scientists were not sure how the cancer spreads among a population, they suspected that it might spread directly from animal to animal as the quarrelsome Tasmanian devils fight face to face over food. This idea was based on laboratory tests that failed to detect any virus particles in the tumors. Laboratory evidence also showed that cells from the tumors all have identical arrangements of *chromosomes* (threadlike structures made of genes), indicating that the same cancer cell line was involved in all the infections.

Conservationists with the Tasmanian government were considering capturing and isolating healthy Tasmanian devils in mid-2005. These animals would be kept in fenced-in areas or other isolated locations outside the disease zones. The healthy Tasmanian devils would serve as an "insurance population" that could later be reintroduced into the wild after the disease had run its course. Authorities were also considering removing ill individuals from the wild populations as a means of suppressing the further spread of the disease.

CONSERVATION continued

The Tasmanian government had appropriated $1.8 million to study the disease plaguing Tasmanian devils in 2003. This funding covered research through mid-2007. Private citizens donated another $50,000 for research purposes.

Amphibian assessment. The first comprehensive global assessment of amphibian populations, reported in December 2004, confirmed earlier studies documenting the dire straits of these animals. More amphibian species are threatened with extinction—with their populations declining more rapidly—than are bird or mammal species. That was the conclusion of a team of biologists headed by Simon N. Stuart of the International Union for the Conservation of Nature and Natural Resources (IUCN). The IUCN, which is also known as the World Conservation Union, is an organization headquartered in Gland, Switzerland, that publishes lists of endangered species.

According to the IUCN, 427 species, or 7.4 percent of all amphibian species, are *critically endangered,* a category indicating the greatest threat to a population. By contrast, 179 bird species (1.8 percent of bird species) and 184 mammal species (3.8 percent of mammal species) fall into the same category. The assessment found that 1,856 amphibian species, or 32 percent of all amphibian species, are *threatened* with extinction, a less serious category of concern.

Stuart said that unless this trend can be reversed, hundreds of species of amphibians will face extinction in the coming decades. Such an outcome would deliver a major blow to Earth's *biodiversity* (variety of species).

Previous studies of individual amphibian species usually indicated habitat loss, disease, or global climate change as likely explanations for population declines. But the new report emphasized that unknown causes are involved in the decline of 48 percent of the imperiled species. These unknown causes are known as *enigmatic declines.* Stuart noted that the mysterious nature of the problem makes the threat much more difficult to remedy.

The scientists discovered that the enigmatic declines occur most often in species that live in or near streams in mountainous habitats of the Neotropics, the tropical regions of the Western Hemisphere. Although many such habitats are being destroyed by human activities, the puzzling population declines were also noted in a number of protected areas, including Monteverde Cloud Forest Preserve in Costa Rica. Other enigmatic sites mentioned in the report included Yosemite National Park in California and Eungella National Park in Australia.

The study found that four groups of amphibians have declined more rapidly than other groups—gastric-brooding frogs, typical Neotropical frogs, true toads, and mole salamanders. Biologists believed in 2005 that the two known species of gastric-brooding frogs had already become extinct; they were last seen in the 1980's. The report stated that unknown causes have played a particularly serious role in the decline of true toads.

According to the IUCN researchers, captive breeding is the only conservation practice available for species threatened by unknown factors. However, many of the threatened amphibian species are difficult to maintain in captivity. Therefore, many scientists believe that extinctions of amphibians are likely to continue until the reasons for the enigmatic declines can be identified and remedied.

Giant panda population. The number of giant pandas living wild in mainland China, which includes their native habitat, increased by more than 40 percent from the 1980's to 2004, according to officials in the Chinese State Forestry Administration. The officials reported that a thorough survey of the wild panda population, completed in June 2004, counted 1,590 of the animals. The survey was the most recent of three population studies of giant pandas conducted in China since the 1970's. In addition to the wild giant pandas, about 160 giant pandas lived in captive breeding programs worldwide in 2005.

Giant pandas, which are recognized around the world as a symbol of endangered species, continue to require protection despite the population growth, conservation experts stressed. The WWF (formerly the World Wildlife Fund), a large conservation organization based in Geneva, Switzerland—and one of the sponsors of the survey—cautioned that improved methods for counting pandas may account for much of the apparent increase in population. Nevertheless, the survey revealed the existence of many more giant pandas in the wild than previously believed.

Many conservationists agreed that the panda numbers in the survey highlighted the effectiveness of conservation efforts. About two-thirds of the pandas included in the survey were found in nature reserves that had been established specifically for the animals.

Habitat loss from logging and *poaching* (illegal hunting) remained the biggest threats to giant pandas in 2005. To help the panda population grow and spread, the Chinese government was developing corridors of forest habitat to connect isolated nature reserves where pandas live. Scientists were also conducting extensive research on panda breeding biology, feeding ecology, and disease prevention. The long-term goal of these conservation efforts was the release of captive-bred giant pandas into well-managed natural areas. Conservationists hoped that such releases could reestablish a healthy, thriving population of wild pandas numbering eventually in the thousands.

Bird populations in decline. Nearly 30 percent of bird species in North America are in "significant decline," according to the National Audubon Society's *The State of the Birds*, a report published in October 2004. The National Audubon Society is a conservation organization based in New York City.

Scientists with the society studied bird population data from 1966 to 2003 for 654 species. They separately examined species that live in North American grasslands, shrublands, forests, wetlands, and urban areas.

Researchers observed the most serious decline among grassland birds. The populations of 70 percent of these species, including the Eastern meadowlark, bobolink, and short-eared owl, declined. Thirty-six percent of shrubland bird species declined in number, and 25 percent of forest bird species declined. Declines among wetland and urban species were less dramatic.

The report stated that these bird losses are

GOOD NEWS ABOUT PANDA POPULATION

A giant panda rests in its mountain habitat in a nature reserve in Sichuan Province, China. The wild population of giant pandas increased by more than 40 percent between the 1980's and 2004, according to a survey reported by Chinese officials in June 2004.

CONSERVATION continued

abnormal and are resulting from environmental problems, including destruction of habitat, overgrazing of grasslands, pollution, and poor management of ecosystems. The society called for improved conservation efforts, including greater protection for bird habitats.

Tsunami affects sea turtles. The disastrous *tsunami* (series of towering ocean waves) that killed almost 300,000 people in the Indian Ocean region in December 2004 also seriously damaged several of the region's sea turtle populations. The tsunami washed away a hatchery for endangered sea turtles in Sri Lanka, destroying about 20,000 eggs and $500,000 worth of research equipment. The eggs were scheduled to hatch on the same day that the tsunami struck.

Beaches in Sri Lanka are nesting grounds for five of the world's eight species of sea turtles. Despite legal protections for the turtles and stiff penalties for harming them, local villagers kill large numbers of turtles for food when the reptiles come ashore to nest. The hatchery was a conservation effort designed to help offset these losses.

The tsunami also washed away the sandy beaches on India's Great Nicobar Island, where leatherback sea turtles nested. The leatherbacks, which can weigh up to 680 kilograms (1,500 pounds), were due to begin nesting in January 2005, just a few weeks after the tsunami struck the island. Sea turtles have nested on Great Nicobar Island for generations, but with suitable habitat no longer available, scientists were not sure where—or if—the turtles would successfully nest again.

In contrast to this bad news, the tsunami may have brought a glimmer of good news for sea turtles in Malaysia, another nation where the powerful waves caused considerable damage. After the disaster, a beach in Malaysia lost its popularity with tourists. As a result, conservationists urged the Malaysian government to turn the beach into a protected nesting area for

The ivory-billed woodpecker, believed to be extinct for some 60 years, is living in a remote hardwood forest in eastern Arkansas. Ornithologist John Fitzpatrick of Cornell University in Ithaca, New York, reported in April 2005 that his team had confirmed sightings of ivory-billed woodpeckers in Arkansas' Big Woods. At 50 centimeters (20 inches) in length, the ivory-billed woodpecker is the largest woodpecker in North America. It is also known as the "Lord God Bird" because of an exclamation people made when seeing it for the first time.

sea turtles, especially the olive ridley sea turtle.

The idea for the sanctuary arose in February 2005, after more than 30 baby olive ridleys were discovered on the beach. Scientists suspected that the young turtles had come from a single clutch laid a few days after the tsunami struck Malaysia. ■ Eric G. Bolen

See also **ENVIRONMENTAL POLLUTION.**

DEATHS OF SCIENTISTS

Notable people of science who died between June 1, 2004, and May 31, 2005, are listed below. Those listed were Americans unless otherwise indicated.

Axelrod, Julius (1912–Dec. 29, 2004), neuroscientist and pharmacologist who won the 1970 Nobel Prize in physiology or medicine for his role in determining how *neurotransmitters* (chemicals in the brain that carry messages from one nerve cell to another) affect a person's behavior and mood. Axelrod's research was widely credited with leading to the development of selective serotonin reuptake inhibitors (SSRI's), a class of antidepressant drug that includes fluoxetine (marketed as Prozac).

Bemer, Bob (1920–June 22, 2004), computer pioneer who helped create and standardize a common computer code known as the American Standard Code for Information Interchange (ASCII). All computers use standard ASCII, which enables them to share information. Standard ASCII is capable of representing 128 different characters, including letters of the alphabet, numbers, punctuation marks, and mathematical symbols. Each character corresponds to a seven-digit *binary number* (a number system containing only 1's and 0's).

Bergstrom, Sune (1916–Aug. 15, 2004), Swedish biochemist who shared the 1982 Nobel Prize in physiology or medicine for discovering the origin of *prostaglandins*, a group of chemical compounds similar to hormones. Prostaglandins play a role in a variety of functions, including allergic reactions, metabolism, and reproduction. They also help control muscle contractions and regulate blood pressure. Bergstrom and his colleagues correctly theorized that prostaglandins could be used to treat high blood pressure, blocked blood vessels, and other circulatory problems because of their ability to relax muscle tissue.

Bethe, Hans Albrecht (1906–March 6, 2005), German-born physicist who received the 1967 Nobel Prize in physics for his formula explaining how stars produce energy. In 1938, during research into nuclear reactions, Bethe showed that virtually all stars fuse hydrogen into helium, releasing nuclear energy that becomes heat and light. During World War II (1939–1945), Bethe worked on the Manhattan Project, a United States government project that produced the first atomic bomb.

Buckley, Sonja (1919–Feb. 2, 2005), Swiss *virologist* (an expert who deals with viruses and viral diseases) who in 1970 helped identify the Lassa virus, a potentially fatal disease that originated in Lassa, Nigeria. The virus causes Lassa fever, the symptoms of which include high fever, massive internal bleeding, and convulsions. In 1969, two American missionary nurses and a laboratory worker were among those who died after contracting the virus, which is carried by mice and rats. The virus may be transmitted in the animals' urine or through dust contaminated with their feces. Buckley, who was part of a research team working in Nigeria, and her colleagues managed to isolate and identify the virus. Her samples were then sent to the United States for further examination.

Crick, Francis (1916–July 29, 2004), British biologist who shared the 1962 Nobel Prize in physiology or medicine with James D. Watson of the United States and Maurice Wilkins of the United Kingdom for their research leading to the discovery of the molecular structure of DNA (*deoxyribonucleic acid*) in 1953. DNA is the double-stranded, spiral-shaped molecule that transmits genetic information from one generation to the next.

Inspired by X-ray images of molecules taken by Wilkins and British chemist and molecular biologist Rosalind Franklin, Crick and Watson constructed a three-dimensional model of DNA. They used pieces of cardboard, sheet metal, wire, and colored beads to depict DNA as a twisted

Francis Crick

DEATHS OF SCIENTISTS continued

ladder consisting of two strands. Crick and Watson theorized that each strand carried chemical instructions for inherited traits. Their model became known as the Watson-Crick model.

Dalton, Katharina (1916–Sept. 17, 2004), British *gynecologist* (physician specializing in diseases of the female reproductive organs) who, during the 1950's, led pioneering studies of *premenstrual syndrome* (PMS). PMS is a condition that affects many women 3 to 10 days before the beginning of their menstrual period. PMS has a variety of symptoms, including anxiety, depression, fatigue, and sudden mood changes. Dalton theorized that PMS was caused by deficiencies in *progesterone* (a female hormone). Dalton's theory was later disproved. Although the exact cause of PMS remains unknown, most physicians believe that the symptoms result from hormonal changes that take place during the menstrual cycle.

Goldstine, Herman (1913–June 16, 2004), mathematician who in the 1940's helped develop ENIAC—the Electronic Numerical Integrator and Computer—one of the first general-purpose electronic computers. ENIAC could add or subtract 5,000 sums or multiply two 10-digit decimals 300 times. However, the machine also weighed 27 metric tons (30 tons) and occupied a room measuring 9 by 15 meters (30 by 50 feet). After ENIAC's first public demonstration in 1946, journalists described the computer as an "electronic brain." Many experts credit the development of ENIAC as the starting point of the information age.

Hilleman, Maurice (1919–April 11, 2005), microbiologist credited with saving tens of millions of lives through his development of 8 of the 14 vaccines routinely recommended for children. These include chickenpox, *Haemophilus influenzae* bacteria (which can cause inflammation of the brain's lining), hepatitis A, hepatitis B, measles, meningitis, mumps, and pneumonia. Hilleman's research also led to the creation of the first vaccines that immunized patients against several diseases at once, including the MMR vaccine for measles, mumps, and rubella.

Hounsfield, Sir Godfrey (1919–Aug. 12, 2004), English electrical engineer who won the 1979 Nobel Prize in physiology or medicine for his role in creating computerized axial tomography (CAT) scanning. The technology later became known as computed tomography (CT) scanning. Radiologists commonly use CT scans to create three-dimensional images of the brain, kidneys, liver, lungs, and other organs and to check patients for major injuries or internal bleeding.

Sir Godfrey Hounsfield

Kübler-Ross, Elisabeth (1926–Aug. 24, 2004), Swiss-born psychiatrist whose investigation of the dying process sparked the development of the hospice movement in the United States. Her research is often credited with changing the nation's perception of death. In her 1969 book, *On Death and Dying*, Kübler-Ross wrote that as a person dies, the human mind prepares itself by going through five stages of grief—denial, anger, bargaining, depression, and acceptance. The book was credited with initiating a dialogue on a subject that, until that time, had rarely been discussed in public. Following the overwhelming success of *On Death and Dying*, Kübler-Ross went on to write more than 20 other books dealing with end-of-life issues.

Westphal, James A. (1930–Sept. 8, 2004), self-tutored astronomer who led the Palomar Observatory in San Diego County, California. He also directed the team that built the first camera for the Hubble Space Telescope, a powerful

Elisabeth Kübler-Ross

telescope that was launched into orbit about 610 kilometers (380 miles) above Earth by the space shuttle Discovery in 1990. Astronomers have used the Hubble to obtain astonishing images of celestial objects and phenomena in unprecedented detail.

Whipple, Fred (1906–Aug. 30, 2004), astronomer who revolutionized the study of comets with his "dirty snowball" theory. In 1950, Whipple correctly theorized that a comet's solid *nucleus* (core) consists of ice and other frozen substances including ammonia, carbon dioxide, and methane. The tail of a comet, he theorized, is formed as particles break away from the icy body as it nears the sun. Further investigation led Whipple to propose that comets form within Earth's solar system. Astronomers later concluded that comets are debris from a collection of dust, gas, ice, and rock that contributed to the formation of some of the planets approximately 4.6 billion years ago.

Wilkins, Maurice (1916–Oct. 5, 2004), British biophysicist who shared the 1962 Nobel Prize in physiology or medicine with James D.

Fred Whipple

Watson of the United States and Francis Crick of the United Kingdom for determining the structure of DNA. As part of the research team, Wilkins devised an X-ray technique to photograph DNA samples. The resulting images led Watson and Crick to create their model of the molecular structure of DNA. During World War II, Wilkins also worked on the development of the atomic bomb as part of the Manhattan Project. ■ Tim Frystak

DRUGS

The United States Food and Drug Administration (FDA) approved 31 new drugs in 2004 and 3 new drugs as of April 1, 2005. Among these drugs were new treatments for leukemia and severe pain. Pharmaceutical companies and the FDA also came under heavy criticism in 2004 and 2005 from scientists, public advocacy groups, and the U.S. Congress on charges of suppressing and ignoring negative information about several widely used drugs.

Snail venom cures pain. The first painkiller based on snail venom won approval from the FDA in December 2004. The drug, ziconotide (sold under the brand name Prialt), is approved for treating patients with severe *chronic pain* who do not respond to traditional pain medications. (Chronic pain is pain that lasts three or more weeks.) About 50 million people in the United States suffer from chronic pain, according to the U.S. National Institutes of Health.

Ziconotide is derived from venom produced by *Conus magus*, a type of cone snail. Named for their cone-shaped shells, these tropical creatures live in the Indian and Pacific oceans, the Caribbean and Red seas, and along the coast of Florida. Some cone snails are harmful to people because they possess a sharp, venomous stinger. These snails are brimming with multiple venoms, often injecting their victims with at least 50 individual toxic *peptides* (chains of *amino acids*, the building blocks of proteins).

Researchers found that certain cone snail peptides block the calcium *ions* (electrically charged particles) that transmit pain signals from one nerve cell to another. This action prevents the pain signal from reaching the brain.

Side effects from ziconotide may include dizziness, headache, or upset stomach. However, unlike morphine and some other pain medications, ziconotide does not lead to addiction or *tolerance* (the need for larger and larger doses to get the same effect), according

DRUGS continued

to the drug's maker, Elan Corporation, which is based in Dublin, Ireland. Peptide drugs such as ziconotide cannot be taken by mouth because they are quickly destroyed by stomach acid. Instead, they must be injected directly into the spinal fluid in order to reach the spinal cord and the brain.

Industry difficulties. In June 2004, New York Attorney General Eliot Spitzer sued British-based GlaxoSmithKline, alleging that the company had fraudulently withheld negative results from clinical trials of the antidepressant paroxetine (sold under the brand name Paxil). Spitzer charged that at least four unpublished studies concluded that the drug was no more effective than a *placebo* (inactive substance) for children under age 18 and, in some cases, had increased the frequency of suicidal thoughts and behaviors among teen-aged participants.

In August, GlaxoSmithKline settled the case by agreeing to pay $2.5 million in fines and to create a publicly accessible Web site offering summaries of company trials conducted since December 2000. In October 2004, the FDA announced it was requiring the packages of all antidepressant medications to carry strict warnings that the drugs increase the risk of suicidal thoughts and behaviors in children and adolescents.

In September, U.S. Senate investigators explored charges that FDA officials had tried to silence agency scientist David Graham, whose research had concluded that high doses of the hugely profitable arthritis drug rofecoxib (sold under the brand name Vioxx) increased the risk of heart attacks and sudden death after 18 months of use. The New York City-based pharmaceutical company Pfizer, Inc., announced in December that its arthritis painkillers celecoxib (sold under the brand name Celebrex) and valdecoxib (sold under the brand name Bextra), which are chemically related to rofecoxib, might increase *cardiovascular* problems (problems of the heart and blood vessels).

A study published in February 2005 and led by Graham indicated that at least 26,000 deaths due to rofecoxib may have occurred in the United States while the drug was available to the public. In April, the FDA announced that rofecoxib must go through a new approval process before it can return to the market. The FDA also prohibited the sale of valdecoxib and declared that dozens of widely used prescription painkillers, including celecoxib, must carry the government's strongest warning that they pose a risk of heart attack and stroke.

New leukemia drug. In December 2004, the FDA approved the new drug clofarabine (sold under the brand name Clolar) for treatment of acute lymphocytic leukemia (ALL). ALL is the most common form of blood cancer in children age 18 and under. Clofarabine was the first leukemia drug approved for children since 1982, according to Genzyme, Inc., the Cambridge, Massachusetts-based pharmaceutical company that developed the drug.

Each year, physicians diagnose an estimated 3,800 new cases of childhood ALL in the United States. About 80 percent of children who develop ALL are cured with *chemotherapy*. (Chemotherapy is the treatment of cancers or in-

FDA WARNING ON PAINKILLERS

New York City-based drug giant Pfizer, Inc., stopped advertising its painkiller celecoxib (sold under the brand name Celebrex) in December 2004 after researchers discovered that it carried an increased risk of heart attacks for users taking high doses. In April 2005, the FDA declared that dozens of prescription painkillers, including celecoxib, must carry the government's strongest warning that they pose a risk of heart attack and stroke.

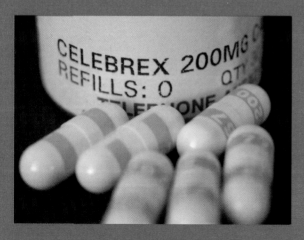

fections with drugs that have a toxic effect on the cause of the illness.) However, the remaining 20 percent of children who do not respond to traditional chemotherapy, or who experience a recurrence of ALL after standard treatment, have a poor chance of survival.

Clofarabine was tested on children who were treated unsuccessfully with other drugs. One in three patients achieved at least a partial recovery, which includes improvements in *bone marrow* (the tissue within bones that produces blood cells) and the disappearance of unhealthy blood cells. About 20 percent of the children were completely cured of their disease. Another 14 percent went on to receive transplants of bone marrow or *stem cells* (young blood cells), which produce healthy blood cells.

Clofarabine is administered by infusion directly into a vein, a procedure that should be performed only under the supervision of a physician with experience in cancer therapy. Doctors should also carefully monitor their patients' blood cell counts during treatments with clofarabine. The most common side effects after clofarabine treatment include vomiting, nausea, diarrhea, low blood cell counts, anemia, and infection.

Unnerving pain. In December 2004, the FDA approved the drug pregabalin (sold under the brand name Lyrica) for the treatment of *neuropathic pain*, chronic pain caused by damage to sensory nerves. Neuropathic pain responds poorly to standard treatment and typically grows worse over time. Pregabalin was the first drug approved for two particular forms of neuropathic pain—*diabetic neuropathy* and *postherpetic neuralgia*.

At least half the 18 million people in the United States with diabetes have some form of diabetic neuropathy resulting from the disease, according to the U.S. Centers for Disease Control and Prevention in Atlanta, Georgia. One in six diabetes patients experiences painful diabetic neuropathy, which is often described as burning, tingling, stabbing, or "pins and needles" in the feet, legs, hands, or arms.

Postherpetic neuralgia often follows an outbreak of blisters on the skin known as *shingles*. Shingles is caused by a reactivation of the same virus that causes chickenpox. Patients describe postherpetic neuralgia as a constant stabbing, burning, or electric-shocklike sensation.

Pregabalin provides rapid and effective pain reduction for both diabetic neuropathy and postherpetic neuralgia, according to Pfizer, the drug's maker. The drug works by blocking the release of a chemical messenger from nerve cells. In addition, pregabalin affects another chemical, called gamma aminobutyric acid (GABA), which also transmits messages in the central nervous system. According to Pfizer, the drug has no serious side effects, and it can be taken by mouth.　　■ Thomas N. Riley

See also **MEDICAL RESEARCH.**

ECOLOGY

The use of radio collars to monitor wild animals for research studies may have an unintended negative effect on the animals, according to a report published in February 2005. Ecologists Tom P. Moorhouse and David W. MacDonald of Oxford University in England reported in the *Journal of Applied Ecology* that attaching radio collars to female water voles (*Arvicola terrestris*) altered the *sex ratio* of their offspring—that is, the ratio of males to females born.

Radio-collaring is a common method used to study the movements of animals in their natural habitat. Researchers place collars containing small radio transmitters on captured animals. The researchers then release the animals and track their movements using radio antennas that resemble television antennas. In these studies, scientists usually compare the survival rates and general health of collared animals with those of a similar group of uncollared animals, which serve as the *control group*.

Before this study, scientists had assumed that animals wearing radio collars suffered no serious effects, though some collared animals experienced changes in weight and behavior and other minor effects. However, Moorhouse and MacDonald found, to their surprise, that the radio-collared females produced fewer female offspring than the control females did. In the control group, males and females were born in approximately equal numbers. Radio-collared females, however, gave birth to approximately three males for every one female born.

ECOLOGY continued

The researchers believe that the presence of the radio collars may have caused stress in the female voles. They note that prior studies showed that stress can cause unbalanced sex ratios in a variety of species. In nature, females that become stressed due to malnourishment or poor habitat may produce more sons than daughters. This behavior is an evolutionary strategy to increase the success of their offspring. The males of many species migrate and so may encounter better conditions, whereas females tend to remain near their birthplace. Thus, under stressful conditions, sons are more likely to survive and reproduce.

In this study, the stress was not poor habitat but the presence of the radio collars. The scientists noted that this was the first study to show a direct correlation between radio collars and sex ratio. They cautioned, however, that

they could not prove that the collars directly caused the change in sex ratios and proposed further research.

Troubled plants? The degree to which current methods used to study plants significantly affect those plants was the subject of a debate in the October 2004 issue of the journal *Ecology*. Both groups of researchers involved in the debate agreed that observers affect the plants they are researching to some degree simply by their interactions with the plants. For example, several studies have shown that plants handled during a field study become more vulnerable to attack by *herbivorous* (plant-eating) insects.

Plant ecologists James F. Cahill, Jr., and David S. Hik of the University of Alberta in Edmonton, Canada, and Brenda B. Casper of the University of Pennsylvania in Philadelphia

PLANNED CANYON FLOOD

A sandbar along a stretch of the Colorado River (below) near the Grand Canyon returns to a more natural size (below, right) after a four-day controlled flood in November 2004. Scientists with the United States Geological Survey planned the flood to help rebuild eroded sandbars and beaches downriver from Arizona's Glen Canyon Dam. The beaches and sandbars serve as habitats for wildlife and

argued that the interactions produce significant effects. They said researchers should use more control groups in order to identify examples of so-called investigator interference and avoid handling plants whenever possible. In a *rebuttal* (alternative perspective), biologist Svata M. Louda of the University of Nebraska in Lincoln and her colleagues examined the same data discussed by Cahill's team. Louda and others argued that any effects resulting from investigator interference are minor. They contended that scientists need not reevaluate past work for evidence of interference or alter current research methods.

Tracking albatrosses. Albatrosses use a surprising variety of routes to find food between breeding seasons, British researchers reported in January 2005. The researchers studying the endangered gray-headed albatross (*Thalassarche chrystostoma*) identified three migration patterns employed by the birds in the 18 months between breeding seasons.

Scientists have long known that albatrosses fly extreme distances looking for food, but scientists had never tracked their exact routes.

Biologist John P. Croxall and his colleagues at the British Antarctic Survey of the Natural Environment Research Council in Cambridge, England, monitored 22 adult gray-headed albatrosses using leg-mounted logging devices. These monitors, like radio collars, allowed scientists to track the positions of the animals. These particular devices recorded two measurements per day covering a total of at least 11,000 days of the birds' activities. Because the birds were not breeding during the study, the scientists were not concerned that the leg monitors would affect the birds' breeding behavior.

The scientists fitted the recording devices at a research station on Bird Island in the South Atlantic Ocean, where the birds gather during breeding seasons. The team found that once the breeding season ended, the birds followed three distinct courses. Some birds traveled only

plants, places for fish to spawn, and campsites for rafters and hikers. The construction of the dam in 1964 reduced by 98 percent the amount of sediment carried by the river. As a result, the natural erosion of the sandbars and beaches far exceeded the gain from river-borne sediment. The flood cleared large amounts of sediment from the riverbed and deposited it along the banks, rebuilding sandbars and beaches.

ECOLOGY continued

short distances within the breeding range in the South Atlantic Ocean. Some birds flew to sites in the south Indian Ocean. Still others *circumnavigated* the globe, flying a complete circle around Antarctica—a trip of about 26,000 kilometers (16,000 miles)—before returning to the Bird Island area. Twelve of the birds in the third group made a total of 15 of these trips, the fastest in just 46 days.

The scientists noted that their findings may prove valuable in efforts to protect these large birds. Some albatross experts have attributed

recent declines in the numbers of the birds to their eating bait fish hooked to fishing lines stretched across the ocean surface by commercial fishing vessels. The hooks harm or kill the birds. Although the birds' home range on and near Bird Island is not a major fishing area, their migration routes cross most of the major tuna-fishing areas. Scientists hope that the findings about the birds' flight paths could spur conservation and protection efforts.

■ Robert H. Tamarin
See also **BIOLOGY; CONSERVATION.**

ENERGY

A racing car designed and built by engineering students at Ohio State University in Columbus became the fastest electric car in the world in 2004. The battery-powered *Buckeye Bullet* set a record on the Bonneville Salt Flats in Utah during speed trials held in October. The car was developed at Ohio University's Center for Automotive Research and Intelligent Operation.

The Buckeye Bullet is 9 ½ meters (31 feet) long and weighs about 1,800 kilograms (4,000 pounds). The vehicle is powered by a battery pack made of 12,000 conventional 1.5-volt rechargeable nickel-metal hydride batteries. Although the huge number of batteries seems an odd choice, they actually weigh much less and perform better than a conventional lead-acid battery system does. The batteries provide a direct current (DC) output of 1,000 volts. An electronic device called an *inverter* converts the DC to alternating current (AC) for the 500-horsepower motor.

During the October speed trials, the *Buckeye Bullet* achieved a speed of 507 kilometers (315 miles) per hour to set a United States record. The previous record—also held by the *Buckeye Bullet*—was 414 kilometers (257 miles) per hour. The race car also broke the international record (which has different judging criteria) with a speed of 438 kilometers (272 miles) per hour.

Electric cars promise quiet operation and a shift of air-polluting emissions from individual autos to central utility power plants, which can be more carefully monitored and regulated. Nevertheless, electric cars still have some hurdles to overcome before they can be considered prac-

SEE ALSO

THE SPECIAL REPORT, **CLEARING THE WAY FOR A HYDROGEN ECONOMY,** PAGE 57.

SCIENCE YOU CAN USE, **SHIFTING GEARS TO HYBRID CARS,** PAGE 152.

tical. A single battery charge for the *Buckeye Bullet* lasts for only one run of about 8 kilometers (5 miles). Recharging the battery pack takes about 30 minutes. Energy researchers noted that a lack of adequate, efficient energy storage continues to limit the usefulness of electric vehicles.

The world's largest wind turbine, with blades sweeping a circle 126 meters (413 feet) in diameter, was dedicated in February 2005 in Schleswig-Holstein, Germany. REpower Systems AG of Hamburg designed and built the 5-megawatt wind turbine, called the REpower 5M. By March, the turbine had produced 1 million kilowatt hours of electric power. The REpower 5M is expected to produce around 17 million kilowatt hours of energy per year at its onshore testing site in Brunsbüttel, Germany, a quantity sufficient for the needs of about 4,500 three-person households. After the testing period, the turbine was to be moved offshore.

The REpower 5M consists of a tower that stands 120 meters (394 feet) high and a rotor made up of three blades. Each blade is 61 ½ meters (202 feet) long and weighs about 18,000

kilograms (40,000 pounds). The blades are constructed of a glass and carbon fiber-hybrid fabric held together by synthetic resins, significantly reducing the weight of the blades. A minimum wind speed of 3 ½ meters (11 ½ feet) per second is sufficient to set the blades in motion.

In 2005, Germany was a world leader in the number of operating wind turbines and in the amount of energy they produced. The German Energy Agency, a company partly owned by the German government, had hoped to fill 20 percent of the country's energy needs using renewable energy by the years 2015 to 2020. However, in a report issued in February 2005, the agency pointed out that accommodating more wind energy generation would result in increased energy costs, because the *power grid* (electric power distribution system) needs to be expanded and portions of it need to be upgraded.

Feeding fuel cells. A robot that digests flies to generate its own energy is under development at the University of the West of England in Bristol. Robotic engineer Chris Melhuish and microbiologist John Greenman reported on their progress in December 2004.

Researchers in many areas of science have long been interested in the development of a robot that would be completely *autonomous* (able to survive without the aid of human beings). Such a robot would be useful in situations that may be hazardous for people. In the early 2000's, researchers created several robots that could make their own energy. However, they needed to be "fed" certain materials, such as sugar cubes, in order to do so.

The robot developed by Melhuish and Greenman, called Ecobot II, "eats" flies and rotten apples that are digested by microbes that live in sewage inside the robot. The microbes generate energy, which the robot uses for power. The researchers expect that, in the field, the sewage would attract flies, allowing the robot to operate autonomously.

The technology behind Ecobot II is based on a new type of *fuel cell* called a *microbial fuel cell* (MFC). Fuel cells are devices that convert chemical energy directly into electric energy. In a microbial fuel cell, microbes convert sewage, also called *wastewater,* into electric current. Researchers at Pennsylvania State University in

ENERGY continued

University Park reported their success in building the first MFC in February 2004.

An MFC is a cylinder that contains eight graphite *anodes* (negative electrodes) and a *cathode* (positive electrode). Bacteria attach themselves to the anodes. The cathode is encased in a hollow tube and exposed to the air. A special membrane that separates the anodes from the cathode allows only *protons* (positively charged particles) through.

Wastewater flows into the anode section of the cylinder. As the bacteria digest the organic matter in the wastewater, they release *electrons* (negatively charged particles). The electrons travel through an external wire to the cathode. The digestion process also releases hydrogen *ions* (electrically charged molecules or atoms).

The protons pass through the membrane to the cathode, where they combine with oxygen from the air and electrons traveling from the anode to create clean water. In this fashion, a microbial fuel cell simultaneously cleans wastewater and generates electric power. Researchers hope that MFC's will make sewage treatment plants affordable for developing nations.

The energy produced by current MFC's is limited. Even with a "stomach" consisting of eight MFC's, Ecobot II can cover a distance of from 2 to 4 centimeters (0.8 to 1.6 inches) in 15 minutes on eight flies. However, the generation process in MFC's can continue for as long as the microbes have food, possibly for years.

Hydraulic hybrids. A new hybrid delivery vehicle—one that uses *hydraulic* pumps to power the *drivetrain* of a diesel-fueled engine—is being developed by a partnership that includes a number of agencies and companies. (A drivetrain consists of all of a car's components that transmit the engine's power to the wheels. A hydraulic pump uses liquid to produce pressure.) The partnership, announced in February 2005, includes the U.S. Environmental Protection Agency (EPA); United Parcel Service of America, Inc., in Atlanta, Georgia; Eaton Corporation of Cleveland, Ohio; International Truck and Engine Corporation of Warrenville, Illinois; and the U.S. Army National Automotive Center in Warren, Michigan.

Hybrid automobiles use a gasoline or diesel engine together with an electric motor. The new hydraulic hybrid vehicle will pair a diesel engine with two hydraulic pumps, one powered by the engine and the other by the energy generated by braking. The two pumps will provide pressure for storage devices called accumulators, the hydraulic equivalent of batteries. The hybrid will be designed for use as an urban delivery vehicle.

Cars and trucks have long used hydraulic pumps and accumulators for power steering and power brakes. In the hydraulic hybrid vehicle, the pumps and accumulators power the drivetrain. EPA researchers estimate that the urban delivery vehicle will improve fuel economy by 30 to 40 percent. ■ Pasquale M. Sforza

ENGINEERING

Research using viruses to assemble molecules into computer components less than one-billionth of a meter wide was honored by the John D. and Catherine T. MacArthur Foundation in September 2004. The Chicago-based grant-making institution awarded a MacArthur Foundation Fellowship, or "Genius Award," to the developer of the viruses—*nanotechnologist* Angela Belcher of the Massachusetts Institute of Technology in Cambridge. The fellowships honor researchers for their "originality, creativity, and potential to do more in the future." A nanotechnologist is a scientist or engineer who works in the field of *nanotechnology,* the manipulation of individual atoms and molecules to create larger structures.

Belcher created *genetically engineered* viruses that interact with *semiconductors,* materials that are used to conduct electric current in computer chips. Genetic engineering involves the manipulation of an organism's genes. A computer chip contains complex electronic circuitry that carries out the instructions that make up computer programs or that holds data or instructions inside the computer.

Belcher's research focused on proteins in the outer coats of certain *bacteriophages,* viruses that infect bacteria. These proteins can *self-*

assemble, or make copies of themselves. Belcher analyzed the *DNA* (the molecule that makes up genes) that carries the instructions for the proteins, and she *cloned* it—that is, she made copies of it. She used these copies to make self-assembling molecular templates on the coats of the viruses. The templates acted like forms to grow tiny wires in solutions of semiconductor molecules. Molecules of zinc sulfide, a semiconductor compound in the solutions, bound to the templates, forming the wires. Because the templates on which the wires were based were self-assembling, the wires also self-assembled.

The MacArthur Foundation praised Belcher's research as a breakthrough in the development of nanoscale-sized electronic devices. Such devices would have many applications in com-

puter design, microelectronics, and other areas. Belcher noted that the modified viruses were *chemically stable*—that is, they did not break down for a long time. Because of this property, she explained, medical personnel might be able to store vaccine compounds bound to the viruses for long periods in remote parts of the world with no refrigeration. Then, when needed, the vaccines could be "dehydrated" for use.

Wired to resist fire. A new insulating material for electrical wiring in buildings could revolutionize the fire-protection industry, according to an August 2004 report. The insulator, called a *ceramifiable polymer,* acts

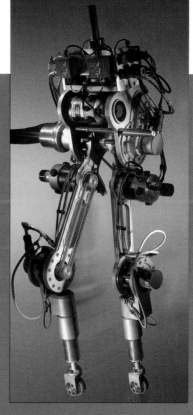

NOT EXACTLY C3PO, BUT . . .

Several technological developments in *bipedal robots*—two-legged walking machines—were reported in 2004 and 2005. Although these machines were still a long way from the imaginative robots seen in science-fiction movies, engineers said that some of the technology developed for the robots might find practical applications in other areas. For example, the way the robotic limbs move might be applied to the movement of advanced prosthetic devices or rehabilitative walking aids for people with physical disabilities.

A robot developed by engineers at Cornell University in Ithaca, New York (right), was one of three mechanical bipeds introduced at the annual meeting of the American Association for the Advancement of Science in Washington, D.C., in February 2005. The shape of the robot's frame and joints were designed to enable it to walk with a minimal use of motors and sensors. (The two "eyeballs" on the front of the robot were added for effect.)

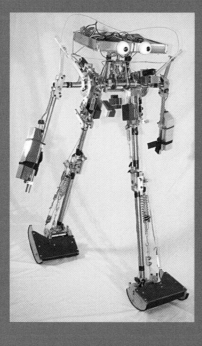

RABBIT (above) is the first known robot to balance like a human being as it walks, according to a May 2005 report by its developers at the University of Michigan at Ann Arbor and several institutions in France. Mathematical equations representing balancing ability were programmed into the robot's computer system. RABBIT's legs end like stilts rather than flat feet, allowing it to pivot on a point as it moves forward.

ENGINEERING continued

like a plastic under mild temperatures but turns into a hard ceramic material under high temperatures. A polymer is a large molecule formed by linking many smaller molecules into a long chain. Engineers Yi-Bing Cheng and Don Rodrigo of Monash University in Melbourne, Australia, developed the material.

Conventional wire insulation can melt during fires, shutting down elevators, sliding doors, computers, telephones, and other equipment that building occupants may need to escape. The new material was designed to withstand the high temperatures of fires.

The engineers compared their ceramifiable polymer with regular plastic insulation as coatings for cables that were heated to 1,050 °C (1,922 °F). In the tests, the regular insulation lasted less than 10 minutes, but the ceramifiable polymer insulation lasted at least 2 hours. In 2005, the Australian team was marketing the polymer material for use in fire-resistant electric cables as well as in wall and ceiling insulation.

Liquid armor. A new liquid that can turn ordinary clothes into body armor may improve safety for police officers, prison guards, and military troops. Norman Wagner, a chemical engineer at the University of Delaware in Newark, led a team that announced the development of this liquid in January 2005. The team also included engineers from the United States Army Research Laboratory in Adelphi, Maryland.

Most bulletproof vests are made of *aramid,* a manufactured fiber that is chemically similar to nylon but, when equivalent weights are compared, is stronger than steel. Aramid vests are sold under the trade names Kevlar and Nomex. Although vests made of aramid are highly protective against most types of bullets, the material is expensive, and many wearers find the vests uncomfortable. In addition, aramid vests cannot prevent penetration by a knife blade or other sharp object.

The fluid developed by Wagner's team was a mixture of silica glass particles and a liquid polymer called polyethylene glycol. The team treated clothing made of nylon, polyester, cotton, and aramid by dipping it in the fluid and then allowing it to dry. The only visual indication of the clothing's altered properties was a slightly oily appearance.

When the treated clothing was shot or jabbed with a sharp object, the material instantly stiffened, preventing the bullet or object from penetrating. After contact with the bullet or sharp object stopped, the material returned to its normal, flexible state. The scientists explained that at low *strain* rates—such as when nothing is contacting the clothing—the hard silica particles flow freely within the applied fluid, allowing the clothing to stay flexible. (Strain measures how much of a given solid changes under stress.) However, at high strain rates—such as when a knife is contacting the clothing—the silica particles form a rigid architecture within the fluid, restricting the ability of the clothing to move.

According to Wagner, clothing treated with the liquid armor could be used to protect the entire bodies of police officers and other law enforcement or military personnel. He said the fluid might also be used for protecting motorcycle riders and extreme-sports enthusiasts.

Making light of LED's. A *light-emitting diode* (LED) that is twice as efficient as previous LED's and lasts about 100 times as long as a standard incandescent light bulb was reported in June 2004 by researchers at Rensselaer Polytechnic Institute in Troy, New York. An LED is a type of electric light that consists of small chips of semiconductor material. LED's give off very little heat and last almost indefinitely. The researchers said the LED they developed could be the first serious alternative to standard light bulbs.

Groups of LED's are used in some pocket calculators and digital watches to form letters or numbers. They are also used in some traffic signals, exit signs, automobile lights, and power buttons on electronic products. LED's have a limited application because they are not as bright as standard light bulbs. To help solve this problem, a Rensselaer team led by engineer Fred Schubert incorporated an *omni-directional reflector* (ODR) into LED chips. The ODR was made of a silver mirror that contacted the LED's semiconductor layer. An electric current flowed through the mirror to activate the semiconductor layer, causing the layer to emit light. The light then reflected off the mirror, increasing the amount of light emitted by the LED. Although still not as bright as a standard light bulb, the new LED was significantly brighter than previous LED's.

Unlike standard light bulbs, the Rensselaer LED emitted more light than heat. Standard incandescent bulbs lose much energy as heat.

Even after an incandescent bulb burns out, it will remain hot for a long time. Another advantage of the Rensselaer LED, according to the researchers, was that it could emit light continuously for roughly 50,000 hours—or 6 years. A standard incandescent bulb lasts only about 500 hours, and a fluorescent bulb might last 5,000 hours. Schubert predicted that LED's could begin to replace incandescent light bulbs by 2010. He added that the high efficiency of the LED's had the potential to decrease the electric power consumption for lighting in the United States by half.

Mind games. Artificial hands, arms, and legs that users could control by thought alone—like natural limbs—moved a step closer to reality in January 2005. Biomedical engineer Daniel Moran of Washington University and neurosurgeon Eric C. Leuthardt of Barnes-Jewish Hospital, both in St. Louis, Missouri, described research that could lead to the development of such *prosthetic* devices.

The researchers first placed electronic grids on the surfaces of the brains of volunteers to record *electrocorticographic* (ECoG) *activity*—that is, electrical signals in the *cortex,* the outer-

most part of the brain. Measurements of ECoG activity provide more precise readings of brain signals than the more familiar *electroencephalographic* (EEG) measurements, which are gathered by electrodes placed on the scalp. The investigators asked the volunteers to perform certain movements, such as opening and closing their hands. The ECoG readings allowed the researchers to associate brain signals with each kind of body movement.

The researchers next hooked the electronic grids on the volunteers' brains to a simple computer game. The volunteers were instructed to move the cursor on the computer screen up and down by imagining these movements. Within about one hour, the volunteers learned to control the cursor with 74-percent to 100-percent accuracy—using only their thoughts.

The researchers planned to use the ECoG technology to teach volunteers to control more complex movements on computer screens. They said they hoped to develop an advanced ECoG grid that would enable patients with motor impairments to easily move prosthetic devices. ■ Celeste Baine

See also **COMPUTERS AND ELECTRONICS.**

ENVIRONMENTAL POLLUTION

Certain environmental pollutants absorbed by the body from food and water and stored in fat cells may play a surprisingly significant role in frustrating dieters' efforts to lose weight, according to a report published in July 2004. Researchers led by metabolism scientist Angelo Tremblay of Laval University in Quebec City, Canada, suggested that the pollutants, released when fat is broken down during dieting, may have a greater effect than a normally occurring hormone on the body's efforts to conserve energy, thus hindering weight loss.

Normally, dieting causes a slowing of *cellular metabolism* (the process by which living things turn food into energy and tissue). This decrease in metabolism, called *adaptive thermogenesis*, is the body's attempt to compensate for receiving less food. Scientists had thought that the hormone leptin, which is produced by fat cells, was one of the chief regulators of this process.

Tremblay's team put 15 obese people on reduced-calorie diets and monitored the levels of pollutants in their blood. After 15 weeks, the

researchers found that blood concentrations of leptin decreased by an average of 33 percent, while concentrations of pollutants called *organochlorines* increased by 23 percent. Organochlorines consist mostly of pesticides and another class of chemicals called chlorinated biphenyls.

Tremblay theorized that organochlorines might interfere with the *thyroid gland*, which produces hormones that control cellular metabolism and, in turn, weight loss. He also speculated that organochlorines may damage *mitochondria*, cellular structures that convert fat and carbohydrates into energy.

Other scientists noted that the study showed a correlation but did not prove that pollutants lead to adaptive thermogenesis. Further research is needed on organochlorines and on natural processes that contribute to changes in metabolism, they contended.

Air pollution and clogged arteries. Additional research linking air pollution to heart disease was reported in December 2004 by re-

ENVIRONMENTAL POLLUTION continued

searchers from the University of Southern California (USC) in Los Angeles. Nino Kunzli, a professor of preventive medicine, and his colleagues concluded that air pollution may cause thickening of the *carotid arteries*, large blood vessels that lead to the brain. Thickening of arteries typically results in deposits of cholesterol and other harmful substances in the affected vessels. This condition, called *atherosclerosis*, is a leading risk factor for heart attacks and strokes.

The researchers studied health care records from about 800 people in the Los Angeles area. They also used atmospheric data to estimate the amount of air pollution near the home of each participant in the study. The team found that people with the highest exposure to air pollution had artery linings that were about 12-percent thicker than those of people with the lowest exposure. This difference translates into a 3- to 6-percent increase in the long-term risk for heart attack, according to the researchers.

The scientists theorized that small airborne particles, each measuring less than 2 ½ micrometers (millionths of a meter) in diameter, irritate the lungs and blood vessels. Air pollution laws in the United States do not currently regulate the emission of such small particles. Over time, the researchers said, these particles cause *inflammation* (irritation) of the arteries, which leads to atherosclerosis.

In late 2004, researchers at the University of Washington in Seattle began a 10-year study to track air pollution exposure and rates of *cardiovascular* (heart and lung) disease, including atherosclerosis, in 8,700 people. The researchers hope their findings will help scientists understand the long-term effects of air pollution on cardiovascular health.

Air pollution and small vessels. Fine airborne pollutants may also disrupt the smallest arteries in the body, according to an October 2004 report by physiologist Timothy Nurkiewicz and colleagues at West Virginia University in Morgantown. These vessels, called *arterioles*, deliver blood to all the body's tissues and organs through even tinier blood vessels called *capillaries*. Arterioles control blood flow to capillaries by *dilating* (opening) and *constricting* (closing) in response to nitric oxide. This chemical is produced locally in many of the body's tissues.

Nurkiewicz put tiny amounts of oily soot— pollutant particles measuring less than 2 ½ micrometers in diameter—into the lungs of rats. He found that the rats' back muscles lost much of their responsiveness to nitric oxide, which suggested that the rats' arterioles were not working properly.

However, the scientists noted, soot could disrupt the arterioles through chemical reactions with other substances in the body. The researchers checked their results by using an *inert* (nonreactive) chemical known as titanium dioxide. Again, the rats' muscles did not respond to nitric oxide. The scientists concluded that the size of airborne particles is the key factor in the relationship between pollution and the regulation of blood flow.

Previous studies of cardiovascular disease in human beings had suggested a link to air pollution. Nurkiewicz's finding offers one explanation for these observations.

Secondhand smoke and mental ability. Exposure to *secondhand smoke* (exhaled smoke from other smokers) may cause small decreases in children's mental abilities, according to a study published in January 2005. Medical researcher Kimberly Yolton and her colleagues at Cincinnati Children's Hospital Medical Center in Ohio and the University of Rochester in New York estimated that nearly 22 million children— more than 40 percent of U.S. children—are at risk of losing some mental ability because of secondhand smoke. The study was the first to use a biological marker—blood levels of *cotinine*, a chemical produced by the breakdown of nicotine—to measure exposure to secondhand smoke. Previous studies relied on data from interviews or questionnaires.

The researchers examined nearly 4,400 students ages 6 to 16. The scientists took blood samples and tested the *cognitive* (memory and problem-solving) abilities of each child in three areas: reading, math, and *spatial skills* (the ability to visualize objects in the mind). The scores of children exposed to secondhand smoke were from two to five points lower than those of children who were not exposed to the smoke, the researchers reported.

Children with the greatest exposure to secondhand smoke scored significantly lower than children with the least exposure. However, the researchers found the greatest difference in scores between children with low exposure and children with no exposure. This unexplained result suggested that even low levels of secondhand smoke can damage the brain, the study authors said. The researchers said their study provided evidence to support laws that reduce childhood exposure to secondhand smoke.

Protection against lung disease. A naturally occurring protein in the lungs may help protect smokers from a debilitating disease called *emphysema*, according to a report published in November 2004. Scientists from Johns Hopkins University in Baltimore, Maryland, found that a protein called Nrf2 activates dozens of beneficial genes in the cells of the *alveoli* (air sacs in the lungs). Emphysema gradually destroys the alveoli. The genes produce chemicals that remove or inactivate harmful chemicals pollutants found in cigarette smoke.

The study compared two *strains* (varieties) of mice—one that had the gene that makes the Nrf2 protein and one that did not. Researchers exposed the mice to cigarette smoke for six months and then examined their lungs. The team found that mice lacking the Nrf2 protein had many more early signs of emphysema—inflammation, dead cells, and *free radicals* in their lungs. Free radicals are unstable molecules that destroy other molecules, including DNA (*deoxyribonucleic acid*, the chemical genes are made of).

The researchers also found 50 genes that were much more active in mice with the Nrf2 protein than in those without it. One of the genes was 11 times as active in the mice with Nrf2. These genes produced *antioxidants* (proteins that fight free radicals) and other proteins that promote cell growth and survival.

Immunologist and team member Tirumalai Rangasamy suggested additional research to determine if the Nrf2 gene and protein act the same way in human beings as they do in mice. If so, then the Nrf2 gene may explain why cer-

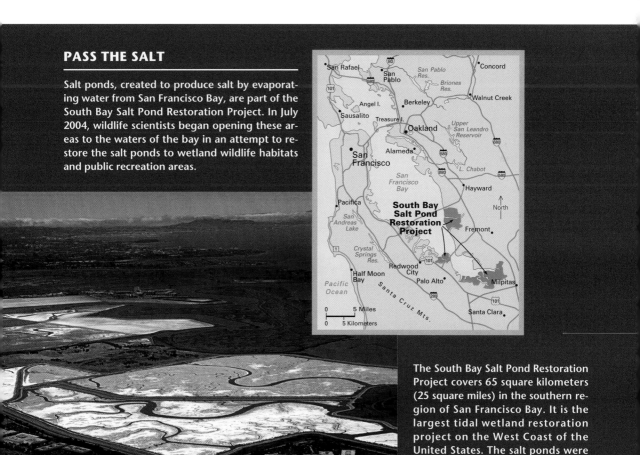

PASS THE SALT

Salt ponds, created to produce salt by evaporating water from San Francisco Bay, are part of the South Bay Salt Pond Restoration Project. In July 2004, wildlife scientists began opening these areas to the waters of the bay in an attempt to restore the salt ponds to wetland wildlife habitats and public recreation areas.

The South Bay Salt Pond Restoration Project covers 65 square kilometers (25 square miles) in the southern region of San Francisco Bay. It is the largest tidal wetland restoration project on the West Coast of the United States. The salt ponds were marsh areas until commercial salt production began in 1854.

ENVIRONMENTAL POLLUTION continued

tain smokers develop emphysema and others do not. Information about the gene may also help researchers determine which individuals have a higher risk of developing emphysema.

Air pollution stunts lung growth. Urban air pollution impairs lung development in adolescents to the same degree as second-hand smoke in the home, according to a study published in September 2004. Medical researchers led by W. James Gauderman of USC focused on teens in 12 southern Californian communities, including some areas with low levels of air pollution and other severely polluted regions. In southern California, airborne pollutants typically come from cars and trucks.

The researchers studied 1,800 children as they progressed from 4th to 12th grade, measuring their lung capacity each year from 1993 to 2001. They also recorded each child's exposure to tobacco smoke and collected air samples for an estimate of local air pollution.

From age 10 to 18 years, lung capacities in boys generally increases by 100 percent. In girls, lung capacity rises 66 percent. However, the scientists found that among about 4 percent of the 18-year-olds, lung capacity fell at least 20-percent short of its predicted rise. The scientists also discovered that teens who grew up in towns with the dirtiest air were up to five times as likely to have smaller lung capacity than teens who grew up in the cleanest communities. This difference, the researchers said, was similar to that observed in studies comparing children with smoking and non-smoking mothers.

Other scientists noted that air pollution damages young lungs in proportion to the pollutants' concentrations—no matter how low they fall—so even small amounts can result in long-term harm. On the other hand, they suggested, improving air quality could prevent disease and significantly improve public health in many areas of the world.

■ Daniel D. Chiras

See also **CONSERVATION; ECOLOGY.**

FOSSIL STUDIES

The theory that mass extinctions on Earth occur in cycles gained new support in April 2005. Mass extinctions are relatively short periods in which huge numbers of unrelated species die out. Physicists Richard Muller and Robert Rohde of the University of California at Berkeley reported finding more evidence for such a pattern, though the cycle they proposed is at least twice as long as the original cycle proposed in 1984.

For many years, paleontologists have studied patterns of *biodiversity* (numbers and variety of animals and plants) on Earth through time. These studies were stimulated in 1984 by the publication of an enormous database on diversity developed by paleontologist J. John Sepkoski, Jr., of the University of Chicago. The database examined the distribution of *genera* (groups of closely related species) and *families* (groups of related genera) of marine animals over a period of 250 million years. Sepkoski and David Raup, also of the University of Chicago, identified an apparent pattern of mass extinctions occurring

roughly every 26 million years during the Mesozoic and Cenozoic eras.

The publication of this theory stimulated intense debate and a great deal of research. However, many doubts remained about whether the pattern was real. Paleontologists wondered why, for example, Sepkoski and Raup's hypothesis did not seem to apply to earlier parts of the fossil record.

Muller and Rohde analyzed Sepkoski's famous database using a different statistical method. They focused only on genera that had existed for relatively short periods (45 million years or less). In addition, they compared the database with a newly developed geologic time scale that provides more precise dates for Earth's various geologic periods. Muller and Rohde reported discovering a pattern of highs and lows in biodiversity over the past 542 million years. This pattern suggests that mass extinctions occur about every 62 million years.

The scientists found, however, that not all types of marine animals seemed to follow this cycle. Corals, sponges, and arthropods exhibit the pattern strongly, but squid and snails do not. Paleontologists had previously noted different patterns of extinction in these two groups but were unsure why such patterns exist.

The Berkeley researchers admit that the causes of such an extinction cycle are almost completely a matter of speculation at this time. They offered different theories to explain the cycle.

Muller offered an explanation similar to one he had advanced in the late 1980's to explain the 26-million-year pattern. He theorized that the extinctions might be linked to comet impacts related to periodic changes in the frequency with which comets cross Earth's orbit. Such disturbance could be triggered by the movement of our solar system through clouds of interstellar dust and gas that have a gravitational effect on the Oort cloud, Muller said. The Oort cloud is a cluster of comets, smaller objects, and perhaps even planets in the outermost region of our solar system. A comet can leave the Oort cloud and enter the inner solar system when disturbed by a large gravitational force, such as the gravity of a passing star.

In contrast, Rohde suggested that the cycle of mass extinctions may be related to massive volcanism caused by periodic disturbances in Earth's mantle, the layer of rock between Earth's crust and core. He suggested that the effects of the eruptions could have caused either extinctions or a growth in Earth's biodiversity.

Ancient predators and prey. Fossilized remains of starfish-like creatures with nibbled arms have provided rare evidence of ancient *predation* (the killing and eating of prey animals by other organisms), according to a September 2004 report by paleontologists Tomasz Baumiller of the University of Michigan in Ann Arbor and Forest Gahn of the Smithsonian Institution in Washington, D.C. The researchers discovered the remains in

PEEKING INTO AN ANCIENT EGG

The fossilized remains of an ancient embryo (left, above), also shown in an artist's rendition (left), reveal the skeleton, wing membranes, and impressions of its skin. The 121-million-year-old fossil, discovered in Liaoning Province in northeastern China, is believed to be the oldest unborn bird ever found. The bird was almost fully formed. Most modern birds are born without feathers and are helpless, remaining in their nest until they are almost full-grown before they learn to fly or feed themselves. The presence of feathers in the prehistoric embryo, the scientists believe, indicates that it was *precocial*, able to feed itself and move about as soon as it hatched.

FOSSIL STUDIES continued

a large collection of fossil crinoids of various ages housed at the Smithsonian. Crinoids, also known as sea-lilies, are a type of echinoderm related to starfish and sea urchins.

Like most echinoderms, modern crinoids can *regenerate* (regrow) parts of their body that have been lost to accidents or predators. The re-grown parts are typically short and stubby compared with normal parts and so can be easily recognized.

Baumiller and Gahn found evidence of re-generated arms—the crinoid's featherlike feeding structures—in a number of fossils. They concluded that the fossilized arms, like those of some modern crinoids, had been damaged by predators. The researchers then charted the frequency of the attacks for various geologic periods. Their data revealed an abrupt increase in the proportion of regenerated crinoid arms starting about 400 million years ago during the Devonian Period.

This discovery of the nibbled crinoids supports a hypothesis made in 1984 by paleontologists Phillip Signor, then of the University of California at Davis, and Carlton Brett of the University of Cincinnati in Ohio that the number of fish predators increased abruptly in the Devonian Period. The paleontologists theorized that the rise in predators had resulted in the development of defensive features among crinoids. Signor and Brett had based their hypothesis largely on indirect evidence—an increase in the abundance of fish species during the Devonian that coincided with the abrupt appearance of spines and thick skeletons in crinoids. Baumiller and Gahn's findings provide direct evidence that crinoids were, in fact, being preyed upon much more frequently from the Devonian onward than in earlier times.

Sleeping dinosaur. The fossil of a small carnivorous dinosaur sleeping in a position similar to that used by modern birds has provided additional support for the theory that birds developed from small predatory dinosaurs. Paleontologists Xing Xu of the Chinese Academy of Sciences in Beijing and Mark Norell of the American Museum of Natural History in New York City reported in October 2004 on their discovery of the fossil in Liaoning Province in northeastern China. The fossil dates from the Early Cretaceous Period, 128 million to 139 million years ago.

The carnivorous dinosaur belongs to the family Troodontidae. Named *Mei long,* from the Chinese words for *soundly sleeping dragon,* it was apparently buried by a volcanic eruption while it slept. The dinosaur is about 53 centimeters (21 inches) long and probably represents a juvenile. *Mei long* had a small skull and long hind limbs. It was preserved with its hind limbs folded beneath its body. Its forelimbs are also folded next to its body in a manner similar to the wing position of resting birds.

The fossil's most striking feature is that its neck is curved to one side, with its head pointed rearward and nestled between its left elbow and body. This posture is identical to that seen in sleeping modern birds. Xu and Norell concluded that the existence of this posture 130 million years ago provides additional support for the theory that small, predatory dinosaurs are the ancestors of modern birds.

Soft tissues in dinosaur bones. The rare discovery of 70-million-year-old *soft tissue* from a *Tyrannosaurus rex* found in Montana was reported by scientists in March 2005. (Soft tissue includes all the tissue of the body except bone.) Soft tissue usually decays within a few days or months after an organism's death. Dinosaur bones, however, are relatively dense and, when fossilized, may survive for millions of years. The discovery may open a new avenue for the study of the relationships between dinosaurs as well as their connections to modern organisms.

Researchers led by paleontologist Mary Schweitzer of North Carolina State University in Raleigh described finding soft tissue in the leg bone of a small *T. rex* from Late Cretaceous sediments. When the scientists dissolved the hard mineralized material of the *T. rex* bone fragments, they found the remnants of slender, flexible tubes floating in the solution. Enlarged images of these tubes, created using a scanning electron microscope, showed details that are almost identical to those found in the outside surface of blood vessels in the *marrow* of modern ostrich bone. Marrow, the soft tissue that fills the center of bones, consists mostly of fat, blood vessels, connective tissue, and blood-forming cells.

Even more surprising, the scientists found small, round, reddish-brown structures inside the tubes that may be the remnants of cells. The scientists speculated that the remnants had survived for so long because they were deeply imbedded in the dinosaur's bone.

Dinosaur-eating mammals. The discovery of the fossil of an ancient mammal with the remains of a dinosaur in its stomach has provided the first evidence that prehistoric mammals fed on dinosaurs. The discovery, made in China, was announced in January 2005 by an international team that included paleontologist Meng Jin of the American Museum of Natural History in New York City. The findings challenged a widely held theory that early mammals were small, insect-eating animals unable to compete for food and territory with dinosaurs.

The unusually complete mammal fossil belongs to the species *Repenomamus robustus,* which lived about 130 million years ago during the Mesozoic Era. Found beneath the mammal's ribs in the probable position of its stomach were the remains of a juvenile psittacosaur (parrot-beaked dinosaur) about 14 centimeters (5 inches) long. The leg bones of the dinosaur were still intact, indicating that *R. robustus* tore chunks of tissue from its prey like crocodiles, rather than chewing the meat as most modern mammalian predators do.

R. robustus had previously been known only from skull fragments. Studies of the new fossil indicated that the mammal had measured about 60 centimeters (2 feet) long and weighed about 7 kilograms (15 pounds), making it a giant among Mesozoic mammals. Most mammals of that period were only about $\frac{1}{20}$ the size of this species.

However, the dinosaur-eating *R. robustus* is not the largest Mesozoic mammal known to paleontologists. In the January 2005 article, the researchers also described the fossils of a second, much larger species of *Repenomamus,* called *R. giganticus.* This creature was more than 90 centimeters (3 feet) long and may have weighed at least 14 kilograms (30 pounds).

The discovery of such large mammals surprised scientists. For many decades, scientists have viewed early mammals as small insect feeders overshadowed by dinosaurs. Prevailing scientific theory states that mammals remained small until after dinosaurs became extinct 65 million years ago. Now, some scientists think that small dinosaurs may have grown larger or

A DINOSAUR-EATING MAMMAL

The remains of a 130-million-year-old mammal called *Repenomamus robustus* (right) is the first proof that prehistoric mammals fed on dinosaurs (artist's rendition, below). The remains of *R. robustus*'s last meal, a tiny Psittacosaurus, was fossilized in the mammal's stomach. Scientists had previously believed that prehistoric mammals were tiny, timid creatures that fled from dinosaurs.

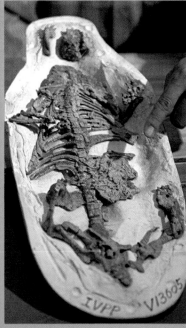

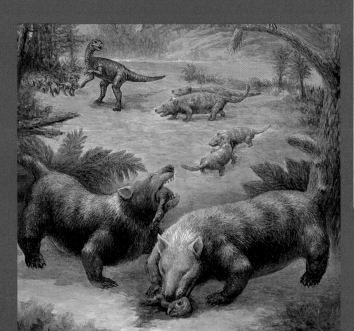

FOSSIL STUDIES continued

developed wings to escape from voracious mammal predators such as *Repenomamus.*

Dinosaur with eggs. The discovery of the first female dinosaur found with its eggs still intact was reported by researchers in April 2005. Although paleontologists had previously found many dinosaur eggs, they had never found a fossilized dinosaur that had died before laying its eggs. The reproductive system of the new specimen shows some features similar to those of birds.

Paleontologist Tamaki Sato of the Canadian Museum of Nature in Ottawa, along with an international team of researchers, found the fossil in China's Jiangxi Province. The specimen, from the mid-Cretaceous Period, may be 98 million years old. The fossil represents the pelvis of a theropod that was from 3 to 4 meters (10 to 13 feet) long. Theropods were a group of dinosaurs that included such carnivores as raptors and tyrannosaurs. Many paleontologists believe one member of this group of dinosaurs was probably the direct ancestor of birds.

The dinosaur pelvis contains two petrified, shelled eggs. The eggs are positioned next to each other, indicating that the dinosaur had two ovaries and two *oviducts* (tube-shaped organs through which an egg passes from the ovary to an opening in the body). The thickness of the shells led the scientists to theorize that the dinosaur probably laid its eggs over a period of days, the way modern birds do. Given that all known dinosaur nests contain many eggs, this finding suggests that dinosaurs also returned repeatedly to their nest to lay more eggs.

Moorpark mammoth. Construction workers excavating for a new housing development in Moorpark, California, uncovered the fossil bones of an ancient mammoth, a relative of modern elephants. Moorpark lies about 80 kilometers (50 miles) northwest of Los Angeles.

Paleontologist Bruce Lander of Paleo Environmental Associates of Altadena, California, and five associates examined the find in April 2005. They reported that the fossils represent about 75 percent of the mammoth's skeleton. Mammoths could grow up to 4 ⅓ meters (14 feet) tall and weigh up to 9 metric tons (10 tons). The Moorpark mammoth's tusks alone are more than 2 ½ meters (8 feet) long.

Lander and his team estimated that the mammoth was from 400,000 to 1.4 million years old. This specimen is much older than the well-known Columbian mammoth from the famous La Brea tar pit in downtown Los Angeles. That mammoth fossil is believed to be about 30,000 years old.

Scientists think the new fossil represents the remains of *Mammuthus meridionalis,* believed to be the first mammoth species to appear in North America. Scientists believe mammoths migrated from Asia perhaps 1.5 million years ago across the Bering land bridge, a now-submerged strip of land connecting Siberia and Alaska. The sea floor there became exposed during ice ages, when ice sheets covered vast regions of Earth. The ice sheets held much of Earth's water, and sea levels dropped.

Mammals into Africa? Contrary to popular scientific theory, Africa may not be the cradle of development for mammal species known collectively as "Afrotheria" or African mammals. This group includes elephants and manatees as well as such unusual relatives as hyraxes and tiny elephant shrews. In April 2005, paleontologist Jonathan Bloch of the University of Florida in Gainesville and researchers from Johns Hopkins University in Baltimore, Maryland, argued that the Afrotheria may have originated in North America.

Bloch and his colleagues reported on the discovery in Wyoming of 54-million-year-old fossilized teeth and bones of a previously unknown elephant shrew. They suggested that this tiny fossil could represent the ancestor of the Afrotheria.

The paleontologists theorized that the group may actually have spread from North America to Africa. There the Afrotheria became established and diversified into a variety of mammals. At some point, the Afrotheres became extinct in their continent of origin.

The theory that these mammals immigrated to Africa is somewhat surprising as no direct land connection existed between the two continents 54 million years ago. The authors note, however, that a brief interval of global warming occurred in the early Eocene Epoch, about 55 million years ago. The warming climates may have also enabled mammals to expand their ranges. Afrotheres may have migrated into Africa through Europe, which was still partially linked to North America at that time.

■ Carlton E. Brett

See also **GEOLOGY.**

GENETICS

Dramatic progress in the ability to produce exact copies of a patient's stem cells from a cloned *embryo* (initial stage of life) was announced in May 2005 by Korean researchers. The team was led by Woo Suk Hwang and Shin Yong Moon of Seoul National University. Embryonic stem cells can develop into virtually any kind of human tissue. Many scientists believe that stem cells hold great promise for replacing damaged tissue or treating disease. However, many people oppose *therapeutic cloning,* the process used to obtain embryonic stem cells, because embryos are destroyed as their stem cells are collected.

To produce new embryonic stem cells, researchers first make a cloned embryo of an individual. Genetic material from the cell of one person is placed into an unfertilized human egg from which the genetic material has been removed. Normally, the embryo is allowed to grow in the laboratory for a few days before the stem cells are collected. The collected cells are then grown in special laboratory dishes to produce what scientists call a *culture* of cells. The Korean researchers produced new cultures, or *lines,* of embryonic stem cells about 10 times as efficiently as any other researchers.

The researchers attributed their high success rate to several factors. These included improvements in methods of handling the cells and growing them in the laboratory and in the skills of the scientists carrying out the cell manipulations. In addition, the Korean scientists used freshly produced egg cells from younger women (under age 30).

The ability to quickly establish new lines of embryonic stem cells was also considered important in light of evidence obtained earlier in 2005 by Ajit Varkri and colleagues at the University of California, San Diego. Varkri's team found that many of the existing cultures of human embryonic stem cells are contaminated with an animal product. As a result, the body would almost certainly reject any therapies based on these cells.

The Korean researchers for the first time used genetic material from patients who had such problems as spinal cord damage or diabetes. The researchers stated that their goal had been only to obtain new cell cultures to study the origin and course of these conditions. Other scientists, however, pointed out that the next step would be research using the cells to correct

SEE ALSO THE SPECIAL REPORT, ADVANCES IN UNDERSTANDING ASTHMA, PAGE 70.

these problems. Once this was accomplished, the cells could be transplanted back into the patients. Because the modified cells would be obtained from embryos that were clones of the individuals themselves, there would be a much smaller chance that the body's disease-fighting immune system would reject the transplanted cells—a common problem in tissue and organ transplants.

A genetic cause of Parkinson disease. A single *mutation* (alteration) in a gene associated with Parkinson disease may cause 5 percent of inherited Parkinson disease cases—more cases than any other gene mutation discovered to date. The gene may also be responsible for from 1.5 to 2 percent of all noninherited forms of the disease.

Three teams of researchers independently reported these findings in January 2005. All three studies focused on a gene, identified in October 2004, called leucine-rich repeat kinase 2 (LRRK2). LRRK2 is one of five genes in which researchers have found mutations linked to Parkinson disease. The mutation in LRRK2 was named Gly2019Ser.

Parkinson disease is a progressive disorder that involves the death of nerve cells in the part of the brain that controls movement. Symptoms of Parkinson disease include tremors, muscular rigidity, and loss of motor control. The disease most commonly affects people age 60 and older but sometimes occurs in younger people.

The largest of the three studies was led by geneticist William C. Nichols of the Cincinnati (Ohio) Children's Hospital Medical Center. Nichols and his colleagues studied the LRRK2 gene in 767 people with Parkinson disease. The group represented 358 families. The researchers found the same mutation in 5 percent of the participants.

Simultaneously, researchers at the Institute of Neurology in London reported that they had found the same LRRK2 gene mutation in 8 of 482 people with Parkinson disease who did not have a known family history of the illness. A third team of investigators from Erasmus Medical Center in Rotterdam, the Netherlands, also reported that they had found the LRRK2 gene mutation in 4 of

GENETICS continued

61 families from Italy, Portugal, or Brazil with a history of Parkinson disease.

The finding of a significant genetic mutation may make it possible to use a process called *genetic screening* to identify people at risk of developing Parkinson disease. Researchers cautioned, however, that the discovery also raises ethical issues: Because there is no preventive treatment for the disease, genetic testing offers no direct medical benefit for patients or relatives.

Muscle baby. Researchers in Germany and the United States have identified a gene mutation that boosts muscle growth. The group, led by pediatric neurologist Marcus Schuelke of the Charite University Medical Center in Berlin, announced the finding in June 2004. Schuelke and his colleagues had been studying a child born in 1999 who, unlike most babies, had clearly defined muscles at birth. By the time he was 4 years old, the boy could hold a 3-kilogram (7-pound) weight in each hand with his arms held straight out, a feat many adults are unable to accomplish.

The researchers found that the child has a genetic defect in both copies of a gene that produces a protein known as *myostatin.* His is the first known case of such a mutation in a human being. (Several breeds of cattle have such a mutation.) The boy's mother, a former professional sprinter, had one mutated copy of the gene and one normal copy. Myostatin works in a delicate balance with other proteins in the body to limit the growth and development of muscles. The defect carried by the boy resulted in a failure to produce enough myostatin to properly limit muscle growth, which resulted in bulging muscles and exceptional strength.

The defect the researchers identified was an example of a *splicing mutation.* As part of the protein-building process, genes first make a molecule known as *RNA* (ribonucleic acid). Sections of the RNA that are not needed for building the protein are normally removed, and the remaining pieces are *spliced* (joined) together. Mutations that disrupt the splicing process interfere with the production of the protein.

Because the mutation produced larger-than-normal muscle mass in an otherwise healthy individual, the researchers hoped that manipulating

GENE THERAPY RESTORES HEARING

Researchers restored hearing in deaf guinea pigs using gene therapy to generate new *auditory hair cells* (right, bottom). The team, led by *otolaryngologist* Yehoash Raphael at the University of Michigan Medical School in Ann Arbor, reported its success in February 2005. (An otolaryngologist is an ear, nose, and throat specialist.) Auditory hair cells, which are located in the inner ear, allow guinea pigs—as well as people and most other mammals—to detect sounds. Many types of hearing loss occur in people because of damage to such cells. The Michigan researchers injected guinea pigs whose auditory hair cells had been destroyed by drugs with a virus that carried a gene called Atoh1. Atoh1 is normally found in a guinea pig *embryo* (initial stage of life) in cells that develop into auditory hair cells. After the cells have developed, the gene shuts down. In the deaf guinea pigs, the injected Atoh1 caused new hair cells to grow. A common hearing test that is also used on people proved that the guinea pigs' hearing had been restored. The researchers hoped that their findings would lead to treatments that could restore hearing in people.

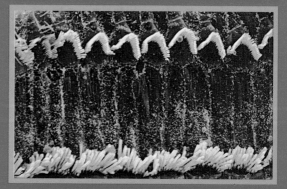

the gene that produces myostatin might lead to new treatments for such diseases as muscular dystrophy. In people with muscular dystrophy, weakness and the loss of muscle mass create potentially fatal problems. Other researchers raised concerns that myostatin blocking may be abused by athletes or bodybuilders seeking to add muscle bulk without the use of steroids or other banned substances.

Timothy syndrome genetic defect. A genetic mutation is responsible for a rare but devastating disorder known as *Timothy syndrome.* The finding was reported in October 2004 by an international group of researchers led by Mark T. Keating, a professor of cell biology, pediatrics, and cardiology, and Igor Splawski, a cardiovascular researcher, both of whom are affiliated with the Howard Hughes Medical Institute, Harvard Medical School, and the Children's Hospital, all of which are in Boston. Katherine Timothy of the University of Utah at Salt Lake City, a *cardiac arrhythmia* (irregular heartbeat) researcher who first described the syndrome in 1989, also participated in the research. Infants born with Timothy syndrome share a number of characteristics that include a rare heart disorder, webbed fingers and toes, an extremely rounded face, and *autism* (a medical disorder characterized by a limited ability to communicate and interact with other people).

To find the defective gene, the researchers obtained genetic material from 13 children affected with Timothy syndrome. In each of the children, the researchers analyzed the chemical subunits known as *nucleotides* that make up the *DNA* (deoxyribonucleic acid—the molecule genes are made of) of five different genes known to be involved in heart problems. They also analyzed several other genes thought to be possible candidates for the Timothy syndrome gene. None of the genes revealed any mutations that could explain the problems common to all the children.

Then the researchers analyzed a gene called $Ca_v1.2$ that has been associated with heart problems. They found that all 13 children carried an identical mutation in this gene. Furthermore, members of their families had no heart problems and carried normal versions of the gene.

The $Ca_v1.2$ gene produces a protein that normally forms a type of gate that controls the amount of calcium flowing in and out of cells. The intake of calcium into certain cells can cause muscle contraction. The scientists showed that the defect in the Timothy syndrome gene could prevent the gate from closing, causing too much calcium to flow into these cells. In heart cells, an excess of calcium can result in irregular muscle contraction and, thus, an irregular heartbeat.

The researchers also found that the gene affected the activity of cells in other areas of the body, including the brain. They suggested that this might help to explain why children with Timothy syndrome also exhibit autism. They stated that though the causes of autism remain mysterious, it was likely that the improper control of calcium flow into brain cells could contribute to the problems in this disorder.

In April 2005, the same researchers reported that they had identified another mutation in a slightly different area of $Ca_v1.2$ that caused a more severe form of Timothy syndrome called TS2. That mutation caused more serious heart irregularities and mental retardation but not webbed fingers and toes.

New Marfan syndrome gene. The discovery of a new genetic defect involved in Marfan syndrome was announced in August 2004 by genetic researchers from Japan and France. The scientists were led by geneticists Takeshi Mizuguchi at Nagasaki University and Gwenaelle Collod-Beroud at the Institut Universitaire de Recherche Clinique in Montpellier.

People with Marfan syndrome tend to have disproportionately long arms, legs, fingers, and toes; loose joints; weak hearts and blood vessels; and such eye problems as nearsightedness or a detached retina. The syndrome is somewhat rare, affecting only 1 in 5,000 to 10,000 people.

Researchers had already identified one cause of Marfan syndrome, a defect in a gene that normally makes a protein called *fibrillin*. The body needs fibrillin to make such connective tissues as bone and muscle. However, researchers knew that defects in this gene explained only about 80 percent of Marfan cases. The new genetic defect identified by the Japanese and French researchers accounts for about half of the remaining cases.

In people without Marfan syndrome, the newly identified gene normally produces a protein called *transforming growth factor-ß (beta)* (TGFß) *type 2 receptor.* Receptor proteins are proteins that help cells communicate with one another. They also send signals that control the activities of a cell. Such signals may include instructions telling the cell to divide, move around, or even die. The TGFß receptor protein also plays an important role in preventing cells from continually dividing.

The researchers found the Marfan gene by analyzing genetic material from a Japanese man who had Marfan syndrome. The man had no defects in his fibrillin-making gene. However, the re-

GENETICS continued

searchers found that part of one of his other genes—the one that makes TGFß—was missing. In disorders such as Marfan syndrome, which is known as a *dominant disorder,* having just one defective copy of a gene is enough to cause the condition.

The researchers next examined genetic material from a French family in which some members also had a form of Marfan syndrome that could not be explained by a fibrillin defect. The family members with Marfan syndrome also had a defect in the gene for TGFß, though in their case the defect was not caused by a missing part. Rather, the defect caused a change in one of the *amino acids* making up the TGFß protein. Amino acids are the building blocks of proteins, and a change in just one block may drastically affect how the protein is able to do its work. None of the family members without Marfan syndrome had a defective version of the gene for TGFß.

The researchers were not certain that the identification of the defect in the signal-transmitting receptor gene would lead to a cure for this form of Marfan syndrome. But they were hopeful that it would help them understand a wide range of other diseases that are either known or suspected to involve problems with receptor proteins.

Human genome variation. In July 2004, a group of researchers from the United States and Sweden, led by geneticist Michael Wigler of the Cold Spring Harbor Laboratory in New York, announced the results of a study comparing large-scale genetic differences between individuals at the level of the *human genome.* The human genome is the complete set of genetic material that an individual has. It consists of roughly 3 billion individual nucleotide subunits—adenine, guanine, cytosine, and thymine—which may be abbreviated as A, C, G, and T.

Wigler and his team were looking for a type of genetic difference called large-scale *copy number polymorphisms* (CNP's). CNP's are blocks of human genetic material, typically 100,000 or more nucleotide subunits long, that are duplicated in some people and missing in others. Wigler's group found differences between individuals in the number of times that CNP's occur.

The researchers analyzed the genomes of 20 people and found, on average, 11 CNP differences between any two individuals. They also found that the duplicated regions of the genome contained several genes, including genes in-

volved in nervous system function, cell growth control, and such diseases as *leukemia* (a form of cancer). The scientists theorized that at least some of these genetic differences between people might explain why some people are more prone than others to certain health problems.

Two other studies of the human genome examined another type of genetic variation between people known as a *single nucleotide polymorphism* (SNP). A SNP is a variation in one of the nucleotides of an individual's DNA. DNA molecules consist of two intertwined strands that carry the four nucleotides A, C, G, and T. The nucleotides always pair up in the same way, A with T and C with G, and so the order of one strand requires a complementary ordering of the other. A SNP occurs in a particular individual when one of the nucleotides in a sequence is replaced with another—for example, finding the sequence TACC in an individual's DNA when most people have the sequence TAGC in that area. SNP differences between people are very common, and they are thought to represent an important tool for understanding human differences.

One study was carried out by a group of researchers from the United States, the United Kingdom, and Sweden. It was led by geneticist Anthony Brookes of the Karolinska Institute in Huddinge, Sweden, who reported the results in July 2004. The group discovered that about 28 percent of the SNP differences between people are found in long, very similar regions of the genome called *duplicons.* This finding suggested that SNP's may not be the factor that increases an individual's risk of disease. Rather, the number of duplicon copies of a gene may play a more important role.

The other study was carried out by a research group led by geneticists David Hinds and David Cox of Perlegen Sciences, Inc., a private company in Mountain View, California. They reported in February 2005 on their study of SNP differences among 71 Americans of African, European, and Asian ancestry. The researchers identified a total of 1.58 million SNP differences among the participants. Many scientists hope that this resource, which the researchers made publicly available, together with information from other sources, would provide a more complete picture of human genetic variation that could be used in a wide range of diagnostic and treatment applications.   ■ David Haymer

See also **MEDICAL RESEARCH.**

■ GEOLOGY

A giant earthquake on the floor of the Indian Ocean on Dec. 26, 2004, caused the most devastating tsunami in history. The Sumatra-Andaman earthquake was the second-largest quake recorded since 1900. Studies of the earthquake made using *seismometers* indicate that it had a *moment magnitude* (level of strength) of at least 9.0. Seismometers detect and measure vibrations called *seismic waves* that are produced by earthquakes.

An analysis of the movement of Earth's crust during the earthquake appeared in a report published in March 2005 by geophysicists S. A. Khan of the Danish Space Center in Copenhagen and Olafur Gudmundsson of the Niels Bohr Institute at Copenhagen University. For their study, the scientists used data from four Global Positioning System (GPS) reference stations in the region. The GPS uses radio signals broadcast by Earth-orbiting satellites to determine the location of points on the surface.

The quake took place along a *fault* (break in Earth's crust) that forms the boundary between two *plates*, the large slabs of crust and mantle that make up Earth's outer shell. This boundary is marked on the ocean floor by the Sunda Trench. There, the relatively dense Indian-Australian Plate is *subducting* (descending) beneath the lighter Burma Plate. These plates normally collide at an average rate of about 6 centimeters (2 ½ inches) per year. On December 26, they moved about 9 meters (29 ½ feet) along one section of the fault.

The researchers reported that one GPS station at Sampali on the Indonesian island of Sumatra moved westward 14.5 centimeters (5.7 inches). This station was 330 kilometers (200 miles) from the earthquake's *epicenter* (point on the surface directly above the point where the rocks first break). Another station, to the north in Singapore, moved westward 2.2 centimeters (0.9 inch). Stations on the Indonesian island of Java and on Cocos Island in the Indian Ocean showed no movement.

Using GPS data and seismic records from *aftershocks* (smaller earthquakes that follow a major quake), the researchers determined that the epicenter of the earthquake lay close to the southern end of the affected area. The researchers found that the earthquake shifted a section of the fault about 200,000 square kilometers (77,200 square miles) in area. The ruptured section of the fault

extended 1,300 kilometers (810 miles) along the Sunda Trench northward from the northeastern tip of Sumatra, westward to the Andaman Islands, and northward toward the coast of Myanmar (formerly called Burma).

Khan and Gudmundsson noted that the quake caused no movement along the trench southeast of the epicenter. On March 28, 2005, only three weeks after their report was published, however, a major earthquake occurred along the previously unaffected area of the fault. Its epicenter was about 160 kilometers (100 miles) southeast of the epicenter of December 26 quake. The March quake had a moment magnitude of 8.7 and caused extensive damage, especially on Nias Island off Sumatra, but did not generate a tsunami.

Ice core yields climate record. The oldest, most detailed record of the climate of the Northern Hemisphere over the last 123,000 years has been recovered from an *ice core* drilled from Greenland's icecap. (An ice core is a long, narrow cylinder of ice.) In September 2004, members of the North Greenland Ice Core Project (NGRIP) reported on their analysis of the new ice core, which is 3,085 meters (10,120 feet) long. Drilling for the core lasted from 1996 to 2003.

In contrast to other Greenland ice cores, the new core reaches back into the Eemian Stage, an *interglacial* that lasted from 130,000 to 120,000 years ago. (An interglacial is a period of warming and glacial melting that follows a period of *glaciation* [glacial formation]). Other cores have not been able to retrieve information from the Eemian because the movement of the icecap has destroyed older layers of ice in many areas. The NGRIP researchers obtained their core from an area where the base had remained stable. The ice core contains about 1 centimeter (0.4 inch) of ice per year for the section of the core dating to 105,000 years ago.

The researchers' analysis of the core revealed that during the Eemian, temperatures over northern Greenland may have been as much as 5 °C (9 °F) warmer than current average temperatures. Nevertheless, Greenland remained ice-covered, in contrast to the rest of the Northern Hemisphere, where glaciers retreated.

According to the study, the return to glacial conditions over northern North America and Europe began 122,000 years ago with a gradual drop in temperatures. But 119,000 years ago, the

GEOLOGY continued

climate grew abruptly colder as the glaciation spread. About 115,000 years ago, glaciation was interrupted by a previously unknown warming period that lasted for 3,000 years. This period was the first of 24 such warming episodes that have occurred over the past 100,000 years. These periods are called Dansgaard-Oeschger (D-O) events after paleoclimatologists Willi Dansgaard of Denmark and Hans Oeschger of Switzerland, who discovered them. The NGRIP core is the first to include a record of all D-O events.

The researchers found that although glacial conditions had become intense by 80,000 years ago, sudden D-O events occurred every 4,000 to 5,000 years. These events lasted from a few hundred to a few thousand years. The most recent D-O event occurred about 13,000 years ago. The cause of these warm episodes in an otherwise frigid climate remains unknown.

Temperature from algae analysis. A new method of analyzing ancient plant material has enabled scientists to more accurately estimate the water temperature of the Arctic Ocean 70 million years ago. Both animal and plant fossils have indicated that temperatures in the Arctic during the Late Cretaceous, from about 100 million to 65 million years ago, were much warmer than they are today. However, scientists had no way of determining exactly how much warmer. Geologist Hugh Jenkyns of Oxford University in England and marine biogeochemists Astrid Forster, Stefan Schouten, and Jaap Sinninghe Damste of the Royal Netherlands Institute for Sea Research in Texel reported on the new method in the Dec. 16, 2004, issue of *Nature*.

The team analyzed membrane molecules from a type of *planktonic* (floating) algae, the Crenarchaeota, found fossilized in a short core of black mud that had been brought up from the floor of the Arctic Sea in 1970. The core was one of several taken from a submarine rise known as Alpha Ridge, which lies close to the North Pole. Although the other cores contained beautifully preserved microscopic fossils, they did not contain enough *organic* (carbon-containing) material for use in determining ancient water temperatures.

Today, the surface air temperature in this region averages –15 °C (5 °F). Jenkyns and his associates found that 70 million years ago, the average annual temperature of the upper layers of water in the Arctic basin was about 15 °C (59 °F). However, this was near the end of the Late Cretaceous, when the world had cooled from its earlier warmer condition. Based on other paleotemperature measurements made in the tropics, the scientists estimate that roughly 90 million years ago, the temperature of Arctic Ocean surface waters may have been at least 20 °C (68 °F).

Superanoxic extinction. Earth's greatest mass extinction, which occurred 251 million years ago, may have resulted from rapid global warming rather than a meteorite impact, a team of scientists reported in the Feb. 4, 2005, issue of *Nature*. Some scientists have suggested that the extinction, which took place at the end of the Permian Period, resulted from the impact of a giant meteorite. An international team of scientists led by geologist Kliti Grice of Curtin University of Technology in Perth, Australia, however, proposed that the extinction resulted from a "superanoxic event" in the ocean.

Anoxic means *without oxygen*. The deep waters of ocean basins may become anoxic if the decomposition of large amounts of decaying plant matter uses up all the free oxygen in the water. After the supply of free oxygen is exhausted, decomposition may continue through the extraction of oxygen in sulfate, a type of sea salt that contains oxygen and sulfur. During the process, however, the sulfur is converted into hydrogen sulfide, a highly poisonous gas that has the odor of rotten eggs, and the water becomes *euxinic*. Today euxinic conditions exist only in the deep waters of the Black Sea and a few smaller areas of the ocean.

Grice and her colleagues studied cores of sediment from the boundary between the Permian and Triassic periods in drill holes taken from the sea floor off the coast of southern China. The cores contain compounds produced by green sulfur bacteria, a special group of organisms adapted for life in water with high levels of hydrogen sulfide. The green sulfur bacteria live in the *photic zone*, the waters near the surface penetrated by light. The researchers found that during the late Permian, green sulfur bacteria were common in the waters off what are now Australia and south China. The scientists concluded that euxinic conditions extended into the photic zone and, periodically, even to the sea surface. They theorized that poisonous hydrogen sulfide gas, which is heavier than air, was released from the water into the atmosphere— causing a mass extinction.

New layer of Earth. The discovery of a previously unknown layer of Earth's mantle about 2,900 kilometers (1,800 miles) below the surface was reported in April 2005 by geophysicists John Hernlund and Paul Tackley of the Institute of Geophysics and Planetary Physics at the University of California, Los Angeles, and Christine Thomas of the Department of Earth and Ocean Sciences of the University of Liverpool in the United Kingdom. The mantle, a layer of partially melted rock between the outer crust and core, makes up about 83 percent of Earth's volume. The newly discovered layer lies just above the boundary between the mantle and the core.

The scientists found the layer by analyzing the *velocity* (speed and direction) of seismic waves traveling through Earth's mantle. The waves' velocity reflects *phase changes* (changes in density) in the minerals that make up the mantle. As depths increase, atoms in the minerals become more closely packed together.

Hernlund's team discovered a previously unknown phase change near the boundary between the core and the mantle. The phase change is well developed beneath Europe and the Caribbean but is absent in other areas. The scientists theorized that these differences result from regional variations in the temperature of the deep mantle. They attributed the temperature variations to the presence of relatively cooler materials from the upper layers that have plunged deep within the mantle at subduction zones.

The researchers believe that this discovery will enable geophysicists to make better estimates of the Earth's internal temperature near the core-mantle boundary. Current estimates of the temperature there range from 3,400 to 4,400 °C (6,200 to 7,460 °F). ■ William W. Hay

See also **ATMOSPHERIC SCIENCE.**

UPDATED GEOLOGIC MAP

The many rock formations in Alaska and northwestern Canada appear in a detail (below) of a new geologic map of North America presented in February 2005 by the Geological Society of America. The new map depicts about 15 percent of Earth's surface and shows more than 900 different types of rock, more than seven times as many as the previous map, which was published in 1965. The 1965 map was created before the advent of the theory of plate tectonics, which states that Earth's outer shell is made up of 30 rigid tectonic plates and that the movement of these plates causes such geologic events as earthquakes and volcano formation. The improved detail is the result of advances in geologic research, including the discovery of more detailed ocean cores and more precise methods of dating rocks.

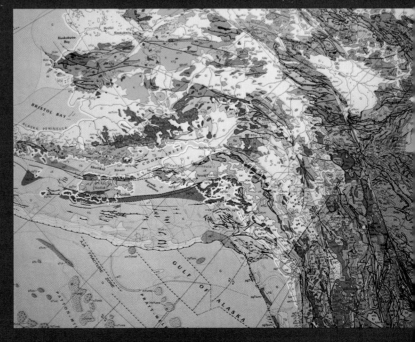

Trembling Earth and Troubled Waters

On Dec. 26, 2004, the world's most powerful earthquake in 40 years shook the bottom of the Indian Ocean, about 255 kilometers (160 miles) southeast of Banda Aceh, on the Indonesian island of Sumatra. The tremors lasted for about three or four minutes, jolting the seabed upward and displacing a vast amount of water. The rising water developed into a series of towering waves, called *tsunami waves*, that spread outward in expanding circles at speeds of up to 800 kilometers (500 miles) per hour.

About 15 minutes after the earthquake—without any warning—waves at least 20 meters (66 feet) high hit the north and west coasts of Sumatra. During the next seven hours, the tsunami waves spread throughout the Indian Ocean, reaching as far as the east coast of Africa—4,800 kilometers (3,000 miles) from the earthquake's *epicenter* (the point on the surface above the first break in the rock).

When it was over, at least 175,000 people were dead, making the tsunami of 2004 the deadliest in recorded history. In addition, the tsunami waves injured hundreds of thousands of people, left millions homeless, and destroyed many buildings, roads, farms, and other types of property.

The earthquake that caused the tsunami had a *moment magnitude* (a number indicating the strength of an earthquake) of at least 9.0. As such, it had the destructive power of 23,000 atomic bombs of the kind that devastated Nagasaki, Japan, at the end of World War II (1939–1945). The quake occurred at the boundary of two *tectonic plates* called the Indian-Australian and the Burma plates.

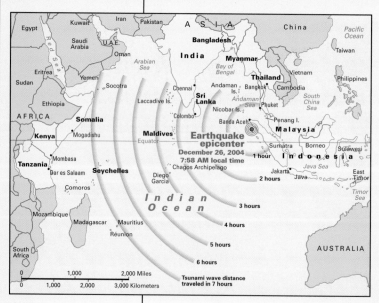

Tectonic plates are large, rigid slabs of Earth's outer shell, consisting of *crust* (the outermost layer of the planet) and part of the *mantle* (a layer of hot rock below the crust). About 30 of these plates slide constantly over a *molten* (melted) layer of the mantle. They move at rates from about 2 to 15 centimeters (1 to 6 inches) per year, carrying the continents and sea floor to ever-changing positions. In some places, such as the boundary between the Indian-Australian and Burma plates, one plate presses against and *subducts* (descends) beneath the other. This process causes a build-up of geological stresses that eventually is released by a sudden, dramatic movement of the descending plate.

The earthquake occurred when the edge of the Indian-Australian Plate lurched beneath the Burma Plate and descended into the mantle along the Sunda Trench. (A trench is a long, narrow valley on the sea floor that marks a subduction zone.) This movement lifted the edge of the Burma Plate about 5 meters (16 feet) along 1,200 kilometers (750 miles) of sea floor parallel to the trench. The movement pushed an enormous column of water upward, causing the tsunami. In other areas near the trench, the geological activity caused the sea floor to sink by as much as 2 meters (7 feet).

Scientists offered several reasons to explain why this undersea earthquake and the resulting tsunami waves were so dramatic. One reason is that the last earthquake along the Sunda Trench occurred in 1833, allowing almost two centuries of geological stresses to build up. When these stresses were finally released, the geological activity was intense.

Another reason for the devastation was the nature of the quake. The quake occurred as the result of *thrust faulting*—a vertical slipping of the sea floor. A different type of plate slippage, called *strike-slip faulting*, results in a more horizontal movement of the sea floor and rarely causes tsunamis. In fact, an earthquake with strike-slip faulting took place on the sea floor near the Macquarie Islands in the southern Pacific Ocean just three days before the December 26 tsunami— without causing a tsunami.

Although geologists understand some of the science behind tsunamis, they were somewhat puzzled on March 28, 2005, when a powerful earthquake with thrust faulting struck the same general area of the Indian Ocean without generating a major tsunami. Scientists noted several differences between the two quakes. The March 2005 quake occurred deeper inside Earth, fractured less of the sea floor, and displaced very little water compared with the December 2004 quake. These were likely important factors in the different outcomes of the quakes.

The force of the December 2004 earthquake along the Sunda Trench permanently altered the geography of the region around Sumatra. The movement of the Indian-Australian Plate toward Indonesia caused the northwest tip of Sumatra to shift toward the southwest, perhaps by as much as 36 meters (118 feet), according to Ken Hudnut, a scientist with the United States Geological Survey. Several small islands off the southwest coast of Sumatra may have been moved to the southwest by 20 meters (66 feet), Hudnut said.

SWAMPED

The northern shore of Banda Aceh, Indonesia, appears before (below) and after (below, bottom) the December 2004 tsunami. Waves swallowed the city's shoreline, and floods drove at least 3 kilometers (2 miles) inland. Tens of thousands of people died in Banda Aceh, the city closest to the earthquake's epicenter.

TOWERING WAVES

When tsunami waves reach the shore, they grow to great heights and then crash onto land. Several cities around the Indian Ocean saw huge waves slamming onto their shores. In Banda Aceh, Indonesia, the first city hit by the tsunami, waves reached heights of at least 20 meters (66 feet), about the height of a six-story building. Seven hours later, after traveling nearly 4,800 kilometers (3,000 miles), the waves crashed into Mogadishu, Somalia, at heights of about 4 meters (13 feet).

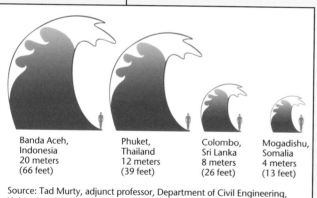

| Banda Aceh, Indonesia 20 meters (66 feet) | Phuket, Thailand 12 meters (39 feet) | Colombo, Sri Lanka 8 meters (26 feet) | Mogadishu, Somalia 4 meters (13 feet) |

Source: Tad Murty, adjunct professor, Department of Civil Engineering, University of Ottawa, Canada.

The tremors from the earthquake were so strong that they actually slowed the speed at which Earth rotates on its axis, according to the National Aeronautics and Space Administration (NASA) Jet Propulsion Laboratory in Pasadena, California. The laboratory estimated that the rotation rate decreased the length of Earth's day by 2.676 *microseconds* (millionths of a second).

Researchers in 2005 were working on various projects to better understand the tsunami of 2004. For example, Vasily Titov, a tsunami researcher at the Pacific Marine Environmental Laboratory in Seattle, Washington, developed a computer model to describe the way the tsunami changed over time. As tsunami waves travel across the ocean, their speed is directly proportional to the sea's depth. That is, the waves travel faster in deep water. At this point, the waves are shallow. Titov's simulation successfully re-created this portion of the tsunami of 2004's journey. As tsunami waves reach the shallow *continental shelf* (the submerged land at the edge of a continent), the waves slow, and the back of each wave catches up with the front. This causes the waves to grow in size and then slam into the shoreline with intense force. A lack of data on shoreline geography and wave heights in the region prevented Titov from accurately modeling this stage of the tsunami.

Perhaps the greatest tragedy of the tsunami of 2004 was the lack of any warning for the dozen affected countries. The Indian Ocean had no warning system because tsunamis rarely occur in this region. About 85 percent of all tsunamis take place in the Pacific Ocean.

In early 2005, government representatives and scientists from many nations met to discuss plans to set up a comprehensive tsunami warning system for the Indian Ocean. This system was to be based on the Tsunami Warning System in the Pacific Ocean, which has been in place since 1968. More than 20 nations participate in the Pacific system, which is headquartered at the Honolulu Observatory in Hawaii. The system includes a number of instrument buoys that are anchored throughout the Pacific Ocean. The buoys are connected to sensors at the bottom of the ocean that measure changes in water pressure, like those that accompany the passage of tsunami waves. The buoys then transmit these measurements to satellites, which relay the data to scientists at warning centers. In case of a tsunami, the scientists can then warn authorities in the threatened countries, providing predictions of when and where the waves will strike.

Scientists hoped to have the Indian Ocean Tsunami Warning System operating by mid-2006. A fully global system could be in place by 2007, according to Koichiro Matsuura, head of the United Nations Educational, Scientific, and Cultural Organization (UNESCO), which is involved in the project. Scientists expect that the tsunami of 2004 will lead to a more complete understanding of tsunamis and better tsunami warning systems for countries around the world.

■ Alfred J. Smuskiewicz

MEDICAL RESEARCH

In 2005, the United States Centers for Disease Control and Prevention (CDC) in Atlanta, Georgia, reported that it had overestimated the number of deaths caused by obesity. Research on breast cancer suggested that a low-fat diet may reduce the risk of a recurrence of the disease. Studies also revealed a possible connection between heart disease and dementia. Investigators presented more evidence for the harmful effects of secondhand tobacco smoke and determined that the human embryonic stem cell lines being used by federally funded scientists have been contaminated. Researchers also identified a new form of muscular dystrophy and revealed new findings about the potentially dangerous side effects of high doses of vitamin E.

Dangers of obesity overstated? In 2005, researchers at the CDC continued their efforts to understand the impact that *obesity* has on an individual's health. However, their efforts caused considerable confusion for the general public and for health professionals. (Physicians generally consider a person obese if the individual scores 30 or above on a measure called the *body mass index* [BMI]. The BMI takes height and weight into account to estimate body fat.)

In March 2004, the CDC had released a report stating that in 2000 (the latest year for which data were available), deaths stemming from poor diet and physical inactivity—two major causes of obesity and overweight—had reached 400,000. Only tobacco use caused more deaths in the United States—435,000 each year. However, in response to questions from researchers both inside and outside the CDC, the agency contracted with two independent statisticians to review these findings. In January 2005, the statisticians reported that they had discovered a mistake in the computer software used to analyze the data. As a result of the review, the CDC revised the number of deaths from poor diet and physical inactivity from 400,000 to 365,000 per year. Obesity fell from second place to seventh place in causes of death in the United States.

In April 2005, researchers at the CDC's National Center for Health Statistics reported slightly different information. Kathleen Flegal, an *epidemiologist* who led the study, explained that she had developed a new statistical method for analyzing the data. (Epidemiologists study rapidly spreading diseases.) Flegal reviewed three na-

SEE ALSO

THE SPECIAL REPORT, **ADVANCES IN UNDERSTANDING ASTHMA,** PAGE 70.

THE SPECIAL REPORT, **STRAIGHT TALK ABOUT BACK HEALTH,** PAGE 84.

SCIENCE STUDIES, **REMEMBERING AND FORGETTING: THE SCIENCE OF HUMAN MEMORY,** PAGE 128.

tional health surveys conducted from the 1970's through the 2000's. She analyzed the participants' BMI and determined the number of deaths associated with being underweight, of normal weight, overweight, and obese. According to these findings, obesity kills about 112,000 people annually. Flegal's study also found a puzzling result that researchers were unable to explain: People who are modestly overweight live longer than people of normal weight.

Flegal's findings caused a backlash against the diet industry and government researchers, as many consumers decided that they did not need to be concerned about excess pounds after all. Nevertheless, health care professionals and the CDC researchers themselves warned that obesity remains a serious health threat. Numerous studies have linked being extremely overweight to heart disease, diabetes, *hypertension* (high blood pressure), and other conditions.

Diet and breast cancer. A low-fat diet may help women with breast cancer avoid a recurrence of the disease. Researchers led by *oncologist* (cancer specialist) Rowan T. Chlebowski at the Los Angeles Biomedical Research Institute in Torrance, California, reported the finding in May 2005. The research was the first controlled, large-scale study to show that a change in lifestyle can affect the risk that a cancer that is considered in *remission* will reappear. (Remission is the disappearance of symptoms in a patient with a chronic illness.)

The researchers studied 2,437 middle-aged or older women with early-stage breast cancer. All the women had had either a *lumpectomy* (a procedure in which only breast tissue surrounding the tumor is removed) or a *mastectomy* (in which the entire breast is removed), followed

MEDICAL RESEARCH continued

by radiation and either hormone therapy or chemotherapy.

The researchers asked 975 of the women to follow a diet that limited fat to 33 grams a day. The remaining women followed a standard diet in which their intake of fat averaged about 51 grams a day. After five years, the researchers found that among the women assigned to a low-fat diet, 9.8 percent experienced a recurrence of their cancer. Among the women who followed the standard diet, however, 12.4 percent developed cancer again. The women on the low-fat diet also lost an average of five pounds.

Some researchers speculated that the weight loss, rather than the low-fat diet, may have caused the reduction in cancer recurrences. However, many oncologists considered the results significant. They also noted that because there are no known drawbacks to a low-fat diet, doctors have no reason not to recommend it to breast cancer patients.

Heart health linked to brain health. Controlling risk factors for *cardiovascular disease* (diseases of the heart and blood vessels), especially high cholesterol and high blood pressure, may help to prevent *dementia* or slow its

THE EFFECT OF STRESS ON CELLS

Chronic stress appears to speed up the aging process in immune system cells, according to a November 2004 study by researchers at the University of California, San Francisco. Cells contain *chromosomes*, which carry the hereditary information for all living things. At the end of each chromosome is a section called a *telomere*. Telomeres are made up of bits of *DNA* and protein. (DNA—deoxyribonucleic acid— is the molecule of which genes are made.) Each time a parent cell divides and produces descendant cells, it loses some of its DNA and its telomere becomes shorter. After many divisions, the telomere becomes so short that the aged cell can no longer divide. Such a cell is at greater risk of disease. The California researchers found that chronic stress also results in shortened telomeres and, thus, increases an individual's risk for disease.

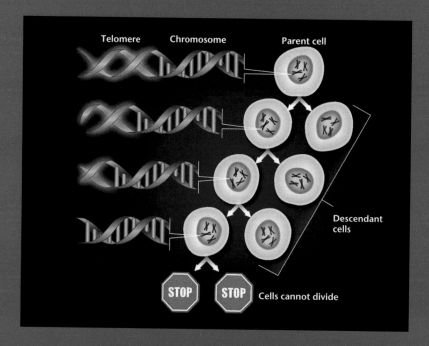

progress. Dementia is an irreversible form of memory loss. A study published in December 2004 helped to explain the connection.

Kenneth M. Langa, an internist at the University of Michigan in Ann Arbor, and his colleagues reviewed the medical literature on Alzheimer's disease, *vascular dementia,* and a condition called *mixed dementia.* In people with Alzheimer's disease, an abnormal protein in the brain triggers cell death that causes irreversible memory loss and other changes. In people with vascular dementia, brain function gradually declines because of a lack of blood flow to the brain. Vascular dementia is usually caused by strokes, high blood pressure, blocked blood vessels, or other problems with blood vessels. Patients with mixed dementia have symptoms of both Alzheimer's disease and vascular dementia.

Langa's group found that mixed dementia was much more common than previously thought. According to the researchers, blood-flow problems affected more than half of all people in the studies with dementia, including those with Alzheimer's disease. The researchers urged doctors to consider whether their Alzheimer's patients may have such conditions as high blood pressure and high cholesterol. Treating these conditions could improve brain function, they said.

Mid-life risk factors for dementia.
People who have one or more risk factors for cardiovascular disease during their 40's may be more likely to develop dementia later in life, according to a study reported in December 2004 by researchers at Kaiser Permanente Division of Research in Oakland, California, and the University of California, San Francisco. Kaiser Permanente is a health maintenance organization (HMO) that also operates a number of medical facilities.

The California team studied the health records of 8,845 people who were members of the Kaiser Permanente HMO. Researchers reviewed health evaluations performed when the participants were from 40 to 44 years old. Investigators looked for such cardiovascular disease risk factors as total cholesterol level, diabetes, high blood pressure, and smoking. Then they looked at the medical records of the same people an average of 27 years later.

In the follow-up evaluations, 721 of the participants (8.2 percent) had been diagnosed with dementia. Those who had all four cardiovascular disease risk factors in their 40's were twice as likely to have developed dementia as those who did not have any cardiovascular disease risk factors in mid-life. Participants who had only one risk factor while in their 40's were 20 to 40 percent more likely to have developed dementia later in life. The more severe and the higher the number of risk factors, the greater was the participants' likelihood of developing dementia.

The California researchers concluded that the presence of multiple cardiovascular risk factors during mid-life substantially increases risk of late-life dementia. They suggested that controlling those risk factors through diet, exercise, and drugs that lower cholesterol and blood pressure may help to prevent dementia.

Secondhand smoke and IQ scores.
Exposure to environmental tobacco smoke (ETS), commonly known as secondhand smoke, may lower a child's intelligence level. A team of investigators at the Cincinnati (Ohio) Children's Hospital Medical Center and other institutions reported this finding in January 2005.

The Cincinnati researchers based their finding on data from the Third National Health and Nutrition Examination Survey (NHANES III), which was conducted from 1988 to 1994. NHANES III included 4,399 children from ages 6 to 16 years. Researchers tested the levels of *cotinine* (a substance formed when nicotine breaks down) in the children's blood to measure their exposure to ETS. (Children with cotinine levels high enough to indicate that they were smokers themselves were not included in the study.)

The children completed standardized tests of reading, math, memory, and the ability to perceive *spatial relationships* (relationships of figures in space), called *visuospatial skills.* The tests were designed to measure the children's intelligence quotient (IQ).

Children who had been exposed to ETS scored lower in tests of math, reading, and visuospatial skills than did children who lived in a smoke-free environment. For every level of exposure, measured in nanograms per milliliter of blood (ng/ml), scores dropped the equivalent of from two to five IQ points. Exposure to as little as 0.1 ng/ml resulted in decreased test scores, suggesting that exposure to even low levels of ETS may be harmful to the brain.

African-American children in the study had higher concentrations of cotinine in their blood than did children from any other ethnic group. Cotinine levels were also higher among children with lower household incomes and those whose parents had lower levels of education.

MEDICAL RESEARCH continued

Children living in the Midwestern United States were also more likely to be exposed to ETS.

Despite mounting evidence that ETS is linked to health problems, more than 40 percent of children in the United States are exposed to tobacco smoke in their homes. ETS has been linked to sudden infant death syndrome, middle ear disease, asthma, and various respiratory problems. The Cincinnati team indicated that their findings provided another reason to keep children away from secondhand smoke.

Stem cell lines contaminated. *Lines* (colonies) of human *embryonic stem cells* that are approved for study using federal funds in the United States are contaminated with a non-human molecule, according to a report published in January 2005 by researchers at the University of California, San Diego (UCSD) School of Medicine and the Salk Institute in La Jolla, California. In a related study published in November 2004, the same group of researchers reported that they had discovered how human cells may become contaminated. Finally, in April 2005, another group of researchers at the San Diego School of Medicine and the Whittier Institute for Diabetes in La Jolla reported that they had developed a method to grow and maintain human stem cell lines that are not contaminated.

Human embryonic stem cells are derived from human *embryos* (the initial stage of life) and have the potential to develop into virtually any kind of human tissue. Researchers believe that stem cells may someday be used to replace damaged tissues and to treat—and even cure—diseases such as Parkinson disease, diabetes, and cystic fibrosis.

However, some people object to the use of human embryonic stem cells in research because the embryos are destroyed in the process of extracting the cells. Because of the ethical debate over this issue, President George W. Bush announced in 2001 that researchers using federal funds were limited to using cell lines created before Aug. 9, 2001. The California researchers found these lines to be contaminated.

Researchers led by Ajit Varki, professor of medicine and cellular and molecular medicine at UCSD, found that federally approved human embryonic stem cell lines contain a substance called N-glycolylneuraminic acid (Neu5Gc). In 1998, Varki and his team had shown that, unlike the bodies of other mammals, the human body cannot make Neu5Gc. In fact, in 2003, the group found that human beings have naturally occurring *antibodies* to Neu5Gc. (Antibodies are proteins produced by the immune system that attack foreign substances.)

In the January 2005 study, Varki and his team exposed the approved cell lines contaminated with Neu5Gc to human antibodies. The antibodies attacked the cells. The researchers concluded that if such cells were to be implanted in people, the human immune system would render the therapy useless.

In 2004, the researchers had found that human cells may incorporate Neu5Gc from the laboratory culture dishes in which they are grown. Traditionally, culture dishes include so-called *feeder layers* that contain connective tissue from mice or calves. The feeder layers maintain cells in an *undifferentiated* (undeveloped) state.

In April 2005, a team at the San Diego School of Medicine reported that they had discovered how to grow and maintain stem cells without animal-derived feeder layers. The team was led by Alberto Hayek, a professor of pediatrics and the director of the Islet Research Laboratory at the Whittier Institute. The researchers identified a molecule called activin A in mouse feeder layers that was responsible for maintaining the stem cells in an undifferentiated state. When Hayek and his team added human activin A to a culture medium, they were able to successfully maintain uncontaminated stem cells in the medium.

New form of muscular dystrophy. A previously unrecognized form of muscular dystrophy was described in January 2005 by researchers at the Mayo Clinic in Rochester, Minnesota. Muscular dystrophy is a group of genetic diseases that cause muscles to progressively weaken and degenerate. It affects about 50,000 people in the United States. Although there is no known cure for muscular dystrophy, treatment can slow the progression of the disease. The researchers named the newly identified form of the disease *zaspopathy*.

The research team, led by neurologist Duygu Selcen, suspected that a protein called ZASP was involved in the development of muscular dystrophy. ZASP, which is found in a part of the muscle cell called the *Z-disk*, plays an important role in heart and skeletal muscle function. The Z-disk is a structure deep within muscle fibers that separates contracting units of muscle cells.

RECOMMENDED HEALTH SCREENINGS FOR ADULTS

Physicians with the United States Preventative Services Task Force, an independent panel of primary care and prevention experts, recommend that Americans obtain regular health screenings to ensure good health. Such screenings may reveal a potentially serious condition when it is still easily treatable. Patients with high blood pressure and high blood cholesterol, for example, may be able to make lifestyle changes that can decrease the risk of developing heart disease. Recommended screenings differ for men and women and also for people at various ages.

SERVICE	GOAL	AGE: 19 TO 39	AGE: 40 TO 64	AGE: 65 AND OLDER
Comprehensive screening exam	To promote wellness	Frequency should be tailored to age and health status. Consult your health professional.		
DIAGNOSTIC TESTING				
Blood Pressure	To identify high blood pressure	Every 2 years		
Cholesterol	To reduce risk of heart disease	At least every 5 years		
Diabetes screening	To test for diabetes	Depends on risk factors and age. Consult your health professional.		
Colon cancer screening: Stool blood (FOBT) Sigmoidoscopy Colonoscopy Barium enema	To detect colorectal cancer			After age 50: frequency depends on test FOBT: every year Sigmoidoscopy: every 5 years Colonoscopy: every 10 years Barium enema: every 5 years
Sigmoidoscopy or colonoscopy	To detect colorectal cancer or large polyps			Every 5 years beginning at age 50
Vision exam	To test vision and screen for glaucoma	Discuss with your health professional.		
Hearing test	To monitor hearing	Every 10 years		Hearing loss increases at age 50 so discuss the frequency of tests with your health professional.
MEN ONLY				
Prostate-specific antigen (PSA)/DRE for prostate cancer	Blood test to detect prostate cancer			Guidelines vary. Discuss with your health professional.
WOMEN ONLY				
Mammogram and clinical breast exam	Early detection of cancer			Every 1 to 2 years starting at age 40
Cervical cancer screening/pelvic exam	To detect cervical and ovarian cancer	Every 1 to 3 years depending on risk		Every 1 to 3 years depending on risk. Over age 65, if negative on previous screens, at your health professional's discretion.
Rubella antibody test	To determine rubella immunity	One time prior to first pregnancy		
Osteoporosis screening	To identify those at risk			At least once after age 65; earlier for high-risk women

Source: U.S. Preventative Services Task Force

MEDICAL RESEARCH continued

Selcen and his colleagues searched for mutations in the gene that contains the instructions for making ZASP among 54 people who had been diagnosed with muscular dystrophy. Of the 54 people, 11 had mutations in the ZASP gene. The researchers identified three different mutations, though they did not determine which of the three could be responsible for causing zaspopathy. They also found that the mutations were passed on from parent to child in a *dominant* manner. That is, a child who inherits one copy of the mutant gene from a parent will develop the disorder.

Zaspopathy occurs in people over the age of 40 and causes damage to heart muscles, weakness in the limbs, and nerve damage. The researchers hoped that identifying a new form of the disease would lead to a greater understanding of muscular dystrophy and more effective treatments.

The dangers of vitamin E. High doses of vitamin E may increase the risk of dying from all causes as well as the risk of heart failure and stroke, according to research reported in 2004 and 2005. Much of the popular and scientific interest in vitamin E has resulted from earlier studies suggesting that vitamin E and other vitamins called *antioxidants* might protect against heart disease and cancer. Antioxidants block the effects of *free radicals,* unstable molecules that form as the result of various processes, including those associated with radiation, cigarette smoke, and air pollution. Our bodies also create free radicals as they burn oxygen for energy. Free radicals can damage cells and cause changes in genes.

Researchers at Johns Hopkins Medical Center in Baltimore reported in November 2004 that people who routinely take high doses of vitamin E supplements may have an increased risk of dying from all causes. The Hopkins team was led by internist Edgar R. Miller, III, an associate professor of medicine.

The researchers analyzed data from 19 clinical trials involving about 136,000 participants. In 11 of the trials, participants had taken more than 400 IU's (international units) of vitamin E per day. (On average, people take in about 10 IU's of vitamin E per day from their diet. Multivitamin pills usually contain from 30 to 60 IU's.)

Miller's team found that in 9 of the 11 trials, the death rate from all causes increased significantly. It was not clear whether taking 200 IU's or less of vitamin E per day increased a person's risk of death. Nor was it clear how vitamin E may increase the risk of death.

The researchers cautioned that most of the participants in the trials were over age 60 and had such pre-existing conditions as heart disease or cancer. They stated that more research needs to be done on the effects of low-dose vitamin E supplements on healthy young adults. Based on the study results, however, the team recommended that people avoid vitamin E supplements containing more than 400 IU's.

In March 2005, another team of investigators also found that high doses of vitamin E may do more harm than good. The researchers reported that in people with blood-vessel disease or diabetes, long-term supplementation with vitamin E does not prevent cancer, sudden cardiac arrest, or stroke. In fact, taking vitamin E supplements may increase the risk of heart failure. The study was led by Eva Lonn of the Population Health Research Institute and McMaster University, both located in Hamilton, Canada.

The clinical trial, called the Heart Outcomes Prevention Evaluation (HOPE), was conducted from December 1993 to April 1999. In 1999, the trial was extended to May 2003 as HOPE-The Ongoing Outcomes (HOPE-TOO). Of the 9,541 people who began the trial in 1993, 3,994 agreed to participate in the extension of the trial. People in HOPE-TOO were at least 55 years old and had blood vessel disease or diabetes mellitus. Study participants took a daily dose of 400 IU's of vitamin E.

Lonn's team tracked the incidence of cancer, cancer deaths, and major cardiovascular events, which it defined as stroke, sudden cardiac arrest, and death from sudden cardiac arrest. The researchers also evaluated the risk of *heart failure* (a decrease in the pumping ability of the heart), heart disease, and blood vessel disease. They found that vitamin E did not affect the incidence of cancer, cancer deaths, or major cardiovascular events. However, it increased the risk of heart failure. The Johns Hopkins and HOPE reports add to a growing number of clinical studies that have consistently demonstrated that commonly used antioxidant vitamin regimens do not significantly reduce cardiovascular events or cancer but may, in fact, be harmful. ∎ Renée Despres

See also **GENETICS.**

NOBEL PRIZES

The 2004 Nobel Prizes in science were awarded in October for the discovery of the way cells break down damaged proteins, the discovery of a phenomenon that explains one of the four fundamental forces of nature, and research into the way in which human beings can distinguish roughly 10,000 different odors. Each prize was worth about $1.3 million.

The prize in chemistry was shared by cancer researcher Irwin A. Rose of the University of California in Irvine and Israeli biochemists Aaron Ciechanover and Avram Hershko of the Technion-Israel Institute of Technology in Haifa. The researchers were recognized for discovering a process called *regulated protein degradation*. In this process, cells break down and dispose of damaged or unneeded proteins.

Rose, Ciechanover, and Hershko found that proteins marked for destruction are tagged with a molecular label that is called *ubiquitin* because it is found in every tissue of nearly every organism. Earlier researchers had discovered ubiquitin in 1975, but had not discovered its function. After being tagged, proteins are carried to *proteasomes,* the "waste disposal" areas of the cells and destroyed. Just before the doomed cells enter a proteasome, the ubiquitin molecule is detached for reuse. A breakdown in the regulated protein degradation process may result in such diseases as cystic fibrosis and cervical cancer.

The prize in physics was awarded to physicists David J. Gross of the University of California, Santa Barbara; H. David Politzer of the California Institute of Technology in Pasadena; and Frank Wilczek of the Massachusetts Institute of Technology in Cambridge. The three researchers were honored for their independent discoveries of a phenomenon that explains the *strong*

2004 CHEMISTRY PRIZE WINNERS

The 2004 Nobel Prize in chemistry was awarded to cancer researcher Irwin Rose of the University of California in Irvine (below, left) and biochemists Avram Hershko (below, center) and Aaron Ciechanover of the Technion-Israel Institute of Technology in Haifa. The scientists discovered the process by which cells break down damaged or unneeded proteins. Cells mark the proteins with a molecular tag called *ubiquitin,* which tells the cells' waste disposal areas to destroy the proteins.

Irwin Rose

Avram Hershko (left) and Aaron Ciechanover

NOBEL PRIZES continued

force (also known as the *strong interaction* or the *strong nuclear force*).

The strong force, one of the four fundamental forces of nature, binds together elementary particles called *quarks*. Scientists believe that quarks make up the protons and neutrons in an atom's *nucleus* (center).

The scientists discovered that the strong force varies according to the distance between quarks. That is, the strong force becomes stronger when quarks move apart and weaker when they move closer together. The scientists termed this characteristic *asymptotic freedom*.

Using this characteristic, the physicists developed the theory of *quantum chromodynamics*, which describes how particles called *gluons* transmit the strong interaction between quarks. The understanding of this theory has enabled physicists to predict the types of subatomic particles that are *emitted* (given off) in high-energy collisions.

The prize in physiology or medicine was awarded to medical researcher Richard Axel of Columbia University in New York City and immunologist Linda B. Buck of the Fred Hutchinson Cancer Research Center and the University of Washington, both in Seattle. The two scientists were honored for solving the mystery of how human beings can distinguish and remember about 10,000 different odors.

In a pioneering study published in 1991, Axel and Buck identified a family of genes responsible for receptor proteins found on *olfactory* nerve cells (those involved in the sense of smell). In later independent research, the scientists identified about 1,000 different olfactory genes, about 350 of which are found in human beings.

The researchers also discovered that each cell in the nasal lining has only one type of olfactory receptor. According to the researchers, the molecules in a specific odor attach to a unique combination of receptors. These interactions cause the nerve cells to signal the brain, which combines the signals to identify an odor by its characteristic signature.

■ S. Thomas Richardson

See also **CHEMISTRY; MEDICAL RESEARCH; PHYSICS.**

NUTRITION

An insufficient amount of sleep may contribute to overeating and weight gain, according to a report published in the December 2004 issue of the *Annals of Internal Medicine*. Sleep researcher Eve Van Cauter and colleagues from the University of Chicago reported on their investigation of the relationship between a lack of sleep and hunger and *satiety* (a feeling of having eaten enough). Previous research had linked sleep deprivation in rodents and in people to overeating. Some researchers had suggested that the long-term trend in the United States toward getting less sleep might be one factor in any explanation for the increase in the the number of people with obesity. (Medical experts define obesity as being about 14 kilograms [30 pounds] over the normal weight for one's height.)

The investigators wondered if reducing the amount of time a person sleeps could alter how much that person eats. Specifically, they questioned whether sleep serves as a major regulator of the hormones *leptin*, which signals satiety to the brain, and *ghrelin*, which triggers hunger. They theorized that changes in the levels of these two hormones could provide a means of describing the relationship between sleep and hunger.

In the study, scientists measured the blood levels of leptin and ghrelin in 12 healthy young men after the men had slept for approximately 4 hours each for 2 nights and again after having slept for up to 10 hours each for 2 nights. (Researchers randomly assigned the men to either of the sleep schedules and then switched them to the other sleep group. Thus, the men served as their own *controls* [standards of comparison] by experiencing both sleep periods.)

The researchers controlled the number of calories in the men's diet as well as the amount of physical activity they participated in. The men also completed questionnaires about their hunger levels and their desire for different types of foods.

When the subjects slept only four hours nightly, their leptin levels decreased by 18 percent and their ghrelin levels increased by 28 percent, compared with their levels after sleeping for the longer period. In addition, the sleep-deprived men reported being hungry for calorie-dense foods with a high carbohydrate content, including candy, ice cream, pasta, bread, and cake.

The study was limited by its small number of subjects. In addition, the researchers did not measure the men's *energy expenditure* (the number of calories consumed compared with the amount of physical activity exerted). Nevertheless, the authors concluded that an in-adequate amount of sleep might increase feelings of hunger among healthy young men.

Fat chances of skipping breakfast. Skipping breakfast might lead to weight gain, according to a study published in February 2005 by bioresearcher Hamid Farshchi and colleagues from the Centre for Integrated Systems Biology and Medicine at the University of Nottingham in the United Kingdom. Previous research had suggested a connection between eating breakfast and a lower *body mass index* (BMI), a measurement used to determine obesity. People with a lower BMI have a lower risk of such chronic diseases as cardiovascular disease and type 2 diabetes.

HEALTHY STEPS

MyPyramid, presented to the public on April 20, 2005, is the visual representation of the new U.S. government food guidelines issued in January. The colored bands correspond to food groups, with the width of each band representing estimates of how much Americans should eat in each food group in relation to the other food groups. For the first time, the guidelines emphasize exercise, represented by the icon of the person going up the pyramid's steps. As a complement to the pyramid, the government also announced a new Web site (www.mypyramid.gov). Web-site visitors can enter their age, gender, and activity levels to reveal 1 of 12 plans, detailing what and how much to eat.

GRAINS Make half your grains whole	VEGETABLES Vary your veggies	FRUITS Focus on fruits	MILK Get your calcium-rich foods	MEAT & BEANS Go lean with protein
Eat at least 3 oz. of whole-grain cereals, breads, crackers, rice, or pasta every day 1 oz. is about 1 slice of bread, about 1 cup of breakfast cereal, or ½ cup of cooked rice, cereal, or pasta	Eat more dark-green veggies like broccoli, spinach, and other dark leafy greens Eat more orange vegetables like carrots and sweetpotatoes Eat more dry beans and peas like pinto beans, kidney beans, and lentils	Eat a variety of fruit Choose fresh, frozen, canned, or dried fruit Go easy on fruit juices	Go low-fat or fat-free when you choose milk, yogurt, and other milk products If you don't or can't consume milk, choose lactose-free products or other calcium sources such as fortified foods and beverages	Choose low-fat or lean meats and poultry Bake it, broil it, or grill it Vary your protein routine — choose more fish, beans, peas, nuts, and seeds
For a 2,000-calorie diet, you need the amounts below from each food group. To find the amounts that are right for you, go to MyPyramid.gov.				
Eat 6 oz. every day	Eat 2½ cups every day	Eat 2 cups every day	Get 3 cups every day; for kids aged 2 to 8, it's 2	Eat 5½ oz. every day

NUTRITION continued

The researchers examined biological changes in healthy women associated with either eating or skipping breakfast. Scientists hoped the study would help them determine whether skipping breakfast alters the person's *resting energy expenditure* (the amount of energy used for normal body function while the body is at rest), blood sugar levels, and protein and fat *metabolism* (the process by which food compounds are broken down into energy). All these factors help determine body weight.

Scientists randomly assigned 10 healthy women to either a 14-day period of eating breakfast or a 14-day period of skipping breakfast. The subjects then returned to their usual breakfast habits for two weeks, after which they were placed in the other group. Thus, each subject participated in both groups and acted as her own control.

During the breakfast period, the subjects consumed whole-grain breakfast cereal with low-fat milk before 8:00 a.m. and a chocolate-covered cookie between 10:30 and 11:00 a.m. The subjects who skipped breakfast consumed the cookie between 10:30 and 11:00 a.m. and the cereal and milk between 12:00 and 1:30 p.m. At predetermined times, all the subjects ate four additional snacks as well as meals similar to those they normally ate. The subjects also recorded their food intake for three days during each period. The scientists collected blood samples before and after each of the two study periods to record blood sugar levels, protein and fat metabolism, and resting energy expenditure.

The researchers found that when the women ate breakfast, they consumed fewer total calories during the rest of the day. Eating breakfast, however, seemed to have no effect on the women's resting energy expenditure. When the women skipped breakfast, their levels of low-density lipoprotein cholesterol (LDL) rose. (Cholesterol is a type of fat, and high levels of LDL cholesterol can increase the risk of heart disease.) In addition, skipping breakfast seemed to lower the women's ability to process sugar. This lowered ability may contribute to weight gain. The authors concluded that avoiding breakfast increased the likelihood of eating more calories. These extra calories, they noted, could lead to weight gain over time.

Eat better, move more. New dietary guidelines that, for the first time, emphasize exercising as well as eating foods with fewer calories were issued by the U. S. Departments of Health and Human Services and Agriculture in January 2005. The new guidelines are the sixth edition of the *Dietary Guidelines for Americans.*

The *Dietary Guidelines* serve as the basis for federal food programs and nutrition education programs. They represent the best science-based dietary advice available to help Americans live healthier, longer lives and to reduce the risk of major chronic disease. An important element of each revision, required every five years by law, is an analysis of new scientific findings on nutrition and health. The new guidelines also provide additional recommendations for pregnant women and other specific population groups and on food handling to avoid microbial food-borne illnesses.

Like previous editions of the guidelines, the new recommendations emphasize eating a healthy, balanced diet of nutritious foods. However, balancing nutrients alone is not enough to maintain good health, according to the guidelines. Total calories are also important, especially as Americans are experiencing an epidemic of obesity. As a result, the *2005 Dietary Guidelines* place a strong emphasis on calorie control and physical activity.

Taken together, the guidelines' key recommendations encourage most Americans to eat fewer calories, be more active, and make wise food choices. The guidelines also stress that nutrient needs should be met primarily through foods rather than supplements. Specific key recommendations include consuming adequate nutrients within calorie needs—that is, consuming a variety of *nutrient-dense* foods within basic food groups. Such foods are high in nutrients but low in calories. In general, people should limit their intake of saturated and trans fat, cholesterol, added sugars, salt, and alcohol.

According to the new guidelines, each day people without special nutritional needs should eat fruit (2 cups), vegetables (2 ½ cups), whole grain products (3 or more ounce equivalents), and fat-free or low-fat milk or equivalent milk products (three cups). People who wish to reduce the risk of chronic disease should exercise for at least 30 minutes daily. To maintain their weight, people should engage in 60 minutes of moderate to vigorous activity daily. To lose weight, people should exercise for 60 to 90 minutes daily. ■ Phylis B. Moser-Veillon

OCEANOGRAPHY

The most devastating *tsunami* in history killed about 300,000 people in southern Asia and eastern Africa on December 26, 2004. (A tsunami is a series of powerful ocean waves produced by an underwater earthquake, landslide, or volcanic eruption.) The 2004 tsunami was caused by a major earthquake at the bottom of the Indian Ocean, about 255 kilometers (160 miles) southeast of Banda Aceh, Sumatra.

Life on underwater chimneys. A previously unknown world of tiny snails and water fleas, transparent worms and crabs, and large mats of bacteria exists in the so-called "Lost City," which lies at the bottom of the Atlantic Ocean, according to a March 2005 report. The Lost City, which was discovered in 2000 on an underwater mountain called the Atlantis Massif, is a field of unusual *hydrothermal vents,* which are chimneylike structures that spew out hot, mineral-rich waters. Most hydrothermal vent have black chimneys and

SEE ALSO THE SPECIAL REPORT, **FISHING POLL: THE CENSUS OF MARINE LIFE,** PAGE 96.

are known as *black smokers.* However, the vents in the Lost City are white, formed by white carbonate minerals released by the vents.

An international team of scientists, led by oceanographer Deborah Kelley of the University of Washington in Seattle and biologist Timothy Shank of the Woods Hole Oceanographic Institution in Woods Hole, Massachusetts, explored the vents in 2003. The scientists vacuumed up water samples and animal specimens from the Lost City and analyzed the material in the laboratory. Their analysis led to the discovery of at least 65 previously unknown animal species.

The scientists said these animals appeared to live off microbes and nutrients produced by

LOST CITY OF WHITE VENTS

Scientists use the robot arm of a submersible to examine the white carbonate "chimney" of a hydrothermal vent in the Lost City, a field of unusual vents on the mid-Atlantic sea floor. An international team of scientists described the white vents, which differ greatly from the more familiar black smoker hydrothermal vents, in March 2005. The scientists reported that many crabs, snails, and other creatures live among the vents.

OCEANOGRAPHY continued

microbes, which themselves derive energy from methane and hydrogen gases erupting from the chimneys. Carbon dioxide, the main energy source at black smokers, is virtually absent at the Lost City. The temperature of the water coming out of Lost City vents averages 65 °C (150 °F), while the water temperature in black smokers is about 370 °C (700 °F). In addition, the water in the Lost City is *alkaline* (basic), rather than acidic, as at black smokers.

The scientists noted that the unusual conditions in the Lost City might mimic conditions early in Earth's history. If that proves to be so, studies of the Lost City might shed light on how life began billions of years ago.

Bone-eating worms. Two strange new species of marine worms were discovered devouring the skeleton of a gray whale at the bottom of Monterey Canyon, off the coast of California, scientists reported in July 2004. The unusual worms were found by a group of marine biologists that included Greg Rouse of the South Australian Museum in Adelaide and Shana Goffredi and Robert Vrijenhoek of Monterey Bay Aquarium Research Institute in Moss Landing, California.

The marine worms have no eyes, mouth, stomach, or legs, according to the scientists. The researchers reported that the worms are closely related to the tubeworms found at many hydrothermal vents. The new worms, however, are sufficiently different from tubeworms to merit classification in their own scientific *genus* (group of species). The scientists named the genus *Osedex,* which is Latin for *bone devourer.*

The worms can penetrate the bones of dead whales using rootlike structures that absorb the bones' nutrients. Special kinds of bacteria living in these structures help the worms digest fats and oils.

At first, the explorers found only female worms, each of which is from 2 to 7 centimeters (0.8 to 2.8 inches) long. Upon examining these worms under a microscope, the researchers dis-

WEIRD WORMS AND DEAD WHALES

A whale carcass (below) lies at the bottom of Monterey Canyon, off the coast of California, where it is being devoured by strange, reddish bone-eating worms (on carcass and at right). Marine biologists from the United States and Australia announced in July 2004 that they had discovered an undersea ecosystem based on the whale carcasses and worms. The worms, which the scientists named *Osedex* (Latin for *bone devourer*), use yellowish rootlike structures to penetrate the bones and to absorb nutrients. Other kinds of animals, such as scavenging sea cucumbers (foreground below), also live among the whale carcasses.

covered that most of the females had dozens of tiny male worms living inside them. The dwarf males are little more than sacs of sperm and bits of yolk. The females were also full of eggs.

The researchers theorized that the worm's unusual sex life is related to its eating habits. A colony of the worms may feed on a single whale carcass for decades, the scientists estimated. However, once a skeleton is entirely consumed, all the worms at the site probably die. Having the males live inside the bodies of the females would help ensure that the females can often release large numbers of *larvae* (young worms). This, in turn, helps guarantee that ocean currents will sweep at least a few offspring to another whale carcass.

Jumbo squid mystery. Thousands of dead jumbo squids washed up on the beaches of southern California between January and March 2005. The beachings puzzled scientists because jumbo squids do not normally inhabit California waters.

Jumbo squids, which are also known as Humboldt squids, usually live and hunt in deep waters off the coasts of Mexico, Central America, and northern South America. These squids are larger than the native squids of California. A jumbo squid can grow to a length of 1.8 meters (6 feet) and weigh as much as 7.7 kilograms (17 pounds).

Marine biologists were uncertain what brought the jumbo squids so far north. Some biologists proposed that the squids were following their prey in a warm current flowing north. Other biologists believed that overfishing in Mexico might have depleted the squids' food sources, forcing the animals to forage far outside their normal range.

The cause of the squids' deaths was also a mystery. According to one theory, a potent neurotoxin called *domoic acid*, which is produced by certain kinds of microscopic marine algae, may have poisoned the animals. Some scientists also speculated that the squids may have spent too much time hunting in warm surface waters. Researchers say that squids are less able to absorb oxygen in warm waters, so they may have suffocated. Scientists hoped to learn more about this mystery with further examinations of the carcasses and regional seawater.

Iceberg threat to penguin chicks. The blockage of McMurdo Sound in Antarctica's Ross Sea by an iceberg in January 2005 placed tens of thousands of Adélie penguin chicks at risk of starvation. The iceberg blocked the sound for about three months, preventing adult Adélie penguins from swimming their normal route in search of food. Biologists feared that the Adélie penguin chicks were in danger of dying of starvation while their parents were being forced to trudge across the ice to look for open water and other food sources.

The iceberg, named B-15A, was 3,100 square kilometers (1,200 square miles) in size. Satellite images from the United States National Aeronautics and Space Administration (NASA) and the European Space Agency showed the iceberg in the sound after it ran aground.

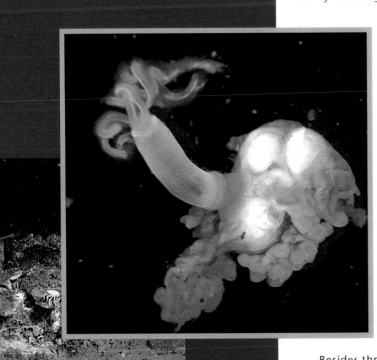

Besides threatening the penguins, the grounded iceberg blocked the path of ships that regularly bring food and supplies to the

OCEANOGRAPHY continued

area's three research stations. Two icebreakers later cleared a narrow path for the ships.

In April, New Zealand officials announced that the iceberg had begun to move again. Satellite images showed that the iceberg then crashed into the Drygalski Ice Tongue, an extension of a land-based glacier stretching into the sea. The iceberg broke off a large section of the tongue, thereby altering the map of Antarctica. As of mid-May, biologists were uncertain how much harm the Adélie penguin population actually suffered.

Phytoplankton photos from space. A breakthrough in the ability to analyze satellite images of seawater was announced in January 2005 by a team of NASA and university scientists. The new technique enabled scientists to measure the abundance and growth rate of single-celled, plantlike organisms called *phytoplankton.*

Phytoplankton are the "lungs" of the ocean because they produce oxygen through the sun-powered process of photosynthesis. As a result, they are the most important indicators of *ocean productivity*—a marine ecosystem's capacity to support fish and other animal life. Chlorophyll, the photosynthetic pigment inside phytoplankton, reflects green light, turning productive water a greenish shade. Therefore, the degree of

"greenness" of seawater indicates the abundance of phytoplankton and ocean productivity.

The researchers, led by biologist Michael Behrenfeld of Oregon State University in Corvalis, analyzed ocean color data from an instrument called the Sea-viewing Wide Field-of-view Sensor (SeaWiFS). SeaWiFS is an optical-scanning instrument carried by NASA's SeaStar satellite. Behrenfeld's team demonstrated how subtle changes in the hue and brightness of green shades of seawater could be calculated from the SeaWiFS data. Knowledge of such changes makes it possible for investigators to study ocean productivity at a level of detail never before possible.

The scientists said their new technique had a number of practical applications. Among these were predictions of the population sizes of fish stocks and evaluations of the effects of pollution on marine *ecosystems* (the biological and physical environment of an area.).

Retiring *Alvin*. In August 2004, the U.S. government announced it would retire the research submarine *Alvin* in 2007. *Alvin*, perhaps best known for its dives to the sunken ocean liner *Titanic* and its role in discovering hydrothermal vents, was to be replaced with a larger, deeper-diving vessel in 2008. ■ Christina S. Johnson

See also **CONSERVATION; ENVIRONMENTAL POLLUTION.**

PHYSICS

The "World Year of Physics," marking the 100th anniversary of Albert Einstein's "miracle year," was launched in January 2005 at an international scientific conference in Paris. In 1905, the German-born physicist, who was just 26 years old at the time, wrote five crucial scientific papers that continue to have a huge impact on the world.

Among Einstein's papers of 1905 was one proposing the special theory of relativity, the revolutionary theory that describes space and time as *relative* concepts—that is, space and time are described as changing, depending on an observer's position. Einstein's other papers described light as occurring as both waves and particles; provided conclusive evidence for the

SEE ALSO THE SPECIAL REPORT, **THE DARK SIDE OF THE UNIVERSE**, PAGE 112.

existence of atoms; presented a formula for measuring the size of molecules; and established that mass can be converted into energy and vice versa. Together, these five papers established the foundation of modern physics.

The international conference was organized by the United Nations Educational, Scientific, and Cultural Organization (UNESCO) as well as various physics societies throughout the world. The conference sponsored a number of events during 2005, including traveling museum exhibits and print and broadcast media presentations. Because a major goal of the organizers of the World Year of Physics was to promote interest in physics among young people, many of the events took place at elementary schools, high schools, and universities.

Einstein passes test. In 2004, Einstein's special theory of relativity passed a unique test that indicated it is just as valid in describing the bizarre world of subatomic particles as it is in describing the world we can normally see. So reported a team of investigators from the Harvard-Smithsonian Center for Astrophysics in Cambridge, Massachusetts, and Indiana University in Bloomington in November 2004.

According to the special theory of relativity, the rate at which a moving clock runs depends on the speed at which it is moving. In other words, clocks traveling at different, fixed speeds relative to one another will tell the time differently. The theory also implies that the rate at which the clocks run should not be related to the direction of motion.

Scientists have verified this effect of time relativity in many experiments using very precise clocks. However, the relationship between time and the direction of motion had not previously been tested at the subatomic scale. The theory of matter and forces at that level—the so-called standard model—was thus incomplete. That is why the Harvard-Smithsonian group, led by physicist Ronald Walsworth, and the Indiana group, led by theorist V. Alan Kostelecky, sought an experimental test to analyze Einstein's equations at this tiny scale.

The "clocks" used in the experiment were made with two types of spinning atomic *nuclei* (center parts of atoms), known as helium-3 and xenon-129. The scientists used each of these nuclei, which spin at different rates, to set the *frequency* (number of vibrations per second) of a *maser,* a laser that operates at microwave wavelengths. By counting the number of microwave vibrations, the scientists were able to use the masers as clocks.

The normal motion of Earth provided the motion for the clocks. The direction in which the clocks moved changed over the course of a day—as they moved along paths traced by both the rotation of Earth around its axis and the orbit of Earth around the sun. If forces operating at the subatomic level were related to the direction of the clocks' motion, then, as the hours of a day went by, the frequency of each maser would continually change. Also, because each maser

was made with a different kind of nucleus, the amount of change in each would be different.

The investigators found no such changes in the frequencies of the maser clocks. These results confirmed that the direction of motion does not affect the passing of time at the subatomic level. The conclusion was strong experimental evidence that the special theory of relativity applies to the world of the very tiny.

Big jolt to Earth's axis. A powerful earthquake off the coast of the Indonesian island of Sumatra on Dec. 26, 2004, shook Earth with so much force that it actually knocked the planet's axis slightly out of position. In January 2005, physicists described the off-kilter axis and an associated decrease in the length of a day. This change in day length, however, was far too tiny for anyone to notice without the aid of an extremely precise scientific instrument.

The earthquake had a *moment magnitude* (strength) of at least 9.1. It struck the bottom of the Indian Ocean in an area where part of the sea floor crust collides with a portion of crust underlying Southeast Asia. The quake thrust a segment of the ocean floor beneath the continental crust and into the planet's interior, in a process called *subduction.* The movement of the sea floor and the water column above it resulted in the development of a *tsunami* (series of huge ocean waves) that killed at least 300,000 people in several coastal nations.

During subduction, a large *mass* (amount of matter) is driven closer to the center of the planet. As a result, Earth's rotation about its axis must speed up in order to conserve *rotational momentum.* Momentum is the quantity of motion of a moving body. Rotational momentum is the momentum that a planet has as it spins on its axis. The laws of physics state that rotational momentum is conserved when changes in the distribution of mass occur inside a planet. The need to conserve momentum after the Indonesian earthquake caused not only a speed up in rotation but also a shift in the orientation of the planet's axis. This axis shift was related to the fact that all the redistribution of mass took place on one side of the planet.

Physicists in New Zealand used the world's largest *ring laser gyroscope* to measure the shift in Earth's axis. A gyroscope is a rotating instrument that detects external changes in direction by resisting any attempt to change its own direction of rotation. Traditional mechanical gyroscopes consist of a spinning *flywheel* or a ball, called the *rotor,* and a support system. Once the flywheel or rotor is set in motion, the

PHYSICS continued

gyroscope maintains a stable direction within the space of its support mechanism.

Ring laser gyroscopes are extremely sensitive gyroscopes used in the navigation systems of the world's newest airliners as well as in ocean ships and spacecraft. They are more precise than mechanical gyroscopes. Instead of containing moving mechanical parts, they contain two beams of laser light moving in opposite directions around a closed path. Special mirrors draw off a small fraction of this light from each beam and combine the light into a single beam. If the path of an airliner or other vehicle rotates, the way in which the two beams combine is altered, producing changes in the brightness of the combined beam. A computer tracks these changes to determine the direction in which the vehicle is moving.

The ring laser gyroscope used to measure the axis shift is located at the Wettzell Fundamental Research Station near Christchurch, New Zealand. The Wettzell instrument measures 4.5 meters (15 feet) in diameter and weighs 9 metric tons (10 tons). It operates in a sealed and pressurized underground chamber to isolate it from vibrations and temperature changes that could distort its readings. Its large size and isolated location make the Wettzell gyroscope sensitive enough to detect the smallest changes in the orientation of Earth's rotation.

The gyroscope's designer, Ulrich Schreiber of the Munich Technical University in Germany, reported that the earthquake caused Earth's North and South poles to shift less than 2.5 centimeters (1 inch).

This finding was complemented by a study of day-length change by geophysicist Richard Gross, at the National Aeronautics and Space Administration (NASA) Jet Propulsion Laboratory in Pasadena, California. Using a computer model, Gross estimated that the Indonesian earthquake sped up Earth's rotation enough to shorten the length of a day by 2.676 *microseconds*. (A mi-

crosecond is one-millionith of a second.) He noted that this effect would be too small to notice by using the motion of stars to measure day length.

Fixing errors in quantum computers. A breakthrough step toward using *quantum mechanics* as the basis for building a new, more powerful kind of computer was announced in December 2004 by physicists at the National Institute of Standards and Technology (NIST) in Boulder, Colorado. Quantum mechanics is the field of physics that describes the structure of atoms and the motion of subatomic particles. It explains how atoms absorb energy and give off

NEW RECORD FOR SEEING SMALL

Straight rows and columns of atoms inside a silicon crystal are seen in this image obtained with a state-of-the-art scanning transmission electron microscope and advanced computer imaging technology at Oak Ridge National Laboratory in Tennessee. Scientists at the laboratory published the image in September 2004, noting that it represented a new record of the smallest thing scientists could see. The scientists said that the ability to see individual atoms at such a fine resolution will enable researchers to better understand atomic bonds and other structural properties of new materials under development.

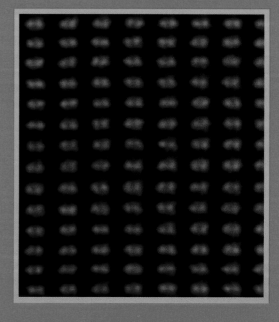

the energy in the form of light. The break-through involved a way to correct errors in quantum computers.

Scientists and engineers have been experimenting with various computing technologies since the 1980's in an attempt to construct a quantum computer. Such a device would be immensely more powerful than the fastest conventional supercomputers. However, serious technical problems have prevented the development of a practical working quantum computer. The NIST research showed more promise for the development of such a system than most previous research in the field.

In an ordinary computer, information is stored and manipulated in the form of *bits* (short for *binary digits),* which are electronic charges that represent numbers. One level of charge represents 0, while the other represents 1. A quantum computer, by contrast, would work with so-called *qubits,* bits of information that can be in two or more states at the same time. A qubit is a mixture of 0's and 1's that does not assume one value or the other until the computation is completed. Such a mixed state is called *coherent.*

A single conventional bit, or even a qubit, is not a particularly useful quantity of information. So computers normally group bits into long strings, referred to as *words.* An ordinary home computer normally works with 32-bit words. Each of these words represents a single number between 0 and 2^{32} (2 multiplied times itself 31 times [4,294,976,296]). However, in a quantum computer, a word of 32 qubits could simultaneously represent all these numbers. Any mathematical operation performed on such a qubit word would, in effect, be 4.3 billion operations performed at the same time. This would make a quantum computer billions of times more powerful than its conventional counterpart.

Computers, like all digital devices, are likely to make occasional errors. For example, a bit might be misread. To guard against this possibility, all computers use a system called *error correction.* In addition to the *real bits* that carry information and are used in computations, a small number of so-called *ancilla bits,* which are not normally used in computations, are parts of the mathematical operations. Computer hardware checks the real bits against the ancilla bits, a process that reveals whether an error has been made. This allows the computer hardware to locate and correct the error.

In a common example of this process, a compact disc (CD) has a few ancilla bits in addition to the bits that encode the music. The CD player has an onboard computer that reads the ancilla bits to correct errors caused by dust or scratches on the CD. As long as the defects are small enough, the listener hears the music exactly as it was recorded.

Qubits are much more fragile and subject to error than conventional bits, so a reliable error-correction system is critical for quantum computers. Previous test systems aimed at incorporating ancilla qubits into quantum computers could not be scaled up to the tens of qubits required to perform useful calculations. The NIST researchers may have found a way to overcome this and other problems.

The test system developed at NIST incorporated three qubits. One served as the real qubit, the other two as ancilla qubits. Each qubit consisted of an *ion* (atom with an electric charge) of beryllium-9 trapped between two gold plates. The nucleus of a beryllium-9 ion can spin with its axis pointed in either of two directions, one of which corresponds to 0 and the other to 1. To serve as a qubit, the direction of the spin axis of beryllium-9 must remain in a coherent mixture of the two different quantum states.

The researchers were able to achieve this quantum state by manipulating the direction of the spin axis with a laser. Tuning the laser to certain desired frequencies caused the spin axis to "flip" from one state to the other. After the real bit was forced into this mixed state, the ancilla bits automatically changed into the mixed state. This change was made possible by a quantum phenomenon known as *entanglement,* in which key properties are transferred from one quantum state to another without any physical contact. Then, after the researchers disturbed the real qubit to produce a deliberate error, entanglement allowed the ancilla bits to restore the real qubit to its original state.

The NIST test used far fewer qubits than a working quantum computer would need. Moreover, the researchers said their experimental system was subject to a much higher error rate than that of conventional computers. Nevertheless, the scientists expected that continued efforts would reduce the error rate as well as make it possible to scale the system up to a practical number of qubits. Although a practical quantum computer likely remained years away, the NIST study demonstrated that error correction in quantum computers is feasible. ■ Robert H. March

See also **COMPUTERS AND ELECTRONICS; ENGINEERING; GEOLOGY; NOBEL PRIZES.**

Tangled Branches:
Art and Physics

"I delight in the way Nature repeats herself, and try to exploit it," says Eric J. Heller of Harvard University in Cambridge, Massachusetts. Heller is a theoretical physicist who describes the forces and building blocks of nature with complex mathematical equations. But Heller is also an accomplished artist who creates stunning digital prints of cutting-edge physics.

Heller's equations express the physics of *quantum mechanics*, the theory that explains the bizarre behavior of atoms and subatomic particles. His artwork reveals this microscopic world of *electrons* (negatively charged particles), atoms, and molecules in striking landscapes. Heller's prints have also offered colleagues new views of physics. In 2005, his artwork was on exhibit in the United States and Canada and was being sold online.

Many of Heller's images focus on the complex interactions between electrons and crystals in layers of *semiconductors* used in computers, CD's, DVD players, and other electronic devices. (A semiconductor is a material that conducts electric current under some circumstances but not others. A computer chip is a piece of a semiconductor, usually silicon, that contains an electric circuit.)

Since 1999, Heller has collaborated with physicist Robert M. Westervelt, also of Harvard. Westervelt conducts experiments on the behavior of electrons sandwiched between layers of semiconductors. A sheet of electrons known as an *electron gas* flows between each semiconductor layer in a chip. To create an image of the atoms on the surface of a semiconductor, Westervelt used an *atomic force microscope* (AFM). This microscope drags a sharp probe over a surface and monitors the mechanical force between the tip of the probe and the surface. By placing the tip near a narrow passage in the electron gas, Westervelt and his colleagues measured the flow of electrons sandwiched between semiconductor layers.

Using a computer, Heller modeled Westervelt's AFM data, creating *algorithms* (mathematical equations that can be used to make computer programs) that simulate the motion of electron gases. His computer models produced detailed pictures of these electron motions. Heller also used image-manipulation software to enhance the color and shading of these images and to create other visual effects.

Heller's pictures of the flow of electrons surprised other physicists by showing complex branching patterns—similar to the branching of certain trees or of a network of blood vessels. Many of the images had shapes known as *caustics*, collections of edges or lines that appear to twist and fold over on themselves. The electrons were forced into these patterns by electric fields from *ions* (electrically charged atoms) implanted in the semiconductors. Heller notes that electron caustics duplicate caustics that are found elsewhere in nature, such as in the patterns of light formed when sunlight shines through a glass of water.

Other pictures made by Heller examine quantum effects that reveal the dual nature of the subatomic world. For example, electrons behave as particles and, at the same time, as waves. In an electron gas, these effects show up as tiny ripples superimposed on the branches of electron flows. The ripples appear when one electron wave interferes with another wave.

Another quantum effect seen in Heller's images is a *quantum dot*. Scientists have created quantum dots in the laboratory by confining one or more electrons to a tiny area using carefully manufactured semiconductors, magnetic forces, or other methods. Heller's pictures show quantum dots that formed naturally between the semiconductor layers. These objects have unique wave behaviors that may eventually be used in *quantum computers*—machines that use the physics of tiny particles to perform certain calculations much faster than conventional computers.

Heller's work may have other practical applications. A complete understanding of the quantum effects of electron motions becomes more important as *transistors* become smaller and smaller. (A transistor is a tiny device that controls the flow of electric current in many electronic devices.) By visualizing the chaotic motions of electrons flowing over semiconductors, Heller is showing engineers how electrons might behave in future computer chips, with even tinier transistors. This knowledge could help engineers design more efficient transistors, which would result in better cell phones, faster computers, and other improvements in electronics.

Scientists value Heller's work for the insights it provides in various fields of research. In 2004 and 2005, for example, Heller, Westervelt, and their colleagues published new findings about quantum dots.

Heller's prints are also admired by art lovers, such as those who attended his traveling exhibit from 2002 to 2005, titled "Approaching Chaos: Visions from the Quantum Frontier." Some of Heller's artwork can be seen on his Web site, at: http://www.ericjhellergallery.com. These precise yet otherworldy images could only be the creation of an artist who, as Heller himself says, uses physics as his paintbrush. ■ Alfred J. Smuskiewicz

BRANCHING OUT

In "Transport II," electrons confined to a sheet so that they are two-dimensional branch outward. Heller and his colleagues didn't expect the electrons to behave this way, a finding that could have implications for the design of small electronic devices.

PSYCHOLOGY

The amount of emotional support that people believe they are receiving from others may depend on their experiences of closeness with childhood caregivers. This finding about the importance of *attachment* was reported by psychologists Nancy L. Collins at the University of California at Santa Barbara and Brooke C. Feeney at Carnegie Mellon University in Pittsburgh, Pennsylvania, in September 2004.

According to the attachment theory, adults have expectations about how close companions or caregivers will respond to their distress. These expectations have been formed through experiences of being listened to and well cared for (or ignored, neglected, and/or abused) during childhood and adolescence. The impact of these past experiences creates expectations called *attachment models* about the reliability, compassion, and trustworthiness of future close companions or caregivers.

Attachment models vary among individuals according to two factors: anxiety and avoidance. People with anxiety about attachment worry about being rejected or abandoned by significant others; people with avoidance limit intimacy and interdependence with others. Psychologists have defined four types of attachment models in individuals. Secure individuals have low levels of anxiety and avoidance. They believe they can rely on significant others for support and form close relationships comfortably. Preoccupied individuals are high in anxiety and low in avoidance. They seek close relationships but doubt the capacity of others to be reliable and supportive. Fearful-avoidant individuals have high levels of both anxiety and avoidance. They avoid close relationships and expect to be rejected. Finally, dismissing-avoidant individuals have low anxiety and high avoidance. They are confident in themselves but view others as unreliable and unsupportive.

Past research has suggested that individuals with insecure attachment models might underestimate the social support that they receive. Collins and Feeney sought to demonstrate that people with insecure attachment negatively misconstrue the meaning or intention of support from others.

The researchers recruited 248 romantically involved couples and administered questionnaires to determine each participant's attachment style. One member of each couple was designated as the caregiver and the other, as the support-receiver. Support-receivers were told that they were to give a speech that would be videotaped and viewed by others. The caregivers were instructed to write supportive ("good luck") or ambiguously supportive ("don't say anything stupid") notes to their partners before and after the speech. The researchers controlled the wording of the notes and had all caregivers give their partner the same set of notes so that they could compare the subjects' responses to the notes. All the support-receivers were also assessed to determine how secure they felt.

The researchers found that the fearful-avoidant and dismissing-avoidant people believed that the low-support notes were more inconsiderate and upsetting than the secure individuals did. The preoccupied (anxious-non-avoidant) individuals perceived the note to be even more upsetting. The researchers concluded that insecure individuals tend to appraise low-support messages differently than secure individuals do.

In a second study designed in the same way, the researchers allowed the partners to write their own notes of either support or low-support in order to test the experiment's *generalizability* (degree to which the finding can be expected to be similar in the larger population). Again, the fearful-avoidant people and the preoccupied ones perceived the low-support notes less favorably than did the more secure people. Independent raters of the notes had assessed their content objectively for their level of supportiveness. The data indicated that insecure individuals misconstrued the notes as more negative than they actually were.

The authors concluded that individuals with less secure attachment models are vulnerable to misperceiving low (or ambiguous) support as negative and that they are, therefore, more likely to suffer by feeling less supported by others. Further research into the long-term consequences of these misperceptions and their underlying causes could lead to better forms of support for insecure individuals.

Rejection and self-control. People who believe that they have been rejected by others become less willing to control themselves in social situations. Researchers in Florida and California reported this finding in April 2005.

For most people, belonging to a group of

peers is an important part of satisfaction with life. Rejection by individuals or groups, however, is a common and painful human experience. Although many factors contribute to social acceptance, one of the most important is the capacity to conform to social expectations by regulating one's behavior. Researchers have long tried to understand the relationship between rejection and subsequent behavior. Prior research has shown that rejected people often behave in ways that are self-defeating and might lead to further social rejection.

Researchers led by psychologist Roy F. Baumeister at Florida State University in Tallahassee described a series of experiments designed to show the effect that feeling rejected has on *self-regulatory* behaviors (behaviors under one's control). The psychologists had 36 college students fill out a personality questionnaire and then divided the students randomly into three groups. The first group was told that the results had indicated that they would end up alone in life. The second group was told that they would have rewarding relationships in the future, and the third group was given information that had nothing to do with social rejection—that they would be accident-prone.

To measure self-control, the researchers offered the subjects a nickel for every ounce they would drink of a bad-tasting beverage that they had been told was healthful. The scientists found that the rejected group drank approximately 2 ounces fewer than the groups who anticipated

TALK TO THE ANIMALS

A border collie named Rico retrieves a toy on command during an experiment at the Max Planck Institute for Evolutionary Anthropology in Leipzig, Germany. The research, reported in June 2004, caused scientists to rethink the nature of language. Researchers tested Rico's ability to understand words by asking him to fetch a series of objects. Rico's owner had taught him the names of some 200 objects. The dog was able to correctly retrieve 37 of 40 familiar toys after hearing the name of the toy. Then the researchers placed seven familiar toys in a room with a toy Rico had never seen before. When his owner used an unfamiliar word to ask the dog to fetch the new toy, Rico retrieved the correct toy 7 out of 10 times and was able to do so even four weeks later. Researchers call the ability to connect a new word with an unfamiliar object *fast mapping*. Children develop fast mapping skills at about the age of three, but scientists had always thought the ability was unique to human beings. According to the German researchers, the experiment with Rico showed that other animals may have fast-mapping ability as well.

future social acceptance or a life filled with accidents.

In a second experiment, 38 students spent 20 minutes getting to know each other. They were then asked to write the names of two peo-

PSYCHOLOGY continued

ple in the group with whom they would like to work. Half of the students, chosen randomly, were told that no one wanted to work with them. The other half heard that everyone wanted to work with them. To test the students' self-control, the psychologists left each in a room with 35 small cookies and asked them to taste and rate the cookies. (A previous survey had shown that most of the students agreed with the statement that eating too much "junk" food is not a good thing to do.) The students who thought they had been rejected ate twice as many cookies as those who thought they had been accepted.

Two other experiments demonstrated that rejection decreases the amount of effort a person will make to try to solve an unsolvable puzzle or to pay attention to sounds played to one ear while being distracted by those played to the other. In both experiments, the rejected students did not perform as well as the accepted students.

Thus, by the end of the fourth experiment, the scientists had demonstrated that social rejection reduces self-control. In a final experiment, the researchers sought to determine whether feeling rejected makes people unable—or unwilling—to control themselves. The researchers offered the participants from $5 to $20 if they performed well on a task. In this situation, the students who had been rejected performed as well as those who had not been rejected.

The researchers concluded that people who feel rejected are still able to control themselves but are less willing to do so. The researchers speculated that such people may be reluctant to examine the reasons for their rejection because such self-examination focuses attention on their possible shortcomings without any guarantee that change will ensure acceptance.

Who are you? Researchers trying to understand how people present themselves to others—and how they are, in turn, perceived by others—found new clues in a relatively recent phenomenon—the personal Web page. Psychologists Simine Vazire and Samuel D. Gosling of the University of Texas at Austin reported in July 2004 that these pages offer a largely accurate portrait of authors' personalities.

People display their interests and personality in many ways, including the cars they drive and the ways they adorn their body. These displays affect the way others perceive us and influence social behavior. The Internet has provided a new way for people to display themselves to others. Many people create their own *Web page,* an Internet-based collection of images and words that communicate the owner's interests, life, and personality. Vazire and Gosling studied personal Web pages to gain insight into the nature and accuracy of these personal displays.

The researchers used an *ecological model* of interpersonal perception to evaluate how effectively personal Web pages portray the personality of their creator. Developed by Gosling and several colleagues in 2002, the ecological model suggests that people perceive each other in two major ways: *identity claims* and *behavioral residue.* Identity claims are stated claims or decorative choices that purposely communicate an aspect of oneself. For instance, wearing a Greenpeace T-shirt communicates an interest in environmental protection. Behavioral residue involves the physical aspects of one's appearance or environment that unintentionally reflect something about one's behavioral characteristics. For instance, having all your books organized alphabetically on a shelf may signify that you are a well-organized person.

The researchers had been trying to understand the relative contributions of identity claims and behavioral residue to the way a person is perceived by others. The personal Web page is uniquely suited for this purpose, because it is an electronic image created with particular care. In addition, a personal Web page cannot be accidentally affected by one's behavior.

Eleven independent raters examined the Web pages of 79 people. The raters assessed the personality of each Web-page author based only on the content of the site. In addition, the Web-page authors were asked to submit descriptions of themselves and to ask two people who knew them well to provide an "informant report." The researchers then compared the self reports and informant reports with the raters' evaluations. In this way, they were able to measure the accuracy of the raters' assessments of the Web-page authors' personality.

The researchers found that, in general, personal Web pages present an accurate impression of the page's author, though the impression is somewhat biased toward a favorable portrait of the author. In other words, the results suggested that identity claims in Web pages are largely accurate.   ■ Michael Murphy

PUBLIC HEALTH

The 2004-2005 influenza (flu) season began, in some parts of the United States, with people waiting in long lines to receive the flu vaccine. On Oct. 5, 2004, the Chiron Corporation of Emeryville, California, a major manufacturer of the vaccine, had notified the Centers for Disease Control and Prevention (CDC) in Atlanta, Georgia, that it would have no influenza vaccine available for distribution in the United States. Chiron's factory in Liverpool, England, had been closed because of bacterial contamination. Consequently, the United States received only half of its expected vaccine doses, which came from two other suppliers.

Immediately, the CDC issued interim recommendations that identified people who would have a priority for receiving the vaccine. These groups included children ages 6 to 23 months; children ages 2 to 18 years on chronic aspirin therapy; adults age 65 or older; people with underlying chronic medical conditions; women who might become pregnant during the influenza season; residents of nursing homes and long-term care facilities; health care workers involved in direct patient care; and caregivers and household contacts of children under 6 months of age.

During the fall and early winter, some states found they had more than enough vaccine for priority groups. On December 17, the CDC allowed state and local authorities in these areas to broaden the list of priority groups to include caregivers and household contacts of people in high-risk groups and all adults ages 50 to 64. By December 31, vaccine had been administered to nearly 59 percent of people age 65 or older, 51 percent of high-risk children, and 43 percent of health care workers.

Meningitis vaccine for adolescents. On Jan. 14, 2005, the U.S. Food and Drug Administration licensed a new vaccine, MCV4 (meningococcal conjugate vaccine) against bacterial meningitis. The Advisory Committee on Immunization Practices (ACIP) at the CDC recommended its use for adolescents.

Meningitis—which is spread by close contact, including kissing or sharing eating utensils—can be caused by either viruses or bacteria. Viral meningitis is the less serious form of the disease. It is characterized by mild, flu-like symptoms and usually does not require special treatment as it runs its course.

In people with bacterial meningitis, however, the flu-like symptoms progress rapidly—usually within hours or days. The bacteria may infect the bloodstream, causing inflammation of the fluid that surrounds the brain and spinal cord and, in some cases, death. In the United States, about 3,000 people contract bacterial meningitis

WHOOPING COUGH ON THE RISE

Cases of pertussis, commonly known as whooping cough, continued to increase in the United States in 2004, particularly in adolescents. Pertussis causes a severe, persistent cough that can lead to vomiting and broken ribs. The cough has a distinctive whooping sound from which the disease gets its name. Whooping cough can be deadly for infants who have not yet been vaccinated. The number of U.S. pertussis cases had fallen dramatically following a vaccination program that began in the 1960's. However, health experts have determined that the effectiveness of the vaccine diminishes within 5 to 10 years. In May 2005, the U.S. Food and Drug Administration approved a new whooping cough booster shot for people from 10 to 18 years old.

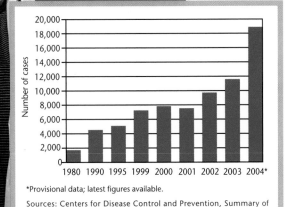

*Provisional data; latest figures available.

Sources: Centers for Disease Control and Prevention, Summary of Notifiable Diseases and Morbidity and Mortality Weekly Report.

PUBLIC HEALTH continued

annually. Among those infected, 10 to 14 percent die and another 11 to 19 percent suffer a permanent disability, such as mental retardation, hearing loss, or loss of limbs.

Adolescents are particularly vulnerable to meningitis because of the close quarters in which they study and sometimes live. The ACIP recommended that the newly licensed vaccine be administered to children 11 to 12 years of age, teens entering high school, and freshmen living in college dormitories.

MCV4 is effective for a period of from 3 to 5 years. (An earlier vaccine lasted for a shorter period and required booster shots.) MCV4 is effective against four of the five most common strains of the bacteria—A, C, Y, and W-135. As of 2005, there was no effective vaccine against the fifth strain, called B.

Dramatic drop in AIDS in U.S. infants. The United States has nearly eliminated AIDS in infants, public health officials in New York City and other areas of the country reported on Jan. 30, 2005. In 1990, as many as 2,000 babies were born with HIV infection acquired from their mother. Human immunodeficiency virus (HIV) causes AIDS. In 2003 (the latest year for which data are available), however, about 200 infants acquired HIV from their mother.

Many doctors attributed the drop to treatment guidelines for pregnant women with AIDS that were first approved in the mid-1990's and updated in 2002. A study released by the National Institutes of Health in 1994 had shown that treating HIV-infected pregnant women with a medication called zidovudine (AZT) reduced to 8 percent the likelihood that an infected mother would transmit the virus to her infant. The transmission rate had previously been as high as 20 to 25 percent. In 2002, researchers recommended that other new and ef-

SUBURBAN SPRAWL AND HEALTH PROBLEMS

Suburban sprawl, the growth of a metropolitan area outward rather than upward, can cause or contribute to a variety of medical conditions, according to research reported in October 2004. In areas of sprawl, stores, schools, and workplaces are usually far from residential areas. As a result, people must drive instead of walking or riding bicycles. Over time, the decrease in physical activity and exercise increases the risk of developing certain physical problems, researchers concluded. (Suburban sprawl did not seem to cause problems with mental health.)

Suburban sprawl may cause or contribute to the following medical conditions to varying degrees:

- Abdominal/digestive problems
- Angina/heart disease
- Arthritis
- Asthma/allergies
- Back pain
- Cancer
- Diabetes
- Emphysema/chronic lung diseases
- Hypertension
- Liver disease
- Migraine/chronic headaches
- Neurological conditions
- Other chronic pain
- Physical disability
- Stroke
- Urinary tract problems

Source: Sturm, R., and Cohen, D.A., "Suburban Sprawl and Physical and Mental Health" in *Public Health,* October 2004, pp. 488-496.

fective medications in addition to AZT be administered to pregnant, HIV-infected women. By 2005, the mother-to-child transmission rate had dropped to about 2 percent.

Polio outbreak spreads. By May 2005, a polio outbreak that began in Nigeria had spread across the Indian Ocean to Indonesia, the world's fourth most populous country. Officials with the World Health Organization (WHO), an agency of the United Nations, determined that the *strain* (variety) of polio virus found in Indonesia most closely matched a strain that had appeared in Saudi Arabia in December 2004. The Saudi Arabian strain, in turn, matched a form of the virus that had been spreading across Africa.

The polio virus lives in the intestine and spreads through fecal-oral contact. People who share food dishes with someone who has polio can become infected, as can those who swim in contaminated water. Some people who become infected with polio suffer only mild symptoms, including fever, headache, sore throat, and vomiting. However, about 1 in 200 people develop neck and back stiffness, muscle weakness, and paralysis.

By early 2003, a vaccination program sponsored by four organizations had virtually eradicated polio throughout the world. These groups included WHO, the CDC, UNICEF (the United Nations Children's Fund), and Rotary International (a humanitarian service organization with headquarters in Evanston, Illinois). Only six countries—Nigeria, Niger, Egypt, Pakistan, Afghanistan, and India—continued to report new cases, which numbered about 200 in 2002. Then, in the summer of 2003, Muslim clerics in northern Nigeria halted polio inoculations there because of rumors that the vaccine could transmit HIV and make girls infertile. By the time inoculations resumed in the summer of 2004, polio had spread to 16 other countries, primarily in western and central Africa and in the Middle East, resulting in 794 new cases.

WHO experts were particularly concerned in 2005 that approximately 2 million Muslims who had made the annual pilgrimage to Mecca, Saudi Arabia, in January may have become carriers of the disease as they returned to their own countries. WHO researchers had found that an Indonesian child who contracted polio in May had been in contact with people in his village who had made the pilgrimage. Hundreds of other children in the area had also become ill and were being monitored for polio-like symptoms. Although only some 125 new cases of polio were reported in the world by May 2005, health authorities were gravely concerned. People who have only mild symptoms can transmit polio to others, making the disease extremely difficult to control. Government officials in Indonesia began a campaign to vaccinate more than 6 million children to contain the disease.

Marburg virus outbreak. The largest and deadliest outbreak of rare Marburg hemorrhagic fever ever recorded erupted in Angola in late 2004. By the end of May 2005, WHO estimated that at least 300 people had died of the disease, many of them children under age 5.

The Marburg virus causes fever, vomiting, and massive internal bleeding. Most victims die of the disease, usually within 10 days after the first symptoms appear. Medical experts have neither a vaccine to prevent the disease nor medications to control it. The Marburg virus is transmitted through bodily fluids, including sweat and saliva. It was first identified in 1967, during a simultaneous outbreak among laboratory workers in Marburg and Frankfurt, Germany, and in Belgrade, Serbia and Montenegro (then Yugoslavia). That occurrence was traced to infected monkeys imported from Uganda.

The Angolan outbreak began in October 2004 in the northern province of Uige. Angolan health officials managed to contain it there, though several cases appeared in the capital, Luanda. As of mid-2005, researchers had still not traced the source of the Angola outbreak.

"Missing" Chinese girls. After many years of silence on the issue, officials in the People's Republic of China began to express concern about the nation's so-called "missing" girls. In January, government officials announced that China's birth ratio had reached 119 boys for every 100 girls. In the rest of the world, the ratio is 105 boys for every 100 girls.

Experts blamed the unbalanced ratio on China's policy of limiting most families to one child. Although the policy has slowed population growth, it has also prompted parents to selectively terminate pregnancies in which the fetus is female. The problem is particularly serious in rural areas, where sons customarily care for parents in their old age.

Some population experts predict that in a few decades, China could have as many as 40 million unmarried men unable to find wives. They predicted that this situation could lead to social instability. In January, China reported the birth of its 1.3-billionth citizen—a baby boy.

■ Deborah Kowal

Avian Flu: A New Pandemic?

Imagine the following scenario: Millions of people around the world are dead. Millions more are seriously ill. The resources of hospitals and other health care institutions have passed the breaking point. Medicines are in short supply. The rapidly spreading illness is taking a huge toll on the economies and social fabric of many nations.

This was the frightening possibility that representatives of the World Health Organization (WHO), presented in February 2005 at an international conference in Vietnam. WHO is a United Nations organization that helps to build better health care systems, mainly in developing nations. The WHO warning was triggered by the emergence of a new, highly *pathogenic strain* (disease-producing variety) of avian influenza—also called bird flu—known as H5N1. Health authorities feared that this strain, which caused its first documented human cases in 1997 in Hong Kong, might *mutate* (change genetically) in such a way that it could cause a global influenza *pandemic*.

In a pandemic, several simultaneous epidemics cause great numbers of illnesses and deaths. Three previous flu pandemics—the so-called Spanish flu of 1918 and 1919, Asian flu of 1957 and 1958, and Hong Kong flu of 1968 and 1969—each killed more than 1 million people. In fact, the 1918-1919 pandemic may have killed as many as 50 million people.

What is this new strain of bird flu that is causing so much concern? And what steps were being taken in 2005 to prevent the WHO prediction from coming true?

Since at least the late 1800's, various strains of the avian influenza virus have been occurring commonly in ducks, geese, and other migratory waterfowl, sometimes spreading to such domestic poultry as chickens and turkeys. In its mild form in birds, avian influenza may cause such symptoms as sneezing, decreased appetite, and reduced egg production. The more highly pathogenic strains, such as H5N1, may cause diarrhea, swollen heads, and respiratory difficulties in birds. Health authorities became alarmed in 1997, when 18 people in Hong Kong became infected by the H5N1 strain. Six of these people died. These were the first cases of human disease attributed to the virus. Apparently, the virus had mutated so that it could spread from birds to people. Subsequently, other worrisome outbreaks of the H5N1 strain among birds and people occurred in various Asian nations in 2003, 2004, and 2005. In people, the symptoms of infection progress from fever and aching joints to coughing and breathing difficulties. Coma and death may result if treatment—usually with the antiviral drug oseltamivir (sold under the brand name Tamiflu)—is not provided within 48 hours of infection. About 70 percent of those infected have died.

From December 2003 to late May 2005, the new strain spread through poultry flocks in several parts of Asia, including Cambodia, China, Hong Kong, Indonesia, Japan, Malaysia, South Korea, Thailand, and Vietnam. Health experts confirmed 97 cases of human infection in Cambodia, Thailand, and Vietnam. Of this number, 53 people died. Health authorities believe that most of the people who developed the disease had inhaled the virus from bird droppings.

As of mid-2005, health authorities had no firm evidence that the germ could pass

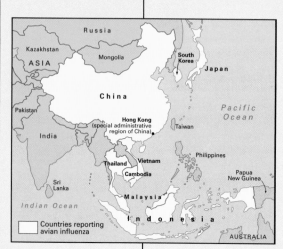

INFECTED AREAS

By May 2005, avian influenza outbreaks or infections caused by the H5N1 viral strain had been confirmed in poultry in nine countries or regions of the world. Government leaders took strong measures to contain the rapidly spreading illness, hoping to prevent it from becoming the latest *pandemic* (simultaneous, widespread epidemics).

easily from person to person within the general population. However, public health care workers in Vietnam and Thailand reported a few cases of possible human-to-human transmission, from one family member to another and from patients to health care workers.

Health officials' biggest concern was that the virus would mutate to allow easy transmission from person to person throughout an entire community. Random genetic mutations in the virus could make this possible. The virus also might mutate by merging its genes with the genes of a regular human influenza virus inside a host who happened to be infected by both germs. Crowded living conditions, especially in Asia, and the modern global transportation system would promote the spread of the deadly new strain around the world within six months, according to WHO.

To prevent this global tragedy, health officials in Asia were moving to aggressively vaccinate or slaughter millions of chickens and other poultry in infected areas. Affected nations also established a network of laboratories to track and identify avian influenza strains. Despite these actions, Asia's traditional open-air farming system presented a major challenge to containment efforts, according to WHO officials. In Vietnam, for example, some 14 million households keep live poultry. About 90 percent of this poultry, according to Vietnamese officials, is raised by small farmers who do not cage their birds. Such farmers are reluctant to destroy birds that may have become infected because they cannot afford to replace them. In addition, the flu virus can survive for weeks in feces during cool temperatures. As one *epidemiologist* from the United States Centers for Disease Control and Prevention working in Vietnam explained, "It's impractical to disinfect all of Southeast Asia." (Epidemiologists are doctors who study epidemic diseases.)

In 2005, researchers were also working to develop vaccines to fight avian influenza in human beings. However, they faced several obstacles. Most vaccines are made by growing a weakened form of the virus in chicken embryos. But the H5N1 virus is so deadly, it kills the embryos before enough weakened virus can be grown for harvesting. Some researchers have developed advanced genetic techniques to develop a vaccine. However, a number of patent issues remained to be resolved. Finally, vaccines, like other medications, must undergo lengthy safety tests before they can be approved for use by the general public. Manufacturers are often reluctant to expose themselves to lawsuits during such trials. As of mid-2005, all avian flu vaccines remained experimental.

The only drug available to treat avian flu, oseltamivir, was expensive to stockpile. It retailed for $68 for a 10-capsule treatment course. In addition, oseltamivir was manufactured by only one company with a single, small factory, and so stocks were limited.

Although vaccine research offered some hope against the spread of avian influenza, the development of a vaccine would not solve all potential problems. For example, WHO officials noted that if a "superflu" pandemic started to spread, existing vaccine production facilities would be able to make enough vaccine to inoculate only a fraction of the population. And even that amount would take several months. If the vaccine was produced in large amounts beforehand and stockpiled, it could lose its effectiveness before any outbreak of the disease. In addition, manufacturers are reluctant to produce costly vaccines with no assurance that anyone will purchase them.

Thus, in 2005, public health officials remained poised between fear and hope. They feared that their concerns of a pandemic may prove true. But they maintained hope because political leaders in many countries had begun to take steps to act on the warnings. ■ Alfred J. Smuskiewicz

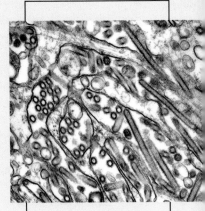

THE H5N1 VIRUS

H5N1 viruses (gold, above) grow inside cells (green) in a colorized transmission electron micrograph. Although the avian flu virus normally infects birds, public health workers in several Asian countries have recorded cases of human infection since 1997.

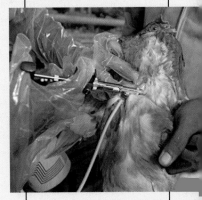

Health workers in Indonesia vaccinate a chicken against avian flu. Millions of birds throughout the country were vaccinated in 2004 and 2005 in an attempt to prevent the spread of the avian flu virus.

SCIENCE AND SOCIETY

The United States government continued to take steps in 2005 to ease restrictions on foreign students and scholars attempting to study and work in the United States. The government had tightened visa requirements after the terrorist attacks of Sept. 11, 2001. As a result, many prospective students and visitors were denied visas or subjected to lengthy processing delays.

In February 2004, the Government Accountability Office (GAO), an agency of the U.S. Congress, had proposed steps to shorten visa processing times without compromising national security. In addition, in May, 25 scientific, engineering, and higher education associations had complained in a widely publicized statement that the restrictions were harming U.S. interests by driving away talented people who posed no threat to the nation's security. In response, various U.S. agencies involved in visa processing, as well as the universities themselves, streamlined procedures to shorten the visa process.

As part of this effort, on Feb. 11, 2005, the U.S. State Department announced that it had extended the duration of security clearances granted to international students in nuclear engineering, computer science, or certain other sensitive fields who were a part of the "Visas Mantis" program. (Visas Mantis, established in 1998, was designed to prevent the entry of people who might try to take sensitive technology out of the United States illegally.)

The rule change allowed Visas Mantis students to receive visas for the length of their academic program, up to a maximum of four years. Previously, such students had to renew their visas every year and undergo an often-lengthy clearance process. The rule change also extended the clearances for temporary workers and exchange visitors granted entry under the Visas Mantis program.

On Feb. 18, 2005, the GAO released a report indicating that the average time for foreign students and scholars to receive clearance under the Visas Mantis program had fallen from 67 days in spring 2003 to 15 days in late 2004. Nevertheless, the Council of Graduate Schools reported in March 2005 that among 450 institutions surveyed, applications by foreign students for U.S. graduate study, which had dropped by 28 percent in 2004, continued to drop in 2005, by 5 percent. (The Council of Graduate Schools is a national association of institutions of higher education located in Washington, D.C.)

The council attributed the continued decline to increased competition from other countries, tougher U.S. visa policies, and the perception that the United States no longer welcomes foreign students. In late 2004, U.S. government officials and university administrators began a campaign to reverse the downward trend in student applications.

Scientific publishing in turmoil. Copies of all published research studies funded by the National Institutes of Health (NIH) must be posted on a free, government-operated Internet site, according to a rule that went into effect on May 2, 2005. NIH is responsible for more than half of all basic research funded by the U.S. government. Legislation passed by the U.S. Congress in 2004 required NIH to take this step.

Scientists traditionally have published their research findings in such *peer-reviewed journals* as *The New England Journal of Medicine, Science,* and *Nature.* (Peer-reviewed journals are those in which articles have been reviewed by professionals within a particular field of study.) Annual subscription fees generally range from less than $100 for journals published by nonprofit organizations to thousands of dollars for journals published by commercial publishers. Some scientists have also developed peer-reviewed online journals that are freely accessible to the public.

Opinion on the merits of the NIH policy and its implications was divided. Taxpayer groups claimed that research supported by public funds should be freely available to the public. Librarians and some scientists saw the policy as a way of reducing the cost of subscriptions. But nonprofit scientific associations, many of which are funded primarily by subscription income from their journals, feared that they would lose much of their income if readers could access their latest articles for free. In November 2004, the NIH adopted a policy that allows researchers to wait up to 12 months before publicly releasing their articles, to protect subscription income.

The theory of evolution continued to be the focus of controversy in the United States in 2005. This theory states that all living things evolved from simple organisms and changed through the ages to produce millions of species. The theory was developed by British naturalist Charles R. Darwin in the mid-1800's.

In October 2004, the Dover (Pennsylvania) Area School Board voted to revise the district's science curriculum to include discussion of what it described as "gaps/problems" in evolutionary theory. The board also voted to require teachers to present other theories about the origin of life, including *intelligent design.* Intelligent design theory accepts the fact that Earth is billions of years old. However, it also states that some structures and processes in nature are so complex that they could not have evolved through small changes over long periods of time and can be explained only as the product of what advocates call "an intelligent cause." Most scientists regard intelligent design as a religious or philosophical idea that cannot be tested scientifically.

In December 2004, a group of 11 local parents sued the Dover school board, arguing that the new policy to teach intelligent design violates the First Amendment to the Constitution, which guarantees that the government will not endorse or aid any religious doctrine. In January 2005, the school board ordered science teachers at Dover High School to read a statement to their ninth-grade biology classes stating that evolution is not a fact and describing intelligent design as an alternative scientific explanation for the origin of life. After the teachers refused, school officials read the statement to the classes themselves.

Also in January, a federal judge in Atlanta, Georgia, ruled as unconstitutional stickers describing evolution as "a theory not a fact" that had been placed in biology textbooks by the Cobb County (Georgia) Board of Education. According to the judge, the stickers could be interpreted as support by the school board for faith-based views on the origin of life.

Some scientists argued that calling evolution "a theory not a fact" may confuse the public. A scientific theory, they said, is an explanation of some aspect of the natural world that has been repeatedly confirmed using scientific methods or observation and experiment. This meaning contrasts with the common usage of the word *theory* to mean *an educated guess.*

Evolution is as well proven as the atomic theory of matter or the germ theory of disease, the scientists said.

Challenges to the teaching of evolution arose in 18 other states. In March, Bruce Alberts, president of the National Academy of Sciences, sent a letter to academy members expressing his concern over what he described as "the growing threat to the teaching of science" from the intelligent design movement. The academy is a nonprofit society of scholars that advises the federal government on scientific and technical matters. Alberts urged scientists to become involved in countering the intelligent design theory by such actions as speaking at school board meetings and writing newspaper opinion pieces.

Nevertheless, in May, when the Kansas State Board of Education held hearings to consider re-

VOTERS APPROVE STEM CELL RESEARCH

A researcher at the Burnham Institute in La Jolla, California, holds a tray of human *embryonic stem cell* cultures. (Embryonic stem cells have the capability to develop into any of the cell types that make up the tissues and organs of the body.) In November 2004, voters in California approved a 10-year, $3-billion bond issue to fund stem cell research in that state. In mid-2005, several other states were either considering or had begun their own initiatives to fund such research. Many people oppose stem cell research because it involves the destruction of human embryos. In 2001, U.S. President George W. Bush had placed strict conditions on embryonic stem cell research conducted with federal funds.

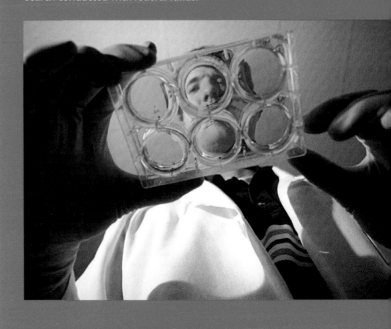

SCIENCE AND SOCIETY continued

vising its science standards, the scientific community refused to attend. A majority of members of the State Board of Education supported the idea that teachers should be required to challenge Darwin's theory of evolution in the classroom. Scientists called the deliberations a "kangaroo court" and argued that it makes no sense to compare evolution, a scientific concept, to intelligent design, which, they said, is based on faith. They expressed concern that if revised standards were adopted, Kansas school graduates would be less qualified to compete in scientific and technical fields and the state would become a less attractive site for high-tech and other information-based businesses.

Human cloning. A nonbinding resolution urging member states to adopt policies that prohibit human *cloning* was adopted by the United Nations General Assembly in March. (Cloning is the creation of a genetic duplicate of an organism.) The U.S. delegation had backed the resolution despite the opposition of many European nations

In addition, many scientists had expressed concern that the resolution's language did not clearly distinguish between *reproductive cloning* (making human babies) and *therapeutic cloning* (using similar techniques to create embryonic stem cells, which can develop into any of the cell types that make up the tissues and organs of the body). Many scientists are eager to pursue research with embryonic stem cells because of their potential use in finding new treatments for spinal cord injuries and such diseases as multiple sclerosis and diabetes. However, many people oppose therapeutic cloning because it involves the destruction of an *embryo* (organism in the first stages of development).

Under a policy announced by President George W. Bush in 2001, the U.S. government placed strict conditions on embryonic stem cell research conducted with federal funds. Legislation introduced in March 2005 in the House of Representatives and in the Senate would ban both reproductive and therapeutic cloning, regardless of its funding source. However, on May 24, the House of Representatives passed a bill that would relax Bush's restrictions on stem cell research. The president had said he would veto the bill.

Meanwhile, stem cell research continued to attract attention at the state level. In November 2004, California voters approved a 10-year, $3-billion bond issue to fund stem cell research in that state. Other states, including New Jersey, Wisconsin, Massachusetts, and New York, were considering or had begun their own initiatives to fund stem cell research.   ■ Albert H. Teich

SPACE TECHNOLOGY

Two-person crews of astronauts and cosmonauts struggled to maintain the International Space Station (ISS) during 2004 and 2005. A privately funded craft carried a pilot into space. And spacecraft were launched to explore the planets Saturn, Mars, and Mercury; the solar wind; a comet; and mysterious gamma ray bursts in space.

The International Space Station. In 2004 and 2005, the United States National Aeronautic and Space Administration (NASA) and its international partners faced the challenge of delivering supplies and crew replacements to the ISS. After the loss of the space shuttle Columbia and its crew on Feb. 1, 2003, NASA halted the flights of the three remaining shuttles—Discovery, Atlantis, and Endeavour.

SEE ALSO THE SPECIAL REPORT, **CLOSE ENCOUNTERS WITH SATURN**, PAGE 12.

Because space shuttles had been the main means of transporting water and other supplies to the orbiting outpost, the number of crew members was cut from three to two to make supplying the station easier. In addition, the amount of time each crew stayed in orbit was lengthened from four months to six to reduce the number of trips needed to replace teams.

Supplies were delivered to the station by Russian Progress cargo ships, and crew members were ferried to and from the station aboard Russian Soyuz vehicles. The crews continued to perform the maintenance and repair work needed to keep the ISS operating safely and conducted scientific experiments when they could.

Space station assembly had stopped in 2003 when the remaining shuttles were grounded. All the major pieces needed to finish the ISS had been designed so they could be carried in a shuttle's cargo bay and attached to the station using a shuttle's robotic arm. Even so, the crews still had to conduct a number of *extravehicular activities* (EVA's, also known as *spacewalks*) to repair the station. They also had to prepare the ISS for the projected arrival in 2006 of the European Space Agency's (ESA's) Automated Transfer Vehicle, a new supply ship.

NASA ground controllers expressed concerns about allowing both crew members aboard the ISS to leave the station at the same time to perform EVA's. On NASA missions, a third crew member had always remained inside the station to help in the event of an emergency. Russian crews had performed two-person EVA's many times aboard the Russian space station Mir, which was allowed to fall to Earth in 2001. Ultimately, in 2004, NASA approved such EVA's. The ISS crews in 2004 and 2005 completed all required EVA's safely, even those in which the crews had to travel the entire outside length of the ISS to reach their work site. Ground controllers in Houston and Moscow watched over the station's systems by remote control while the space-suited crew members worked outside.

In October 2004, Russian cosmonaut Gennady Padalka and U.S. astronaut Michael Fincke were replaced by U.S. astronaut Leroy Chiao and Russian cosmonaut Salizhan Sharipov. Chiao and Sharipov, in turn, were replaced in April 2005 by Russian cosmonaut Sergei Krikalev and U.S. astronaut John Phillips.

Returning the shuttles to flight. During 2004 and 2005, NASA engineers worked to prepare the remaining three space shuttles for a return to space. Their greatest concern was ensuring that an accident such as the one that brought down Columbia and its crew would never occur again. Accident investigators had determined that a piece of insulation had broken off Columbia's main fuel tank and shattered a critical heat shield on the aircraft's left wing. The crack in the wing allowed superhot gases generated by the friction of reentry into Earth's atmosphere to melt Columbia's aluminum structure. All seven astronauts aboard died as the shuttle broke up.

To limit the risk that a similar accident might occur, NASA engineers designed a special boom that would allow space shuttle crews to inspect the delicate ceramic tiles and carbon composite panels that protect the shuttle wings and belly. Lacking such a boom, Columbia's crew had no way of knowing that their ship had been badly damaged by the insulation fragment as it ascended into space. If future shuttle crews spot damage, they would be able to repair small cracks and holes with kits specifically developed for that purpose. If the damage is too extensive, the crews are to take shelter in the ISS until NASA launches a second shuttle to return them safely to Earth.

NASA originally planned to launch Discovery in spring 2005. However, a series of safety concerns led NASA to postpone the shuttle's return to space until summer.

The Hubble Space Telescope. In April 2005, NASA Administrator Michael Griffin promised that if the first two shuttles scheduled to return to flight did so successfully, he would reconsider the issue of sending astronauts to repair the Hubble Space Telescope (HST). After 14 years in orbit, the HST needed to have its aging batteries replaced and the gyroscopes that help it maintain its position in space repaired. NASA had decided in April 2004 not to send a shuttle crew to repair the HST, in part, because of a new mandate announced by U.S. President George W. Bush in January. Bush had directed NASA to begin preparing for a human presence on the moon by 2020 and for using a moon base to test equipment for a trip to Mars. Astronomers, educators, and the public strongly opposed NASA's decision, citing the importance of the HST in astronomical exploration. Bush appointed Griffin to replace former administrator Sean O'Keefe in April 2005. The U.S. Senate confirmed Griffin's appointment on April 14.

Mars rovers' mission extended. In 2004 and 2005, NASA's Mars Exploration rovers performed far better than even the most optimistic scientists had hoped. Although the rovers had been designed to work for only 90 *Martian days* after their landing on opposite sides of the Red Planet in January 2004, both Spirit and Opportunity continued to function well beyond that date. (A Martian day is the equivalent of about 24 hours and 40 minutes on Earth.) Like a pair of robotic geologists, they trundled across the planet's surface, searching for life—or evidence of it. They found evidence of liquid water in the planet's past virtually everywhere they went.

Spirit explored the Columbia Hills, which were visible in the distance from Gusev Crater, its landing site. In the hills, it found layered

SPACE TECHNOLOGY continued

rocks showing evidence that they had been altered by water. Opportunity drove to a crater the size of a football stadium, dubbed Endurance, and found a way down its steep sides and back out again. Opportunity was able to plot the water history of the Meridiani Planum, its landing zone. Scientists believe that the area once may have been a salty sea. In April 2004, the Mars rover mission had been extended to March 2005. In April 2005, NASA again extended the mission for an additional 18 months.

As the rovers forged ahead, they left tracks on the dusty surface of Mars that were clearly visible from three satellites orbiting the planet:

SPIRIT KEEPS GOING AND GOING

NASA's Spirit rover uses its robotic arm to position a microscopic imager for a photo of a rock on Mars in June 2004. Spirit and its identical twin, Opportunity, landed on Mars in January 2004 for what was to be a 90-day mission. However, both rovers far surpassed their controllers' expectations with their durability and the wealth of data they collected about the dry, frozen surface of the planet. In April 2005, NASA scientists extended the mission for the second time, for an additional 18 months.

Mars Global Surveyor, which began orbiting Mars in 1997; Mars Odyssey, which arrived at the planet in 2001; and the ESA's Mars Express, which reached Mars in 2003. In April 2005, Mars Global Surveyor photographed the other two satellites, creating the first images of a spacecraft orbiting another planet taken by another spacecraft orbiting that same planet.

Cassini-Huygens at Saturn. In mid-2004, after a journey that lasted seven years, the Cassini-Huygens spacecraft reached Saturn and began orbiting the ringed planet. Less than one month later, scientists got their first close look at Saturn, as Cassini returned hundreds of images that revealed the planet's rings, clouds, and other features in unprecedented detail.

In January 2005, Cassini released the Huygens probe—named for the Dutch astronomer Christiaan Huygens (1625-1695)—into the dense, orange atmosphere of Saturn's largest moon, Titan. Huygens was developed by the ESA. As the probe parachuted to the surface, it collected data about various aspects of Titan's atmosphere, including temperature, winds, and chemical composition. Huygens also captured images of Titan's surface. Cassini was to continue gathering data about Saturn and its moons and rings for an additional four years.

Genesis falls to Earth. Scientists who study the sun experienced a setback on Sept. 8, 2004, when the Genesis spacecraft crashed in the Utah desert. For 26 months, Genesis had been parked in an orbit outside Earth's magnetic field. There, the spacecraft had collected atoms streaming from the sun in a flood of particles known as the *solar wind*, storing the samples on an array of delicate, hexagonal collectors. A helicopter was to have caught the capsule containing the samples in midair as it descended through Earth's atmosphere. Instead, the capsule's parachute failed to open, and it hit the ground at an estimated speed of nearly 320 kilometers (200 miles) per hour. In October, a NASA investigating board determined that a design error had caused engineers to install critical sensors upside down. In that position, the sensors were unable to trigger the deployment of the capsule's parachute.

Nevertheless, when the recovery team examined the damaged craft, the scientists found that the collectors—some coated with thin layers of gold, diamond, and sapphire—were in relatively good condition. Some of the collectors were only slightly damaged. Other collectors, while shattered, held clues to their original position that scientists could use in their analysis. Ultimately, the Genesis team believed, scientists would be able to separate the tiny collection of solar samples—weighing only as much as one or two grains of salt—one molecule at a time for study.

Deep Impact, a spacecraft launched by NASA on January 12, was scheduled to fire a missile at Tempel 1, a comet that regularly passes through the inner solar system. The projectile was due to hit the comet's icy core on July 4.

The missile, which will be traveling at a speed of 37,000 kilometers (23,000 miles) per hour, was to hit with enough force to blow a hole the size of a football stadium in the core. The blast should expose materials scientists believe hold clues to the nature and origin of the solar system, which formed some 4.6 billion years ago. Researchers will analyze the exposed materials of the comet using instruments on the Deep Impact spacecraft itself, which will pass within about 500 kilometers (300 miles) of the core. On Earth, astronomers will turn powerful telescopes on the comet at the moment of impact, so they can also use their Earth-bound instruments to analyze the composition of the cloud of debris expected to be ejected from the comet.

Messenger to Mercury. The Romans knew Mercury as the messenger of the gods, but astronomers today know it as the mysterious planet closest to the sun. In honor of the planet's ancient namesake, NASA named the spacecraft it launched to Mercury on Aug. 3, 2004, Messenger (*Me*rcury *S*urface, *S*pace *Env*ironment, *Ge*ochemistry, and *R*anging). If Messenger reaches its destination, it will become the first spacecraft to orbit Mercury and the first to visit the planet in 30 years, since Mariner 10 completed

BRACING FOR IMPACT

Rock and dust explode from comet Tempel 1 after NASA's Deep Impact spacecraft fires a missile at the comet, in an artist's drawing of an event planned for July 2005. After creating a crater the size of a football field, the spacecraft, launched on January 12, was to study the material exposed in the crater's walls. NASA scientists hoped that the mission would allow them to analyze material that had remained unchanged since the formation of the solar system, about 4.6 billion years ago.

its mission in 1975. Messenger was to begin returning data about the planet after its arrival at Mercury in 2011.

Although Mercury lies only 77 million kilometers (48 million miles) from Earth at its closest approach, Messenger's journey will actually cover about 8 billion kilometers (5 billion miles). The trip will be so lengthy because today's chemical rockets lack the power to produce the drastic cut in speed needed to put a spacecraft hurtling toward the sun into orbit around Mercury. As a result, engineers will use the gravity of Earth, Venus, and Mercury itself to slow Messenger enough for it to enter Mercury's orbit. Messenger is scheduled to fly by Earth once, in August 2005; Venus, twice, in October 2006 and June 2007; and Mercury, three times.

Once in orbit around Mercury, Messenger is to study the planet's surface features, including

SPACE TECHNOLOGY continued

volcanoes and ice, which may lie hidden in deep craters near the north and south poles. To survive the heat of the nearby sun, the probe will carry a sunshade that is expected to grow as hot as 370 °C (700 °F) as it casts a cooling shadow on Messenger and its delicate instruments. Messenger is to remain in orbit around Mercury for 12 months.

Europe reaches the moon. In November 2004, the ESA's first moon mission—called Smart-1 (*Small Missions for Advanced Research in Technology*)—reached the moon and began its orbit of Earth's only natural satellite. Smart-1 took 14 months to enter lunar orbit. Built in Sweden, the spacecraft collects energy from the sun with its solar arrays, converts the energy to electric power, and feeds it to the engine.

Smart-1's engine uses xenon gas as fuel. Inside the engine, electric power generated by the sun strips *electrons* (negatively charged particles) from xenon molecules to create *ions*

(electrically charged atoms). The ions are forced through a nozzle in a high-speed beam from the back of the probe to provide *thrust* (the force that propels an airplane or spacecraft). A xenon ion engine produces very low thrust—about as much as a piece of paper against the palm of the hand—but it can burn much longer than conventional rockets without exhausting its fuel.

To reach the moon, Smart-1 fired its engine 289 times to gradually raise the high point of its Earth orbit—called the *apogee*—until it was close enough for the moon's gravity to take over and pull the spacecraft into lunar orbit. The process required Smart-1 to orbit Earth 332 times and consume 59 of the 82 kilograms (130 of the 181 pounds) of xenon fuel that the spacecraft carried at liftoff. After being pulled into the moon's orbit, the spacecraft used the rest of its fuel to gradually lower its orbit.

Smart-1's mission was to take close-up photographs of the surface and use its instruments to study the moon's chemical composition. The spacecraft will also try to peer into deep craters near the moon's north and south poles, which always lie in shadow. Some scientists believe these regions may hold water ice left by comets that bombarded the surface.

First private flight into space. On Oct. 4, 2004, a privately owned, three-person spacecraft called SpaceShipOne reached outer space for the second time in two weeks. The feat earned a group of California engineers the $10-million Ansari X Prize. The prize had been established to encourage the development of private space flight. American aviator Charles Lindbergh won a similar prize, the $25,000 Orteig Prize, in 1927 for making the first nonstop solo flight across the Atlantic Ocean.

SpaceShipOne, which was made of plastic and had movable wings, was designed to be carried aloft by a jet called the White Knight. After it is released high up in Earth's atmosphere, SpaceShipOne ignites its *hybrid rocket motor.* The engine burns a mixture of liquid and solid propellant. The solid propellant is made of a type of synthetic rubber called hydroxyl-terminated polybutadi-

NEW VENTURE INTO SPACE

SpaceShipOne, a privately funded three-person rocket, prepares to land in California's Mojave Desert on Sept. 29, 2004, after completing the first stage in the Ansari X-prize competition. To win the competition, a commercial aircraft had to fly to the edge of space—100 kilometers (62.5 miles) above Earth's surface and return successfully to Earth twice within two weeks. SpaceShipOne captured the $10-million prize one week later, after its second successful flight.

TRACKING GAMMA RAY BURSTS

The Swift satellite focuses on the afterglow of a *gamma ray burst* in an artist's rendering of the spacecraft launched on Nov. 20, 2004. Gamma ray bursts are mysterious, high-energy flashes that scientists believe may be the last gasps of massive dying stars. Discovered in the 1960's, gamma ray bursts have since been observed exploding in all areas of the sky. NASA developed Swift to detect a burst, relay its coordinates to telescopes on Earth, and then swivel its own instruments to track the burst's afterglow. Astronomers use the afterglow to measure the distance to the burst's origin.

ene (HTPB). Nitrous oxide, the liquid propellant, acts as an *oxidizer,* a substance that enables the fuel to burn without drawing outside air into the combustion chamber. The combination of HTPB and nitrous oxide provides a stable, nontoxic fuel.

After the fuel is used up, the engine shuts down, and SpaceShipOne coasts into space, propelled by its own momentum. When it reaches its highest altitude—about 100 kilometers (62 miles), the widely accepted boundary between Earth's atmosphere and space—the pilot folds up SpaceShipOne's wings so that the spacecraft resembles a shuttlecock. That position increases the spacecraft's *drag* and allows SpaceShipOne to reenter Earth's atmosphere relatively slowly, without overheating. (Drag is the opposing force that an airplane or spacecraft encounters as it moves through air.) At the end of its reentry, SpaceShipOne glides onto a runway at Mojave, California, where it was built.

SpaceShipOne was developed by Burt Rutan, an American aerospace engineer who also designed the GlobalFlyer airplane. The GlobalFlyer completed the first solo nonstop, nonrefueled flight around the world in March 2005. After the successful flights of SpaceShipOne, Sir Richard Branson, a British billionaire and owner of Virgin Atlantic Airways, Ltd., bought the rights to use SpaceShipOne technology from Paul Allen. Allen, a co-founder of Microsoft Corporation of Redmond, Washington, had paid Rutan to develop the spacecraft.

Branson planned to spend an additional $100 million to have Rutan build a five-seat version of SpaceShipOne. The new venture, to be called Virgin Galactic, was to carry a pilot and several space tourists into the vacuum and weightlessness of space. Virgin Galactic planned to begin operation in two to three years.

Mysterious gamma ray bursts. On Nov. 20, 2004, NASA launched a spacecraft dubbed Swift for its ability to turn quickly in space to focus its telescopes on *gamma ray bursts.* First discovered in 1967, gamma ray bursts are short-lived, extremely powerful blasts of energy that occur randomly across the sky. Swift will detect bursts, turn toward them, and try to determine their cause. The spacecraft has an X-ray telescope as well as a telescope that collects light from the ultraviolet to the visible ranges of the electromagnetic spectrum. Swift will also relay the coordinates of the bursts to telescopes on Earth, which astronomers can use to study the bursts' afterglow to determine the distance of the gamma ray bursts from Earth.

Scientists are not certain what causes gamma ray bursts. However, they suspect the bursts are related to stellar explosions or collisions between stars or black holes. ■ Frank Morring, Jr.

See also **ASTRONOMY.**

WORLD BOOK SUPPLEMENT

Five new or revised articles reprinted from the
2005 edition of *The World Book Encyclopedia*

Special effects created by computer graphics merge with a shot of an actor in the motion picture *The Mask.*

© New Line from Shooting Star

Computer graphics is a term that refers both to the use of computers to create or change images and to the images themselves. Such images can be individual pictures, such as photographs or diagrams, or part of a motion picture, such as an animated cartoon, music video, or feature-length movie. The use of computer graphics to create a realistic three-dimensional image is called *rendering.*

Computer graphics uses various optical cues to give viewers the perception of three-dimensional depth through a flat image. Such cues include *perspective,* which causes objects farther away to appear smaller, and *occlusion,* in which closer objects block the view of farther objects. A type of computer graphics called *virtual reality* uses additional techniques, such as *stereopsis,* in which each eye sees a different image, and *view tracking,* in which an image changes when the viewer's head moves. These techniques help create for the viewer a powerful illusion that he or she is actually in the environment represented by the images.

Uses of computer graphics

Computer graphics is best known for its applications in entertainment. However, it also makes important contributions in science, engineering, and medicine.

In entertainment and the arts, computer graphics provides animation and special effects for motion pictures. This use of computer graphics is called *computer-generated imagery* (CGI). Animators use CGI to give the illusion of motion and personalities to dinosaurs, toys, insects, and other cartoon characters. Filmmakers use CGI to create artificial environments for motion pictures. For example, CGI may create an ocean setting for scenes shot in a studio rather than at sea.

The ultimate goal of computer graphics in entertainment is to simulate human actors. Such simulation is challenging because most viewers are too familiar with human appearance and movement to be fooled by imprecise representations.

Computer graphics also creates images for video games played on personal computers and game consoles. The computer graphics used for video games must react to a player's control. It must also render images at least 20 times per second to provide the illusion of fairly smooth movement.

In science, computer graphics helps researchers produce images of real objects that cannot be seen clearly because of their size or location. The use of computer

David W. Deerfield II and Greg Foss, Pittsburgh Supercomputing Center

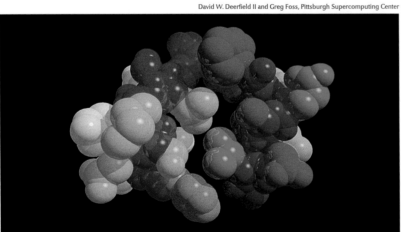

A computer-generated frame from an educational motion picture shows how groups of atoms fit together to form a molecule. The molecule shown is lysozyme, a substance found in human tears and other body fluids. Lysozyme can destroy many kinds of bacteria.

graphics to convey such information visually is called *scientific visualization.* For example, scientists use computer graphics to draw pictures of DNA (deoxyribonucleic acid) molecules, which play a key role in heredity and cell development. The pictures enable scientists to better understand the functions of DNA.

Computer graphics can also be used to graph or chart abstract mathematical values or measured physical quantities. These graphs can be simple, such as one that plots the vertical position of points as a function of their horizontal position. Or the graphs can be quite sophisticated, using differences in position, color, brightness, or other features to indicate different aspects of the data. Scientists can use such graphs to gain insight into physical processes. For example, a chemist might create a graph that shows the energy levels at which molecules react with one another to produce a certain substance. The "valleys" in this graph would indicate how the substance could be produced using less energy.

In engineering, computer graphics can enable a machine designer to create a three-dimensional computer representation of the shape of an object, called a *geometric model.* Using a process called *computer aided design* (CAD), the designer can see how a new part would appear, and even how it would function, before physically making the part.

In medicine, computer graphics enables physicians to "see" inside the body. *Computed tomography* (CT) involves many X-ray images of a body, taken from a number of different directions. A computer combines the X-ray images to create a three-dimensional image called a *volumetric model.* A volumetric model incorporates information about the size, shape, texture, and density of structures inside the body. Doctors might then use this volumetric model to pinpoint the location of a tumor, and even to practice the surgery for removing it.

How a computer creates images

A computer-created picture consists of many points of color called *picture elements* or *pixels.* If you look closely at a computer screen, you can see the pixels. Pixels are so small that more than 1 million fit on some screens. The computer must calculate a color for each pixel based on a three-dimensional model of a scene it holds in its memory. In one technique, called *ray tracing,* the computer traces a line from the viewer's eye to the image's light source through each pixel. The computer then figures out the first object in the scene this line intersects and represents the color of the object at each such intersection point. Ray tracing produces highly realistic images, and filmmakers commonly use it for motion-picture special effects.

A technique called *rasterization* produces the graphics for most personal computer applications and video games. This technique is faster but creates less realistic images. It finds the pixels through which a viewer would see each object in the scene. It then colors each pixel according to the colors of the object. Unlike ray tracing, rasterization does not represent how light sources affect an object's colors. But the method is constantly improving, providing ever more realistic images.   John C. Hart

Glacier is a large mass of ice that flows slowly under the influence of gravity. Glaciers consist of packed snow that has built up over many years. The snow's weight eventually compresses its lower layers into ice. Glaciers scrape the ground as they move over it, eroding old landforms and creating new ones. They range in thickness from several feet or meters to 10,000 feet (3,000 meters) or more.

Glaciers form in the colder regions near the North and South poles and in mountainous areas. During periods called *ice ages,* glaciers can grow to cover large portions of Earth's surface.

Kinds of glaciers. Scientists classify glaciers according to size and shape. An *ice sheet* is a dome-shaped glacier covering an area greater than 19,300 square miles (50,000 square kilometers). The ice in an ice sheet flows slowly outward from one or more central domes. Faster moving glaciers called *outlet glaciers* flow outward from the edge of an ice sheet. Ice sheets can reach a thickness of more than 2 miles (3 kilometers). They often conceal the entire landscape beneath them except for the tallest mountain peaks, called *nunataks.* Huge ice sheets cover most of Antarctica and Greenland.

An *icecap* is a dome-shaped glacier that covers an area of 19,300 square miles (50,000 square kilometers) or less. Icecaps resemble ice sheets, with outlet glaciers flowing outward from a central ice dome. Icecaps occur in Iceland and Norway and on several Arctic islands.

In some high mountain areas, glaciers form in a *cirque,* a bowl-shaped hollow with steep walls. A relatively small glacier confined to a cirque is called a *cirque glacier.* A *valley glacier* is a long, narrow stream of ice that flows down a mountain valley. Valley glaciers occur in mountainous regions worldwide.

Different valley glaciers flowing downhill sometimes come together, much as the tributaries of a river merge. Unlike tributaries, however, each of the glaciers remains a separate mass and continues to flow on its own. Rock debris carried by the glaciers accumulates at the boundaries between them. Some valley glaciers flow out of the mountains and onto flatter ground. No longer confined by valley walls, the ice spreads out to form a rounded lump called a *piedmont glacier.*

Scientists also classify glaciers by comparing the temperature of a glacier's ice with the ice's *melting point,* the temperature at which it turns to water. Within a *temperate glacier,* the ice remains at or near its melting point throughout most of the year. Temperate glaciers contain ample *meltwater* (water from melted ice). They are not frozen firmly to the ground. The ice in a *polar glacier* remains well below its melting point throughout the year. Polar glaciers contain little or no meltwater. Most polar glaciers are frozen to the ground and cannot slide over it. A single large glacier can stretch across different climate zones or elevations that have different temperatures. One portion of such a glacier might be temperate, and another portion might be polar.

How glaciers form. Glaciers form in areas where some snow remains on the ground throughout the year. This snow accumulates in layers over hundreds

A valley glacier flows down this mountain valley in Alaska. Dark strips of rock debris called *moraines* run through the ice. Melting ice forms a lake, *foreground,* at the end of the glacier.

Bob and Ira Spring

or thousands of years. Eventually, the weight of the upper snow layers compresses the lower layers into tiny pellets of ice called *firn.* At greater depths, the weight further compresses firn into solid ice. As snow turns into firn and ice, the frozen mass becomes more dense. With enough pressure, the ice can begin to flow, and the mass becomes a glacier.

Meltwater plays an important role in the formation of most glaciers. As ice on the glacier's surface melts, meltwater seeps deep into the ice mass, filling open spaces between ice crystals and particles and then re-freezing. Meltwater also reduces the friction between ice particles, speeding the internal movement of the glacier as well as the rate at which the glacier slips over the ground. An abundance of meltwater makes temperate glaciers move faster than polar glaciers.

Glaciers grow and shrink with seasonal variations in temperature and snowfall. Typically, lower air tem-peratures in winter and spring prevent a glacier from melting, and heavy snowfall causes it to grow. In summer and autumn, higher air temperatures can

melt portions of a glacier, causing it to shrink.

In frigid regions, glaciers can shrink as they enter the sea. The ice on a glacier's leading edge, which floats, is pushed upward by seawater. Huge chunks of ice break off in a process known as *calving.* The chunks, called *icebergs,* are carried away by wind and ocean currents.

Glaciers also grow and shrink with changes in Earth's climate. During an ice age, lower air tempera-tures and increased snowfall cause glaciers to thicken and expand. During an *interglacial period,* higher air temperatures and lower snowfall cause glaciers to thin and retreat.

Glaciers covered vast areas of Asia, Europe, and North America during the Pleistocene Epoch, a period in Earth's history from about 1,700,000 to 10,500 years ago. Many ice ages occurred during that time. During the Pleistocene Epoch, the huge Laurentide Ice Sheet covered much of what are now Canada and the north-ern United States. Today, many valley glaciers around the world are retreating and thinning in response to a

A sectional view of a valley glacier

A valley glacier moves downslope from a *cirque,* a bowl-shaped hollow near a mountain peak. As the glacier travels over uneven terrain or changes its velocity, its surface forms cracks called *crevasses.* The glacier picks up rocks and other materials and piles them up in ridges called *moraines.*

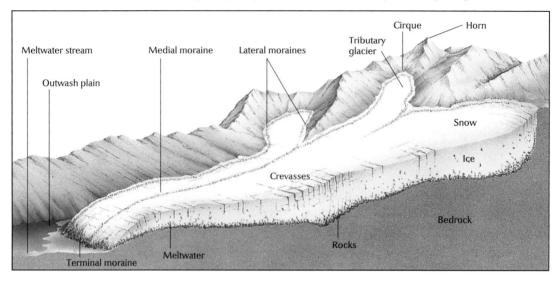

global warming trend that began in the late 1800's.

How glaciers move. Gravity causes the ice in a glacier to move. From the surface down to a depth of about 130 feet (40 meters), the ice is brittle. This area can become stretched or compressed as the glacier changes its speed or moves over uneven or steep terrain. The ice often breaks, forming deep cracks called *crevasses.* At greater depths, the ice in a glacier flows like a thick plastic without breaking. At these depths, the pressure of the overlying layers causes ice crystals to change shape and regroup. These small changes in the individual crystals cause the entire ice mass to move internally.

Glaciers move over the ground at different speeds. Heat from the ground and friction causes some melting at the bottom of a temperate glacier. The meltwater lubricates the bedrock, causing the glacier to slide over the ground more quickly. Temperate glaciers typically advance only 1 inch (2.5 centimeters) or so a day, but, in steep terrain, such glaciers can move as much as 20 feet (6 meters) per day. Pressure from an icecap or ice sheet can push some outlet glaciers from about 30 to 100 feet (9 to 30 meters) per day. The various parts of a glacier can also move at different speeds. For example, the central and uppermost portions of a valley glacier flow the fastest. Friction with the valley walls and floor causes the sides and bottom of the glacier to move more slowly.

How glaciers shape the land. The impact of prehistoric glaciers can be seen in many modern landscapes. For example, the rolling terrain of the northern United States was shaped by glaciers that melted more than 10,000 years ago. Geologists believe ancient glaciers also carved long, narrow inlets called *fiords* in Norway and similar features found in Alaska, British Columbia, Maine, Newfoundland and Labrador, Greenland, and New Zealand.

Land forms created by a glacier

As a glacier melts, it leaves behind humps of hard bedrock, and rounded hills and narrow ridges of rock debris. Hollows in the loose rocks trap water from the melting glacier, forming lakes.

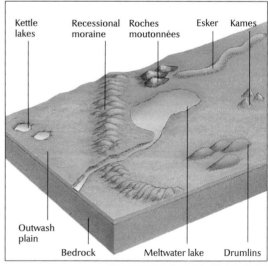

WORLD BOOK illustrations by Oxford Illustrators Limited; adapted from a drawing by Janet Allin

Advancing glaciers create a variety of landforms by eroding, transporting, and depositing rock debris. Meltwater from glaciers can enter cracks in the bedrock. This water then freezes and expands, breaking away pieces of rock that are carried off by the glacier. Glaciers also scoop up rock debris and drag it along at their bases. This debris polishes, scratches, or grooves exposed bedrock as the glacier scrapes over it. Valley glaciers can carve sharp-bottomed, V-shaped river valleys into gently curving, U-shaped valleys. An advancing glacier can shape a rocky knob into a formation called a *stoss-and-lee* feature. The side that faced the approaching glacier, called the *stoss* side, is smooth and gently sloping. The opposite side, called the *lee* side, is rough and steep.

A moving glacier transports and deposits *till,* angular rock fragments that range in size from gravel to boulders. Glaciers deposit till in uneven ridges known as *moraines.* A *ground moraine* forms under the glacier and features an irregular surface. Ridges called *lateral moraines* develop along the sides of a valley glacier. Where two valley glaciers come together, their lateral moraines merge to form a *medial moraine* where the two streams of ice meet. A *terminal moraine,* or *end moraine,* marks the farthest point of advance of a valley or piedmont glacier. A *recessional moraine* forms when a glacier that was retreating begins to advance or temporarily halts. Advancing glaciers can also deposit till in an oval-shaped hill called a *drumlin.*

Glaciers also shape the land as they thin and retreat. Meltwater flows over, under, and through the ice of a retreating glacier. Streams of meltwater carry rock fragments freed from the ice by melting. This process polishes and rounds the fragments and separates them by size, leaving fragments of different sizes in different deposits. An *esker* is a narrow, winding ridge of sand and gravel deposited by a stream of water flowing through a tunnel or crevasse in a melting glacier. Sometimes, large chunks of melting ice become buried by sediment. These chunks melt slowly, leaving behind a *kettle,* a circular or oval depression that fills with water. Streams draining a melting glacier transport sediment over a broad, flat area known as an *outwash plain.*

Famous glaciers. The French and Swiss Alps feature some of the world's best-known glaciers, including the Mer de Glace on Mont Blanc and the Aletsch Glacier near the Jungfrau. Europe's largest glacier, Vatnajökull in Iceland, covers 3,130 square miles (8,100 square kilometers). Jostedalsbreen in Norway, the largest glacier on the European continent, covers about 190 square miles (490 square kilometers). The largest North American glacier outside Greenland is the 1,930-square-mile (5,000-square-kilometer) Malaspina Glacier near Yakutat Bay in Alaska's Saint Elias Mountains. Other North American glaciers include those in Banff National Park in Alberta, Glacier National Park in Montana, and on Mount Rainier in Washington. Some other well-known glaciers are in the Andes Mountains of South America, the Himalaya of southern Asia, and the Southern Alps of New Zealand.   Joseph M. Moran

Additional resources

Gallant, Roy A. *Glaciers.* Watts, 1999. Younger readers.
Knight, Peter G. *Glaciers.* Stanley Thornes, 1999.
Sharp, Robert P. *Living Ice: Understanding Glaciers and Glaciation.* 1988. Reprint. Cambridge, 1991.

WORLD BOOK photo

From iron ore to steel. Steelmakers work with many forms of iron and steel. For example, they convert pellets of concentrated ore into pig iron, which is refined into steel.

Iron and steel are the world's cheapest and most useful metals. These hard, durable metals are used in making thousands of products, from paper clips and refrigerators to automobiles and ships. Machines made of iron and steel help produce almost everything we use, including our clothes, our homes, and even our food.

The word *iron* can refer to both an element and a number of *alloys* (chemical mixtures) of iron and other elements. As an element, iron is one of the most common chemical substances in Earth's crust, but it is almost never found in pure form there. Almost all iron occurs in ores, though some meteorites also contain iron.

Iron ores are mineral or rock deposits in which geological processes have concentrated iron. Manufacturers crush and process these ores to produce high-grade iron *concentrates.* The concentrates are turned into metallic iron by heating them with other raw materials in huge furnaces. Most metallic iron is used to make steel, but some is made directly into iron products.

Thomas J. Misa, the contributor of this article, is Associate Professor of History at the Illinois Institute of Technology and author of A Nation of Steel: The Making of Modern America, 1865-1925.

A modern steel mill, such as this plant at Handan in Hebei Province, China, may perform all the steps in steelmaking, from smelting iron ore to producing steel in useful shapes and forms.

Iron is the basic material of steel, and all steel contains iron. However, the *properties* (characteristics) and uses of iron and steel vary widely. Steelmakers first refine liquid iron in furnaces, often along with recycled iron and steel scrap. They produce steel by alloying the purified iron with carbon and often with certain metals as well. The liquid steel is then formed into sheets, beams, rods, wire, tubing, and other shapes.

Some modern steel mills perform all the steps in steelmaking, from smelting iron ore to producing steel in useful shapes and forms. Other modern mills, called *minimills,* perform only the steps needed to melt scrap steel into new raw steel.

As early as 4000 B.C., people used iron from meteorites to make ornaments, weapons, tools, and utensils. The making of iron from ores developed independently in several parts of the world, including the Middle East, China, and India. The technology spread quickly to other regions. By about 1000 B.C., many civilizations had mastered the art of ironmaking. Early ironmakers sometimes produced small quantities of steel. However, steel could not be manufactured cheaply in large quantities until the second half of the 1800's. The technology of steelmaking developed rapidly from 1850 to 1930.

Today, the production of iron and steel is one of the world's most vital industries. Throughout the world, steelmaking plants employ about a million workers. Millions of additional workers provide machinery, raw materials, and energy to iron and steel companies, or manufacture consumer products from iron and steel.

Kinds of iron and steel

The metals called iron and steel are alloys of the element iron and at least one other element. In general, steel is any alloy of the elements iron and carbon that contains less than 2 percent carbon. Most types of steel also contain some manganese, and many kinds also include other elements. The properties of any kind of iron or steel depend largely on the chemical composition of the alloy. Heating and *working* (shaping) the metal can change its physical properties.

There are thousands of kinds of iron and steel. Iron can be classified as (1) pig iron, (2) cast iron, or (3) wrought iron. Steel can be grouped as (1) carbon steel, (2) alloy steel, (3) stainless steel, or (4) tool steel.

Pig iron is the crude iron produced in a blast furnace from iron ore. Most pig iron contains 3 to 4 percent carbon and smaller amounts of other elements. The term *pig iron* comes from an early method of pouring liquid iron from a blast furnace into molds set around a central channel. The molds looked somewhat like a group of baby pigs around their mother. The bars of iron that formed in the molds were called *pigs.* Today, most pig iron is used in making steel. However, a small amount is made into cast iron or wrought iron.

Cast iron is any iron alloy that contains from 2 to 4 percent carbon. It often contains silicon as well. Because of its high carbon content, solid cast iron cannot be hammered or welded, no matter how hot it is heated. At an elevated temperature, it simply melts. Cast iron is made into useful objects by pouring the liquid metal into molds and letting it cool and harden.

Wrought iron is nearly pure iron, with essentially no carbon alloyed with it. It has glasslike fibers of melted sand called *silicate slag* mixed with the pure iron. Unlike cast iron, wrought iron is *malleable*—that is, it can be shaped by hammering or rolling.

Wrought iron was once used in making many products now typically made from steel. Today, manufacturers produce only small amounts of wrought iron. Most wrought iron is made into porch railings, gates, fences, and other decorative items.

Carbon steel is the most widely used steel. The properties of carbon steel depend primarily on how much carbon it contains. Most carbon steel has a carbon content of less than 1 percent. Carbon steel can be cast, rolled, or hammered into useful shapes. It is made into a wide range of products, including structural beams, automobile bodies, kitchen appliances, and cans.

Alloy steel contains some carbon, but its properties result chiefly from the addition of other chemical elements. These elements improve one or more of the steel's properties. For example, manganese increases strength and toughness. Nickel provides greater toughness, especially in steels used at extremely low temperatures. Molybdenum increases hardness and resistance to corrosion. Other elements frequently used in alloy steels include chromium, titanium, tungsten, and vanadium. Many alloy steels contain more than one alloying element in addition to carbon.

Stainless steel resists corrosion better than any other type of steel. Chromium is its chief alloying element. Most stainless steel contains between 12 and 18 percent chromium. Many stainless steels also contain nickel. Such household items as knives, flatware, and pots and pans are made of stainless steel. Various kinds of stainless steel are used in a large number of products, including automobile parts, hospital equipment, and razor blades. Equipment made from stainless steel is widely used in the dairy, food, and chemical industries.

Tool steel is an extremely hard, wear- and heat-resistant steel used to make metalworking tools. Tool steels are produced by heat-treating certain types of high-carbon alloy steel. Most tool steels contain mixtures of chromium, manganese, molybdenum, nickel, tungsten, and vanadium. In the heat-treating process, steel is heated to a high temperature and then cooled quickly.

Sources of iron ore

The term *iron ore* commonly refers to any rock or mineral that contains enough iron to make it possibly worth mining. The location and characteristics of an ore deposit may at first make it undesirable as a source of iron. However, developments in transportation, mining techniques, or mineral processing may later make a deposit commercially valuable. Changes in demand for iron, or changes in government policies or world trade, can lead to the opening or closing of ore mines.

The supply of iron ore in the world remains plentiful even though the steel industry continually uses huge amounts of it. In some countries, much of the richest ore has been used up. As a result, steel companies must use lower-grade ores. They may also import ore from other countries. The leading iron ore mining countries, in order of production, are China, Brazil, Australia, Russia, and India. Most of China's iron ore comes from large, low-grade deposits in the northeastern provinces. Brazil has large deposits of rich ores that contain up to 65 percent iron. The state of Minas Gerais has most of Brazil's ore. Most of Australia's iron ore deposits occur in Western Australia. Other nations that have large deposits of iron ore include Kazakhstan and Ukraine.

The most important iron ore deposits in North America lie near Lake Superior. The Mesabi Range in Minnesota has produced more ore than any other area in the United States. Alabama, California, Michigan, Missouri, and Wyoming also have major deposits. Canada's chief deposits lie along the border between Quebec and Labrador and north of Lake Superior in Ontario.

Kinds of iron ore. In nature, iron always occurs in chemical combination with other elements, especially oxygen, carbon, sulfur, and silicon. Iron ores thus contain chemical compounds made up of iron and one or more other elements. The principal ores from which iron is obtained include hematite, magnetite, limonite, pyrite, siderite, and taconite.

Hematite and magnetite are the richest iron ores. They are *iron oxides* containing about 70 percent iron and 30 percent oxygen. Hematite is typically steel-gray, dull red, or bright red in color. Magnetite is dark gray to black and has magnetic properties that make it easy to locate and to concentrate.

Limonite has an iron content of about 60 percent. It is yellow-brown to black in color, and it consists of iron oxide and water.

Pyrite is about half iron and half sulfur. It is pale yellow to brassy-yellow in color and is sometimes mistaken for gold.

Siderite contains about 50 percent iron, plus carbon and oxygen. It occurs in a wide range of colors, including white, yellow, brown, greenish-gray, and gray. In the past, it served as an important source of iron in the United Kingdom and Germany. However, those two nations have exhausted their siderite deposits.

Taconite is a low-grade ore that serves as a chief source of iron in North America. It may be either magnetic or nonmagnetic. Magnetic taconite is a hard, fine-grained rock. The magnetic taconite mined today typically contains 17 to 35 percent iron in the form of magnetite and 40 to 55 percent silica. Nonmagnetic taconite contains iron in the form of limonite or hematite. Taconite is typically gray in color.

Iron ore deposits. The world's largest deposits of iron ores were formed by a geological process that began more than 2 billion years ago. This process began in Earth's shallow seas. Iron compounds in the water gradually settled to the bottom of the seas. There, together with sand and silt, they formed rock. Earthquakes and the movements of Earth's crust later raised this rock above the level of the water. In some areas, rich concentrations of ore were left behind as water trickled through the rock, interacting with and breaking down some of the other minerals in the rock.

Other iron ore deposits formed in different ways. For example, the slow cooling of *molten* (melted) volcanic rock produced iron ore deposits in Sweden and some other areas. Elsewhere, tiny organisms in the water caused iron oxide to form. Today, iron oxides accumulate in marshy areas and on beaches.

Mining and processing iron ore

There are two basic methods of mining iron ore, *open-pit mining* and *underground mining*. After the ore has been removed from the earth, it must be processed to make it suitable for use in making iron.

Open-pit mining is used to dig out deposits of iron ore that lie near the surface. First, bulldozers and other earthmoving equipment remove the soil and rocks that cover the deposits. This material is called the *overburden*. Next, miners use explosives to break up the mass of ore. Power shovels then scoop the ore into trucks and railroad cars for delivery to a central processing station.

Most of the world's iron ore comes from open-pit mines. The largest of these mines extend over several square miles or square kilometers and may measure more than 500 feet (150 meters) deep.

Underground mining, also known as *shaft mining*, involves digging tunnels into an ore deposit. Miners then go into the tunnels to remove the ore. To mine iron ore far below the surface, they dig a shaft into the rock next to the deposit. From this shaft, the miners drill horizontal tunnels into the ore at various levels. Conveyor belts or special railroad cars transport the ore to the shaft, where it is hoisted to the surface in buckets.

Underground mining is much more expensive and hazardous than open-pit mining. Today, this method is rarely used except to mine extremely high-grade ores.

Processing. Ores with a high iron content may need only to be crushed, screened, and washed to remove particles too small for use. However, most iron-making nations rely heavily on taconite and other ores that require extensive processing. These ores must be broken

Leading iron ore mining countries

Usable iron ore produced in a year

China	⬤⬤⬤⬤⬤⬤⬤⬤⬤⬤⬤⬤ 242,508,000 tons (220,000,000 metric tons)
Brazil	⬤⬤⬤⬤⬤⬤⬤⬤⬤⬤⬤◖ 231,485,000 tons (210,000,000 metric tons)
Australia	⬤⬤⬤⬤⬤⬤⬤⬤⬤⬤ 200,128,000 tons (181,553,000 metric tons)
Russia	⬤⬤⬤⬤◖ 90,941,000 tons (82,500,000 metric tons)
India	⬤⬤⬤⬤◖ 87,303,000 tons (79,200,000 metric tons)
Ukraine	⬤⬤⬤ 60,241,000 tons (54,650,000 metric tons)
United States	⬤⬤◖ 50,918,000 tons (46,192,000 metric tons)
South Africa	⬤⬤ 38,313,000 tons (34,757,000 metric tons)
Canada	⬤◖ 29,894,000 tons (27,119,000 metric tons)
Sweden	⬤ 21,480,000 tons (19,486,000 metric tons)

Figures are for 2001.
Source: U.S. Geological Survey.

Leading iron ore mining states and provinces

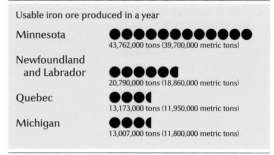

Usable iron ore produced in a year

Minnesota	⬤⬤⬤⬤⬤⬤⬤⬤⬤⬤ 43,762,000 tons (39,700,000 metric tons)
Newfoundland and Labrador	⬤⬤⬤⬤◖ 20,790,000 tons (18,860,000 metric tons)
Quebec	⬤⬤⬤◖ 13,173,000 tons (11,950,000 metric tons)
Michigan	⬤⬤⬤◖ 13,007,000 tons (11,800,000 metric tons)

Figures are for 2002.
Sources: U.S. Geological Survey; Statistics Canada.

apart so that the particles of ore can be separated from the sand and rock. The rich ore is called *concentrate,* and the waste materials are referred to as *tailings*.

Chunks of taconite are crushed to fine powder by tumbling them with steel rods or balls in large, rotating barrels. Powerful magnets then remove particles of magnetite from the powder. If the taconite contains nonmagnetic hematite, the hematite can be converted to magnetite by roasting the ore in a furnace without oxygen. Or workers can mix the crushed taconite with a dense *slurry* (soupy mixture) of water holding finely ground particles of an alloy of iron and silicon. The waste particles remain suspended in the slurry. But the particles that contain iron are denser and so settle to the bottom. This concentrated iron oxide is then removed and dried.

Iron oxide produced from taconite must be converted into a form suitable for shipping and for use in making iron. In the most widely used process, the concentrate is mixed with a little moist clay, which binds the concentrate so that it can be formed into pellets. The pellets, which measure $\frac{1}{2}$ inch to 1 inch (1.25 to 2.5 centimeters) in diameter, are dried and baked to a hard finish.

Taconite produces about 2 tons (1.8 metric tons) of tailings for every 1 ton (0.9 metric ton) of iron-oxide pellets. Therefore, iron ore is processed near the mine to save the cost of transporting huge quantities of waste.

How iron is made

To convert iron oxide into metallic iron, ironmakers must remove the oxygen from the ore. This process requires heat and a *reducing agent,* a substance that chemically combines with the oxygen that is released.

Iron is made either in a blast furnace or by a method called *direct reduction*. In a blast furnace, iron ore is combined with a reducing agent at high temperatures to produce liquid iron. In direct reduction, the temperature remains below the melting point of iron.

The blast furnace process. A blast furnace is a huge cylinder made of steel and lined with *firebrick* (heat-resistant brick). Some blast furnaces stand more than 100 feet (30 meters) tall and measure over 30 feet (9 meters) wide at the base. Structures for loading raw materials and recovering waste gases are on top. Blast furnaces operate continuously until their brick lining wears out. A furnace typically functions for 5 to 10 years before it must be rebuilt.

© G. Lucas, Stone/Getty Images

Open-pit mines, such as this one in southern Ontario in Canada, produce most of the world's iron ore. Open-pit mining is used to mine deposits of ore that lie near the surface.

The term *blast furnace* comes from the blast of hot air that is constantly forced into the lower part of the furnace. This air is heated by two or more giant stoves that can be as tall as the furnace itself. The air is blown through a stove into the furnace. The production of molten iron in a blast furnace generates waste gases that are, in turn, used to fire the stoves. These gases are often mixed with natural gas for the firing. The blast of hot air enters the furnace through pipes called *tuyères* at between 1600 and 2300 °F (870 and 1260 °C).

While air is blown through one stove, the other stove or stoves are being heated.

In addition to iron ore, *coke* and limestone are raw materials used for making iron in a blast furnace. Coke is a hard substance that consists of about 90 percent carbon. It is made by heating coal in airtight ovens. Heat drives out gases and tar from the coal, and coke remains. Limestone helps remove impurities from iron ore. Many of these impurities do not usually melt at temperatures as low as the melting point of iron. But

Hanna Mining Company

Rod and ball mills are used in processing *taconite,* a low-grade iron ore. Steel rods or balls in rotating barrels crush the taconite into powder, from which particles of iron oxide can be removed.

Hanna Mining Company

Rotating drums roll a mixture of iron oxide particles and moist clay into balls. The balls are dried and hardened into pellets rich in iron, which are shipped to steel mills to be made into steel.

limestone, when mixed with iron ore, acts as a *flux*—that is, it combines with impurities in the ore and causes them to melt at lower temperatures.

The iron ore, coke, and limestone together are called the *charge.* Open cars carry the charge to the blast furnace up a ramp called a *skip hoist.* At the bottom of the ramp, each skip car is filled with a carefully weighed load of the charge. At the top of the ramp, the skip car dumps its load into the furnace. Many modern plants use a continuous conveyor belt rather than a skip hoist to load the furnace.

As the materials in the charge drop into the furnace, they contact the blast of hot air. The hot air causes the coke to burn. Oxygen in the air combines rapidly with the coke to produce carbon monoxide gas. This gas serves as the agent, removing oxygen from the ore and chemically combining with it to form carbon dioxide. The burning of coke also produces intense heat, which melts the iron. Temperatures rise above 3000 °F (1600 °C) at the bottom of the furnace. In this area, called the *hearth* or *crucible,* the molten iron forms a pool 4 to 5 feet (1.2 to 1.5 meters) deep. Impurities referred to as *slag* float to the top of this pool.

Waste gases rise to the top of the furnace. Devices called *gas scrubbers* use water to clean these gases of dust and other impurities. The gases are then burned as fuel in the stoves that heat air for the furnace.

Molten iron is typically tapped from a furnace every 3 to 5 hours. Workers burn out a plug called the *iron*

notch, and a white-hot stream of iron rushes through the hole. The iron flows into a hot-metal car, which can hold more than 150 tons (135 metric tons) of iron.

Traditionally, slag was tapped once or twice between each tapping of iron. Workers removed it through a *slag notch* located above the level of the iron. The slag flowed into a *slag ladle* mounted on a railroad car. At many blast furnaces, slag is now removed through the same notch through which the iron is tapped. Manufacturers use slag in making portland cement, as a material called *aggregate* to be mixed into concrete, and as ballast to make the beds for railroad tracks.

The direct reduction process converts the iron oxide in ore into *direct-reduced iron.* There are several methods of direct reduction. The main methods all use gases obtained from natural gas as agents. Each of these processes combines iron ore and reducing gases in a large furnace. Other methods use coal as the reducing agent. Direct reduction is a major method of producing iron in India, Iran, Mexico, Venezuela, and several other nations.

Furnaces used in direct reduction can be built much more quickly and cheaply than blast furnaces and coke ovens. Because it does not use coke ovens, direct reduction causes much less air pollution than blast furnaces do. But metallic impurities in iron ore are not removed in a direct reduction furnace as they are—by the formation of slag—in a blast furnace. Therefore, the

How a blast furnace operates   Iron is made in a blast furnace by means of chemical reactions among iron ore, coke, limestone, and a blast of heated air. Cars carry the *charge* (solid materials) up a ramp and dump them into the furnace. Air is heated in giant stoves and blown into the lower part of the furnace. Liquid iron also settles to the bottom of the furnace and is tapped into a *hot-metal car.* The limestone combines with impurities and forms *slag* (waste), which flows into a *slag ladle.*

WORLD BOOK illustration by Oxford Illustrators Limited

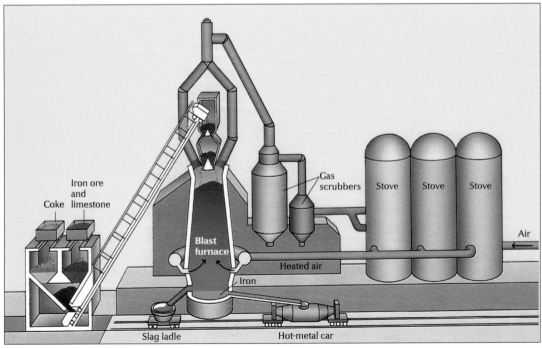

solid iron produced in a direct reduction system must be further processed before being made into steel.

Making iron products

More than 90 percent of the iron produced in blast furnaces and nearly all direct-reduced iron is used in making steel. The rest is cast into pigs and shipped to plants called *foundries,* which produce cast iron and wrought iron.

Casting iron pigs. A pig-casting machine has two conveyor belts that carry shallow molds. Workers pour molten iron from a ladle or hot-metal car into a channel that divides and flows into the molds. Water cools the iron in the molds. By the time the molds reach the end of the conveyor belt, the iron has hardened into pigs that weigh about 40 pounds (18 kilograms) each.

Making cast iron products. At a foundry, workers melt pig iron in a furnace called a *cupola* and then process it into various types of cast iron. The iron is cast in molds to manufacture such products as pipe, automobile engine blocks, and fire hydrants.

Making wrought iron products. To produce wrought iron, workers melt high-quality pig iron and remove most of its impurities. They pour the molten iron over a glassy mass of silicate slag. The iron and silicate form spongelike balls. These balls are placed in presses that squeeze out the excess slag and form blocks of wrought iron called *blooms.* The processes used to shape wrought-iron blooms into various products are the same as those used with steel blooms. For a description of these processes, see the *Shaping and finishing steel* section of this article.

How steel is made

Most steel is produced from molten pig iron and scrap iron or steel. Steelmakers recycle steel scrap from rolling or casting mills along with scrap recovered from recycled steel cans and junked automobiles. Steelmaking primarily involves the removal of excess carbon and other unwanted substances from these materials and the addition of other desired materials in carefully controlled amounts.

There are three chief methods of making steel: (1) the basic oxygen process, (2) the electric furnace process, and (3) the open-hearth process. In each of these processes, the materials making up the charge are placed in a furnace, where the necessary reactions are carried out to produce a batch of refined steel. The rate of steel production varies greatly among the three processes. A basic oxygen furnace produces a batch of steel in about 45 minutes. An electric furnace does the job in about four hours, and an open-hearth furnace takes about eight hours. Steelmaking furnaces range in capacity from less than 50 tons (45 metric tons) to more than 500 tons (450 metric tons).

The basic oxygen process (BOP) produces steel by blowing oxygen at high pressure into molten iron and scrap. This method was commercially developed in Austria in 1952 and has since grown in importance throughout the world. Today, about 60 percent of the world's steel is produced by the basic oxygen process.

A basic oxygen furnace, usually called a *BOF,* is a pear-shaped steel vessel with an open top and heat-resistant lining. The furnace is mounted on pivots so it

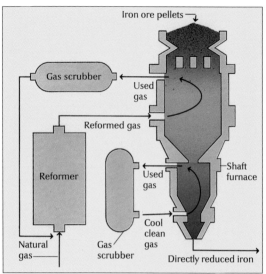

WORLD BOOK illustration by Oxford Illustrators Limited

Direct reduction produces solid iron. In the system shown here, the *reformer* converts natural gas into hydrogen and carbon monoxide. These gases remove oxygen from the hot ore in the furnace, converting the ore into metallic iron. Cool gas circulates through the lower part of the furnace and cools the iron.

can be tilted for charging and emptying. Basic oxygen furnaces are usually operated in pairs. While one produces steel, the other is being charged.

The usual charge in a BOF consists of molten iron combined with 20 to 35 percent scrap steel. The molten iron is typically about 4 percent carbon, and it contains smaller amounts of silicon and other impurities. After tilting the furnace and adding cold scrap, workers pour in the molten iron and return the furnace to its upright position. Then they lower an oxygen *lance* (pipe) into the furnace to blow pure oxygen onto the charge. Typically, a blast of 22,500 to 31,500 cubic feet (640 to 900 cubic meters) of oxygen per minute is blown at supersonic speed into the metal. The oxygen penetrates into the charge and reacts rapidly with the carbon, silicon, and other impurities. These reactions generate the heat necessary for melting the scrap while also bringing about the refining process. Fluxes are then added, and a slag soon forms. A hood on top of the furnace traps the waste gases. When steel is ready to be poured, the BOF is tilted, and the molten steel flows out through a tap hole near its top. The steel flows into a ladle, to which workers can add alloying materials.

During the 1970's, European steelmakers developed a process called Q-BOP. In this process, oxygen is blown into the charge at the bottom of the furnace. Powdered fluxes are blown in along with the oxygen. The *Q* stands for the German word *Quell,* which means *fountain* and refers to the manner in which the oxygen enters the charge. A Q-BOP unit stirs the charge vigorously, and it can melt larger chunks of scrap. Today, many oxygen furnaces combine top and bottom blowing.

Both BOP and Q-BOP produce steel at relatively low cost, largely because they require no additional fuel to create heat. The two processes also produce steel rapidly. In addition, steel produced by these methods is low in nitrogen. Nitrogen reduces the toughness of certain kinds of steel. However, BOP and Q-BOP do not permit as much precision as other processes do in the control of the chemical composition of steel. They also can use only a limited amount of scrap.

The electric furnace process uses strong electric currents to produce the heat needed to make steel. The *electric arc furnace* is the most widely used type of electric furnace. Other types of electric furnaces melt steel by using an *oscillating* (vibrating) magnetic field to induce current in the steel. This field is created in a coil that encircles the part of the furnace that holds the charge. Electric furnaces account for 35 percent of the world's total steel production.

An electric arc furnace consists of a shallow steel cylinder lined with firebrick. The roof has holes through which up to three graphite or carbon rods called *electrodes* are inserted. A powerful electric current *arcs* (jumps) from one electrode to the charge material and then to another electrode. This arcing produces intense heat, which melts the charge. Electric arc furnaces that use direct current (DC) power sources have a single rod inserted through the cylinder's roof. The arc passes

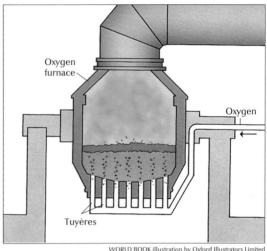

WORLD BOOK illustration by Oxford Illustrators Limited

Q-BOP is a version of the basic oxygen process. A Q-BOP furnace has no overhead oxygen lance. Instead, the oxygen is blown in through *tuyères* (pipes) at the bottom of the furnace. Q-BOP makes steel faster than the basic oxygen process.

Making steel by the basic oxygen process

In the basic oxygen process, steel is produced by blowing oxygen at high pressure into molten iron and scrap. The oxygen combines with carbon and other impurities, converting the charge into steel. Reactions between oxygen and the charge produce the heat used in the refining process.

WORLD BOOK illustrations by Oxford Illustrators Limited

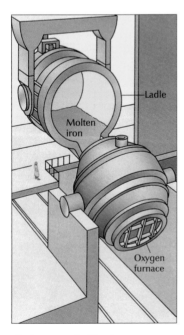

The furnace is tilted for charging. Workers dump in scrap steel and add a ladle of molten iron. Then they return the furnace to its upright position.

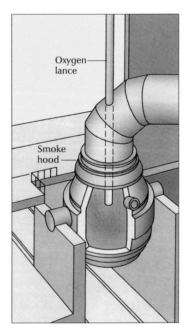

Oxygen is blown into the charge through a *lance* (pipe) lowered into the furnace. A smoke hood on top of the furnace captures waste gases.

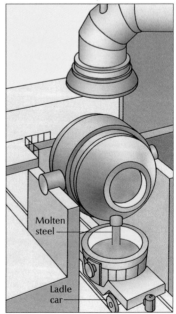

When refining is complete, the smoke hood and oxygen lance are removed. The furnace is then tilted to pour out the steel through the taphole into a ladle.

Iron and steel 291

Making steel by the electric furnace process

These diagrams show steel being made in an electric arc furnace, the most widely used type of electric steelmaking furnace. The roof of an electric arc furnace has holes through which three carbon rods called *electrodes* are inserted to conduct electric current to the charge.

WORLD BOOK illustrations by Oxford Illustrators Limited

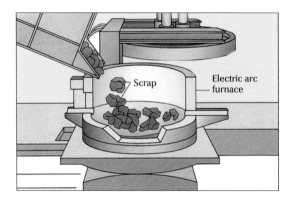

The furnace, with its roof swung aside, is charged with scrap. Steelmakers rarely use pig iron in an electric arc furnace but may use directly reduced iron if it is available at low cost.

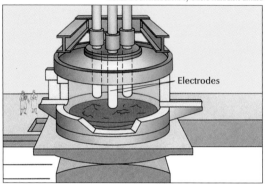

A powerful electric current *arcs* (jumps) between the electrodes and the charge. This action produces intense heat, which melts the charge and promotes chemical reactions that produce steel.

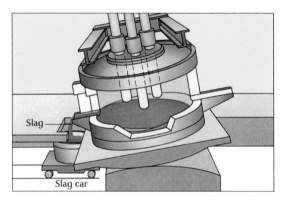

Workers turn off the power to the electrodes at the end of the refining process. Then they tilt the furnace, which is mounted on rockers, to pour out the slag.

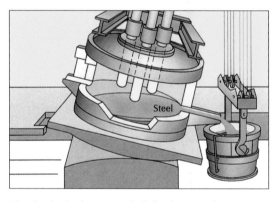

After the slag has been poured off, the electric arc furnace is tilted in the opposite direction. The liquid steel rushes out through the taphole and is collected in a ladle.

from that electrode through the charge to an electrode in the bottom of the furnace.

The charge in an electric arc furnace consists mostly of scrap steel and alloy materials. Steelmakers rarely use molten pig iron in this type of furnace. But they sometimes use pellets of direct-reduced iron in the charge. The furnace roof is raised and swung to one side so the charge can be dumped in. After the charge has melted, fluxes and additional alloying material are added through a charging door on the side. The furnace stands on rockers and so can be tilted to pour off the slag through the charging door. Later, it is tipped in the opposite direction to pour out the molten steel through the tap hole.

Electric arc furnaces are used in minimills. Their advantages over other furnaces include efficient operation, economical construction, and low emissions of pollutants into the air. Electric arc furnaces are ideal for making alloy steels and tool steels. These steels require the addition of alloying elements that readily combine with oxygen. Such elements, which include chromium

and vanadium, would be oxidized rapidly in an open-hearth or basic oxygen furnace and thus lost in the slag. The steel and slag in an electric arc furnace contain so little oxygen that alloying elements are not oxidized.

The open-hearth process got its name because the hearth of the furnace is open directly to the flames that melt the charge. The furnace has a lining of firebrick, and a low, arched roof covers the hearth. A typical open-hearth furnace measures about 90 feet (27 meters) long and about 30 feet (9 meters) wide. Most open-hearth plants have several furnaces end to end in one long building. Workers use heavy-duty cranes and special charging machines to fill the furnaces through doors on one side and tap the steel on the opposite side. The floor on the loading side is higher than that on the tapping side.

Each end of an open-hearth furnace has a fuel burner and a *checker chamber*. This chamber contains firebricks arranged in an open, checkered pattern that provides many passages through which air and waste gases can flow. While the burner at one end of the furnace sends flames onto the hearth, the hot exhaust gases are drawn through the checker chamber at the other end. These hot gases heat the chamber, then eventually exit out the smokestack. The furnace automatically switches burners about every 15 minutes, reversing the flow of gases through it. Thus, the air on its way to the hearth is preheated by passing through the hot checker chamber. Many open-hearth furnaces also have an oxygen lance in the roof. Pure oxygen is forced through this pipe into the furnace to speed the melting process.

Open-hearth furnaces can combine molten pig iron and cold scrap in widely varying proportions, but most steelmakers use about equal amounts of each. First, a charging machine dumps limestone and scrap steel into the furnace. After these materials have melted, molten iron is poured into the furnace. As the heating continues, most of the carbon from the iron is driven off in the form of carbon monoxide gas. Other impurities are oxidized and become part of the slag. Workers take a sample of the molten steel and may add materials to obtain the desired composition.

To tap the steel, workers blow out the tap-plug with a small explosive. The steel flows into a large ladle. Workers may then add alloying materials or substances to remove oxygen from the steel. When the slag appears, it overflows from the ladle into a smaller container called a *slag thimble.*

The open-hearth process can use gas, oil, or even powdered coal as fuels, but it makes steel much more slowly than other methods do. It also produces large volumes of polluting waste gases. For these reasons, use of the open-hearth method has declined steadily since 1950, when it was the chief steelmaking process. Today, only India, Russia, and Ukraine make significant amounts of open-hearth steel.

Special refining processes. Steel tapped from a furnace may require additional refining and alloying. Such special processes are necessary to produce the highest grades of steel, such as that used in the manufacture of jet airplanes. Steelmakers may put molten steel into a vacuum chamber to remove hydrogen, oxygen, and other gases. They may mix the molten steel by bubbling argon gas through it to distribute alloy elements, make the temperature uniform, or make it easier to remove tiny particles of sulfur or other contaminants. Steelmakers may also add additional alloying elements in precise quantities.

Shaping and finishing steel

Liquid steel must be cast into a solid form before it can be made into useful objects. Steelmakers cast most steel by means of *continuous casting* or *ingot casting.* These processes result in solid steel that must be further formed by *rolling, forging, extruding,* or other processes.

Making steel by the open-hearth process   In an open-hearth furnace, the charge is melted by flames from fuel burners. A charging machine dumps limestone and scrap into the furnace. Oxygen is forced in through a lance in the roof to increase the temperature and thus speed the melting. Workers add molten iron, and continued heating converts the charge into steel. Air used in the furnace is preheated by passing it through hot *checker chambers.* The steel is tapped into a ladle below the level of the furnace.

WORLD BOOK illustration by Oxford Illustrators Limited

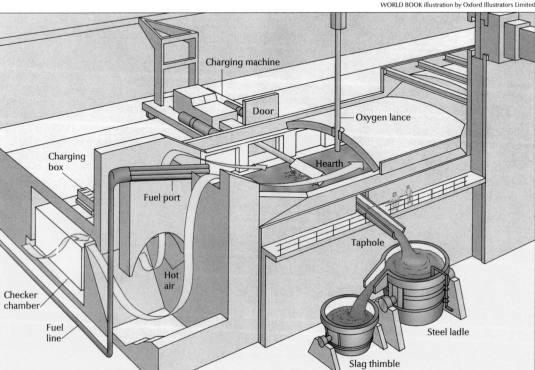

Charging machine

Door

Oxygen lance

Charging box

Hearth

Fuel port

Taphole

Hot air

Checker chamber

Fuel line

Steel ladle

Slag thimble

In *mold casting,* a small amount of steel is cast in a mold that gives it the shape of a finished product. Some types of steel receive a special finish or coating.

Continuous casting, sometimes called *strand casting,* produces *blooms, slabs,* or *billets*—three semifinished forms of steel—directly from molten steel. Blooms have a square cross section, and slabs are rectangular in cross section. Billets are square like blooms, but they have a smaller cross section. Most billets are much longer than blooms.

In continuous casting, workers pour liquid steel from a ladle into a *tundish* (flow control dish) at the top of the machine. The steel flows at a controlled rate from the tundish through a mold that forms the metal into the desired shape. Cold water quickly cools the steel, causing it to solidify even as it continues to move through the caster. As the steel leaves the caster, cutting torches or mechanical shears cut it into desired lengths.

Beginning in the 1960's, steelmakers in Japan and Western Europe rapidly adopted continuous casting. Today, it accounts for more than 85 percent of raw steel production worldwide. In many countries, including the United States, it accounts for 95 percent or more.

Ingot casting is the casting of steel into blocks called *ingots.* Steel ingots vary widely in size, depending on the type of steel and the kind of product to be made. For example, ingots of tool steel may weigh only a few hundred pounds or kilograms. In contrast, huge ingots weighing up to 300 tons (270 metric tons) are made into parts for enormous industrial machines. Most ingots weigh between 2 and 40 tons (1.8 and 36 metric tons).

To cast ingots, workers pour liquid steel from a ladle into molds made of cast iron. Most of these molds have a tapered, rectangular shape. The molds are placed on special railroad cars, and steel is poured into them from above. After the steel hardens, which may take up to three hours, the mold is lifted off by giant tongs that grip it by handles on the sides. Iron contracts as it cools, and the outside of an ingot cools faster than its center. As a result, a funnel-shaped depression called a *pipe* forms in the top of an ingot. The portion of the ingot that contains the pipe—as much as 20 percent by weight—is removed and remelted as scrap.

Ingots are then placed in a furnace called a *soaking pit,* where they are heated to a temperature of about 2200 °F (1200 °C). The heated ingots travel to a *roughing mill,* a machine that squeezes them between heavy rollers to form billets, blooms, or slabs.

Since the 1960's, most steelmakers have switched from ingot casting to continuous casting. The processes of casting, heating, and rolling ingots are more costly and time-consuming than continuous casting methods. Continuous casting avoids inconsistencies that result from the slow cooling of ingots. It also generates less scrap than ingot casting produces.

Rolling is the most commonly used method of shaping steel products. In this process, billets, blooms, or slabs pass between heavy rollers that squeeze them into the desired size and shape. The major products made by rolling include (1) sheet and strip, (2) bars, (3) railroad rails and structural beams, and (4) plates.

Sheet and strip are flat products, generally less than $\frac{1}{4}$ inch (6.4 millimeters) thick. Strip is much narrower than sheet, which may be up to 100 inches (250 centimeters) wide. Sheet and strip are the main products of the steel industry.

Steelmakers produce most sheet and strip in the form of large coils that the user can cut into pieces of any desired length. However, some sheet and strip is cut into specified lengths at the plant. A great deal of sheet and strip is used in automobile bodies, but thousands of other products also contain these forms of steel.

Machines called *hot-rolling mills* produce sheet and strip from slabs and billets. The process is known as *hot rolling* because the steel is reheated to about 2200 °F (1200 °C) before being rolled. A hot-rolling mill has many sets of rollers called *roll stands* arranged in a long line. In each roll stand, the rollers are closer together than in the preceding stand. As a result, the steel is squeezed thinner and thinner as it travels through the mill. As the thickness decreases, the length increases.

A hot-rolling mill can convert a slab 5 inches (13 centimeters) thick and 8 feet (2.4 meters) long into a sheet $\frac{1}{16}$ inch (1.6 millimeters) thick and 1,400 feet (430 meters) long. The process takes only a few minutes. A hot-rolling mill may be housed in a building up to 1 mile (1.6 kilometers) long. This great length is necessary because of the large number of roll stands and the

Casting steel ingots Steelmakers cast molten steel into blocks called *ingots* by pouring it from a ladle into molds made of cast iron, *left.* After the steel hardens, giant tongs remove the molds. The ingots are then put into a *soaking pit, right,* where they are heated to about 2200 °F (1200 °C).

WORLD BOOK illustrations by Oxford Illustrators Limited

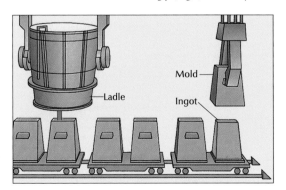

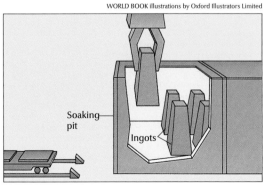

How steel is shaped and finished

Steelmakers use a wide variety of shaping and finishing processes. These diagrams show two processes that produce semifinished forms of steel called *blooms, billets,* and *slabs;* four methods of shaping these forms into steel products; and a technique used to coat steel products.

WORLD BOOK illustrations by Oxford Illustrators Limited

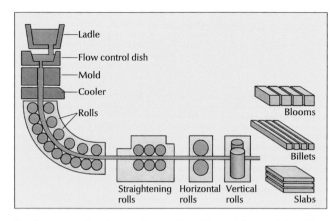

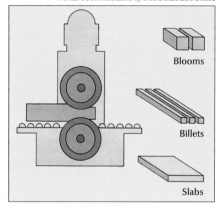

Continuous casting shapes molten steel into blooms, billets, and slabs. The steel flows through a specially shaped mold. Cold water quickly cools the steel, causing it to harden as it moves through the rolls of the caster.

A roughing mill converts heated ingots of steel into blooms, billets, and slabs by squeezing the ingots between heavy rollers.

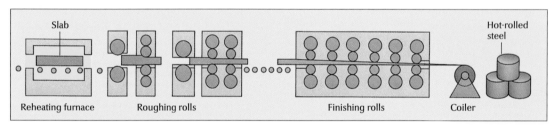

Hot rolling produces sheets of steel. In a *hot-rolling mill,* the roughing rolls reduce the thickness of a reheated slab. Then the finishing rolls squeeze the steel into extremely thin sheets. As the steel comes out of the finishing rolls, it is wound into large coils.

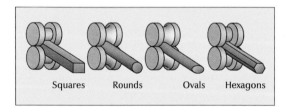

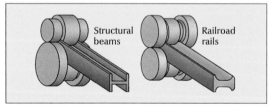

Rolling of steel bars takes place in a *bar mill,* which resembles a hot-rolling mill. A bar mill has rolls that are grooved to roll hot billets into square, round, oval, or hexagonal bars.

Rolling of railroad rails and structural beams is performed by mills similar to bar mills. However, steel companies manufacture most rails and beams from blooms.

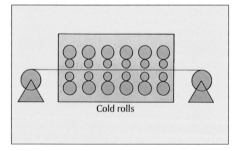

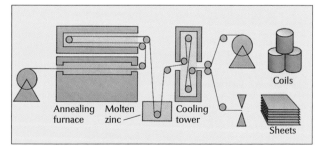

Cold rolling smooths and thins steel sheets. In a *cold-rolling mill,* steel travels at room temperature through a series of rollers and then is re-coiled.

Galvanizing involves coating steel with zinc to make it resist corrosion. The steel is *annealed* (heated and slowly cooled), passed through molten zinc, and then cooled to harden the coating.

Continuous casting is a common method of producing semifinished steel directly from molten metal. This continuous caster at a steel mill in Kimitsu, Japan, produces an unbroken slab of steel that can then be rolled to produce sheet steel or steel plate.

AP/Wide World

tremendous increase in the length of the steel. As the hot-rolled steel comes out of the last stand, it is wound into large coils.

After cooling down, the coils of steel may be shipped to customers, or they may be processed further. Much hot-rolled sheet and strip is *pickled* and then *cold-rolled.* Pickling involves passing the steel through vats of acid to remove oxide that formed on it during hot rolling. In a *cold-rolling mill,* the steel travels rapidly at room temperature through a series of roll stands and then is re-coiled. Cold rolling gives steel the ability to be stretched and shaped without cracking. It also makes steel thinner and smoother and gives it a bright finish.

Bars are made in many sizes and in such shapes as round, square, oval, and hexagonal. They are hot rolled by *bar mills,* which resemble the machines used for sheet and strip. However, a bar mill has grooved rolls that squeeze a hot billet into the desired shape. Many bars receive further processing after being hot rolled. They can be pulled at room temperature through an opening in a tool called a *die.* This process strengthens the steel and gives it a bright, smooth finish. Products made from steel bars include hand tools and auto parts.

Railroad rails and structural beams are hot-rolled into long lengths in the same way as bars. Steelmakers produce diverse structural shapes, such as I-beams, angles, tees, zees, and channels. Most railroad rails and structural beams are made from blooms.

Plates are flat and measure more than $\frac{1}{4}$ inch (6.4 millimeters) thick. They are used in the construction of ships and bridges and in many kinds of industrial and scientific equipment. Steel plants roll most plates from slabs, but some come directly from ingots. Machines called *reversing mills* produce the majority of plates. The heated steel passes back and forth between the rollers of a single roll stand. The distance between the rolls decreases with each pass until the steel reaches the desired thickness. Some plates are made by continuous rolling mills like those that produce sheet and strip.

Forging is a process in which steel manufacturers heat ingots or billets and hammer or press them into the desired shape. Many products that must withstand great stress are made by forging. This process changes the internal structure of steel to give it the greatest strength

where needed. The largest forging presses shape huge ingots of steel weighing several hundred tons.

Extruding involves forcing heated steel through an opening in a die. A ram at one end of a cylinder pushes the steel through a die at the other end. Molten glass serves as a lubricant to help the hot steel slip through the die. The steel comes out shaped like the die opening. Steel firms use extrusion to make seamless tubing and products of complicated shapes.

Other shaping processes are used in making a variety of small steel products. Automatic machines stamp, hammer, and press steel into such products as bolts, nails, screws, and tools. Wire is made by drawing steel rods through a series of successively smaller dies.

Finishing. Many types of steel receive a special finish or coating. For example, some stainless steel goes through special grinding and polishing. The most important coating processes include (1) galvanizing and (2) electroplating.

Galvanizing is the process of coating steel with a thin layer of zinc. The zinc coating makes the steel highly resistant to corrosion. Galvanized steel sheet is made into such products as heating ducts and storage tanks. The most widely used method of galvanizing, called *hot-dip galvanizing,* starts with coils of steel sheet. The steel is *annealed* (heated and then cooled slowly) to make it more flexible. Next, rollers carry the steel into a pot of molten zinc. The steel then travels through a cooling tower, where the zinc coating hardens. The finished product is wound into coils or cut into sheets.

Electroplating coats steel with another metal by means of electric current. Steel companies use this process in producing tin-plated steel, which is made into tin cans. Steel is electroplated with chromium to make *tin-free steel.* This metal can be used instead of tin-plated steel to produce cans and other containers.

The steel industry

Steelmaking ranks among the world's most important industries. Steel products play an essential role in almost all major economic activities, including manufacturing, mining, construction, transportation, and agriculture. In addition, military forces depend on steel for tanks, ships, and aircraft components. China produces

Leading steel-producing countries

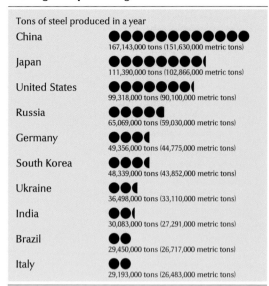

Tons of steel produced in a year

China
167,143,000 tons (151,630,000 metric tons)

Japan
111,390,000 tons (102,866,000 metric tons)

United States
99,318,000 tons (90,100,000 metric tons)

Russia
65,069,000 tons (59,030,000 metric tons)

Germany
49,356,000 tons (44,775,000 metric tons)

South Korea
48,339,000 tons (43,852,000 metric tons)

Ukraine
36,498,000 tons (33,110,000 metric tons)

India
30,083,000 tons (27,291,000 metric tons)

Brazil
29,450,000 tons (26,717,000 metric tons)

Italy
29,193,000 tons (26,483,000 metric tons)

Figures are for 2001.
Source: U.S. Geological Survey.

World iron and steel regions

● Steelmaking center

● Iron ore deposit

⟿ Coking coal field

WORLD BOOK map

more steel than any other nation. Japan and the United States are also leading steel producers.

In some countries, the government owns and manages the steel industry. In others, the industry consists of privately owned companies. Still other countries have a mixture of private and public ownership. Even in nations where the entire steel industry is privately owned, the government generally plays a major role in regulating it.

The manufacturing plants that make up the steel industry vary greatly in size. The largest, called *integrated steel mills,* have a full range of equipment, including coke ovens, blast furnaces, steelmaking furnaces, and rolling mills. Most of these plants produce from about 1 million to 10 million tons (900,000 to 9,000,000 metric tons) of steel annually. *Minimills* generally consist of one or more electric furnaces to melt scrap and a mill that produces bars, rods, or flat rolled steel. A minimill may produce less than 100,000 tons (90,000 metric tons) of steel in a year. However, some minimills produce well over 1 million tons (900,000 metric tons) yearly.

Few of the major steel-producing countries produce as much steel as the capacity of their plants. Actual production varies with the general level of economic activity. The demand for steel rises when there is expansion in construction and manufacturing activities. When these activities decline, so does steel production.

Modern steelmaking methods and equipment enable steel plants to operate with far fewer employees than was possible many years ago. In nearly all major steelmaking countries today, the steel industry employs less than half the people it did in 1975. Most employees are production and maintenance workers. Others have professional, administrative, sales, and clerical positions. Steelmaking also offers opportunities for chemists, engineers, *metallurgists* (experts on metals), and technicians.

In China, the steel industry has undergone astonishingly rapid growth since the 1980's. During the early 2000's, China's steel production grew by 15 to 20 percent each year. The country is the world's leading producer and consumer of steel. Its leading steelmaking company is Shanghai Baosteel Group Corporation. Other major steel companies include Anshan Iron and Steel Group Corporation and Shougang Group.

Steel produced by the basic oxygen process accounts for about 70 percent of China's total production, and electric processes account for about 15 percent. More than 90 percent of China's steel is continuously cast. China has most of the raw materials it requires to produce steel. However, its domestic iron ore and coal are of low grade. Consequently, its steel industry is a major source of air and water pollution. China imports more steel than any other country except the United States. It also imports high-grade iron ore.

In Japan, nearly all materials for steel production must be imported. The country's steel mills are among the most modern and efficient in the world. Japan exports about 25 percent of the steel it produces. Its leading steel companies are JFE Steel Corporation; Kobe Steel, Ltd.; Nippon Steel Corporation; and Sumitomo Metal Industries, Ltd.

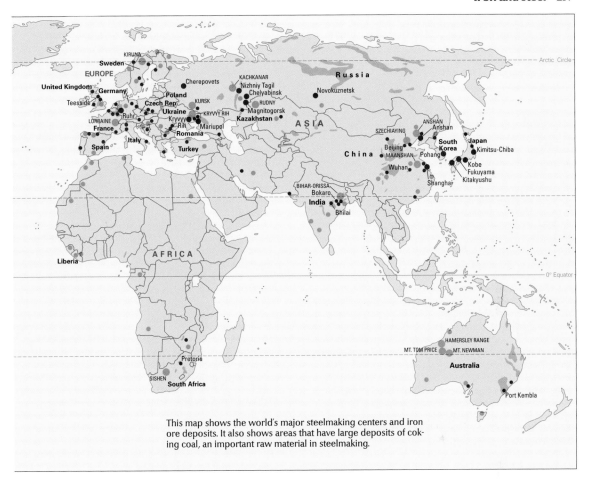

This map shows the world's major steelmaking centers and iron ore deposits. It also shows areas that have large deposits of coking coal, an important raw material in steelmaking.

In the United States, nearly all the coal used by steel companies is domestic coal. United States steel companies import about 10 percent of their iron ore, mostly from Canada and Brazil. They also import such alloying elements as chromium, cobalt, manganese, and vanadium. The United States Steel Corporation has been the country's largest steel company since its formation in 1901. It operates not only steel mills but also coal mines, iron ore mines, limestone quarries, and transportation systems. The second largest steel producer is Nucor Corporation, which operates many minimills. Minimills produce more than half of the country's steel.

Indiana is, by far, the leading steel-producing state, and Ohio ranks second in steel production. Together, these two states account for nearly 40 percent of the steel made in the United States. Other important steel-producing states include Illinois, Michigan, Pennsylvania, and Texas.

Nearly all employees in the steel industry below the level of management belong to one labor union, the United Steelworkers of America (USWA). The USWA, one of the largest labor unions in the United States, has done much to gain higher wages and better working conditions for steelworkers.

The United States government regulates the steel industry in a number of ways. It sets federal standards for emissions of pollutants from plants. The Occupational Safety and Health Administration (OSHA) establishes regulations to protect the health and safety of workers. From time to time, the U.S. government has also taken actions to control the price of steel.

In other countries. Other major steel-producing nations include Germany, India, Russia, South Korea, and Ukraine. Before about 1950, the less developed countries imported nearly all their steel from the United States and other major industrial nations. Since then, however, many developing nations have established their own steel industries. This development has been especially important in countries that have plentiful natural gas and iron ore, such as Mexico and Venezuela. These nations operate plants that produce directreduced iron and refine it into steel in electric arc furnaces. Iran and India also make substantial amounts of direct-reduced iron. Blast furnaces produce most of Brazil's iron, and the country uses basic oxygen furnaces and electric arc furnaces to make steel. South Korea's POSCO, a private company that began as a government-owned operation, is one of the world's largest steel companies. Even in nations with limited raw materials, governments have helped establish modern steel industries.

Canada's steel industry produces about 15 million tons (14 million metric tons) of steel annually. Ontario is by far the leading steel-producing province. Quebec is also an important steel producer. Stelco Inc., Canada's largest steel company, makes about a third of the nation's steel.

History

The Iron Age. Prehistoric people obtained iron from meteorites and used it to make tools, weapons, and other items. In several early languages, the word for iron meant "stone from heaven" or "star metal." People used such iron as early as 4000 B.C., but it is not clear when or where they first made iron by smelting ore.

The first people known to have large supplies of iron were the Hittites, who lived in what is now Turkey. By about 1400 B.C., they had learned to make iron weapons and tools. People in China and India also developed methods of making iron. By 1000 B.C., many of the world's civilizations knew ironmaking techniques, and the Iron Age was well underway (see **Iron Age**).

The early ironmaking furnaces were shallow, bowl-shaped hearths in which people heated iron ore and charcoal. After several hours, the ore released its oxygen to the surrounding hot carbon and formed small spongy bodies of metallic iron. But before it could be used, this iron had to be reheated and hammered repeatedly to force out the remaining hard, brittle impurities. By 1200 B.C., ironworkers could reheat, work, and cool this iron to make wrought iron, which could be hammered into useful shapes.

Ironmakers soon learned that blowing air into the furnace made the fire hotter and thus improved the quality of the iron. Later, they used a device called a *bellows* to blow air through openings into the furnace. In the A.D. 700's, ironworkers in Catalonia, in what is now northeastern Spain, developed a better type of hearth furnace, called the *Catalan forge*. A water-powered pump forced air in at the bottom of the furnace. The Catalan forge made up to 350 pounds (160 kilograms) of iron in five hours, far more than earlier furnaces could make.

Historians believe that by about the 400's B.C., the ironworkers in China had developed furnaces that could melt ore to make liquid cast iron. The ironworkers would pour this iron into molds to make various objects. The Chinese were the first ancient people to shift from making wrought iron to making mostly cast iron. In China during the Han dynasty, which ruled the country from 206 B.C. to A.D. 220, the use of cast iron became widespread. Ironmakers cast such varied products as cooking pans, weapons, plows, and many kinds of tools. They made cast iron in small furnaces, into which a bellows blew air. These furnaces were perhaps 7 feet (2.1 meters) in height. The Chinese probably began smelting with coke about the time of the Song dynasty, also called *Sung,* which ruled China from 960 to 1279. Blast furnaces, with tall brick or stone shafts up to 30 feet (9 meters) in height, appeared in China by the 1300's. About this same time, the Chinese began making cast iron firearms.

Blast furnaces developed independently in Europe. They evolved from earlier methods of smelting iron. European ironmakers built many types of shaft furnaces. A typical shaft furnace around 1350 was probably be-

tween 10 and 16 feet (3.0 and 4.9 meters) in height. Workers dumped iron ore and charcoal into the top of a brick-lined shaft, which was 3 to 4 feet (0.9 to 1.2 meters) across at its widest point. Often these furnaces produced the standard spongy masses or "blooms" of wrought iron. But if temperatures were high enough and the metallic iron absorbed enough carbon from the fuel, the furnace would instead produce carbon-rich molten cast iron.

By around 1450, ironmakers, especially those in long-standing ironmaking districts in Italy, France, and Germany, were using blast furnaces to produce sizable amounts of molten cast iron. About that time, Europeans began casting iron into cannons, pans, and many other types of new iron goods. During the 1700's, a shortage of wood forced British ironmakers to begin using coke instead of charcoal in their blast furnaces.

The English colonists brought ironmaking with them to the New World. An ironworks operated briefly on the James River in Virginia before being destroyed during an Indian raid in 1622. In 1646, the first successful North American ironworks opened in what is now Saugus, Massachusetts. It continued to produce iron until 1668. By 1775, plentiful supplies of charcoal and iron ore had enabled American blast furnaces to reach an annual output of 30,000 tons (27,000 metric tons) of cast iron. This production accounted for 15 percent of the world's annual production of cast iron

The first steel. People made small amounts of some forms of steel during the early part of the Iron Age. For example, the Haya people of eastern Africa made steel in a cone-shaped furnace driven by bellows. In southern India, as early as 300 B.C., a type of carbon steel called *wootz steel* was made by heating and melting high-grade ore with wood chips or charcoal in closed crucibles or by melting cast iron and wrought iron together. By the A.D. 500's, the Chinese were producing steel by melting bars of wrought iron with molten cast iron. Ironmaking was introduced into Japan from Korea, probably in the A.D. 300's or 400's. During the 700's, Japanese sword makers began using *Tatara steel,* which the Japanese made from iron sands. By about the 700's, Middle Eastern sword makers began to import wootz steel from India. They forged this steel into blades of fine layered steel that became known as *Damascus steel.*

Europeans used various *cementing* processes throughout the Middle Ages, which lasted from about the A.D. 400's through the 1400's. In cementing, two substances, such as iron and powdered charcoal, are heated together to produce a chemical change in one of them. The Europeans baked wrought iron bars in sealed pots with charcoal or wood chips for seven days or more. The wrought iron absorbed carbon and became a type of steel known as *cemented steel* or *converted steel.* However, such steel was scarce and expensive.

In 1740, Benjamin Huntsman, a clockmaker from Sheffield, England, invented a crucible process for steelmaking. The carbon content of cemented steel was uneven, with more carbon near the surface, where the iron came into contact with the charcoal or wood chips. Huntsman melted cemented steel in sealed clay pots called *crucibles* at high heats. Huntsman's process produced steel that was more uniform in quality and freer from impurities than any previously produced. But his method required a great deal of highly skilled labor. In addition, the largest crucibles could produce only about 100 pounds (45 kilograms) of steel. Still, steelmakers in Sheffield became world famous for their high-quality crucible steels.

The birth of modern steelmaking. During the 1850's, Henry Bessemer, a British inventor, developed the first method of making steel cheaply in large quantities. This method became known as the *Bessemer process.* An American ironmaker named William Kelly patented a similar process in the United States.

In the Bessemer process, workers took molten iron from the blast furnace and poured it into a large pear-shaped container called a *converter.* They then pumped a large blast of air into the iron through openings in the bottom of the converter. The oxygen in the air reacted rapidly with the carbon, silicon, and manganese in the molten iron. This action removed the impurities and converted the iron into steel. Robert Mushet, a British metallurgist, found that adding an iron-carbon-manganese alloy, called *spiegeleisen,* after the blowing process helped remove oxygen and adjust the steel's carbon content.

The Bessemer process was used in the United States for the first time in 1864. By 1880, the method accounted for more than 90 percent of U.S. steel production.

The open-hearth process appeared soon after the Bessemer method became widespread. In 1861, Charles William Siemens, a German-born scientist living in the United Kingdom, proposed melting steel in a gas furnace his brother Friedrich had patented several years earlier. This furnace, called a *regenerative gas furnace,* used hot waste gases to preheat the fuel and air put into it. In 1864, two French brothers, Pierre and Émile Martin, made steel in a furnace that incorporated the Siemens regenerative design. The resulting Siemens-Martin, or open-hearth, process had many advantages over the Bessemer process. Most importantly, it pro-

duced steel from scrap and allowed greater control over the chemical composition of the product. Few Bessemer plants were built after 1910, but existing ones continued to operate until the 1960's.

In 1878, William Siemens demonstrated that steel could be melted in an electric arc furnace. But at that time, electric power was limited in supply and was extremely expensive. In 1899, Paul L. T. Héroult of France, who had invented an electric process for making aluminum, opened the first steel mill equipped with electric arc furnaces.

Growth of the steel industry. After the introduction of the Bessemer and open-hearth processes, steel manufacturing expanded rapidly. Germany and the United Kingdom became the leading European steel producers.

Rich iron ore ranges opened in the Lake Superior region of the United States, and that nation's annual production of steel increased tremendously. Between 1880 and 1910, production rose from about 1,400,000 tons (1,300,000 metric tons) to more than 24 million tons (22 million metric tons). In 1875, Andrew Carnegie's Edgar Thomson Works went into operation in Braddock, Pennsylvania. This steel plant's design served as the model for many later plants. Carnegie later built or bought up a number of other steel plants.

In 1901, Carnegie sold his mills to the newly formed United States Steel Corporation. Through this purchase, U.S. Steel gained control of 60 percent of the nation's steelmaking capacity. But its share of the industry gradually declined as other major steel firms grew.

Much of the steel produced in the late 1800's was used to make rails for the railroads of the United States and Europe. During the 1900's, production continued to increase to meet the rising demand for steel for automobiles, ships, skyscrapers, and countless other products. Other developments included new processes for rolling steel and the creation of new alloys.

Most of the world's major steel industries, except that of the United States, were severely damaged during

The Bessemer process was the chief method of making steel during the late 1800's. This picture of a Bessemer plant shows workers charging molten iron into a Bessemer converter and pouring liquid steel into ingot molds.

Computer-controlled equipment performs many operations in steel plants. This worker directs steel-finishing operations from a control room at a steel mill in Sault Ste. Marie, Ontario, Canada.

© Paul A. Souders, Corbis

World War II (1939-1945). As a result, U.S. companies dominated world steel production during the postwar years. However, Japan and many European nations rebuilt their steel plants in the 1950's and 1960's. The new mills used the most modern and efficient techniques, including the basic oxygen process and continuous casting. This modernization gave the Japanese and European steel industries an advantage over the American industry, which was slow to adopt the new techniques.

The U.S. steel industry faced many difficulties during the 1980's. Competition from imported steel and declining domestic consumption reduced demand for U.S.-made steel. Many plants were forced to close. Some mills continued to operate using outdated equipment and production methods. By the 1990's, several large U.S. steel companies had modernized their facilities enough to compete effectively in the world market. Minimills sprang up, and by the early 2000's, they had surpassed integrated steel mills in total steel production. In the early 2000's, the United States imported nearly 30 percent of the steel it consumed.

Recent developments. During the late 1900's and early 2000's, steelmakers and steel processors in many countries suffered financially because of unprofitable pricing. Prices for hot-rolled coil steel, a common form of steel made and sold worldwide, fell by nearly half between 1995 and 2001. In the United States, many companies sought bankruptcy protection. During 2002 and 2003, the U.S. government imposed duties of up to 30 percent on many steel imports to help protect U.S. companies. Steelmakers in some countries responded to financial difficulties by merging to create larger companies. For example, steelmakers in France, Luxembourg, and Spain merged to form Arcelor, the world's largest steelmaker. Other companies expanded into markets outside their home countries. For example, LNM Group of the Netherlands and its London-based subsidiary Ispat International operate plants in Europe, Asia, Africa, and North America.

World steel production has continued to rise, primarily because of rapidly expanding output in the developing nations of South America and Asia. By the early 2000's, yearly steel production exceeded 1 billion tons (910 million metric tons). Thomas J. Misa

Questions

What are the main raw materials used to make iron in a blast furnace?
What determines the physical properties of a particular kind of iron or steel?
How were the world's largest deposits of iron ore formed?
What are some reasons continuous casting expanded rapidly since the 1960's?
What is the principal alloying element in stainless steel?
Which steelmaking process produces most of the world's steel?
Which state ranks as the leading steel producer in the United States?
What is pig iron? How did it get its name?
What is the most commonly used method of shaping steel products?
Where did prehistoric people obtain the iron they used to make tools and weapons?

Additional resources

Level I
Curtis, Neil, and Greenland, Peter. *How Steel Is Made.* Lerner, 1992.
Kassinger, Ruth G. *Iron and Steel: From Thor's Hammer to the Space Shuttle.* 21st Century Bks., 2003.
Martin, John H. *A Day in the Life of a High-Iron Worker.* 1985. Reprint. Troll, 1996.

Level II
Bjorhovde, Reidar, and others. *Structural Steel Selection Considerations: A Guide for Students, Educators, Designers, and Builders.* Am. Soc. of Civil Engineers, 2001.
Llewellyn, D. T., and Hudd, R. C. *Steels: Metallurgy and Applications.* 3rd ed. Butterworth, 1998.
Misa, Thomas J. *A Nation of Steel: The Making of Modern America, 1865-1925.* Johns Hopkins, 1995.
Sutherland, R. J. M., ed. *Structural Iron, 1750-1850.* Ashgate Pub. Limited, 1997.
Thorne, Robert, ed. *Structural Iron and Steel, 1850-1900.* Ashgate Pub. Limited, 2000.

© Tony Linck

Great Serpent Mound, near Hillsboro, Ohio, was built by people of the Fort Ancient culture. It resembles a huge snake and measures about $\frac{1}{4}$ mile (0.4 kilometer) long. Its purpose is unknown, but many Indian mounds were used as burial places or as platforms for important buildings.

Mound builders were early groups of North American Indians who built large earthwork structures. They built more than 5,000 mounds throughout North America between 7000 B.C. and A.D. 1700. Most mounds are in the eastern regions of the United States, with the greatest number around the Mississippi and Ohio rivers. Mounds are also found throughout eastern Canada and the southeastern United States.

Mounds in North America occur as single structures or in groups and in a variety of shapes and sizes. Some mounds were used to bury the dead. Others provided foundations for houses and temples or served to identify or mark the territories of different groups.

In the 1800's, some scholars thought that the mounds were remains of an ancient civilization. They theorized that the ancient mound builders came to North America from Europe, from Egypt, or even from the legendary continent of Atlantis. However, by 1894, archaeologists from the Smithsonian Institution had excavated several mounds and proved that the mound builders had been the ancestors of modern American Indians.

The mound builders were not a single group of people. Instead, different American Indian cultures built the mounds over thousands of years. The mounds were entirely built by people transporting and depositing loads of soil and rocks by hand without the use of wheeled vehicles or *draft* (work) animals, such as horses or oxen. Archaeologists recognize three broad prehistoric periods in which mound building occurred in North America. They are the Archaic Period (7000 B.C. to 1000 B. C.), the Woodland Period (1000 B. C. to A.D. 1100), and the

Mississippian Period (A.D. 900 to A.D. 1700).

Archaic Period. American Indians of the Archaic Period lived in small, seasonally occupied camps, and survived by hunting, fishing, and gathering wild plants. In some areas, however, a few groups began to cultivate sunflowers, gourds, and other plants. They made tools of chipped stone. They also manufactured various items from bone, hides, and other animal products; and wood and other plant materials. By the end of the Archaic Period, some groups had begun to make and use pottery.

The earliest evidence of Archaic Period mound building is at a site called L'Anse Amour, near Forteau, on the island of Labrador, Canada. There, Archaic Period Indians built a circular pile of boulders in about 5500 B.C. to mark the grave of a child. By 3,000 B.C., Archaic peoples were building low, circular burial mounds throughout the Mississippi Valley and nearby areas.

A site called Poverty Point, near Epps, Louisiana, preserves some of the most unique mounds of the Archaic Period. Archaeologists believe that this site was an important center for trade among Indian groups in the region. Archaic people built a large group of mounds there between about 1800 B.C. and 500 B.C. The mound complex is composed of six semicircular earthen ridges, each more than $\frac{1}{2}$ mile (0.8 kilometer) in diameter. The ridges were about 80 feet (24 meters) wide and nearly 10 feet (3 meters) high. The ridges surround two large mounds up to 65 feet (20 meters) in height. Many smaller mounds stand nearby. Archaeologists believe that the mounds were built as foundations for houses that stood on top.

An eagle made of rocks spreads across the top of a circular mound near Eaton- ton, Georgia. It is not known who built this mound, but many mounds in the south- eastern United States were built by Indians who be- longed to the Mississippian culture.

Woodland Period. Many early Woodland peoples moved seasonally to hunt, fish, and harvest wild plants, as their Archaic ancestors had done. Over time, Wood- land groups became more reliant on cultivated plants and settled into small communities. The communities grew gourds, squash, sunflowers, and other food crops, and tobacco. *Maize* (corn) became an important crop during the later Woodland Period. The Woodland Peri- od is also characterized by widespread use of pottery and mound building. Many Woodland mounds were cone-shaped. Some were as high as 30 feet (9 meters).

Archaeologists recognize two major mound-building cultures of the Woodland Period, the Adena and Hopewell. People of the Adena culture built many large mounds beginning about 600 B.C., centered in what is now southern Ohio. Over time, the Adena culture gave way to the more widespread and complex Hopewell culture, which flourished from about 100 B.C. to about A.D. 500. It extended throughout present-day Ohio, Indi- ana, Michigan, Illinois, Wisconsin, Iowa, and Missouri.

Adena and Hopewell mounds usually contained one or more burials, often accompanied with finely made pottery and objects fashioned from imported materials. Hopewell traders obtained shells and shark teeth from what is now Florida and *pipestone,* a soft stone used to make pipes, from present-day Minnesota. They also traded for volcanic glass from the Wyoming area and silver from what is now Ontario. Archaeologists believe that the people buried in the mounds were high-ranking members of the society.

The Hopewell trade network collapsed by about A.D. 500, and mound building ended throughout much

Monk's Mound, built by the Mississippian peoples, is the largest of over 100 mounds near Cahokia, Illinois. It covers about 16 acres (6 hectares) and is bigger at the base than the Great Pyramid of Egypt.

of the region. However, some regional mound-building traditions emerged toward the end of the Hopewell culture. Prehistoric Indians in what are now Iowa, Minnesota, and Wisconsin built many *effigy mounds* in the shapes of birds and other animal forms. Other Woodland societies began settling in more permanent villages and gave rise to the cultures of the Mississippian Period.

Mississippian Period. Mississippian communities became established in the river valleys across what is now the southeastern United States after A.D. 900. Mississippian people raised livestock and grew crops. They built some of the earliest towns and cities of North America. The larger towns often centered around mounds and other earthworks bordering a plaza where public events took place. The mounds ranged from 10 feet (3 meters) to 40 feet (12 meters) in height. Many Mississippian mounds were pyramid-shaped with flat tops, though the Mississippian builders also erected cone-shaped and linear mounds. Archaeologists believe that temples stood on top of the mounds along with buildings for the ruling chiefs. *Stockades* (log walls) protected many towns, indicating that warfare was common.

The largest Mississippian city was Cahokia, in present-day Illinois. Archaeologists estimate that it had a population of between 10,000 and 20,000 residents. Monk's Mound, the largest mound in Cahokia, rises about 100 feet (30 meters) and covers about 16 acres (6 hectares). Cahokia had more than 100 other mounds. Many were burial mounds, and others served as foundations for temples or for the houses of city officials.

Mississippian people made varieties of decorative pottery, much of it in the shapes of animals and human beings. Stone pipes in the form of human figures and crafts of imported shell and copper are also found at many Mississippian sites. The imported materials are evidence that Mississippian people traded with other groups through an exchange network that extended over much of eastern North America.

In what is now Ohio, people known as the *Fort Ancient culture* built mounds, earthen forts, and other structures. These people were culturally distinct from other Mississippian Period communities to the west. The name of the culture comes from one of their largest forts, Fort Ancient, near Lebanon, Ohio. A famous mound built by the Fort Ancient people is the Great Serpent Mound, near Hillsboro, Ohio. It looks like a huge snake from the air and is about $\frac{1}{4}$ mile (0.4 kilometer) long. The mound's purpose is unknown.

Conflicts with the Europeans and diseases introduced by them led to the destruction of Mississippian culture and brought an end to the mound-building traditions in the early 1700's. Since then, construction and land clearing have destroyed many mounds. Some states now have laws to protect mounds.   Roland L. Rodell

Additional resources

Birmingham, Robert A., and Eisenberg, L. E. *Indian Mounds of Wisconsin.* Univ. of Wis. Pr., 2000.
Denny, Sidney G., and others. *The Ancient Splendor of Prehistoric Cahokia.* 2nd ed. Ozark, 1997. Younger readers.
Young, Biloine W., and Fowler, M. L. *Cahokia, the Great Native American Metropolis.* Univ. of Ill. Pr., 1999.

Squid is any of a number of soft-bodied marine animals that have 8 or 10 limbs around the mouth. Squids are *invertebrates,* or animals that lack a backbone. They belong to a group of invertebrates called *cephalopods,* which also includes octopuses, nautiluses, and cuttlefish. Squids live in all seas and at all depths.

The body of a squid has two fins, one on each side of the tail. In most squid *species* (kinds), the head is surrounded by eight arms and two often longer limbs called tentacles. The arms and tentacles possess rows of suckers. Instead of bones, the animal has a *pen* (reduced shell) inside its body. Squids range in length from less than 1 foot (0.3 meters) to about 60 feet (18 meters), including the tentacles.

A squid's head has two well-developed eyes, a pair of powerful beaklike jaws, and a toothed structure called a *radula.* The radula assists the jaws in tearing up food, and it also helps move the food into the digestive system. A muscular, tubelike structure called the *mantle* forms the main part of the body. Attached to the body below the head is a smaller tubelike structure called the *funnel.* A squid propels itself through the water by filling its mantle with water and then forcing the water back out through the funnel. Squids also have three hearts—a main *systemic heart* and two additional *branchial hearts.* The branchial hearts supply blood to the animal's gills.

The life of a squid. Many types of squids live close to the ocean surface or near shores. Coral reefs house some of the most colorful varieties. Other types inhabit the dark, cold waters of the deep sea. Some species have structures called *photophores,* which emit light. Scientists do not completely understand the function of photophores, but a squid may use them for signaling other squids, luring prey, or scaring away predators.

A squid's diet consists of various sea animals, including fish, shellfish, and plankton. Squids often catch their prey by attacking with sudden bursts of speed. They then hold onto the prey using the suckers on their arms and tentacles. Many squids also have glands that emit a poison for stunning prey.

Numerous animals eat squids, including toothed whales, seals, sharks, and bony fishes. Squids avoid these animals in a variety of ways. For example, all squids have an ink sac that spurts out a dark fluid when the squid flees from a predator. This fluid may conceal

Parts of a female squid

WORLD BOOK illustration by Oxford Designers and Illustrators

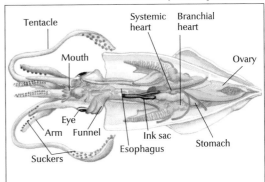

A **Caribbean reef squid** inhabits coral reefs off the Caribbean island of Grand Cayman. This small squid resembles most other squid species. It has a soft, torpedo-shaped body with huge eyes. Two transparent fins grow on either side of the tail.

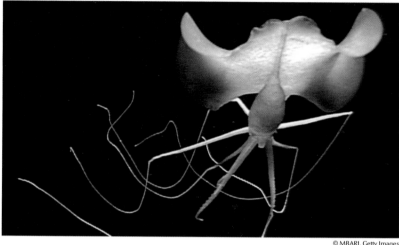

A **deep-sea squid** inhabits dark waters near the ocean floor. Sometimes called the longarm squid, this unusual creature has 10 long, string-like arms. It also possesses huge, flapping fins that resemble elephant's ears. Deep-sea explorers first discovered this squid in the late 1980's.

the squid as it escapes. Many species can also escape danger by rapidly changing color. Skin cells called *chromatophores* contain a colored pigment. When a squid is threatened, these cells contract or expand to produce sudden color changes. Such color changes can either startle the predator or enable the squid to hide by blending into its environment.

Squids have large brains and often exhibit complex behaviors. Many types swim in large groups. To attract females or ward off rivals, male squids sometimes change color and wave their arms as a form of display.

The number of eggs produced by females varies from a few dozen to many thousands. Newborn squids resemble miniature versions of the adults. Squids generally do not live long. Lifespans typically range from a few months to a few years.

Kinds of squids. Some of the best-known squids live in shallow waters near coasts. The *Caribbean reef squid,* for example, inhabits coral reefs throughout the Caribbean Sea. This small squid grows to about 12 inches (30 centimeters) long. It feeds on crustaceans and small fish.

Two related species, the *longfin inshore squid* and the *veined squid,* rank among the most commercially important types. People around the world eat them and use them as fish bait. Longfin inshore squids inhabit the western Atlantic Ocean from Newfoundland to Venezuela. Veined squids live in eastern Atlantic waters and the Mediterranean Sea. Both species gather in shallow coastal areas to breed and lay eggs. They range from 15 to 36 inches (38 to 91 centimeters) long.

Many squids inhabit deep ocean waters around the world. Scientists know little about most of these animals, which have rarely been seen alive. Deep-sea squids include the huge *giant squids,* which may reach about 60 feet (18 meters) in length. Giant squids probably eat other mollusks, including squids, as well as fish.

In the late 1980's, scientists discovered an unusual deep-sea squid. Sometimes called the *longarm squid,* it has 10 extremely long, threadlike arms of equal size. The arms bend to create elbowlike forms. Nearly all other squids possess eight arms and two tentacles. The longarm squid also has two huge fins that flap as the animal moves. The total length of this creature probably reaches 10 to 20 feet (3 to 6 meters).

Squids and people. Squids have captured people's imaginations for centuries. Many seafaring cultures, such as those of Japan and Polynesia, created stories of large sea monsters that probably represented squids. Such cultures often prized squids as a source of food. Today, squids play an important role in the fishing industry worldwide, both as food and as bait.

Scientists from a variety of fields study squids. Researchers analyze the nervous systems of squids to learn more about how the human nervous system functions. Biologists and deep-sea explorers continue to discover new squid species.   Robert S. Prezant

Scientific classification. Squids belong to the class Cephalopoda, and they make up different orders and families. The scientific name for the Caribbean reef squid is *Sepioteuthis sepioidea.* The longfin inshore squid is *Loligo pealei,* and the veined squid is *L. forbesi.* Giant squids make up the genus *Architeuthis.*

INDEX

How to use the index
This index covers the contents of the 2004, 2005, and 2006 editions.

Each entry gives the edition year and the page number or page numbers—for example, **Gene therapy.** This means that information on this topic may be found on the pages indicated in the 2006 edition.

When there are many references to a topic, they are grouped alphabetically by clue words under the main topic. For example, the clue words under **Genetic engineering** group the references to that topic under several subtopics.

A page number in italics means that there is an article on this topic on the page or pages indicated. For example, there is an Update article on **Genetics** on pages 233-236 of the 2006 edition. The page numbers in roman type indicate additional references to this topic in other articles in the volumes covered.

The "see" and "see also" cross-references refer the readers to other entries in the index. For example, additional information on **Genetics** will be found under the headings indicated.

An entry followed by WBE refers to a new or revised *World Book Encyclopedia* article in the supplement section, as in **Glaciers.** This means that there is a *World Book Encyclopedia* article on pages 280-283 of the 2006 edition.

The indications (il.) and (ils.) mean that the reference on this page is to an illustration only, as in **Graupel** in the 2006 edition.

ACKNOWLEDGMENTS

The publishers gratefully acknowledge the courtesy of the following artists, photographers, publishers, institutions, agencies, and corporations for the illustrations in this volume. Credits are listed from top to bottom, and left to right, on their respective pages. All entries marked with an asterisk (*) denote illustrations created exclusively for this yearbook. All maps, charts, and diagrams were staff-prepared unless otherwise noted.

6	Jacques Desclioitres, MODIS Land Rapid Response Team, NASA/GSFC
7	Dale DeBolt*
8	© Peter Brown; AP/Wide World
9	NASA/JPL/Space Science Institute
10	Chandler Wilkerson, Institute for Molecular Design, University of Houston
12-13	NASA/JPL/Space Science Institute
15-16	NASA/JPL
17	NASA/JPL/Space Science Institute; NASA
18	NASA/JPL/University of Iowa
19	NASA/JPL/Space Science Institute
20-21	NASA/JPL/Space Science Institute; Precision Graphics; NASA/JPL/Space Science Institute
22-24	NASA/JPL/Space Science Institute
25-27	NASA/JPL/ESA/University of Arizona
28-39	Electron Microscopy Unit/ARS/USDA; © PhotoDisc/Getty Images
40-41	© M. Gunther from Peter Arnold, Inc.
42	© Steve Bloom, Alamy Images
43	© Michael Neugebauer, The Jane Goodall Institute; © Steve Bloom, Alamy Images
44	© Anup Shah, Getty Images
47	© Michael Neugebauer, The Jane Goodall Institute
49	© Anup Shah, Nature Picture Library
50	© Steve Bloom, Alamy Images; © Karl & Kay Amman, Bruce Coleman Inc.
52	© Bruce Davidson, Nature Picture Library
53	© Sven Torfinn, Panos Pictures
54-55	© Martin Harvey
56-57	© AFP/Getty Images
59	Paul Perreault*
61	Ford Motor Company
62	WORLD BOOK diagram by Sarah Woodward
63	Lanny Schmidt, University of Minnesota; National Renewable Energy Laboratory; © Microfield Scientific Ltd./SPL/Photo Researchers
64	WORLD BOOK diagram by Linda Kinnaman
65	© AFP/Getty Images
67	© AFP/Getty Images; © Corbis/Bettmann
68	Shell Hydrogen
70	© Marc Asnin, Corbis
74	WORLD BOOK illustration by Barbara Cousins
75	Nizar Jarjour, University of Wisconsin, Department of Medicine (photo by LaCinda Burchell)
76	© Eddy Gray, Photo Researchers
79	© Saturn Stills/SPL/Photo Researchers; © SIU/Peter Arnold, Inc.
80	Adapted from artwork originally created for the National Cancer Institute. Reprinted with permission of the artist, Jeanne Kelly. Copyright 2004.
82	WORLD BOOK illustration by Barbara Cousins
84-85	© David Grossman, The Image Works
86	WORLD BOOK illustration by Barbara Cousins
87	© Siri Mills, Phototake
88	WORLD BOOK illustration by Barbara Cousins
91	WORLD BOOK illustration by Barbara Cousins and Rolin Graphics
92	© Corbis
95	© David Young-Wolff, PhotoEdit
96	© SCALA/Art Resource; National Undersea Research Center
97	Kevin Raskoff, Mar-Eco; Marsh Youngbluth, Mar-Eco; National Undersea Research Center
99	Tracey Sutton, Mar-Eco; Mar-Eco
100	Tracy Sutton, Mar-Eco
101	Mar-Eco
102	Richard Young, Mar-Eco
103	Klockargaardens Film AB/Mar-Eco; Oceanlab/Mar-Eco
104	Margaret Butschler, Vancouver Aquarium Marine Science Centre
105	Monterey Bay Aquarium
107-108	National Undersea Research Center
109	NOAA Ocean Explorer
110	NOAA
111	Census of Marine Life
112-113	© Lynette R. Cook
115	Max Tegmark/Sloan Digital Sky Survey; Paul Perreault*; NASA/WMAP Science Team
116	NASA/CXC/IoA/S. Allen
117	Paul Perreault*
118	NASA/The Electronic Universe Project; Paul Perreault*
119	NASA/J. Bahcall; Paul Perreault*;